Anchoritic Traditions of Medieval Europe

The practice of anchoritism – religious enclosure which was frequently solitary and voluntarily embraced, very often in a permanent capacity – was widespread in many areas of Europe throughout the middle ages. Originating in the desert withdrawal of the earliest Christians and prefiguring even the monastic life, anchoritism developed into an elite vocation which was popular amongst both men and women. Within this reclusive vocation, the anchorite would withdraw, either alone or with others like her or him, to a small cell or building, very frequently attached to a church or other religious institution, where she or he would – theoretically at least – remain locked up until death. In the later period it was a vocation which was particularly associated with pious laywomen who appear to have opted for this extreme way of life in their thousands throughout western Europe, often as an alternative to marriage or remarriage, allowing them, instead, to undertake the role of 'living saint' within the community.

This volume brings together for the first time in English much of the most important European scholarship on the subject to date. Tracing the vocation's origins from the Egyptian deserts of early Christian activity through to its multiple expressions in western Europe, it also identifies some of those regions – Wales and Scotland, for example – where the phenomenon does not appear to have been as widespread. As such, the volume provides an invaluable resource for those interested in the theories and practices of medieval anchoritism in particular, and the development of medieval religiosity more widely.

T0366952

Anchoritic Traditions of Medieval Europe

Edited by Liz Herbert McAvoy

THE BOYDELL PRESS

First published 2010
The Boydell Press, Woodbridge
Paperback edition 2019

ISBN 978 1 84383 520 2 hardback
ISBN 978 1 78327 380 5 paperback

The Boydell Press is an imprint of Boydell & Brewer Ltd
PO Box 9, Woodbridge, Suffolk IP12 3DF, UK
and of Boydell & Brewer Inc.
668 Mt Hope Avenue, Rochester, NY 14620–2731, USA
website: www.boydellandbrewer.com

The publisher has no responsibility for the continued existence or accuracy
of URLs for external or third-party internet websites referred to in this book,
and does not guarantee that any content on such websites is,
or will remain, accurate or appropriate

A CIP catalogue record for this book is available
from the British Library

This publication is printed on acid-free paper

Typeset by Tina Ranft

Contents

Acknowledgements

The production of this volume has been a lengthy task, initially beset by problems arising from translation issues and dearth of funding. It has, however, been deeply stimulating and rewarding, and would certainly not have come to fruition had it not been for a determination to continue in the light of unwavering support from its publishers. I am, therefore, highly indebted to Caroline Palmer at Boydell and Brewer, not only for persuading me (in what now seems like a very distant past) to take the task on, but also for her help, advice and encouragement as the project appeared variously to develop, to become derailed, or to founder. The volume's successful completion is as much a result of her sustained belief in its value as my own, for which I am most grateful. I am also indebted to the volume's reader, Eddie Jones, whose careful consideration of the proposal and advice proffered during the course of its production, have helped considerably to improve and refine the end product. Thanks are also due to the volume's contributors' whose patience and willingness to alter and amend their essays, frequently at short notice, have been exemplary; indeed, their professionalism and dedication to their studies have made it a great pleasure to work with them. All, without fail, have responded readily and fully to my editorial requests and demands, and have been exceptionally patient whilst issues arising from translation into English have held up the volume's production.

Particular thanks must be proffered to Swansea University's School of Arts (more recently the School of Arts and Humanities) Research Committee for a generous subvention towards translation costs at the eleventh hour which, combined with their granting me a period of study-leave, has been pivotal to the project's completion. Without this assistance and encouragement, the project would almost certainly have suffered further delay.

My thanks are also due to the interested, efficient and sensitive treatment of the non- English language essays by their translators: in particular, Alex Sagar, Robert Olsen, Ceridwen Lloyd-Morgan and Ruth Evans who produced nuanced and effective translations of the essays by Gabriela Signori, Anneke B. Mulder-Bakker, Paulette L'Hermite-Leclercq and Mario Sensi respectively. Their professionalism has contributed much to the end product. I am also grateful to my colleague Helen Fulton for generously taking time out of her busy schedule to offer a careful reading of my own contribution on Welsh reclusion. Her comments and suggestions have proved invaluable.

Finally, as ever, thanks are due to my family who continue to take interest in and support my academic endeavours, in spite of the inevitability of my periodic metamorphosis into one of those very anchoritic women who form the primary focus of this study.

List of Contributors

G. Cavero Domínguez is Lecturer in Medieval History at the University of León, Spain. Her current research focuses on monasticism and reclusion. Among her latest publications are 'Fuentes para el estudio del emparedamiento en la España medieval (siglos XII–XV)', *Revue Mabillon* 17 (2007), pp. 105–26; and *Inclusa intra parietes: la reclusión voluntaria en la España medieval* (2009).

P. L'Hermite-Leclercq is Professor Emerita at the University of the Sorbonne in Paris. Her work has focused primarily on religious history and women's history, within which fields she has published widely. Her principal works include: *Le monachisme féminin dans la société de son temps* (Paris, 1989); *L'Eglise et les femmes dans l'Occident chrétien* (1997); *Vie de Christina de Markyate*, 2 vols (2007). She is currently preparing a study on religious reclusion in the Middle Ages.

Mari Hughes-Edwards is Lecturer in English Literature at Edge Hill University, having taught at the universities of York, Manchester, Liverpool, Salford and Liverpool John Moores. Originally a medievalist by training, she has research interests in medieval anchoritism, solitude and space, and a monograph entitled *The Ideology of English Anchoritism* forthcoming with the University of Wales Press. Her research now focuses on contemporary British literature, her publications having concentrated on contemporary poetry, especially on the work of Carol Ann Duffy and Lee Harwood.

Liz Herbert McAvoy is Senior Lecturer in Gender Studies and Medieval Literature at Swansea University. Her research interests lie in medieval anchoritism; female mysticism; medieval women's writing; representations of alterity; and critical theory, particularly post-structuralist feminist theory. She has published widely in these areas, including *Authority and the Female Body in the Writings of Julian of Norwich and Margery Kempe* (2004); ed. with Mari Hughes-Edwards, *Anchorites, Wombs and Tombs: Intersections of Gender and Enclosure in the Middle Ages* (2005); ed., *Rhetoric of the Anchorhold: Space, Place and Body within the Discourses of Enclosure* (2008); ed., *A Companion to Julian of Norwich* (2008), as well as journal articles, book chapters and encyclopaedia entries. She is currently working on a book which examines the intersections of gender and space within representations of the medieval anchorite.

Anna McHugh is a Junior Research Fellow at Harris Manchester College, Oxford. Her research interests include anchoritism in the British Isles; meditative praxis and its transmission in poetic texts; the frame-tale in different cultures; medieval formulations of truth; and theories of memory from classical antiquity to 1500. Her most recent publication is a study of inner space as a speaking space in *Ancrene Wisse*, published in *Rhetoric of the Anchorhold, Space, Place and Body within the Discourses of Enclosure*, ed. Liz Herbert McAvoy (2008).

Anneke B. Mulder-Bakker taught Medieval History and Medieval Studies at the University of Groningen, The Netherlands. She is now Professor Emerita at the University of Leiden. Her publications on historiography, hagiography and gender include *Sanctity and Motherhood* (1995), *De Kluizenaar in de Eik: Gerlach van Houthem en zijn Verering* (1995); ed. with Renée Nip, *The Prime of Their Lives: Wise Old Women in Pre-industrial Europe* (2004); *Lives of the Anchoresses: The Rise of the Urban Recluse in Medieval Europe* (2005); ed. with Jocelyn Wogan-Browne, *Household, Women and Christianities in Late Antiquity and the Middle Ages* (2005); *Mary of Oignies: Mother of Salvation* (2006).

Colmán Ó Clabaigh is a Benedictine monk of Glenstal Abbey, Co. Limerick, Ireland, where he teaches in the abbey school and is the monastery archivist. A graduate of NUI Galway, he specialises in the history of monastic and religious orders in late medieval Ireland. He is the author of *The Franciscans in Ireland 1400–1534* (2002) and editor (with Martin Browne OSB) of *The Irish Benedictines: a History* (2005), and (with Salvador Ryan and Rachel Moss) of *Art and Devotion in Late Medieval Ireland* (2006). His book *The Friars in Ireland 1224–1534* will appear in 2010. His other medieval research interests include anchorites and hermits, Irish library catalogues, religious patronage and monastic delinquency.

Mario Sensi obtained a doctorate in Theology in 1967 from the Pontifical Lateran University in Rome and a doctorate in Letters and Philosophy from the University of Perugia in 1970. He is Professor of Ancient and Medieval Church History at the Pontifical Lateran University and a member of the Pontifical Board of Historical Knowledge [Pontificio Comitato di Scienze Storiche (CPSH)]. Notable among the many books which he has published are: *Vita di pietà e vita civile di un altopiano tra Umbria e Marche (secc. XI–XVI)* (1985); *Le osservanze francescane nell'Italia centrale (secoli XIV–XV)* (1985); *Dal movimento eremitico alla rego-lare osservanza francescana, l'opera di fra Paoluccio Trinci* (1992); *Storie di biz-zoche tra Umbria e Marche* (Rome, 1995); *Il Perdono di Assisi* (2002); *Santuari, pellegrini, eremiti nell'Italia centrale*, vol. 3, Centro Italiano di studi sull'Alto

Medioevo (2003). In addition, he has published more than 380 articles in Italian and foreign journals, and contributed entries on aspects of Church History to a wide range of encyclopaedias and dictionaries.

Gabriela Signori has been Professor of Medieval History in the Department of History and Sociology at the University of Konstanz, Germany, since 2006, before which she was Professor at the Westfaelische Wilhelms University of Muenster (2001–6). Her main area of research is social history of late medieval towns, in particular law, gender, culture and religion, in which areas she has published widely. Her recent publications include *Das dreizehnte Jahrhundert. Eine Einführung in die Geschichte des spätmittelalterlichen Europas* (2007); ed. with Birgit Emich, *Kriegsbilder. Bilder und Abbilder vom Krieg in Spätmittelalter und Früher Neuzeit* (2009); and ed., *Die lesende Frau. Traditionen, Projektionen, Metaphern im fächer- und epochenübergreifenden Vergleich* (Köln, 2009).

Abbreviations

AASS	*Acta Sanctorum*, 68 vols (Antwerp and Brussels: Societé Bollandistes, 1643–)
BHL	*Bibliotheca Hagiographica Latina antiquae et mediae aetatis*, ed. Socii Bollandiani, 4 vols (Brussels, 1898–1986)
CAHMER	Centre d'archéologie et d'histoire médiévale des établissements religieux [Centre of Medieval Archaeology and the History of Religious Establishments]
CCh.R	Calendar of the Charter Rolls
CPR	Calendar of the Patent Rolls
EETS	Early English Text Society
MED	*Middle English Dictionary*
MGH	*Monumenta Germaniae Historica*
MGH Script.	*Monumenta Germaniae Historica Scriptorum*
MGH. SRMer.	*Monumenta Germaniae Historica. Scriptores Rerum Merovingicarum*
OED	*Oxford English Dictionary*
PL	*Patrologia Cursus Completus: Series Latina*, ed. J. P. Migne (Paris 1841–64)
RCAHMS	Royal Commisssion on the Ancient and Historical Monements of Scotland
SPCK	Society for Promoting Christian Knowledge
VCH	*Victoria County History*
VSBG	*Vitae Sanctorum Britannia et Genealogiae*, ed. A. W. Wade-Evans (Cardiff, 1944)

Editor's note

Considerations of space have precluded the inclusion of quotations in their original languages, unless absolutely essential to the arguments being promoted. They therefore appear, in the main, in modern English translation with key words and phrases from the original inserted in square brackets where necessary. In all cases, full references to the original sources appear in the notes. Similarly, the differences between accepted Continental and Anglophone referencing styles have been acknowledged and respected and are retained in the respective footnotes to each essay.

Introduction

Liz Herbert McAvoy

[T]here radiates about this centralized solitude a universe of meditation, prayer, a universe outside the universe ... As destitution increases it gives us access to absolute refuge.[1]

Anchoritic Studies: a background

This volume comes together as a result of a recent upsurge in scholarly interest in the medieval solitary life and its legacies, both in Continental Europe and the more anglophone regions of the world. Increasingly, those of us whose research areas lie somewhere embedded within the complex web of medieval religiosity have begun to recognize the pivotal role played by the reclusive way of life within much wider-reaching cultural contexts during the Middle Ages. This is something which was prefigured by the words of Dom Jean Leclercq in 1965 who saw the life of the medieval solitary as 'exercis[ing] an influence, direct or indirect, on every manifestation of spiritual life'; moreover, for Leclercq, whilst the eremitic impulse that characterized the age 'does not perhaps explain everything, yet there is hardly anything that can be completely understood without it'.[2] Like many scholars of his day, Leclercq's interest was in the medieval solitary in a multifarious sense which encompassed traditional hermits, both solitary and communal, and what we would recognize as 'anchorites', all of whom were high-status figures – if, more often than not, anonymous ones – strewn across the map of medieval Europe. As Leclercq's work demonstrates too, the distinction between hermit and anchorite has not always been a clear-cut one, either in pre-modern categorizations or, indeed, within our own contemporary discussions (and this is something I will deal with in more detail later in this introduction); their roles, both public and private, have often been amalgamated in popular imagination, resulting in their occupying the shadowy ground beneath the overarching umbrella of 'medieval eremitism'. In this context, the very specific way of life and role of the anchorite, as opposed to the hermit, has frequently been subsumed into the larger category and the socio-religious project of medieval anchoritism has thus frequently been occluded. When definitive categorization has been forthcoming, in

---

[1] Gaston Bachelard, *The Poetics of Space* (Boston, 1964), p. 32 (first published as *La poétique de l'e-space* [Paris, 1958]).
[2] Jean Leclercq, *L'Eremitismo in Occidente nei secoli XI e XII*, Miscellanea del Centro di Studi Medioevali IV (Milan, 1965), p. 594.

traditional terms the hermit has been defined as a solitary who can both live alone or within a community of other hermits and who is very often peripatetic – indeed, his/her ability to move about is paradigmatic of the vocation. In contrast, the anchorite is one who has made a solemn vow of stability of place before the bishop or his representative and lives out his or her life in a locked or walled-up cell. Both, however, have opted for the solitary life for purposes of spiritual development and both undertake important work on behalf of the community which, discursively at least, they have left behind.

This volume, therefore, aims to pick up the mantle where Leclercq dropped it, focusing in particular on the medieval anchorite in Western Europe and offering wide-ranging evidence to corroborate the central role played by religious solitaries throughout Europe during the Middle Ages. In so doing, it will acknowledge the multiple nature of medieval reclusion, the similarities and differences which manifested themselves between European regions and temporalities and allow the figure of the walled-in anchorite, particularly the female anchorite, to emerge from the shadows of history. On reading the essays collected here, the reader is offered an insight into a teleology of reclusion which permeated all walks of life throughout the European Middle Ages and infiltrated the mind-sets of its peoples, its cultures and its belief-systems.

Leclercq's research on medieval reclusion, however, operated within a European research context which, until the late twentieth and early twenty-first centuries, had rarely entered into close communication with its Anglophone counterparts working on medieval reclusion within Britain and Ireland. Whilst scholars from the Netherlands, Germany, France, Italy and Spain were in dialogue with each other, meeting regularly at conferences which focused on a range of experiences of religious reclusion, the same cannot be said of their English-speaking counterparts, whose research into the phenomenon tended until very recently to be both Anglocentric and androcentric in the development of its paradigms. Whilst, too, the pivotal works in English on the topic, such as Rotha Mary Clay's *Hermits and Anchorites*, Francis Darwin's *The Mediaeval Recluse*, and, more recently, Ann Warren's *Anchorites and their Patrons*, made their way into research across the Channel,[3] the widespread dissemination of Continental material in the English-speaking world did not take place in the same way. As a result, the paradigmatic nature of English anchoritism became established with little reference to what was going on in Europe during the same period, a lack of cross-pollination which, in many ways, left our understanding of the impetuses behind the phenomenon and the multiplicity of its expressions wanting. Moreover, to this day, the paradigm of English anchoritism and its conflation with a notion of its 'Britishness' has left its expression in medieval Scotland, Wales and Ireland completely unexplored, something which again this present volume attempts, in part, to redress.

---

[3] The earliest concerted study of medieval reclusion in England is that of Rotha Mary Clay, *The Hermits and Anchorites of England* (London, 1914). Whilst Clay's seminal examination is yet to be surpassed, both Francis Darwin, *The Mediaeval Recluse* (London, 1954) and Ann K. Warren, *Anchorites and their Patrons in Medieval England* (Berkeley, Los Angeles and London, 1985) have drawn upon and developed aspects of her study in the context of anchorites in particular.

The problem of scholarly non-communication was first confronted in 1992 with the visit of Anneke Mulder-Bakker, the first contributor to this volume, to a conference organized at the then University of Wales' conference centre at Gregynog in Powys, entitled *Anchorites, Wombs and Tombs: Intersections of Gender and Enclosure in the Middle Ages*. This conference was to pave the way for increased international traffic between European anchoritic scholars and their English-speaking counterparts elsewhere, which resulted in, for example, a round-table session at the International Leeds Medieval Congress in 2005 in which several of the contributors to this volume took part. Again in 2005, a second three-day conference was convened entitled *Rhetoric of the Anchorhold: Space, Place and Body within the Discourses of Enclosure* and, in April 2007, interaction between this new community of anchoritic scholars and their counterparts in Ireland was forged in a three-day symposium, *Medieval Anchoritism*, held at Glenstal Abbey.[4] This type of interaction resulted in the formation of the International Anchoritic Society in 2006–07 which now has members worldwide – including a substantial number from all of those regions represented here. This volume, therefore, represents fully this new liaison and dialogue, and its compilation has been driven by three primary imperatives: the pedagogical, the historical and the conceptual.

The demands of pedagogy, history and the conceptual

On the level of pedagogy, this volume brings together in English for the first time – and under one cover – much of the most important work on medieval anchoritism undertaken in recent times, enabling the reader to access far more varied expressions of the anchoritic life and within a comparative setting. Shot through with points of coincidence as well as contrast, paradox and other types of resonance, it presents the anchoritic life as a much more varied, dynamic and organically productive way of life than has perhaps been previously understood. Pedagogically, too, it is hoped that this volume will facilitate both the teaching of anchoritism and its adjuncts and provide a spring-board for future research at postgraduate and postdoctoral levels; in this capacity it should also mitigate against the type of 'reinvention of the wheel' which anglophone scholars were certainly in danger of having to undertake upon entering the field.

The second imperative behind this collection is to open up the wider historical plane in which the phenomenon of anchoritism was played out in its various manifestations. Medieval anchoritism has long fallen away from our collective consciousness, of course, and few people outside academic circles – nor, indeed, many within – have any clear conception about what the medieval anchorite was or

---

[4] Two of these events were to lead to edited collections: *Anchorites, Wombs and Tombs: Intersections of Gender and Enclosure in the Middle Ages*, ed. Liz Herbert McAvoy and Mari Hughes-Edwards (Cardiff, 2005); *Rhetoric of the Anchorhold: Space, Place and Body within the Discourses of Enclosure*, ed. Liz Herbert McAvoy (Cardiff, 2008). A further collection of essays is also forthcoming, based on recent anchoritic conference sessions at the international medieval congresses of Kalamazoo and Leeds: *Anchoritic Spirituality: Enclosure, Authority, Transcendence. Selected Proceedings from the International Medieval Congresses at Leeds, UK and Kalamazoo, MI.*, ed. Susannah Chewning (Turnhout, forthcoming 2010).

how s/he functioned within the whole. If we return to the words of Jean Leclercq, however, it is important to attempt to reconstruct historically the important figure of the medieval anchorite and the range of meanings attached to his/her body, as well as identify the myriad ways in which s/he functioned both diachronically and synchronically. This is paramount if we are to gain in our understanding of how the cultures under scrutiny operated, how solitude functioned within those cultures and – crucially – the legacy of those operations to our own 'postmodern' cultures.

It is thus this issue of cultural legacy which also forms the conceptual rationale behind this volume. Medieval anchoritic reclusion constitutes just one expression of a human impulse towards withdrawal into solitude which takes on many forms and guises within virtually all cultures. In the words of John D. Barbour, writing on the traditional ethics of solitude: '[S]ocieties need, sustain and value solitaries. Every human society creates niches where solitude can be practised.'[5] For Barbour, moreover, a human withdrawal into solitude is an important 'critical practice' whereby society can be viewed – and therefore view itself – from a different perspective, that is to say through the eyes of the solitary, who is both part of and apart from that same society.[6] Solitary reclusion therefore provides a critical practice which allows for a productive critique of society, its mores and, as Pierre Bourdieu has expounded, its *habitus*.[7] As such, the potential of the solitary life within any given society lies embedded within its ethical and spiritual values: it is not a way of life which aims to escape the world in its entirety (whatever it claims within discourse) but, to adapt the words of Barbour, its intervention is brought about in order to enact a different type of participation within it.[8]

The importance to human culture of the solitary life and those who have espoused it is something which has also been explored by Gaston Bachelard in his *The Poetics of Space*. Rather than configuring solitude in terms of a social practice as does Barbour, however, Bachelard visualizes it as a primary, semiotic space of 'homecoming', somewhere where the loss which underpins the human psyche may at least gain a glimpse at its own healing:

> And all the spaces of our past moments of solitude, the spaces in which we have suffered from solitude, enjoyed, desired and compromised solitude, remain indelible within us, and precisely because the human being wants them to remain so.[9]

These words, from the reveries on space undertaken by Bachelard in his book, point towards what he recognizes as a perennial, even essential, human desire for a return to solitude, that space of endless creativity once enjoyed, but now for the

[5] John D. Barbour, *The Value of Solitude: The Ethics and Spirituality of Aloneness in Autobiography* (Charlottesville and London, 2004), p. 31.

[6] Ibid., p. 200.

[7] For Bourdieu the *habitus* is the system of structured and structuring dispositions which dictate the operations of any given society. These are both conscious and unconscious and are based upon accepted practices and past experiences. Like the workings of language, the *habitus* also reflects, articulates and constructs what constitutes 'reality' in any given social context. On this, see Pierre Bourdieu, *The Logic of Practice*, trans. Richard Nice (Stanford, 1992).

[8] Barbour, *Value of Solitude*, p. 201.

[9] Bachelard, *Poetics*, p. 10.

most part lost and only accessible via the traces of memory. For Bachelard, solitude remains one of the indelible blue-prints of what it is to be human; much of our lives are therefore spent in attempts to recapture or reconfigure a primary isolation which is restored to us only through the medium of day-dream or – in more contemporary terms – performative re-enactment through memory or imagination. This ritualistic re-enactment is not only undertaken by the solitary her/himself, but also by the onlooker by proxy – in Bachelard's terms the traveller who sees the candle in the window of the hermit's hut shining from afar in the darkness of the night.[10] Elsewhere, he configures this 'place' of primary solitude metaphorically as the 'garret' or 'attic', with obvious connotations of the 'rooms' of the mind, the imagination or memory – the womb, even – and thus he allies it with intense creativity and the commemoration of a lost realm: the human 'knows instinctively that this space identified with his solitude is creative'.[11] Ironically, however, this creative individuality is also compromised by the fact that the longed-for attic room is common to all humanity and is the place to which that same humanity craves return, 'even when … the attic room is lost and gone'.[12] In identifying the solitary's space in paradoxical terms as both primary isolation and primary unity, Bachelard anticipates the work of Julia Kristeva for whom the hermit's hut, the attic, the garret, the draw of solitude, all conflate in a conceptualization of the primary realm as the *chora*, a prediscursive space of origins where a '*pre-thetic*' unity with the (m)other within the isolation of the womb is fleetingly experienced and quickly lost forever. This loss, however, embeds itself into both human psyche and culture to emerge in a range of metamorphosed forms: poetic language, being one of the primary examples.[13] For Kristeva, the medium of poetic language can allow access to the vestiges, the traces, of the *pre-thetic*. However, when allied to Bachelard's use of spatial poetics of the eremitic, which incorporate unity, loss, desire and longing, both Bachelardian poetics and Kristevan semiotics transport us directly back to the Edenic stage and the performance of biblical origins enacted there. In this realm, love, transgression and loss tragically converge to produce the always already fallen state which has traditionally lain behind the impulse towards a specifically Christian religious reclusion.

Biblical precedent and the solitary impulse

As the Book of Genesis tells us of Adam (and in so doing, recaptures the rupture which constitutes the birthing of the human): 'And the Lord God sent him out of the paradise of pleasure, to till the earth from which he was taken. And he cast out Adam'.[14] Adam's expulsion from paradise simultaneously severs him from the womb of Eden, the site of his soil-bound birth, and causes him to 'know' his wife,

---

[10] Ibid., p. 31.

[11] Ibid., p. 10.

[12] Ibid., p. 10.

[13] See, for example, Julia Kristeva, 'Revolution in Poetic Language', in *A Kristeva Reader* , ed. Toril Moi (Oxford, 1986), pp. 93–8.

[14] Genesis 3:23–4.

Eve, in the first of the sexual encounters which will forever attempt to compensate for, and yet forever announce, the loss of primary unity within the fertile garden, Eden. Now the destiny of humankind is carnal knowledge and fleshly birthing, an inheritance passed immediately and ever onwards as a reminder of primary and perpetual loss. In the words of Cain, also recounted in Genesis: "'Behold thou dost cast me out this day from the face of the earth, and I shall be hidden from thy face, and I shall be a vagabond and a fugitive on the earth" … And Cain went out from the face of the Lord, and dwelt as a fugitive on the earth, at the east side of Eden.'[15]

In this way, the implications attached to the spaces of solitude and the loss they attempt to remedy, whether on an individual basis or experienced communally, lie at the heart of the Christian faith, as well as many other belief-systems of the world, both past and present. No less urgent than the Genesis exiles just recounted, for example, is the figure of Moses guiding the Israelites through their forty-year exile in the harsh and unforgiving Egyptian desert, as recounted in the Book of Exodus. By now, however, solitude and exile have become factors which serve to carve out for the biblical prophets such as Moses a perspective which allows for the addressing of social injustices: for Moses and others like him, withdrawal into isolation constructs an arena which God himself may enter in order to converse directly with the prophet in order to allow him some kind of intervention.[16] Similarly, the desert and wilderness meander prominently throughout the New Testament's geography: John the Baptist, the 'precursor to Christ', calls out from the wilderness about Christ's coming ministry; Christ himself withdraws periodically to desert or wilderness to formulate his thoughts and consolidate his resolve; Mary Magdalen will retire to the desert at the end of her life to live as a contemplative and ascetic. For all of these biblical figures, withdrawal, spiritual growth and a type of rebirth in the face of loss become the pattern which will eventually lead them to transcendence of their earth-bound state and to unity with divinity.

Early Christian solitude

In his 1951 play *Le Diable et le Bon Dieu,* Jean-Paul Sartre examines the nature of religious belief and its discourses of good and evil, having his newly absolved war-criminal protagonist, Gœtz, declare to Heinrich ('le curé'):

> Tu vois ce vide au-dessus de nos têtes? C'est Dieu. Tu vois cette brèche dans la port? C'est Dieu. Tu vois ce trou dans la terre? C'est Dieu encore. Le silence, c'est Dieu. L'absence, c'est Dieu. Dieu, c'est la solitude des hommes.

> [You see this emptiness above our heads? It's God. You see this breach in the door? It's God. You see this hole in the ground? It's God again. Silence, it's God. Absence, it's God. God is the solitude of men.][17]

[15] Genesis 4:14–15.
[16] This is something discussed by Barbour, *Value of Solitude*, p. 11.
[17] Jean-Paul Sartre, *Le Diable et le Bon Dieu* [*The Devil and the Good Lord*] (Paris, 1951), Act X, scene iv, p. 267. My translation.

Whilst in this scene Sartre's anti-hero, a professed atheist, articulates what he sees as a human impulse not only to *play* God but to *be* God too, these words also summon up an emptiness of being which tends to be both reified and deified by the human mind in its search for transcendence and the recapturing of lost unity. This may indeed be true of the earliest of adherents to Christianity; however, withdrawal into the desert in the wake of Christ's execution was, in truth, a two-fold necessity: not only was it a means of recapturing the life of Christ himself, holding it tight within the memory by means of re-enactment and contemplation (what Bachelard terms 'the daydream'), it was also a response to the physical dangers resulting from the inevitable persecutions which took place in the aftermath of the crucifixion. These first followers of Christ – men, women and their children – fled to the safer caves and hills on the fringes of the Egyptian desert where they could live out their lives and their faith without the danger of persecution – or worse. In time, the most zealous were to withdraw further into individual solitude, living out ascetic, contemplative lives as holy men and women, the first Christian hermits and precursors of the medieval anchoritic tradition. In the words of John Cassian (d. *c*.435), one of the earliest commentators on this Christian tradition, writing in the fifth century about the origins of Christian monasticism:

> Those in whom the apostolic fervor still existed, however, were mindful of that earlier perfection. Abandoning their towns and the company of those who believed the negligence of a more careless life was lawful for both themselves and the Church of God, they began to live in rural and more secluded places and to practice privately and individually what they remembered had been taught by the apostles [...]. [T]he disciples who removed themselves from contamination [...] gradually separated themselves from the crowds of believers by reason of the fact that they abstained from marriage [and] cut themselves off from the company of their parents and from the life of this world, and were called monks or μοναζοντες [solitaries] because of the strictness of their individual and solitary lives.[18]

The writings of Cassian on the origins of Christian institutional life, which remained popular throughout the Middle Ages in Europe, suggest that the cornerstones of the holy life – chastity, poverty and obedience – which were to have such a bearing upon both monastic Christianity and medieval anchoritism in the West, were laid down by these early Christian solitaries, the so-called Desert Fathers and Mothers. Many of these men and women, whether 'real' personages or 'imagined' ideals, went on to find lasting renown in the earliest Christian writings: in particular, the first hagiographies which recorded their extraordinary lives as exempla for future generations.

This early life of withdrawal and ascesis, however, was frequently episodic and transient in nature: solitude was a condition practised in close proximity to village

---

[18] John Cassian, *The Conferences*, ed. Boniface Ramsey (New York, 1997), 3, 18, ch. 5, p. 638. For the original Latin text see *PL* 49, cols 477–1328. For some recent studies on Cassian and his writings, see, for example, Richard J. Goodrich, *Contextualising Cassian* (Oxford, 2007); and Thomas Merton, *Cassian and the Fathers* (Kalamazoo, 2005).

and community rather than in complete isolation within the desert expanses. As Athanasius of Alexandria (d. 373), an early Christian hagiographer, points out in his account of the life of Saint Anthony, one of the first Christian hermits, the remotest parts of the desert remained as yet unpenetrated by the early Christians:

> For there were not yet so many monasteries in Egypt, and no monk at all knew of the distant desert; but all who wished to give heed to themselves practised the discipline in solitude near their own village.[19]

Here Athanasius points inadvertently towards the figurative – if not metaphorical – nature of the original notions of desert retreat and solitariness which were to become a major discourse within the anchoritic ideal in the later Middle Ages. Adhering to a common hagiographic topos, Athanasius tells how Anthony, a wealthy young man by birth, chose to relinquish his inheritance upon the death of his parents and withdraw into desert solitude in order to live closer to God. And yet, his withdrawal was never a complete one. Like many other solitaries, he lived close enough to the community to have sporadic interaction with them, whilst at the same time aiming to focus on unceasing prayer at some distance apart. This liminal state of belonging and yet not belonging soon began to attract more followers, many of whom opted initially to live their spiritual lives in solitude, but who later went on to found communities of solitudes who grouped together to form the first coenobites. As a result, solitude as the fundamental core of an elite and transcendent spirituality became a basic tenet of both forms of religious life, that is the monastic and the eremitic, although in the former state it came to be exercised communally whilst in the latter solitude and quasi-independence were to become paramount.

The Lives *of the (female) saints and the anchoritic body*

Also popular amongst the writings which emerged during this period were accounts of the tribulations and persecutions of early female adherents to Christianity; indeed these *vitae* or Lives were to retain widespread popularity throughout the Middle Ages. In particular, the *Acts of Thecla* and *The Passion of Saint Perpetua* captured Christian imagination, not least because both women had been reputedly known to Saint Paul.[20] Whilst for Maud Burnett McInerney, these two texts 'herald the battle for control of the female body', something which would become a major discourse and material focus within the Christian tradition,[21] for Amy Hollywood, such stories formed part of a male fetishization of the female body, an attempt to recapture the lost realm of the (m)other within a male imaginary, as alluded to above, a fetishization which was to continue to display

---

[19] Athanasius, *Select Works and Letters*, ed. Philip Schaff and Henry Wace, Nicene and Post-Nicene Fathers ser. 2, vol. 4 (1892), p. 196.

[20] Whilst Thecla of Iconium was said to have been a companion to Saint Paul, Perpetua was supposedly martyred in Carthage with Saint Paul bearing witness to the event. On this see Maud Burnett McInerney, *Eloquent Virgins: From Thecla to Joan of Arc* (New York, 2002), ch. 1, pp. 15–45.

[21] Ibid., p. 17.

itself in the cultural imperative of the anchoritic woman of the later Middle Ages.[22] For Peter Brown, however, writing on the history of the relationship between Church and body, these early female martyrs, whose place became central within medieval religiosity, 'could be used "to think with" by Christians who faced the crucial issue of loyalty in a pagan environment ... [T]he bodies of women ... were potentially the most vulnerable of all bodies, and their resilience, for that reason, was the most impressive.'[23] Again, if we return to the notion of the enclosed body as 'critical practice', in many ways the critical practice of late medieval female anchoritism, which constitutes the main focus of this volume, was decidedly gynaecentric, if not proto-feminist, in its tenor. Simultaneously appropriated by an intensely patriarchal socio-religious culture and yet also in some ways self-deployed, that anchoritic female body carried with it the potential to become the type of 'blind-spot in the eye of the patriarchy'[24] which led to the huge groundswell in female reclusion throughout Europe in the thirteenth and fourteenth centuries, providing an ideal conduit for the flocking of women in their hundreds to the anchoritic life. By the thirteenth and fourteenth centuries ubiquitously throughout Europe, female anchoritism formed part of a 'window of opportunity' never before experienced by religious laywomen. In their thousands, they strove for spiritual lives which lay outside the jurisdiction of the monastic orders: as beguines; as tertiaries; as hospital sisters; as carers of the poor; as communal solitaires on the peripheries of town; and as anchorites. Whilst the distribution of these vocations was by no means equal in the regions under scrutiny here (England, for example, never had a significant beguine community, nor were groups of women living in extra-monastic communal solitude ever a commonplace phenomenon as they were in Italy, for example), a much clearer picture of the enormity of what can only be termed a 'women's movement' may be gleaned if we look in a comparative way at some of those areas of Western Europe which were most affected.

Problems of terminology and definition

This diversity of vocation, all falling under the aegis of the 'solitary' one, along with the issue of haphazard distribution, calls attention to two problematic issues which need at this point to be addressed. The first of these is that of terminology: with so many different expressions of the anchoritic life at any particular historical moment within the areas included in this volume, and with its being recorded in so many different languages, how do we homogenize our reference points and

---

[22] Amy Hollywood, *Sensible Ecstasy: Mysticism, Sexual Difference and the Demands of History* (Chicago, 2002); see, in particular, pp. 236–78.

[23] Peter Brown, *The Body and Society: Men, Women and Sexual Renunciation in Early Christianity,* Twentieth-Anniversary Edition with a new Introduction (New York, 2008; first edn 1988), p. 154.

[24] This is a term first coined by Luce Irigaray regarding women's ability to destabilize the hegemony of patriarchal discourse by means of mimesis and disruption from within; for which see, for example, *Speculum of the Other Woman*, trans. Gillian C. Gill (Ithaca, 1985), ch. 1, pp. 13–29; and 'The Power of Discourse and the Subordination of the Feminine', in *This Sex Which Is Not One*, trans. Catherine Porter (Ithaca, 1985), pp. 68–85.

produce a methodology to ensure that we are even speaking about the same thing? Secondly, any discussion of medieval 'Europe' within a twenty-first century context is also beset by problems because of the perpetual redrawing of boundaries and the creation of nation-states that form part of those national – and nationalistic – geographic imperatives which have come to fruition during the modern period. It is therefore necessary at this point to lay out the rationale of this volume as far as these two potentially problematic issues are concerned.

It is now widely accepted that the colourful term 'anchorite' derives from the Greek ἀναχωρέα (*anachōrein*) meaning 'to withdraw' or 'to retire'.[25] An anchorite was therefore considered to be 'one who has withdrawn' and, in many of the early sources which document the solitary way of life, the term seems to be used interchangeably with ἔρῆμος (*erēmos*), signifying 'desolate', 'lonely', 'solitary' (and thus, eventually, 'desert'); it is from this term that the word 'hermit' is derived.[26] Whilst this points towards the common origins of the two ways of life, as documented above, it also suggests that the religious solitary life's evolution into two distinct categories, that is to say anchoritism and eremitism, was a gradual process which, I argue, was further underscored when women began to make up the larger proportion of adherents to the solitary life in Europe from the thirteenth century onwards. This is further demonstrated if we look at the proliferation of anchoritic guides outlining how an anchoritic recluse should live her or his life which sprang up during the later Middle Ages – particularly within the English tradition.[27] The earliest extant guide, however, was written specifically for religious recluses within a monastic setting by the German Benedictine monk Grimlaïcus (and, not surprisingly, is based closely on the Rule of Saint Benedict). This guide, *The Rule of Grimlaïcus*, sees little difference between a monk and a recluse:

> We must first indicate why someone is called a 'monk' or 'solitary', and then, with God's gracious help, proceed to explain other matters. The word monk [*monachus*] comes from Greek and means that a person is single [*singularis*]. 'Monas' is Greek for the Latin singleness [*singularitas*]. Hence 'solitary' translates the word 'monk'. That is why, whether one says 'monk' or 'solitary', it is one and the same thing.[28]

Grimlaïcus was writing in the ninth century and attempting to refine the Rule of Saint Benedict for those monks who had opted to move up the vocational ladder and withdraw into seclusion. Three hundred years later, however, and in England, the author of the anchoritic guide *Ancrene Wisse* was to direct his text specifically

---

[25] See *A Greek-English Lexicon*, ed. Henry George Liddell and Robert Scott (Oxford, 1925). The word ἀναχωρέα can mean both 'to withdraw from battle' and 'to retire from public life'.

[26] Ibid.

[27] As Mari Hughes-Edwards points out in her essay on the English tradition, there are thirteen such guides extant within the English tradition, some written in Latin, others in the vernacular. However, as she argues, these do not necessarily give us an accurate idea of what English anchoritic practice may have been; instead, they offer us 'rich sources of spiritual ideology'. See p. 136 below.

[28] The Latin edition of this text, edited by Lucas Holstenius in 1759, can be found in *PL* 103, cols 574–664. This has also been published in *Codex Regularum Monasticarum et Canonicarum*, ed. Lucas Holstenius, vol. 1 (Augsburg, 1759), pp. 291–344. It was reprinted in 1957 by the Akademische Druck- und Verlagsanstalt in Vienna.

at women, regarding the profession, in England at least, as decidedly female and lay, referring to his enclosed women as *ancren* or, sometimes, *reclus,* but never 'hermit', 'nun' or 'coenobite'.

Existing between these apparent polarities are the categories adopted by other authors, many of whom are discussed in the essays collected here, categories which (at least at the level of the linguistic gendering of nouns in the various languages represented) allowed for an incorporation of the recluse's gender: we have in Latin, for example, *inclusa/us* and *reclusa/us*,[29] with a good many other terms appearing in the various European vernaculars which were used in some of the sources. For example, in Spain there was the *emparedada* [walled-up woman] and, in Italy, the *incarcerate.* Such a proliferation of terminology, and the fact that some regions (Italy, for example) retained for much longer the conflation between *eremitus/a* and *anachoreta* and its variations, has made it decidedly difficult to speak generically of what it was to be an 'anchorite' within the European context. It is hoped, therefore, that this present volume and its linguistic definitions will go a long way towards resolving this particular difficulty. Indeed, each essay included here helps to clarify the use of such terms in its own area, whilst confirming the overwhelming generalization that, in the later Middle Ages, anchoritism was primarily a lay women's preserve and was characterized by a vow of permanent stability and a walling-up in a sacred space which ultimately became her tomb, a spatial configuration which located her on the very threshold between this life and the next. One could also argue that the many exceptions to this 'rule' ultimately serve to prove it. On the other hand, eremitism in the form of a solitary hermit's life (whereby the hermit lived as a solitary but was free to move about) became primarily a male preserve, the gendered ideological climate of the later Middle Ages militating entirely against individual female expressions of a relatively unregulated reclusive life. And yet this is complicated, as suggested earlier, by those groups of female 'hermits' who lived a communal life on the margins of Italian cities, for example.

Within English scholarship, it has long been customary to identify the female anchorite by the gendered term 'anchoress' and the male by the generic 'anchorite', although there is absolutely no evidence that the feminized form of the noun was used in Middle English before the fifteenth century.[30] Indeed, with the prevalence of female anchoritism outnumbering the male expression sometimes as much as five-to-one in the later Middle Ages,[31] one could argue that the anchorite was, indeed, generically female and there was thus no requirement for

[29] Interestingly, another Latin term, *anachoreta*, is only found in its feminine form.

[30] During the fifteenth century the word *ancres* begins to appear in connection with female anchorites. However, prior to that it appears to have been a generic form of the noun which was used to refer to anchorites, both male and female. The *MED* cites the first instance of this generic usage as dating from 1200: *MED, ancre/auncre/anker/ancren* 1c.

[31] I am drawing here upon the statistics of Warren in *Anchorites and their Patrons*, p. 20. However, Warren's study has relied solely on published sources and, as current scholarship is uncovering, there are hundreds of anchorholds and occupants documented in unpublished sources and in material traces which her survey overlooks. If the distribution remains the same, then women were flocking to the anchoritic life in England in even greater numbers than previously appreciated. E. A. Jones is currently updating the statistics, based on the work of both Clay and Warren.

the female ending. In any case, in modern English usage, the feminizing suffix *–ess* has become subject to negative hierarchizing practices, rendering it frequently a patronizing and demeaning linguistic construction. This is something which has been acknowledged by commentators such as Dale Spender, who remarks on the ways in which words associated with women tend to become 'perjorated' over time: 'irrespective of origin or intent, words which are marked female are marked negative'.[32] The *–ess* noun ending, therefore, no longer bears the value-neutrality which it once did, one reason, of course, why contemporary actors and poets who just happen to be female have dropped this once-preferred ending from these designations. Such a rejection of the term 'anchoress' in favour of the term 'female anchorite' is something I first posited in the introduction to the volume co-edited with Hughes-Edwards, *Anchorites, Wombs and Tombs: Intersections of Gender and Enclosure in the Middle Ages* (2005), although I do recognize that there are equally weighted arguments to be made against this term too: an insistence upon the use of the qualifying adjective 'female' could also serve to render the term 'anchorite' as default male. Again, here I am reminded of the words of Spender, who acknowledges that for women 'who do not wish to be compared to men, there is nowhere to go in the language'.[33] In truth, however, as I have stated earlier, the default sex of anchoritism was certainly female for much of its history and, in the face of such linguistic limitations, I have opted for the terms 'male anchorite' and 'female anchorite' in those contexts where the unqualified use of the noun would create confusion. In this capacity, I concur with Christopher Cannon, who has recently noted that the use of the term 'anchoress' remains unsupported by Middle English grammar and who thus similarly rejects it.[34] Continuing in this vein, therefore, this volume makes use of 'anchoress' only in quotation from secondary sources or from those primary sources which originate during the late fifteenth century and onwards,[35] considering it a term which is both anachronistic and somewhat misleading for a modern audience.

Similar problematics concerning anachronicity arise in any attempt to discuss medieval Europe in terms of discrete units of separate identities with national(istic) consciousnesses built upon local cultural traditions, inheritances and language. This type of mapping out of 'fixed' and 'policed' European boundaries constitutes a social practice which is very much part of the 'modern' moment; in the words of Irit Rogoff, 'maps do the work of making present both materially and temporally the accumulated thought and labor of the past'.[36] Within the modern period, too, it is clear that the mapping and recording of boundaries becomes increasingly a deeply urgent and entrenched national project, 'a political and epis-

---

[32] Dale Spender, *Man Made Language* (London, Boston and Henley, 1980), p. 16.

[33] Ibid., p. 21.

[34] Christopher Cannon, *The Grounds of English Literature* (Oxford, 2004), p. 143, n. 10.

[35] See, for example, the second edition of the redaction of *The Book of Margery Kempe*, printed by Henry Pepwell in 1521. Here Kempe is referred to as 'deuoute ancres'. *The Book of Margery Kempe*, ed. Hope Emily Allen, EETS o.s. 212 (London, 1997), p. 353 (p. 357, n. 11). See also my brief discussion of contemporary attitudes towards Kempe below.

[36] Irit Rogoff, *Terra Infirma: Geography's Visual Culture* (London, 2000), p. 74.

temological activity … deeply imbricated in nations' narratives of their own formation'.[37] Moreover, the assigning of specific names to certain regions, the drawing of them into, or relinquishing them from, previous classifications, along with their own self-determined designations – all of these naming strategies imposed upon swathes of land form part of a linguistic code which seeks to classify and assert ownership: these are all, again to use the words of Rogoff, 'a code of invention'.[38] Thus, the 'countries' identified in this present volume – the Low Countries, Germany, Italy, Spain, France, Ireland, along with the 'British' regions of England, Scotland and Wales – are similarly editorialized here as a 'code of invention'. As such, whilst recognizing their ultimate limitations, these terms facilitate for the modern reader a codification of this volume's comparative and contrasting discussions of a ubiquitous phenomenon which made its presence felt across much of medieval Europe and was as much part of the region's social history as its politico-religious one. It was, however, a phenomenon which was characterized by as many regional differences as similarities but, as will become clear, there were no clear-cut divisions reliant on 'national' boundaries in its expression. Instead, what we have is a widespread phenomenon distributed across Western Europe, but with pockets of varying intensity and concentration based on the particular micro and macro influences to which they were subject. The division of this volume into discrete chapters based on 'national' boundaries then, rather than offering an 'accurately historical' account of anchoritism and its adjuncts in bordered and water-tight geographies, is more a methodological tool to offer simplification of – as opposed to imposing reductionism upon – a distribution and expression of a way of life which was far more complex and diverse than rigid categories allow for.

In this context of arbitrarily invoked boundaries, Saskia Sassen has argued that the Europe of the Middle Ages, particularly the early period, was an area where various types of 'territorial fixity' interacted with an absence of 'territorial authority'.[39] Moreover, this was a time when rights were embedded in social class rather than bestowed according to territorial precepts. The demands of the Holy Roman Empire operated alongside those of the Church, interacting with the preconditions of a feudal existence to form what Sassen coins 'multiple crisscrossing jurisdictions'.[40] Thus, the types of authority to which the European peoples were subject were both multiple and frequently conflicting, whilst giving rise to a veneer of homogeneity in the discourses and projects exercised by both Church and Empire. Meanwhile, in many ways, neither Church nor Empire recognized the notion of boundaries in the modern geographical sense: for the community of believers, faith had no geographical limits and any expression of an *amor patriae*, love for one's country, was directed, of course, at the transcendent heavenly Jerusalem and the ultimate 'homecoming'. The only geographically conceived boundary to be

---

[37] Ibid., p. 74.

[38] Ibid., p. 75.

[39] Saskia Sassen, *Territory, Authority, Rights: From Medieval to Global Assemblages* (Princeton and Oxford, 2006), here at pp. 32–3.

[40] Ibid., p. 33.

crossed was that which lay between this world and the next. In this context, one can now perhaps see the allure of the anchoritic life within this socio-religious faith system. If national boundaries fail to signify in any significant way, then the 'international' figure of the anchorite is part of a homogenizing strategy which functions to break down the barrier between the human and God, situated as s/he is on the very threshold between her/his more prosaically local environment and that of the heavenly city. Thus, despite a very material 'separation' – permanent or otherwise – from the community, enforced by walls of stone, s/he simultaneously serves to both dismantle and deconstruct those boundaries, allowing vicarious access across the border into the life of the sacred and thus dissolving that border itself.

Situating the European anchorite within the type of strategic geographical configuration adopted by this volume can, I think, also help us understand not only the extraordinary explosion in the popularity of this type of holy life throughout the regions under scrutiny – and amongst the female population, in particular – but also its metamorphoses as it made that journey. As many of these essays attest, this relentless exodus of women from the familial to the independent, or quasi-independent, religious life operated like a tidal wave sweeping through Europe, crossing the North Sea into England and Ireland – although, apparently not making its mark in any significant way in Wales and Scotland.[41]

Anchoritism and the medieval town

Early medieval anchoritism began as a rural phenomenon, cascading into a widespread practice in the high to late Middle Ages at the same time as long-distance trading opportunities gave rise to a proliferation of wealthy economic centres where people began to group themselves into larger urban conglomerates: the cities and towns. Developing alongside a new commercial and agricultural prosperity, late medieval solitary enclosure reflected this economic revival and also depended upon it. The growing wealth of towns created incentives for aristocratic patronage and the granting of protection rights, something soon to be emulated by the new upwardly mobile artisan and mercantile classes. In turn, this gave rise to a new sense of territory, emphasized further by the high city walls surrounding these centres of new commercial activity. As well as attaching themselves to the churches within these new communities, recluses were also active in structures or small communities along the city walls – termed by Mario Sensi in his essay on Italy, 'the sacred perimeter' – again mapping out inviolate sacred spaces which would synecdochically offer the citizen a glimpse at heaven in its midst; as wills and testaments throughout the period attest, supporting an anchorite was a sure-fire way of guaranteeing a secure place in the hereafter, whilst also establishing

---

[41] This dearth of female anchoritic expression in both Scotland and Wales is, perhaps, a result of the multiple colonial projects to which these regions were subjected throughout the Middle Ages as well as to greater levels of poverty and less dense populations. These issues will be discussed, in part, in this volume's two concluding essays focusing on these countries. The reasons for the Irish experience's being rather different, in spite of its own problems with colonization, are also posited by Ó Clabaigh in his essay on the Irish experience.

one's place and status in the here-and-now. And, as ever, prosperity brought with it expansionism: between the eleventh and thirteenth centuries, Christian territory more than doubled in size and its population increased accordingly. Sassen notes the extraordinary statistic of five thousand cities being founded in Europe between the mid-eleventh century and the early thirteenth,[42] many of which were in Italy where they became virtually autonomous city-states with their own legislative powers and where large armies were housed for purposes of protection.[43] It is hardly surprising, then, with a greatly increased population, half of which was presumably female, that we should see a large increase in women entering the holy life during this period – and various forms of its solitary expression at that. With a new sense of autonomy being generated by urban life, opportunities offered themselves to women, both within a religious capacity and an economic one, within these environments. Whilst laywomen were beginning to have access to the trades and other urban employment,[44] their more devout sisters were searching out a range of religious options which would allow for the expression of an individualized spirituality at the heart of the community.

During this period, too, Western Europe was expanding via conquest and encroachment: Spain was seized back from Moorish control; the Normans spread into the reaches of Sicily and southern Italy; and the 'English' begin to expand into Wales, Scotland and Ireland. New trade routes, both local and long distance, were established, forming a network for information dissemination and the construction of 'virtual' communities within which anchoritism was a major actor. For Max Weber, in his seminal focus on the development of the city in Western Europe,[45] this type of multi-expansionism and optimism was a dynamic combination which necessarily was productive of innovation and change. Moreover – and this is crucial to my argument here – for Weber, the birth of the city provided the environment which allowed the practices of the marginalized or excluded to come to the fore in the making of history.[46] And, by its very nature, medieval anchoritism was a practice of the deliberately marginal: those who chose a liminal life on the discursive 'margins' of society. Moreover, those women who were drawn to various expressions of it in their droves throughout Europe during the period were doubly elevated because doubly marginalized: as women and as recluses. They were (again to adapt the words of Sassen) 'a built-in capability'.[47]

---

[42] Sassen, *Territory, Authority, Rights,* p. 60.

[43] Ibid., p. 58.

[44] On women and work in medieval Europe see, for example, David Herlihy, *Opera Muliebria: Women and Work in Medieval Europe* (New York and London, 1990); and Martha C. Howell, *Women, Production and Patriarchy in Late-Medieval Cities* (Chicago, 1986). For an overview of their wider roles within European society, see Margaret Wade Labarge, *Women in Medieval Life* (London, 1986; repr. 2001); and Shulamith Shahar, *A History of Women in the Middle Ages* (London, 1983).

[45] Max Weber, *The City* (London and New York, 1958).

[46] Ibid., but see, in particular, ch. 4 'The Plebeian City', pp. 157–95.

[47] Sassen, *Territory, Authority, Rights*, p. 73. H. G. Koenigsberger suggests that the citizens of these new towns and cities developed a sense of 'privileged separateness' from those who lived outside the city, something which came to be represented by the city walls themselves. See H. G. Koenigsberger, *Medieval Europe 400–1500* (London, 1987), p. 146.

The essays: outline and rationale

Just what this 'built-in capability' was able to achieve during its height is reflected in all its diversity in the essays collected together in this volume. Each contributor combines closely researched historical data from a wide range of sources with interpretive analysis and a number of case studies, producing evidence to suggest that the medieval anchorite in Europe was more often a woman and fulfilled a plethora of socio-religious roles. She could be teacher, counsellor, advisor; she could be highly literate or completely unread; she could care for the sick and the marginalized; she could sometimes prophesy or ordain miracle cures; at other times she could confess others and adopt a quasi-priestly role; frequently she withdrew entirely and permanently; in other instances she withdrew only periodically in order to do penance. Always, however, she had the precepts of her desert forebears at the front of her imagination. Always, too, she was elevated above the common *mêlée* of the faithful, taking up a position somewhere between this world and eternity. Whilst the male anchorite would build upon his former role as already sanctified monastic or priest and intensify it, the female anchorite's journey was a much longer and more precipitous one – one of the primary reasons for the almost ubiquitous anxiety which she generated within both Church and community as the flip-side to her sanctified and privileged status. Whilst at her most prolific, ironically she was at her most policed.

The first essay in this collection focuses on the expression and development of anchoritism in the Low Countries, a region which its author, Anneke Mulder-Bakker, defines as stretching from the Seine to the Elbe where these rivers enter the North Sea. This is an area which the present-day reader would recognize as encompassing northern France, Belgium and the Netherlands and it was here that the ground-swell of extra-monastic female religious activity alluded to earlier was first felt; in particular, via the activities of the beguines and the women of the *Devotio Moderna* [Modern Devotion].[48] Mulder-Bakker rightly identifies this as a 'trail-blazing' of lay female religiosity within an expanding urban culture which operated variously under the aegis of the French king or German emperor. And it was here, so she argues, that the ground was rendered fertile enough for a rich expression of female anchoritism to develop, indeed a 'built-in capability' which would ultimately shape the religious sensibilities of the entire region and make its presence felt in the anchoritic life as it developed elsewhere in Europe. Mulder-Bakker begins her essay by retracing the origins of European anchoritism, both male and female, following its progress from the Desert Fathers and Mothers, through the hermit-knights of the early Middle Ages, to the rich and varied expressions of independent female anchoritism which characterized the later Middle Ages. Mulder-Bakker's wide-reaching approach serves not only to develop some of the issues raised during this introduction but also to underpin many of the

---

[48] The *Devotio Moderna*, or 'modern devotion', refers to a movement towards the regeneration of the spiritual life that was initiated in the Netherlands during the late fourteenth century and whose influence was felt also in Germany, France and parts of Italy, as Mulder-Bakker, Signori and Sensi all demonstrate in their essays included here.

other essays which follow, in particular that of Signori, whose preferred methodology is to scrutinize closely some of the plethora of literary sources pertaining to female anchorites and their confessors in the German-speaking regions of the Middle Ages. Unlike the English tradition, the German tradition and that of the Low Countries are rich in literary sources which recount the lives of their female anchorites (written frequently for purposes of proposed canonization) and who were evidently of central importance to their local communities, and in many cases to the wider intellectual and spiritual community. Signori, therefore, takes up where Mulder-Bakker leaves off, demonstrating the ways in which the extant literary evidence, in particular the male-authored *vitae* of such women, confirms the high esteem in which female anchorites were held and the investment made in them by those learned men who were frequently also their confessors and biographers. There are, of course, some problems with a methodological reliance on these types of sources for ascertaining the actual *practice* of female anchoritism during the period: almost every male biographer had an urgent agenda or vested interest in presenting his female subject in the holiest possible light and thus such texts contain concerted performances of both an ideal and idealized gender and holiness.[49] Indeed, Mulder-Bakker in her own essay has already posed the question as to the historical reliability of the *vitae* of such women because of the cultural work which they are devised to undertake, but she also rejects the possibility that they are tales of complete fantasy. Her conclusion is that they are neither historically accurate, nor entirely fantastical, adding most elegantly: 'The history of eremitism is just as much an *histoire des mentalités* as an *histoire des réalités*.' Signori's focus, therefore, read alongside Mulder-Bakker's treatment, is ideally placed to offer us a clear idea of the type of *mentalités* which led to such texts and the performances constructed within them. Her essay also goes some way to revealing what went into producing those *mentalités* in the first place, particularly on the local level where the women under scrutiny were frequently venerated as living saints and developed into cult figures soon after death.

In contrast to this wealth of extant *vitae* in northern Continental contexts, the situation in Italy was somewhat different. As Mario Sensi asserts at the beginning of his essay on the region, in spite of the extremely popular nature of the eremitic life amongst women south of the Alps during the period covered, very few literary accounts of their lives remain – and those Sensi approaches with caution for the reasons already recounted above. Like Signori, he recognizes the cultural project invested in the production of such writings, sometimes – but not always – in the context of attempts to effect canonization; whatever their purpose, however, successful investment in a written Life could have desirable political and economic repercussions. What made this cultural project more urgent, too, was the civic nature of the Italian political scene of the day: large cities constituted independent realms which often accrued large armies to protect their autonomy and,

---

[49] This is an issue which has been examined in some depth by Catherine M. Mooney in *Gendered Voices: Medieval Saints and their Interpreters* (Philadelphia, 1999). Particularly useful here is Mooney's comparison of the ways in which the women depict themselves and their vocation (when their own writings are extant) and the representation of those same women by their male biographers.

whilst ultimately answerable to the Roman Church, nevertheless developed distinctive expressions of what Sensi refers to as 'civic religion'. Moreover, a distinctly female eremitic religiosity lay at the very heart of such distinctive expressions, particularly from the thirteenth century to the fifteenth, helping to define and demarcate the civic and religious spaces which its adherents in all their forms occupied. Whilst, according to Sensi, it is impossible to overstate the extent and importance of the burgeoning of independent female religious expression during the period or the 'profound traces' which it left on the fabric of society, he picks out some of the most influential for particular scrutiny: the *bizzocaggi* [communal groups]; the *carceri* [solitaries]; the female penitentials. All of these groups took as their base the extra-monastic eremitism of their desert forebears, although not all of them sought to live out a life in solitary confinement in a single location. Many, however, lived in places which in common parlance were deemed to be 'prisons' but which were often referred to in synodal constitutions as *domi* [houses] or *cell[a]e* [cells], belying in some ways the more ascetical nature of such women's lives. Sensi finishes his essay with a summary of the official institutional interventions aimed at controlling these women and their lives, providing a useful context in which to read the 'women's movement' dealt with by all the contributors to this book. Ecclesiastical anxiety about quasi-independent holy women was writ large across Europe and was felt as much in the far reaches of Ireland as it was in the Italian cities. As Sensi takes pains to emphasize, however, such interventions failed entirely to halt the tide of independent spiritual expression. Rather, what these women demonstrated time and again was an ability to adapt, metamorphosing their groupings and shaping their *modus operandi* to fit the shifting political and religious influences to which they were subject.

This type of expedient metamorphosis is also characteristic of the recluses of the Iberian peninsula who form the focus of Gregoria Cavero Domínguez's essay. Offering an overview of the phenomenon from the fourth century onwards, Cavero asserts the popularity of this way of life in Spain from very early times. Particularly popular amongst the aristocracy, its main premise during this early period seems to have been penitential rather than contemplative, something reflected in the word which came to be associated with cells, *ergastulum*, which has the alternative meaning of 'prison'. Expansion under Visigoth influence and survival under Muslim rule led to an explosion in its expression from the twelfth century onwards, as was also witnessed in most of the other European regions examined in this volume. Thereafter, the records present women locked up in great numbers, both in urban and in rural settings: next to village churches, alongside cathedrals, abutting collegiate churches, parish churches and chapels. Known as the *emparedadas* or 'walled-up women', they lived a life of meditation and prayer combined with a more active life of charitable activity and social projects: textile work, teaching etc. Most interestingly, Cavero presents a rare text purporting to be a prayer focusing on the passion of Christ and written in the first-person by one such *emparedada*. The *Oración de la Emparedada* [Prayer of the Walled-up Woman] appeared in the fifteenth century, gaining widespread popularity, even read within royal circles. However, reflecting the type of male institutional anxiety about unregulated female religiosity which seems to have impinged upon medieval anchoritism ubiquitously, this highly popular text rapidly found its way into the library of banned books and came to be associated with the malign spells of witchcraft. This, more than anything, demonstrates clearly the thin line trodden by many anchoritic women between orthodoxy and heresy in the eyes of the authorities.

In contrast with the essays that precede it, Paulette L'Hermite-Leclercq's contribution on the French tradition chooses to focus primarily on those anchoritic men and women whose experiences of separation from the world were fully concretized by surrounding walls of solid stone. Such recluses, like their English counterparts, professed stability of place and took solemn vows before the bishop, although they had begun as part of a much wider eremitic movement (which L'Hermite-Leclercq also traces in the first part of her essay). Whilst acknowledging the importance of the vocation as a material reality undertaken by a living person (who was more often than not a woman) inhabiting a cell of solid stone, L'Hermite-Leclercq also gives voice to the vocation's discursive transformation into the type of mythical homecoming which we saw in Bachelard's invocation of the hermit's candle in the window of his cell, to which I alluded at the beginning of this introduction. The symbolic elements of the immurement – the cell as holy vessel, the door as a closed threshold, the windows which no longer signify as a conduit of sunlight and air and vision – all combine to transform the occupant into an other-worldly figure who is both absent and present simultaneously. The anchorite lives, in effect, 'between two deaths', offering the faithful of the community an example of both how to live – and how to die. What is particularly remarkable about the French experience, however, is the wealth of disparate sources it generated, which allows us to corroborate these insights, suggesting in turn a hugely widespread phenomenon which has left significant material traces in its wake. These sources include chronicles, obituaries, cartularies, notarial registers, even specifications for building suitable anchorholds. In addition, there are anchorites' wills, royal charters and accounts, records of proceedings and parish accounts, all adding to the findings of archaeological research and place-name studies, along with the usual iconographical and literary sources.

What they do not include, however, are any guidance texts written specifically for the anchorite and crafted towards teaching her/him how to successfully live out a life of perpetual and permanent solitary enclosure. The proliferation of this type of source seems to be particular to the English tradition, perhaps because in England there were far fewer opportunities available to women in particular to live an extra-institutional religious life. Except for one possible site in Norwich during the fifteenth century, for example, there are no records of any beguinages existing in an insular context.[50] Nor do there appear to have been communities of extra-institutional female hermits, which were common in some areas of Europe during the period. In fact, as is evidenced by the fifteenth-century *Book of Margery*

---

[50] In the fifteenth century there emerged briefly in Norwich two groups of women living unregulated, quasi-beguinal lives, on which see Norman P. Tanner, *The Church in Late Medieval Norwich 1370–1532*, Pontifical Institute of Mediaeval Studies, Studies and Texts 66 (Toronto, 1984), pp. 64–6.

Kempe, women who aspired to live a holy life outside of nunnery and anchorhold were constantly under suspicion in England for harbouring heterodox tendencies and were closely policed in all their activities. As one particularly fraught and anxiety-ridden monk articulates to the laywoman with holy aspirations, Margery Kempe, 'I wold þow wer closyd in an hows of ston þat þer schuld no man speke with þe',[51] suggesting that some kind of enclosure – whether anchoritic, monastic, domestic or penitential – is far preferable to having her wandering about of her own volition and discussing the word of God with whomever will listen. In this context, it is also interesting that, by the time a redacted version of Kempe's book reached its second imprint in 1521, as author she had already been safely categorized as 'a deuoute ancres called Margerye kempe of Lynne',[52] although there is no other evidence to suggest that Kempe entered the anchorhold after her book was written in the late 1330s.

The category of 'deuoute ancres' is one presumed upon for his audience on many occasions by the author of the popular guidance text *Ancrene Wisse*, a text which has long dictated our understanding of the English expression of anchoritism. Indeed, the comparative wealth of guidance-text material in England is something outlined by Mari Hughes-Edwards in her essay on the English experience. Here, Hughes-Edwards argues cogently for the ideological nature of the surviving guidance texts, dovetailing effectively with L'Hermite-Leclercq's analysis of the mythologizing project attached to literary responses to the anchoritic life. As both contributors would concur, such guidance texts, far from outlining the 'actual' day-to-day practices of the anchorite, are more helpful for the slippage they produce in revealing the *mentalités* behind the vocation and its particular expression in England. Again, in the most colourful and lyrical of these texts, *Ancrene Wisse*, written in the first instance for three anchoritic sisters, then rewritten, redrafted, amended and translated for generations of English anchorites – Anglophone, Latinate, Anglo-French, male and female – deep anxieties about independent and unregulated female religiosity predominate, anxieties that helped to shape both the female and male expressions throughout the regions under scrutiny.[53]

Methodologically, Hughes-Edwards draws closely upon the two most fundamental studies of English anchoritism to date which have long formed the basis of our understanding of the phenomenon, those studies by Clay and Warren cited at the start of this introduction. Indeed, these seminal works on the English tradition are yet to be surpassed, and it is for this reason too that Colmán Ó Clabaigh draws upon Warren's methodological tools in particular to examine and codify the anchoritic tradition in medieval Ireland. As Ó Clabaigh rightly points out, to date there have been no concerted studies into Irish anchoritism beyond his own and the research field is, therefore, still in its infancy. Moreover, research is impeded

[51] Kempe, *The Book of Margery Kempe*, p. 27.
[52] See p. 12, n. 35 above.
[53] The importance of *Ancrene Wisse*, not only to female and male anchorites but also to lay spirituality more generally in England, has been addressed by Cate Gunn in her book *Ancrene Wisse: from Pastoral Literature to Vernacular Spirituality* (Cardiff, 2008).

by a scarcity of material on which to base a comprehensive survey, the complete antithesis to what we have seen in the context of some of the other European regions. As Ó Clabaigh documents, the poverty of the medieval Irish church precluded it from efficient and comprehensive record-producing and the enormous and protracted upheavals of Irish history put paid to the survival of many of the records which were produced (and the same can be said, in part, for both Scotland and Wales). Ó Clabaigh's task, therefore, has been to piece together a likely picture of the Irish anchoritic tradition and its prevalence from a kaleidoscope of fragments which he proceeds to uncover and reassemble. Nevertheless, the picture which is emerging is sufficiently clear to suggest that both hermits and anchorites were familiar figures within the topography of medieval Ireland and, indeed, continued to appear in the records well into the seventeenth century.

The case for Scotland and Wales is radically different, as the two concluding essays within this collection demonstrate. Whilst there is fragmentary and sometimes tantalizingly obscure evidence to suggest that both hermits and anchorites were part of the cultural landscape in both countries, written evidence for the latter is particularly hard to come by – and there is virtually no evidence at all to support any kind of tradition of female reclusion as having existed in any significant way. In her survey, Anna McHugh recounts much of the extant evidence which supports the existence of the hermitic life in Scotland, whilst at the same time lamenting the absence of material pertaining to the anchoritic existence. She also astutely assesses why this may have been the case, taking into consideration the influences of the Celtic church and its reforms, as well as both geographical and economic considerations. And the same may well be the case for Wales although, as I point out in my own essay on the Welsh experience of anchoritism, no research has ever been undertaken into the solitary life in this region and, even more so than in medieval Scotland, the incidences of the solitary life have been subsumed into hagiography, legend and pseudo-histories such as those articulated by Gerald of Wales, for example. Indeed, any such anchoritism which existed in Wales seems to have allowed itself to be completely overshadowed by the proliferation of that way of life – and its female expression, in particular – along the Marches which separated the Welsh territories from their English counterparts and where *Ancrene Wisse* is thought to have originated. As I argue, it is almost certainly the case that in Wales an admixture of a small, frequently oppressed population, geographic inaccessibility, a clan- or family-based monastic structure working for many centuries outside the jurisdiction of the Roman Church, and a dearth of 'excess' women meant that all were absorbed into the local socio-political economy with social reclusion taking on, perhaps, the status of unobtainable 'luxury' for anybody other than tried and tested monks. Until a new generation of anchoritic scholars takes up the challenge presented by this lack of research, the anchoritic tradition which almost certainly existed within these two overlooked regions, and the Bachelardian 'universe outside the universe' which it represented, will remain a closed and hidden chapter within their respective histories.

1 Anchorites in the Low Countries

Anneke B. Mulder-Bakker

This chapter focuses on eremitism in the Low Countries, the delta region between the Seine and the Elbe where the great rivers flow into the North Sea. Politically speaking, it encompasses the present Northern France (medieval Flanders), Belgium and the Netherlands, and the adjacent areas along the Lower Rhine up to the Elbe in Germany. Numerous independent principalities and city republics operated here under the formal sovereignty of the French king or the German emperor. In socio-economic terms, they comprised the prosperous commercial centres of the Low Countries with their expanding urban culture and trailblazing religious developments. The Beguine movement originated here as well as the Modern Devotion [*Devotio Moderna*] of the Sisters and Brethren of the Common Life, both with a preference for a non-monastic form of religious life often characterized as the *mixed life*. In cultural and religious terms, beginning in the thirteenth century, far more women were active here than anywhere else in Europe.

The example of Saint Martin

When Count Ansfried of Hamaland surrendered his title and family life and ascended at an advanced age to the Utrecht episcopal see in 995, he had a small monastery with a hermitage built outside of Utrecht on the Eem River, which he called the Hohorst or Heiligenberg. He was, in this respect, following the example of Martin of Tours, who had built a similar complex on the Loire in France. Ansfried (d. 1010) was consequently placing himself in the tradition of the famous Saint Martin, prototype of ascetic and eremitic Christianity in Western Europe and patron of the church of Utrecht (and the Hohorst monastery as well).[1] A few centuries before Ansfried, the Flemish missionary Amandus (*c*.600–*c*.680) had done something similar. In his youth, Amandus made a pilgrimage to Saint Martin's grave in Tours and took a container of hallowed ground as a talisman for his

---

[1] The survey of Latin saints' Lives edited by the Socii Bollandiani, *BHL*, Subsidia Hagiographica 6, 12, 70, makes an inventory of all Latin *vitae* (referred to in this essay as *BHL* followed by the number). It has Ansfried's listed under no. 543. Alpertus Mettensis, *De Diversitate Temporum*, c. 11–17, in *Gebeurtenissen van deze tijd en Een fragment over bisschop Diederik I van Metz,* ed. and trans. Hans van Rij (Amsterdam, 1980), pp. 22–41 (p. 31). Johanna Maria van Winter, 'De Rijksbisschoppen in de elfde eeuw', in *Geschiedenis van de provincie Utrecht tot 1528*, ed. C. Dekker, et al. (Utrecht, 1997), pp. 115–30.

further course in life. In imitation of Saint Martin, he allowed himself to be shut up as an anchorite in Bourges in order to prepare himself mentally for his ministerial task. After a trip to Rome, he then wandered around the lands of the Meuse and Scheldt rivers in order to organize Christianity in these regions. He founded monasteries and converted the people, sometimes to an asceticism as rigorous as he himself practised. The converts included Bavo, on whom I will focus below. For later generations, Amandus embodies the ideal of true eremitism because he is reported to have retreated into a hermitage not only at the beginning but also at the end of his life.[2]

Similar to Ansfried in the tenth and Amandus in the seventh century, Wulfilaïcus was inspired by Saint Martin as early as the sixth century. He, too, made a pilgrimage to Saint Martin's grave and took a container of consecrated ground back with him. He then became a stylite who had himself nailed to a column outside Trier; he incited all passers-by to convert to the Christian faith, because people passed his column when they secretly wanted to do service to idols in the forest. His activities were a thorn in the side of the bishops in the region. According to church leaders, ascetics were supposed to withdraw into monasteries and concentrate on the contemplative life of prayer and pious manual labour; they should not preach, the latter being the work of bishops. The bishops therefore summoned the hermit to them; he, of course, had to come down from his pillar, and they quickly had it chopped down.[3]

The above-mentioned ascetics – and many others – saw Martin of Tours (c.316–396) as the great example for them. This Roman, who began his career as a soldier in service of the emperor, learned about Christianity in Trier and there heard stories about the great desert father Anthony (251/2–356). Smitten with this man's ascetic ideals, Martin left military service and lived for a while as a hermit on an uninhabited island. He subsequently joined the learned Bishop Hilarius of Poitiers in the then barely Christianized Gaul. He was there elected bishop of Tours by the enthusiastic population in c.370, after which he continued his Christianizing work with all the greater authority from that city. He established a hermit colony on the Loire River and experimented there with a form of life that combined missionary work among the people with contemplative existence in the hermitage.

Sulpicius Severus (c.360–406), who visited Martin in his hermitage several times, wrote a *vita* immediately after Martin's death that provides a character sketch of the man of God (*Vita Martini*). Sulpicius also wrote a few letters and dialogues, the wording of which reminds us of the *vita* of Anthony the Great.[4] He compared Martin with the desert father Anthony but replaced the *anachoresis*

---

[2] Amandus: *BHL* 332–48. *Vita Amandi prima*, in *MGH. SRMer.*, vol. 5, 395–485; in a later interpolation in this *vita* Amandus is retrospectively fashioned into the model of the true hermit. É. de Moreau, *Histoire de l'église en Belgique*, vol. 1 (Brussels, 1940), pp. 77–90.

[3] Gregory of Tours, *Historiarum Libri Decem*, Book 8, 15, in *Gregor von Tours, Zehn Bücher Geschichten*, ed. Rudolf Buchner (Darmstadt, 1955), vol. 2, pp. 176–82.

[4] Jacques Fontaine (ed. and trans.), *Sulpicius Severus, Vie de Saint Martin*, 3 vols, Sources Chrétiennes 133–5 (Paris, 1967–1969). The dialogues have been edited by Carolus Halm in *Sulpicii Severi, Libri qui supersunt*, Corpus Scriptorum Ecclesiasticorum Latinorum 1–2 (Vienna, 1866).

(which signified complete withdrawal into the uninhabited desert) with a *peregrinatio* [wandering] among pagans. He wrote that Martin was often

> compared with hermits and even *anachoretae*. These are said to have performed
> their miracles free from all impediments with only the heaven and angels as wit-
> nesses. Saint Martin however, living in the midst of the people – among quar-
> relling clergy, ferociously ranting bishops, weighed down by what were nearly
> daily scandals, first here, then there – Martin nevertheless persevered. He was
> rooted in an invincible power, confronting the entire world, and he did more than
> even those individuals about whose life in the desert we have just learned.[5]

Sulpicius's *Vita Martini* would become one of the most influential texts in
Western church history. As a result, Saint Martin would come to embody the
Western asceticism of the mixed life, a combination of eremitic asceticism and
pastoral work among people, a way of life that would later become so characteristic of the Low Countries.[6]

It is for this reason that Saint Martin is given pride of place at the beginning
of this chapter. In my sketch of hermits and recluses in the Low Countries which
follows, I will join in the tradition of Saint Martin and focus on the type of informal eremitism which kept the adherent in contact with his/her fellow human
beings, whilst laying the greatest emphasis on female anchorites specifically. It
will become clear that medieval sources frequently document a retrospective creation of an image rather than any verifiable factual history of the anchorites
themselves. Indeed, we are often left with scant information about the historical
'reality'. The history of eremitism is just as much an *histoire des mentalités* as an
histoire des réalités.

The ideals of the Desert Fathers

As mentioned, Martin of Tours stood in the tradition of the Egyptian Desert
Fathers, leading to, on the one hand, the hermits and anchorites of the later periods and, on the other, the monks. After all, both forms of religious life in the
Middle Ages had their origins in the Desert Fathers,[7] those virtuosos of the third
and fourth centuries who freely and unconditionally dedicated themselves to the
service of God. Anthony the Great was the prototype for both.[8] But in the course
of the following centuries the two strands moved in opposite directions as the

---

[5] Sulpicius Severus, *Dialogus Primus*, 24, op. cit, pp. 176–7.

[6] Saint Martin was also the patron saint of the diocese of Utrecht, and many of the old city and parish
churches in the Netherlands are dedicated to him. Along with Saint Nicholas, he is the best-known male
saint: see Henricus Josephus Kok, *Proeve van een onderzoek van de patrocinia in het middeleeuwse bis-
dom Utrecht* (Assen, 1958).

[7] For an excellent introduction to this, see Marilyn Dunn, *The Emergence of Monasticism: From the
Desert Fathers to the Early Middle Ages* (Oxford, 2000).

[8] G. J. M. Bartelink (ed. and trans.), *Athanase d'Alexandrie, Vie d'Antoine*, Sources Chrétiennes 400
(Paris, 1994).

monastic life became incorporated in ecclesiastical structures and the eremitic life was pushed away into the desert. Church fathers preferred the monastic communities of monks and nuns who replaced the Desert Fathers' mental rejection of the world with physical avoidance. Monastics lived in the isolation of an abbey, protected from the world outside by thick walls, at least in Western Europe where Benedict created a strict regime for his followers. In monasteries, monks and nuns devoted themselves to a life of self-sanctification and contemplation. From the church leaders' perspective, this was an orderly and manageable, and thus beneficial, institution. They strongly promoted it.

Benedict, who began his religious career as a hermit in a cave near Subiaco, nevertheless created the possibility in his monastic rule of living as an anchorite under strict conditions. Experienced monks could obtain permission to leave the community and live further as a hermit. To quote from his rule: 'they have built up their strength and go from the battle line in the ranks of their brothers to the single combat of the desert'.[9] In their case, the desert was life in a hermitage in the mountains or as a recluse enclosed in an anchorhold at the abbey church. In Carolingian times, the Benedictine Grimlaïcus wrote a rule for this latter group: the *Regula solitariorum* (discussed briefly by Signori in her contribution to this volume).[10] This is not a general rule for the anchoritic life, as is often believed,[11] but is specifically tailored for recluse-monks, for students of the 'graduate class', as it were.

Hermits, on the contrary, were rough warriors of God who did not conform to this monastic ideal. Church leaders had admiration only for hermits who withdrew completely from society, the *anachoretae* deep in the desert, or the dendrites high in the trees. With a mix of admiration and horror they talked about the *subdivales*, who lived like hares in the field without any form of protection, or the *bosschoi*, the grass-eaters, who like grasshoppers ran away as soon as they saw a living creature approaching (at times ecclesiastical busybodies tried to catch them with large butterfly nets). And they told each other anecdotes about hermits living between the ceilings of a church building, only stretching out their arm once a week to be given bread. The stories about these heroes of the faith still haunt our memories and distort our image of (Western) eremitism. Martin of Tours tried some of these extreme forms but saw the danger and turned back to the human world. He subsequently allowed himself to be led by the original ideals of the Desert Fathers, living on the edge of the human world rather than by the principles of the 'true' *anachoretae*. Western Europe would follow him in this respect. Extreme anachoresis is not a Western European phenomenon.

Independent of the two strands of monasticism and anachoresis, actual historical men and women were drawn through the ages to the more humane ideal of

[9] *Regula Benedicti*, 1, 3–5, ed. Timothy Fry, et al., *The Rule of St. Benedict in Latin and English* (Collegeville, MN, 1981), pp. 168–9.

[10] Grimlaïcus, *Regula solitariorum*, *PL* 103, cols 577–664.

[11] See Karl Suso Frank, 'Grimlaicus, "Regula solitariorum"', in *Vita religiosa im Mittelalter. Festschrift für Kaspar Elm*, ed. Franz J. Felten and Nikolas Jaspert (Berlin, 1999), pp. 21–36.

the Desert Fathers and Mothers. They radically cut all ties with family and Church, but not necessarily with society as such. They opted for free submission to God but, as Peter Brown has shown in his magisterial study of the 'Holy Man in Late Antiquity', usually went no further away than the edge of the desert. Combining contemplation with pastoral care, they felt called to respond to the desires and needs of the faithful around them. They functioned as personal counsellors and as intermediaries between ordinary mortals and their masters, between human beings and God. They had prophetic quality, were mediators of salvation and agents of happiness. Their social role was not a sideline that distracted them from their main task of contemplation and avoidance of the world; it was rather a matter of the 'incarnation' thereof, of concretization of this primary task. They were 'holy men' and 'holy women', living in a patch of paradise on earth – with a tamed lion at their feet – as instances of salvation. Martin's life in Tours stands in this tradition.[12]

The Peregrinatio *of the Irish*

Still another tradition had a crucial influence on the eremitism of the Low Countries: the Irish tradition of *peregrinatio*. As Colmán Ó Clabaigh demonstrates in his chapter on Ireland, Irish ascetics eagerly chose a religious life outside the clan and the clan monastery. They left their homeland and settled on an uninhabited island, with or without a group of companions, or in an unknown, preferably pagan area. They called this their *peregrinatio Dei*, their wandering around for God. Often, they combined it with active preaching of the Gospel. They settled among the Angles and Saxons in England, and stimulated these peoples to undertake a similar *peregrinatio*, or they struck out for the Continent. Especially in Northern France and Belgium, these Irish pilgrims founded hermitages and monasteries between the fifth and seventh centuries. They worked in concert with aristocratic women in the area, such as Aldegondis and the sisters Gertrudis of Nivelles and Begga.[13] In the seventh and eighth centuries, Anglo-Saxon *peregrini* undertook missionary work in the Low Countries and Germany. Willibrord and Boniface were great organizers and they in their turn involved female family members from England who were living in convents on the Continent. Their

---

[12] Peter Brown, 'The Rise and Function of the Holy Man in Late Antiquity', repr. in Peter Brown, *Society and the Holy in Late Antiquity* (London, 1982), pp. 103–52. On the Desert Mothers, see Joseph M. Soler, 'Les mères du désert et la maternité spirituelle', *Collectanea Cisterciensia* 48 (1986), pp. 235–50. For an evaluation of Brown's ideas, see *The Cult of Saints in Late Antiquity and the Early Middle Ages*, ed. James Howard-Johnston and Paul Antony Hayward (Oxford, 1999). For Gaul, see R. van Dam, *Saints and their Miracles in Late Antique Gaul* (Princeton, 1993).

[13] De Moreau, *Histoire de l'église en Belgique*, vol. 1, pp. 115–40. Each of these women also became a popular saint herself. Their reputations were strongly influenced by the eremitic ideal and the Irish *peregrinatio*, as I will show below. An example can be found in Aldegondis, *BHL* 244–50. In her third Life, published in *AASS*, 30 Jan., vol. 3, pp. 655–65, Aldegondis escaped a threatening marriage by walking across a river without getting wet (p. 658). She then entered an uninhabited area and lived there. See also Anne-Marie Helvétius, 'Ste Aldegonde et les origines du monastère de Maubeuge', *Revue du Nord* 74 (1992), pp. 221–37.

ambition was to establish a well-organized church with a network of dioceses in which orthodox worshippers would worship in obedience to the pope in Rome. They were missionary preachers just like Martin of Tours, and their ideals were similar. Amandus, for example, was captivated by both Martin and the Irish *peregrinatio* ideal.[14]

In the wake of these apostles of the faith, other men and women came to the Continent; they were more concerned with individual devotion to God. Some entered the new monasteries, while others became hermits. They journeyed for God without attaching themselves to any settled form of life or place of residence. All these individuals are to be regarded as hermits, believers who individually and without status spent their life in the service of God, not living in a monastery under a rule and an abbot, nor teaching and preaching as a priest or bishop. They were individual virtuosos who combined ascesis and contemplation with pastoral attention to visitors. If they had already enjoyed clerical status as a monk or an ordained priest in a previous phase of life, they did not rely on this standing during their eremitic existence. They were hermits, simple warriors for God, who formed the ideal image of perfection for ordinary believers. They found disciples among the native religious population, both men and women.

The early Middle Ages

From late antiquity we find dozens of examples of this free anchoritic ideal in Western Europe. Jean Heuclin has provided a survey of them in Northern France and the Low Countries in his exhaustive study *Aux origines monastiques de la Gaule du Nord. Ermites et Reclus du ve au xie siècle.*[15] He mentions more than 100 hermits by name, most alive in the sixth to eighth centuries, followed by a regression under the Carolingians, after which there was a resurgence until the eleventh century (as McAvoy has suggested in her introduction, society changed radically after the eleventh century, and anchoritism also followed suit, as I shall demonstrate further). Of the 100 anchorites in our research area, approximately a quarter came from abroad and about a quarter of them were women.

After an initial generation of foreign ascetics, including the above-mentioned Amandus from Aquitaine, native believers were increasingly gripped by the ascetic ideal. Allowinus, later named Bavo (d. before 659), a nobleman from Hesbaye, attached himself to the preacher Amandus after the death of his wife. He became an ordained priest, preached the Gospel and, towards the end of his life, had himself enclosed in an anchorhold at a monastery in Ghent which he had entered as a monk shortly before. He was one of the first locally born recluses. His *vita*, written in the Carolingian period two centuries after his

---

[14] Lutz E. von Padberg, *Bonifatius: Missionar und Reformer* (Munich, 2003).

[15] Jean Heuclin, *Aux origines monastiques de la Gaule du Nord. Ermites et Reclus du ve au xie siècle* (Lille, 1988).

death, was used to elaborate an ideological programme.[16] It reads like an exemplification of the Rule of Grimlaïcus.

Female solitaries

Heuclin recorded an exceedingly large number of female hermits and independent religious women in his study.[17] He identifies Dympna, the Irish princess who, according to her Latin *vita,* supposedly fled from the incestuous desires of her father, as if she were a second fairy-tale princess Donkeyskin. Thereupon, she is supposed to have come to the Continent and entered a hermitage at Geel in the Kempen region, where her father is said to have followed her and killed her with his own hands.[18] Another Irish princess, Oda of Saint Oedenrode, fared a little better, at least according to her *vita.* After she was healed of blindness at the grave of Saint Lambert in Liège, she reportedly became a hermit in the reclaimed area of Brabant, where the farmers built the same sort of hut for her as those in which they lived themselves in the twelfth and thirteenth centuries.[19] Both female hermits (or should we categorize them as Irish *peregrinae?*) were, according to their *vitae,* buried in old sarcophagi, which would become the locus of their veneration. We must recognize, however, that no such Irish female hermits ever existed in historical reality. The legends about them stem from the twelfth and thirteenth centuries and emanated from remarkable sarcophagi found by the colonists in the areas that they were reclaiming. Elaborating on the old Irish *peregrinatio* ideal, these legends reflect the religious fantasies of the colonists.

There were also female solitaries who were reportedly born in this area. Landrada, for instance, sojourning in the midst of the wilderness, was thrown a stone cast from heaven on which the cross of her beloved was carved. She built a monastery around the site.[20] It is said Alena of Dielbeck died when she ventured all alone in the Kolenwoud forest near Brussels.[21] Berlindis devoted her life to

---

[16] For Bavo, see *BHL* 1050–51. *Vita Bavonis prima, AASS,* 1 Oct., vol. 49, pp. 229–35, here at p. 233: even as a recluse he remained obedient to his abbot. According to the *Vita tertia* in *AASS Belgii,* vol. 2, pp. 511–32 (p. 519), written in the twelfth century, Bavo was characterized as a knight-hermit; just like Gerlach of Houthem (see below), he first lived in a tree in the forest. In the late Middle Ages, he was remembered in Saint Baaf's church in Haarlem as the knight with sword in hand and falcon on his arm, who liberated the people of Haarlem. Compare Adriaen Verhulst, 'Saint Bavo et les Origines de Gand', *Revue du Nord* 69 (1986), pp. 455–70.

[17] For modern bone research on the relics of the legendary female hermits, see *Relieken: echt of vals?* ed. Mark van Strydonck, Anton Ervynck, Marit Vandenbruaene and Mathieu Marit en Boudin (Louvain, 2006); furthermore, see Anneke B. Mulder-Bakker, 'Saints without a Past: Sacred Places and Intercessory Power in Saints' Lives from the Low Countries', in *The Invention of Saintliness,* ed. Anneke B. Mulder-Bakker (London, 2002), pp. 38–57; and 'Gendering Medieval Martyrdom: Thirteenth-Century Lives of Holy Women in the Low Countries', in *More than a Memory: The Discourse of Martyrdom and the Construction of Christian Identity in the History of Christianity,* ed. Johan Leemans (Leuven, 2005), pp. 221–39.

[18] For Dympna, see *BHL* 2352–5; *AASS,* 15 Maii, vol. 16, pp. 478–95.

[19] For Oda Rodensis, see *BHL* 6263–68; and Joseph van der Straeten, 'Sainte Ode, patronne de Sint-Oedenrode', *Analecta Bollandiana* 76 (1958), pp. 65–117 for an edition of the Latin *Vita.*

[20] For Landrada, see *BHL* 4711–14; *AASS,* 18 Julii, vol. 29, pp. 619–29.

[21] For Alena, see *BHL* 265; *AASS,* 17 Junii, vol. 24, pp. 315–23.

God in her own house in Meerbeek, just like Ermelindis of Meldert.[22] These two women, Berlindis and Ermelindis, were, according to their *vitae*, types of elite hermits. Withdrawing into their own country estates, they became devoted to the service of God. Berlindis would later be included as one of the 'Three Maidens', a reminder of the Three Mother Goddesses or Matrons from pagan times.

How should we, from our vantage-point, explain this type of independent, self-reliant *mulieres religiosae* [religious women] from local stock in the early Middle Ages? Their *vitae* do not seem particularly historically reliable. Are they products of fantasy? The British historian Sarah Foot has noted that, in addition to the pastor in Anglo-Saxon England, there was sometimes an elderly female *nunne* active in the religious community, 'a title usually given to elderly persons'. The word is derived from the Latin *nonna* = grandmother. The *nunne* was not 'the cloistered woman meant by the modern term but rather the female counterpart to the secular priest or canon'.[23] To date, no-one has embarked upon researching whether a similar phenomenon existed on the Continent. Did Berlindis and Ermelindis and other maidens such as Pharaïldis play a comparable role?[24] Were they, along with many other nameless women, not hermits in the wilderness but, perhaps, a type of religious leader in the local community? And did the married women who had themselves enclosed as recluses at a mature age play a similar role in the period? For example, the noble matron Berta of Blagny (d. 725), together with her five daughters, withdrew after the death of her husband into a convent that she had founded. One of her daughters became abbess, while she had herself enclosed as a recluse. Her *vita*, written after Grimlaïcus had established his rule, has the main points of the monastic rule for recluses elegantly 'worked into' it, but what did the *historical* Berta do?[25]

Sacred places
All these ascetics (insofar as they are historical) came in contact with people for whom Christianity still meant virtually nothing.[26] We must remember that in these regions people still lived together in small groups in the middle of vast forests, swamps and impenetrable landscapes. They lived semi-nomadically from herding

---

[22] For Berlindis, see *BHL* 1184; *AASS*, 1 Febr., vol. 4, pp. 381–88 (together with the other Maidens, Nona and Celsa); for Ermelindis, see *BHL* 2605–07; *AASS*, 29 Oct., vol. 60, pp. 843–72.

[23] Sarah Foot, *Veiled Women I: The Disappearance of Nuns from Anglo-Saxon England* (Aldershot, 2001), p. 105.

[24] For Pharaïldis (Dutch: Veerle), see *BHL* 6791; *AASS*, 4 Jan., vol. 1, pp. 170–3, *vitae* from the tenth to fifteenth centuries. Pharaïldis supposedly remained a virgin during her marriage and reportedly applied herself to the 'scientien': J. van Loon, 'De heilige Farahildis: haar naam en de historische waarde van haar vita', *Naamkunde* 14 (1982), pp. 103–15.

[25] For Berta of Blagny, see *BHL* 1266–70; *AASS*, 4 Julii, vol. 29, pp. 47–60. I did not mention Oda of Amay because she is not hailed as an anchorite. But she was a widow who withdrew from court, founded convents and was buried in a sarcophagus. In her case, archaeologists found the sarcophagus underneath the floor of the church of Amay, while she herself is mentioned in documentary sources dating from the seventh century. See my 'Gendering Medieval Martyrdom', pp. 221–42.

[26] Joris van Einatten and Fred van Lieburg, *Nederlandse Religiegeschiedenis* (Hilversum, 2005), pp. 25–41; and Arnold Angenendt, *Geschichte der Religiosität im Mittelalter* (Darmstadt, 1997).

cattle and a little agriculture. There were hardly any cities; nor was there any net-work of dioceses and monasteries – and therefore no network of religious pastors and preachers. Bishop Servaas founded the diocese of Tongres-Maastricht-Liège in the fourth century, and Willibrord established Utrecht at the beginning of the eighth century. Two bishops had to serve nearly all of the Netherlands and Belgium from Liège and Utrecht. The first monastery in the Northern Netherlands, the Benedictine abbey of Egmond, was only founded in the tenth century by the first counts of Holland. In brief, concentrations of recognizable Christianity with the capacity to propagate the faith were lacking throughout the period. Hermits and *peregrini* were the only religious individuals whom the rural population had any chance of encountering – and the same may well be true of rel-atively well-educated noble matrons.

The religious landscape was not marked by churches and monasteries but by sacred places in the fields and woods where people performed their rituals and devotions. Daily life was dominated by what later came to be regarded as magical practices intended to ensure protection of cattle, horses and the harvest, or to ward off disease and harm. Above all, a mother earth-goddess and the triad of matrons enjoyed a great deal of devotion. After the Carolingian kings proclaimed Christianity, the rural population was required to give up 'heathen' practices. But religious needs remained intact, of course: sickness and harm also had to be fend-ed off within Christianity; protection still had to be invoked. Though 'beheaded', so to speak, the needs of devotion remained intact and the hermits and recluses proved to be the holy men and women administering to this need.[27] During their lives and especially through the legends and reputations propagated after their deaths, they became the holy patrons and matrons of the rural population. The anchorite Gerlach of Houthem (d. 1165) became, for example, the patron of cat-tle and horses. Farmers strewed soil from his grave on their stalls to protect their cattle.[28] And in case of the miraculous discovery of the sarcophagi, suitable holy figures were 'devised' who assumed the roles of female patrons caring for the reli-gious community. The religious landscape was, in this way, at least partly defined by hermits, male and female, and their places of worship.

The later Middle Ages

The emergence of urban civilization in Western Europe, starting in the eleventh and twelfth centuries, radically changed the nature of society and therefore the anchoritic ideal. In particular, the emerging cities gave rise to a middle class that participated much more actively in life. The new citizens learned how to build up a comfortable existence using their own business sense and wished to prosper equally well in religious life. Not only were parishes being founded everywhere,

---

[27] Heuclin, *Aux origines*, p. 15: 'le seul à pouvoir y jouer un véritable rôle religieux et à y créer une civil-isation particulière fut l'ermite' [the only one who could play a true religious role and create a particular civilization was the hermit].

[28] Anneke B. Mulder-Bakker, *De kluizenaar in de eik. Gerlach van Houthem en zijn verering* (Hilversum, 1995); and see below 'Hermit knights'.

each with a parish priest for the Sunday mass and daily ministering, ordinary believers also gave active form to their own belief and became interested in a sincere personal devotion. Faith acquired an ethical and moral dimension. Within all this, the desire for the anchoritic life persisted, but in another form: a large number of the common faithful now had the desire to devote themselves entirely to God.

An additional new development stemmed from the fact that the religious options for men and women began increasingly to diverge. During the implementation of the Gregorian Reform (beginning in the 1070s), priests and clergy – always men, therefore – were separated from ordinary believers within church doctrine. They were forged into a separate group, the *sacerdotium* [priesthood] with its own rights and duties. Priests now had to embrace a celibate life, were recognizable by their clothing and were the only ones who could serve salvation. The common faithful, both male and female, were now denied the right to interfere within this sphere of activity: only an ordained priest would be allowed to administer the sacraments, to preach or hear confession; only he was to be considered an intermediary between God and mankind. An unordained and therefore 'lay' person, no matter how divinely gifted, had to abstain from such activities. If ordinary believers wanted to devote themselves full time to religion, they were supposed to withdraw into the contemplative life and enter a cloister. The consequence of this new doctrine was that the 'old' anchorites, the hermits, male and female – which is to say the living holy men and women who had, until then, been the actual spiritual guides of the common faithful – were stripped of their role by church doctrine; within church doctrine lay hermits and recluses only had a life of prayer and contemplation available to them.[29]

Men who opted for a full-time religious career in this new constellation had, after a 'transitional period' which lasted until the thirteenth century, the choice between the priesthood in the midst of the community or the monastic life outside it. The option of the mendicant order, monasteries in the world, was added in the thirteenth century. But there were still men who felt an attraction to the old anchoritic ideal, especially nobles of advanced age: knights who converted after an adventuresome life, for example, or aristocrats who withdrew from active government. They would enter one of the anchoritic orders as lay brothers or dwelled for set periods in a hermitage, a place of retreat that was built near certain monasteries.

In the vision of the church hierarchy, only the contemplative life in a convent was open to women. Even the mendicant orders did not provide them with a way out as even the Poor Clares and Dominican sisters were supposed to withdraw from the community into a cloistered convent. But many women were not satisfied with this role. Accustomed to looking after religious affairs within the family structure, they began to develop new forms of religious life. For the first time in the history of Western Europe, increasingly large groups of women made faith the substance of their lives. While there had only been a few abbeys for noble women in previous centuries, along with a small number of secular convents for aristocratic

---

[29] Robert I. Moore, *The First European Revolution, c.970–1215* (Oxford, 2000).

canonesses[30] – and perhaps a scattering of religious women living independently – late medieval women began to cultivate a whole range of unique forms of piety, as Mario Sensi comprehensively demonstrates in the Italian context elsewhere in this volume. For example, they followed travelling preachers, began to live together in house communities or convents, some of which sought affiliation with the new monastic orders, and from the thirteenth century onwards they went in their hundreds to live in beguine convents and beguinages. There were also women who went from door to door praying and begging, who cared for the sick and the lepers, and who met to discuss the Bible and the basic tenets of the Christian faith. A sizable number of women had themselves enclosed as anchorites near a parish church or city chapel.[31]

In the transitional period of the eleventh and twelfth century, while increasingly large groups of common believers were enthralled by the new zeal, the church hierarchy was not strong enough to enforce its strict new structures. Professionals, monastics and lay persons all proved to be inspired by the *vita apostolica* [apostolic life]. Just as Christ and his disciples (apostles) had wandered around ancient Palestine as homeless paupers, their medieval emulators also wanted to strive after the perfection of poverty: *pauper sum et peregrinus* [I am a pauper and a wanderer]. They endeavoured to realize a life devoted to poverty and self-chosen ascesis, often combined with apostleship, preaching and ministering. The twelfth century was also a period in which a growing desire for a personal relationship with God erupted. At least in the transitional period, this found expression in forms beneficial to the anchoritic ideal. As a result, religious practice turned out to be much richer than the conceptions of church ideology allowed. Giles Constable, in his authoritative work *The Reformation of the Twelfth Century*, therefore correctly concludes that the free anchoritic existence, with its unregimented devotion to God, was the ideal of the age: it 'permitted a more personal type of religious life than was possible in most monasteries'.[32] Knights became hermit knights, women urban recluses.

Mindful of the aims of this section focusing on the later Middle Ages, I will now concentrate primarily on the independent 'lay' hermits and recluses, the men and women who, acting on their own authority, gave form to the ideal life dedicated to God.[33]

---

[30] De Moreau, *Histoire de l'église en Belgique*, numbers forty-five convents in the Southern Low Countries in the eighth century, of which there were a dozen for women. Hardly any others were added in subsequent centuries.

[31] Most of the interest of modern scholarship has focused on the beguines: see Walter Simons, *Cities of Ladies: Beguine Communities in the Medieval Low Countries, 1200–1565* (Philadelphia, 2000); and the older work by Ernest W. McDonnell, *The Beguines and Beghards in Medieval Culture: with Special Emphasis on the Belgian Scene* (New Brunswick, 1954).

[32] Giles Constable, *The Reformation of the Twelfth Century: The Spirituality of Reform* (Cambridge, 1996), p. 261.

[33] There is no work surveying the hermits and anchorites in the Low Countries, only a few inventories in regional studies mainly for the southern regions. See C. Dereine, 'Ermites, reclus et recluses dans l'ancien diocèse de Cambrai entre Scarpe et Haine (1075–1125)', *Revue Bénédictine* 97 (1987), pp. 289–313; L. Dewicke, *Eremitisme en kluizenarij in de Zuidelijke Nederlanden en het prinsbisdom Luik, 13ᵉ –18ᵉ eeuw. Een geografische en socio-religieuze studie* (Gent, 1984); L. G. C. M. van Dijck, 'Kluizenaressen

Hermit knights

For the lay world in northwest Europe the anchoritic ideal was a new revelation. For example, Aybert of Crespin (Hainaut, c.1060–1140) was said to have been a young man dissatisfied with his life on the family manor.[34] He longed for something else. When he, by chance, heard songs about Count Theobald of Champagne who became a charcoal burner in the forest, he went seeking a hermit in his own environment and found Jan, a monk who lived as a hermit near the Crespin monastery. Aybert wanted to follow this lowly figure. Together they travelled to Italy and dwelled for a while with the strict monks of Vallombrosa. Having returned to Hainaut, Aybert also became a monk. As this life did not turn out to be satisfying for him, he had himself shut into an anchorhold on the island in the Haine (1115) and gave himself up to extreme starvation. He only ate roots and grasses, refusing any form of cooked or baked food (bread). Though he was not a priest, Pope Paschalis II granted Aybert permission to preach and hear confession.[35] Contrary to church ideology, he therefore took on a recognized function in the community of the faithful and consequently became the prototype of the hermit knight, mortifying the flesh and opening his hermitage for his fellow men. Like the 'holy man' of Peter Brown's figuration,[36] he was a personal advisor, an agent of salvation, a source of happiness for his fellow believers. Aybert's reputation as a minister and performer of miracles attracted so many visitors to his anchorhold that, over time, this location seemed like a beleaguered fortress. Visitors wanted to confess their sins to him, and if they could not press through, they would at times shout out their spiritual anguish in public.

There are three remarkable elements in this history. The first is that young noblemen were indeed gripped by the ideal of perfection but did not wish to become monks – evidently, they wanted to remain in contact with their fellow men. In this way, they knowingly became involved in spiritual guidance in a manner at odds with the claims of the Gregorian Reform, according to which the agency of salvation was reserved for the ordained priesthood. In practice, howev-

in en rond 's-Hertogenbosch ca. 1370–1630', *Varia Historica Brabantia* 9 (1980), pp. 1–20; J. Habets, 'Kluizen en kluizenaars in Limburg', *Publications de la Société d'Histoire et d'Archéologie dans le Duché de Limbourg* 7 (1870), pp. 351–62; A. Welters, *Kluizenaas in Limburg* (Heerlen, 1950); A. C .M. Kappelhof, 'Kluizenaressen in en rond Den Bosch: a supplement', *Noordbrabants Historisch Jaarboek* 5 (1988), pp. 178–80; Michel van Maarseveen, 'Middeleeuwse reclusen. Kluizenaressen en hun besloten bestaan', *Spiegel Historiael* 30 (1995), pp. 307–12; 319–20; Ludo Milis, *L'évolution de l'érémitisme au canonicat régulier dans la première moitié du douzième siècle: transition ou trahison?* Studia Historica Gandensia 235 (Gent, 1979); Floris Prims, 'Kluizen, kluizenaars en kluizenaressen in Brabant', *Bijdragen tot de Geschiedenis* 14 (1922–1923), pp. 616–24; V. Sempels, 'Opkomst en bloei van het kluizenaarsleven te onzent in de bloei van de twaalfde en dertiende eeuw', *Collectanea Mechlininensia* 32 (1947), pp. 357–76; E. van Wintershoven, 'Recluseries et ermitages dans l'ancien diocèse de Liège', *Bulletin de la Société scientifique et littéraire du Limbourg* 23 (1905), pp. 97–158.

[34] For Aybert of Crespin, see *BHL* 180. For his *vita* written by his contemporary Robert of Oostervant before 1148, see *AASS*, 7 Aprilis, vol. 10, pp. 669–79. See also Charles Dereine, 'La critique de la Vita de Saint Aybert reclus en Hainault', *Analecta Bollandiana* 106 (1988), pp. 121–42; and Charles Dereine, 'Ermites', pp. 301–5.

[35] Dereine, 'Ermites', p. 303.

[36] Brown, 'Rise and Function of the Holy Man', op. cit.

er, parish priests were simply not up to the task of preaching and ministering. The popes knew this, and charismatically gifted men continued to be supported by papal privileges.[37] The second intriguing point is that common believers evidently trusted these non-professionals. They were not just dependent on church authorities for their heavenly salvation; they knew how to find hermits (later female recluses as well) whose ascesis visibly manifested that they were inspired by God. These holy men and women had salvation in their bones, so to speak. A third element is the fact that the hermits and recluses often lived in places that had an age-old numinous atmosphere attached to them; these were more or less sacred places where salvation was visible and tangible. The anchorite's presence enabled the pre-Christian mythical geography to be overwritten by a Christian sacred landscape. A good example of such overwriting – as well as of the hermit knight – is provided by Gerlach of Houthem.[38]

Gerlach (d. 1165), who fought as a knight in the army of Frederik Barbarossa in Italy and probably came into contact with eremitism as a result, established himself as a hermit living in a hollow oak on his own property near Maastricht. The oak, with the spring that bubbled up beside it, must have been sacred. After his death, believers attributed a type of miraculous power to the oak wood and the spring water, resembling their numinosity in pre-Christian times, and a similar power was attributed to the earth in which Gerlach was buried. As a result, believers strewed earth from the grave in the stalls to protect their cattle and horses or drank water from the well to cure their fevers. During his life, Gerlach garnered great admiration for his strict ascesis (he walked barefoot daily to the grave of Saint Servaas in Maastricht) and with his call for conversion he influenced the ethical and moral observances of the people living in the region. He personally shaved the luxuriant hair of former fellow soldiers, the sign of their 'effeminacy'. His hermitage became a centre for proclaiming faith and attracted many more visitors than the abbey of Meerssen, whose monks held the position of parish priests. All in all, Gerlach christianized both people and the sacred place in which he lived. After his death, he grew into a miracle-worker and patron saint.

We see here a miraculous interaction. Originally, Gerlach's oak emitted a numinous, sacred glow, which benefited the knight and rendered him a holy man. The holy man then christianized the pagan numinous site, transforming it into a Christian 'power-station' from where salvation was extracted. Gerlach (just like Aybert) returned from Italy with a papal bull. The old magical practices, which were 'beheaded' by the emergence of Christianity, found a wonder-working patron in him. Through him, cattle and horses were in saintly hands. In the vicinity of Brussels, Guido of Anderlecht, also a hermit pilgrim, was supposed to pro-

---

[37] See Herbert Grundmann, 'Zur Vita S. Gerlaci eremitae', *Deutsches Archiv für die Erforschung des Mittelalters* 18 (1962), pp. 539–54. Gerlach also received a papal bull, as did Hildegard of Bingen.

[38] Mulder-Bakker, *De kluizenaar in de eik*. See also the twelfth-century *vita* of the legendary hermit knight Mengold of Huy in Philippe George, 'Noble, chevalier, pénitent, martyr: l'idéal de sainteté d'après une "Vita" mosane (Mengold) du xiie siècle', *Le Moyen Age* 89 (1983), pp. 357–80; and Peter Jan Margrie and Charles Caspers (eds), *Bedevaartsplaatsen in Nederland, vol 3: Provincie Limburg* (Hilversum, 2000), pp. 324–50.

vide exactly the same protection. Horses still trot around the church on his feast day. While in other regions, the Irish anchorite Brigida of Kildare had livestock under her mantel of protection.[39]

There were also groups of knights that sought unity together. According to the twelfth-century foundation chronicle of the Afflighem monastery, six knights were supposed to have retreated into the Brabant forest as hermit knights. A rich monastery grew from their huts; 'by accident' an abbey was created and hermit monks are said to have remained living in a hermitage near the monastery.[40] A certain ambivalence permeates this and similar cases; Ludo Milis even speaks about possible 'betrayal' of the original eremitic ideal. According to Henrietta Leyser, however, such a founding of a monastery was intended, and she qualifies this in her *Hermits and the New Monasticism*.[41]

The twelfth century constituted the 'high time' of chivalric eremitism, after which its popularity declined rapidly. In the thirteenth century, the mendicant and anchoritic orders began to appear. Studious types who were attracted to solitude became Carthusian or else Augustinian hermits. And the mendicants provided a challenge to be taken up by active city-dwellers. Only simple folk were still hermits. A hermit residing near Groningen on the busy traffic route to the south earned his living as a road worker. By the time of the Protestant Reformation, his type of eremitism had become a position of respectable labour passed down from father to son.[42]

Interest in the reclusive life was waning among men, moreover. Emo, the abbot of the Bloemhof monastery in Frisia, reported the tragic adventures of two male recluses at the beginning of the thirteenth century. One was killed in a fire at the church of Usquert; the other was thrown in prison because he harassed Dominican preachers from his anchorhold in Stitswert.[43] Both appear to be old-style monk-hermits of the 'graduate class', such as I have mentioned before. In the new relationships of the later Middle Ages, these types of male recluses are no longer to be found.

---

[39] For Guido (Wido Anderlacensis), see *BHL* 8870–72; *AASS*, 12 Sept., vol. 44, pp. 36–48; see also J. Lavalleye, 'Notes sur le culte de Saint Guidon', *Annales de la Société royale d'archéologie de Bruxelles* 37 (1934), pp. 221–48 (245). For Brigida Kildariae, see *BHL* 1455; *AASS*, 1 Febr., vol. 4, pp. 245–48; see also Edda Frankot, 'Brigida. Een Ierse maagd op reis. Het beeld van Brigida van Kildare in haar vitae. Levens en verering' (Groningen: unpublished thesis, 1999).

[40] V. Coosemans and C. Coppens (eds), 'De eerste kroniek van Affligem', *Affligemensia* 4 (1947), pp. 1–41. See G. Despy, 'Les Bénédictins en Brabant au xiie s.: la "Chronique de l'abbaye d'Afflighem"', *Problèmes d'histoire du Christianisme* 12 (1983), pp. 51–116; see also the critical review thereof in Charles Dereine, 'Les origines érémitiques d'Afflighem (1083). Légende ou réalité', *Revue Bénédictine* 101 (1991), pp. 50–114; and W. Verleyen, 'L'Exordium Affligemense. Légende ou réalité?', *Revue d'Histoire Ecclésiastique* 99 (1995), pp. 471–83.

[41] Henrietta Leyser, *Hermits and the New Monasticism: A Study of Religious Communities in Western Europe, 1000–1150* (London, 1984); Ludo J. R. Milis, 'Hermits and Regular Canons in the Twelfth Century', in *Religion, Culture, and Mentalities in the Medieval Low Countries*, ed. Jeroen Deploige and M. De Reu (Turnhout, 2005), pp. 181–246.

[42] B. Lonsain, 'De kluizenaar in het "Harener Holt"', *Maandblad Groningen* 111 (1920–1921), pp. 101–3.

[43] *Kroniek van het klooster Bloemhof te Wittewierum*, ed. H. P. H. Jansen and A. Janse (Hilversum, 1991), p. 232 and p. 242.

The urban recluses

Women had much less choice. They could not hold any priestly position, of course; nor could they become itinerant mendicants. Many were attracted by travelling hermit preachers and joined their followers: Norbert of Xanten had a whole flock of women disciples whom he accommodated in double monasteries he founded, and these women therefore became nuns. Others had themselves individually enclosed as recluses. In the new male abbey founded at Rolduc, the noblewoman Reinwidis had herself enclosed in an *inclusorium* when, at an advanced age, she decided to devote herself to the service of God. Such an *inclusorium* was a cell or complex of cells in which one or more women lived in obedience to the abbot and in accordance with the rule of the male abbey. They thus constituted an informal community of cloistered nuns.[44]

Reinwidis's contemporary and fellow countrywoman, Guda, widow of the count of Valkenburg (d. 1125), did things differently: she was one of the first examples of the new reclusion.[45] She specifically sought an anchorhold in an urban setting and withdrew into a cell near the Saint Jacques convent in Liège. Before long many were following in her footsteps, as the socio-economic and religious climate flourishing in the commercial centres of the Low Countries increased female city dwellers' attraction to the anchoritic life rather than a cloistered community outside the city. Ordinary urban young women as well as older widows wished to dedicate themselves to God in their own surroundings. They sought to free themselves from the entanglements of family and society just as Christ did (the above-mentioned *vita apostolica*), but not to turn their backs on society as such. They therefore had themselves enclosed at parish churches and chapels in the city, thus fundamentally changing the nature of the old monastic ideal of the nun-recluse.

Like Reinwidis and Guda, they had often already fulfilled their 'communal duties' concerning housekeeping and maternity over a number of years; only then did they grasp the opportunity to release their personal desires and assume responsibility for their own lives. As already mentioned, a life as a priest, itinerant mendicant or even a hermit was inconceivable for them as women, while the anchorhold offered them a feasible alternative. It was a setting where they found spiritual liberty, inwardness and the possibilities of inner freedom and knowledge. Without a fixed rule and without an imposed form of life, they were free to act as the spirit, the Spirit, moved them. This meant listening to people, instructing them if they lacked knowledge, hearing their confessions and helping them to find answers to questions of life and death. It also meant taking authoritative action against those who behaved immorally. In most cases, these women chose to live in an anchorhold near the main church in a town or near some strategically located church or chapel.

---

[44] L. Augustus (ed.), *Annales Rodenses* (Maastricht, 1995), p. 150; Habets, 'Kluizen in Limburg', p. 354. For the meaning of *inclusorium*, see my *Lives of the Anchoresses* (Philadelphia, 2005), pp. 4–6, especially notes 14–16.

[45] H. Demaret, 'Guda, veuve de Thiebauld comte de Fouron, recluse à Saint-Jacques au commencement du xiie siècle', *Bulletin de la Société d'art et d'histoire du diocèse de Liège* 4 (1884), pp. 37–50.

Unlike nuns, especially those in the new orders, recluses did not cut all ties with society. The pressure to enter the cloistered life, to which nuns yielded, continued to meet with their resistance. As part of the social 'upper-crust', they probably could have entered a convent, but they chose not to do so. Even though they often had close bonds with beguines and sometimes lived in a beguinage cell – in the beguinage of 's-Hertogenbosch (or Den Bosch) it was the 'task' of one of the beguines to be enclosed in the community's own anchorhold – their life was dedicated to God in a much more drastic and demanding way. Their stance towards the world, forsaking but not avoiding it, was an essential distinguishing feature.

The anchoritic existence actually approached that of the parish priest. Like priests, recluses distinguished themselves from the ordinary faithful by maintaining a recognizable way of life, marked in the one case by celibacy and a cassock and in the other by a cell and a grey habit. For both of them, dedicating themselves to God included serving their fellow human beings. Both underwent a solemn ritual that confirmed their choice of life. The ordination of the priest into the Church, it is true, was defined in canon law in terms fundamentally different from the benediction of a recluse. But unlike the priest, the father (*pater*) of the community of believers, who was present in the church only when services required him to be, the female anchorite (*mater*) actually lived in the church. Present day and night, she was like a mother, always at home.

There must have been hundreds of this type of recluse in the Low Countries and surrounding regions. Nearly every city parish and many villages must have had their own. For the Southern Low Countries, contemporary Belgium, we have overabundant historical evidence in the sources: complete saints' Lives were written for some recluses such as Mary of Oignies (d. 1213), Yvette of Huy (d. 1228), Odilia of Liège (d. 1220), Christina the Astonishing (d. 1225) and Juliana of Cornillon (d. 1258). Brief reports of others appear in chronicles, such as the chronicles of the Cistercian Villers Abbey. Often, their names are mentioned without further information in necrologia. Moreover, mention of gifts to recluses is found in wills, which indicate that there were hundreds of them in the region of contemporary Belgium from the thirteenth century onwards.[46] These types of sources are lacking for the Northern Low Countries (the current Netherlands without North Brabant).[47] This can partly be blamed on the loss of episcopal and monastic records during protestantization – or the lack of research on the surviving remnants. Nearly the entire medieval archive of the diocese of Utrecht was lost when it was placed in carts and taken to the safe south to protect it against the threat of emerging Protestantism. If, by chance, a single document is preserved, such as the formulary of Bishop Frederick of Blankenheim, recluses figure prominently in it. Thirteen women received permission to move into an anchorhold sometime during the years 1396 to 1423. Agnes in Zaltbommel was one of them,

[46] See the references to inventories in note 33 above, but there are many more.
[47] We only have such wills and other documentary sources for North Brabant: see Van Dijck 'Kluizenaressen', op. cit.

but local monastic archives report that another recluse also lived there.[48] The city of Utrecht certainly had five anchorholds in the fifteenth century.[49] Surviving accounts of Rijnsburg Abbey from 1380 record that ironwork and wood were acquired for 'a lock that a female anchorite had on her door'. Was a new recluse perhaps being shut in?[50] And the chronicle of the Nieuwe Kerk in Delft relates how Truysuster led a strict spiritual life in the anchorhold attached to the church for nearly fifty years until she died in 1459. Sometimes, her confessor came to visit her through a door in the churchyard and met her in 'enraptured contemplation'. He then crept silently away, in order not to disturb her. Citizens of Delft occasionally met her in the churchyard late at night, creeping around the church on her bare knees: she 'thus was frequently seen behaving austerely' (in passing, such anecdotes make it clear to us that a recluse was certainly 'enclosed' but not necessarily 'locked up'). A stained-glass window made for Truysuster after her death suggests that she enjoyed a certain lasting veneration.[51] Most of the other recluses did not share her continued renown: they had their significance during their lives but not after their death.[52]

There may be a substantial number of traceable recluses in the Dutch sources available to us; still, there are reasons to believe that the popularity of the anchoritic ideal in the Northern Low Countries cannot automatically be regarded as the equivalent of the motivations in the south. Apart from the lack of source material, something peculiar is at stake. Whereas the bulk of references to anchorites and recluses in the Southern Low Countries (and in England as well) are met in special dispositions and wills, these types of sources in the Netherlands (among those preserved) do not contain any names of recluses, nor do they mention any gifts to them. Wills certainly contain references concerning gifts made to convents and religious institutions, but only rarely do any such benefactions relate to recluses. Believers definitely felt involved in the building of anchorholds, as indicated in the formulary of Bishop Frederick, but this was not manifested in their wills. How can this point be explained? As yet, I have no answer.

All in all, the state of the sources pertaining to the Netherlands and the research conducted prevent us from obtaining any definite insight into recluses who, as shown in the surviving sources, must certainly have existed. Hermits and anchorites functioned in the oral world of lived Christianity. They were not part of the institutional structure of the Church and had no status in church law. Their life was not governed by ecclesiastical laws and regulations. But with the advancing

---

[48] Utrechts Archief: Bisschoppelijk archief, regs. 9 and 10; see also S. Muller (ed.), *Regesten van het Archief der Bisschoppen van Utrecht (722–1528)*, 4 vols (Utrecht, 1917), vol. 1, nos 1369–565.

[49] See the introduction in *Mi quam een schoon geluit in mijn oren. Het werk van Suster Bertken*, ed. José van Aelst et al. (Hilversum, 2007) and the references given there.

[50] Maria Hüffer, *Bronnen voor de geschiedenis der abdij Rijnsburg*, 2 vols (The Hague, 1951), p. 758 and p. 199.

[51] *Kroniek van de Nieuwe Kerk te Delft*, ed. D. P. Oosterbaan, *Haarlemse Bijdragen* 65 (1958), pp. 197–98 and p. 218; see also my *Verborgen Vrouwen. Kluizenaressen in de middeleeuwse stad* (Hilversum, 2007), pp. 27–9.

[52] Only Eve of Saint-Martin in Liège enjoyed lasting veneration as the originator of the Feast of Corpus Christi.

bureaucratization of the Church and the reforming zeal of some of its leaders, it became clear that they could not escape some form of institutionalization. First steps were taken in this direction around the middle of the thirteenth century. Jacques Pantaleon, Archdeacon in Liège and friend of recluses, wanted to bring all free-roaming religious women living at home in an informal convent or in an anchorhold under some kind of *forma vitae* and urged them to live some sort of communal life. Once he had become Pope Urban IV (1261–4), he proved to be a strong proponent of closed convents. The Clares obtained a new rule from him, the first rule to impose total enclosure. Regulations (not rules) were established in the Low Countries according to which recluses were supposed to live in total seclusion, separated from the world outside by a stone wall and a black curtain at their window. Once a week they were allowed to hold 'office hours', at a time set by the parish priest, in order to control the crowd of believers.[53] The implication here is that female anchorites were supposed to devote their entire lives to penitence and prayer, not to pastoral work or to teaching their fellow citizens.

References in the life-stories of late medieval recluses, one of which I outline in my conclusion to this essay, indicate that these regulations met with little success. Coletta of Corbie (1381–1447), later reformer of the Poor Clare Order, began her religious career as a recluse at Corbie (1402–6). In the anchorhold, she discovered her calling to convert people to a strict religious life. She travelled around France and the Netherlands and founded several convents for the Poor Clares. Truysuster was well known in Delft, as she regularly came out of her anchorhold. Another noteworthy example is the recluse Bertke of Utrecht, mostly referred to as Sister Bertken. At the boundary of the (Catholic) Middle Ages and (Protestant) modernity, she occupied a spiritual leadership role in the Northern Low Countries that does not pale in comparison to the roles of the great female anchorites in the south during the preceding centuries.

Sister Bertken of Utrecht

Born in 1427 as an illegitimate daughter of Jacob of Lichtenberg, the provost of Saint Peter and deputy to the bishop for a number of years, Bertke belonged to a powerful Utrecht family.[54] At the age of thirty, she used her own money to build an anchorhold at the Buurkerk. Viewed from the Church's centre of power around the cathedral where she probably grew up, the Buurkerk was the church on the other side of the Oude Gracht [the Old Canal] in the dazzling mercantile quarter. It was the parish church (*buur* means 'neighbour') where citizens came together and where the civic government announced council decisions. Bertke therefore sought out the heart of the city community.

---

[53] Van Dijck, 'Kluizenaressen', pp. 16–18 (see note 33 above), published the *Ordinantiën en regulen* of the anchorhold of Vught (sixteenth century).

[54] Van Aelst (ed.), *Mi quam een schoon geluit* (see note 49), pp. 13–27; José van Aelst, 'Het leven van Suster Bertken. Kanttekeningen bij de recente beeldvorming', *Ons Geestelijk Erf* 72 (1998), pp. 262–72; Llewelyn Bogaers, 'Kluizenares midden in de wereld. Suster Bertkens antwoord op haar beladen familiegeschiedenis', *Trajecta* 7 (1998), pp. 296–318.

She was enclosed there in the busy city centre for fifty-seven years until her death in 1514. Her name remained known to later generations because the prior of the Regulierenconvent, who kept the key to her anchorhold (and is therefore likely to have been her confessor), had a note made in an *incunabulum* of his convent, the *Legenda Aurea*, indicating that, having departed at the age of eighty-seven, 'the devout maid Berta Iacobs daughter [...] was a professed sister according to the rules that all those who are enclosed in anchorholds are supposed to follow'. She had accepted these rules and was immured by 'the honourable father in Christ Lord Joest, bishop of Hieropolis [? Jheropolitaen], suffragan of Utrecht'.[55] But above all, she is known by the songs and tracts found in her anchorhold after her death. They were printed in 1516 by Jan Berntz and then further distributed in various reprints. A few of these songs still belong to the standard repertoire of Dutch poetry. Her Christmas vision also still enjoys some repute.

Based on this information, previous generations assumed that Bertke must have been a secluded penitent, unknown and unloved, escaping oblivion after her death only because of the fortuitous discovery of her writing. In recent decades, however, a few surprising finds in the archives (including material regarding her origins) and the study of devotional manuscripts surviving from the late Middle Ages have begun to reveal that Bertke must also have been an influential personality during her lifetime. Her songs were already being sung outside of her anchorhold and included in songbooks. Even her devotional and mystical ideas must have been in circulation. In the oral culture of medieval Christianity, she must have played a role that has entirely escaped us because we have abandoned ourselves to one-sided written source material. This is demonstrated by notes which appear in Buurkerk's account book for 1514: when Bertke died and was buried in her anchorhold, six guards had to be hired in order to govern the circulation of the masses of faithful who wanted to honour her. The parishioners evidently had a great emotional bond with the recluse. This must mean that Bertke had an enormous impact on daily practices in medieval Utrecht. She was not the unknown recluse turned in on herself as she has been regarded by subsequent generations, but was a loved and inspiring force for the city dwellers amongst whom she lived. By choosing to locate her dwelling place near the Buurkerk, the 'city hall' of Utrecht, she was publicly acknowledging that she had something to say to the city. And we might assume she accomplished her aim in the years that followed. Despite the restrictive policy of the church authorities, the civic community of Utrecht, like those in the cities of the twelfth and thirteenth centuries, was strong enough to decide that it wished to listen to this recluse. And the clergy still proved unable to impose its will.

Bertke had a great deal to say to the community. According to her songs, she resembled her predecessors in the manner by which she wrested herself away

---

[55] On the title page of an *inculabulum* of the *Legenda Aurea* (Straatsburg, 1496) in Utrecht, Universiteitsbibliotheek H fol. 252 rariora: 'die deuote maghet berta iacobs dochter [...] Ende sy was een professide suster nae die reghel die alle die gheenen toe behoert te houden die in der enicheyt ende in clusen besloten werden. Welke reghel sy an ghenomen heeft ende is besloten van den eerwardighen vader in Christo heer Joest biscop van Jheropolitaen, suffragaen tutrecht.'

from the limitations of human existence through the strength of her ascesis and an exemplary yearning for virtue. She possessed the true quietude necessary to hear God's voice. It resounds in her songs and tracts; it must also have echoed in her discussions with visitors. Although we know nothing about Bertke's upbringing and religious education, her texts suggest a highly cultured woman, very familiar with theology and the mysticism of her time. We might suspect that she had access to a library located close to her anchorhold, where there was a rich collection of manuscripts and *incunabula*, the basis of the Utrecht university library.

Bertke also experienced mystical ecstasies. In her Christmas vision, she described how Mary, when she knew that her hour had come, was taken up by angels into heaven. Mary felt the 'sweet yearning and urging' of her loving soul for the Lord, words that remind us of the mystical ecstasies of Hadewijch and Ruusbroec. Raised by angels into an ever higher sphere, she knew the Lord and bore His son. The angels received the small King in their arms and carried him to earth. They also carried Mary back to the stall in Bethlehem, where the infant was presented to her. He made soft noises so that Mary came to herself and began to care for him. It is a moving and highly original vision that reads as an evocative portrayal of Mary's ecstatic act of giving birth to the Living Word, one that serves as a metaphor both for Bertke's ecstasies and for the birth of God's Word in her heart. Like several recluses in earlier centuries, Bertke had a special relationship with Mary. She followed in her footsteps and felt, in her own ecstasies and in the words that she incorporated into her poetry, that she was the disciple of the queen of heaven who gave birth to the Living Word.

Bertke lived the life of angels. Living on holy ground, she made salvation present, made it visible and understandable, indeed tangible to believers. The long lines of people who came to pay their last respects to her after her death are evidence of this fact: she was a living saint. Her confessor's inclusion of her life story in the *Legenda Aurea incunabulum* in his library can hardly be viewed as evidence of anything else. Bertke's task was on earth, in Utrecht, and not in heaven after her death. She saw it as her work to interpret God's Word for her fellow believers. Her written words, recorded on the pages of her little notebooks, are preserved and have penetrated written history: they can be studied. Her spoken words circulated by oral transmission: they cannot be studied but have to be listened to. And whoever listens well will hear Bertke's words resounding in the heavy bells of the cathedral. For when Bertke died, the bells rang out twice, as they do on the death of a prelate.

Conclusion

Hermits and female anchorites in the Low Countries proved to be fervent supporters of the mixed life throughout the Middle Ages. To the extent that we can discover in the sources, they never sought anachoresis far outside the community. They always remained in contact with their fellow men and women and were crucially important for the religious community, an importance that is manifested in historical reality. They were living saints. As I perceive it, they had significance on three levels. First, their lives exemplified that lay believers could also have an independent religious existence for which they were fully responsible. This was eminently important, especially in the case of women. They made the idea of 'independent religious women' conceivable.

Second, while anchoritism is noteworthy for its absence in church organization and canon law (there were only rules for monastic anchoritic orders), the virtuosos in the early Middle Ages, both male hermits and female recluses, were the ideal of religious perfection for the common faithful. The ideal enjoyed so much attention that even several non-anchorites were, in the posthumous re-creation of their image, transformed into hermits. There are many *vitae* and anecdotes about anchorites in the early Middle Ages that have no foundation in historical reality. Anchoritic practice changed in the later Middle Ages, both in terms of the historical reality and retrospective revisionism. For men, there were then sufficient 'historical' opportunities to lead a life of perfection. Socially motivated men could become parish priests and fulfil a central function in medieval parish life; or they could become mendicants and popular preachers. These outlets were unavailable to women. However, the civic emancipation of the late Middle Ages left the entire fallow field of lay religious leadership to women. They could flourish as urban recluses, even if it was only because they had a genius for gossip. In documented sources and anecdotes (many exempla), we encounter them everywhere and almost always in a positive light.

Third, when Christianity began to penetrate daily life, anchorites helped believers to make the step to a Christian community with Christian practices of devotion and a Christian 'sacred geography'. After the 'conversion en profondeur' (a term coined by Ludo Milis)[56] was fully complete, this function was lost. For Truysuster and Bertke, this did not seem to have any significance, as they discovered a new function. Due to Bertke's aristocratic background and knowledge and Truysuster's lived devotions, they participated in the theological and spiritual culture of their time while remaining understandable and affable to the common faithful around them – in Bertke's case partly on account of her writing in the vernacular.

As I concluded in my *Lives of the Anchoresses*, both holy laymen and holy laywomen living in their anchorholds were devoted messengers of God. Although neither were authorized to preach or hear confession, living in the midst of humanity they were easily induced to convey God's grace to their fellow human beings. The faithful knew this and flocked to these holy individuals in large numbers.

---

[56] See Ludo Milis, 'Conversion: A Never-Ending Process', in *Religion, Culture, and Mentalities* (op. cit. n. 41 above), ed. Deploige and Reu, pp. 153–65.

2 Anchorites in German-speaking regions

Gabriela Signori

Traditions

Over the centuries – millennia, even – the lives of the Desert Fathers, as recorded in the so-called *Vitae patrum*, furnished models and inspiration for believers striving after the perfect Christian life.[1] In Germany their influence would even transcend confessional boundaries.[2] These naked, emaciated figures with long hair and beards lived together in small ascetic communities or, like wild animals, kept themselves hidden in caves or old pagan gravesites. Their lives were recorded in the early fifth century by travellers from both the East and the West.[3] Later generations of monks would expand the collection of short *vitae* when the need arose.[4]

Writing some two centuries after these first monastic accounts, Gregory of Tours (d. 594) proposed a different model of the ascetic ideal, one more strongly oriented towards the realities of the 'Western' Church.[5] One half of his *Liber vitae patrum* deals with saintly bishops and abbots, the other half with anchorites who

---

[1] On the reception of the *vitae patrum* in the later Middle Ages see Louise Gnädinger, 'Das Altväterzitat im Predigtwerk Johannes Taulers', in *Unterwegs zur Einheit. Festschrift für Heinrich Stirnimann*, ed. Johannes Brantschen and Pietro Selvatico (Freiburg/CH, 1980), pp. 253–67; Carlo Delcorno, 'Le *Vitae Patrum* nella letteratura medievale (secc. XIII–XV)', *Lettere italiane* 53 (1991), pp. 187–207; Werner Williams-Krapp, '*Nucleus totius perfectionis*. Die Altväterspiritualität in der "Vita" Heinrich Seuses', in *Festschrift Walter Haug und Burghart Wachinger*, vol. 1, ed. Johannes Janota (Tübingen, 1992), pp. 405–21; Rüdiger Blumrich, 'Überlieferungsgeschichte als Schlüssel zum Text. Angewandt auf eine spätmittelalterliche bairische Übersetzung der Vitaspatrum', *Freiburger Zeitschrift für Philosophie und Theologie* 41 (1994), pp. 188–222.

[2] Ernst Benz, 'La littérature du Désert chez les Évangéliques allemands et les Piétistes de Pennsylvanie', *Irénikon* 1 (1978), pp. 338–57; Klaus Klein, 'Frühchristliche Eremiten im Spätmittelalter und in der Reformationszeit. Zu Überlieferung und Rezeption der deutschen *Vitaspatrum*-Prosa', in *Literatur und Laienbildung im Spätmittelalter und in der Reformationszeit*, ed. Ludger Grenzmann and Karl Stackmann (Stuttgart, 1984), pp. 686–95.

[3] *Des Palladius von Helenopolis Leben der Heiligen Väter*, ed. and trans. S. Krottenthaler, Bibliothek der Kirchenväter 5 (Kempten/München, 1912); *Tyrannius Rufinus, Historia monachorum sive de vita sanctorum patrum*, ed. Eva Schulz–Flügel, Patristische Texte und Studien 34 (Berlin/New York, 1990). See also Georgia Frank, *The Memory of the Eyes: Pilgrims to Living Saints in Christian Late Antiquity* (Berkeley, 2000).

[4] Walter Berschin, *Griechisch-lateinisches Mittelalter. Von Hieronymus zu Nikolaus von Kues* (Bern/München, 1981), pp. 77–81; Eva Schulz-Flügel, 'Zur Entstehung der Corpora Vitae Patrum', *Studia Patristica* 20 (1989), pp. 289–300.

[5] As the manuscript history shows, however, the *Liber vitae patrum* was not a great success.

renounced the world and had themselves shut up like prisoners in cells, towers, or old buildings.[6] For the bishop of Tours, these *inclusi* were the real virtuosi of the ascetic life.[7] Many of them had been monks living in community before opting for total isolation. The same author's *Historia Francorum* also contains several accounts of recluses. One of these figures, a certain Hospitius, was able to succeed where Gregory's other *vitae* had failed.[8] He became famous. As the exemplar from the Carthusian monastery in Basel shows, Hospitius found entrance into the living corpus of the *Vitae patrum*.[9] In fact, he was to become the very prototype of the *inclusus* in the Western Church.[10] He had himself walled up naked and in chains in a tower in the vicinity of Nizza. Under his iron fetters his flesh began to putrefy, and the worms that had tormented him his whole life left his body only after his death.[11] Hospitius restricted his diet to dates and bread, during Lent to roots and herbs. And, at last, he obtained the divine gift of prophecy.

Grimlaïcus and Benedictine monasticism

Although institutional forms of monastic life became more prevalent in the period that followed,[12] nonetheless the Desert Fathers lived on in the books and in the minds of the monks who read and copied them. The Rule of St Benedict prescribes daily reading from Cassian's (d. 430) *Conlationes, Institutiones* and

---

[6] František Graus, *Volk, Herrscher und Heiliger im Reich der Merowinger. Studien zur Hagiographie der Merowingerzeit* (Prag, 1965), pp. 109–11; Maria-Elisabeth Brunert, *Das Ideal der Wüstenaskese und seine Rezeption in Gallien bis zum Ende des 16. Jahrhunderts*, Beiträge zur Geschichte des alten Mönchtums und des Benediktinertums 42 (Diss. Bonn, Münster 1994), pp. 344–407.

[7] Sometimes he uses the term *reclusus* simply as a synonym for hermit. See Gregory of Tours, 'Liber vitae patrum', in *Gregorii episcopi Turonensis miracula et opera minora*, ed. Bruno Krusch, Scriptores rerum merovingicarum I/II (Hannover, 1885), pp. 255–9; Gregory of Tours, *Liber vitae patrum/Life of the Fathers*, trans. and intro. Edward James, Translated Texts for Historians, Latin Series 1 (Liverpool, 1985), pp. 83–7. See also Brunert, *Das Ideal der Wüstenaskese*, p. 397.

[8] Gregory of Tours, *Zehn Bücher Geschichten*, vol. 2, books 6–10, trans. Rudolf Buchner (Darmstadt 1967), p. 12. See also Gregory of Tours, 'De gloria confessorum c. 95', in *Gregorii episcopi Turonensis miracula et opera minora*, p. 359; Gregory of Tours, *Glory of the Confessors*, trans. and intro Raymond van Dam, Translated Texts for Historians, Latin Series 4 (Liverpool, 1988), p. 99. See also Brunert, *Das Ideal der Wüstenaskese*, pp. 352–60.

[9] Basel University Library, B V 2; see *Die mittelalterlichen Handschriften der Universitätsbibliothek Basel. Beschreibendes Verzeichnis. Abteilung B: Theologische Pergamenthandschriften*, vol. 1: *Signaturen B I 1–B VIII 10*, ed. Gustav Meyer and Max Burckhardt (Basel, 1960), pp. 417–33.

[10] There were numerous later imitators and imitations; see for example Michael Zozmann, 'Rainer von Osnabrück. Wiedergeboren im Dienste der kirchlichen Erneuerung', in *'Heiliges Westfalen'. Heilige, Reliquien, Wallfahrt und Wunder im Mittelalter*, ed. Gabriela Signori, Religion in der Geschichte 11 (Bielefeld, 2003), pp. 151–61.

[11] On this tradition, see Giles Constable, *Attitudes toward Self-Inflicted Suffering in the Middle Ages* (Brookline, 1982).

[12] Heinrich Fichtenau, *Askese und Laster in der Anschauung des Mittelalters* (Vienna, 1948); Friedrich Prinz, *Askese und Kultur. Vor- und frühbenediktinisches Mönchtum an der Wiege Europas* (Munich, 1980); Friedrich Prinz, *Frühes Mönchtum im Frankenreich: Kultur und Gesellschaft in Gallien, dem Rheinland und Bayern am Beispiel der monastischen Entwicklung (4.–8. Jahrhundert)* (Munich, 1965); Karl Suso Frank (ed.), *Askese und Mönchtum in der Alten Kirche*, Wege der Forschung 409 (Darmstadt, 1975); Karl Suso Frank (ed.), *Frühes Mönchtum im Abendland*, 2 vols. (Zürich, 1975).

the *Vitae patrum* at community mealtimes.[13] This intensive repetition of and rumination over the same body of texts exercised a powerful influence both on how the monks lived their own lives and how they wrote about the lives of later ascetic saints.

The oldest rule dealing with the life of a recluse, the tenth-century *Regula solitariorum* written by a certain Grimlaïcus, clearly shows the overwhelming influence of the *Vitae patrum*.[14] It was primarily in the centres of Benedictine monasticism (Regensburg, St Gall, Scheyern, Tegernsee, St Maximin in Trier etc.) that the Latin rule was read and copied. Once again, we see how closely linked the two forms of monastic life – eremitic and coenobitic – were at the beginning.[15] Two Upper German translations of the *Regula solitariorum* from the late 1300s and early 1400s reveal a persistent connection to traditional monasticism. The earlier originated in the Benedictine monastery of St Emmeram in Regensburg;[16] the later was written in 1425 by a conventual of St Gall, Johannes Hertenstain, for the female anchorites in Steinertobel.[17] The translation bears the title 'Rule of the Forest' [*Waldregel*], reflecting the wide-

---

[13] *Die Benediktsregel. Eine Anleitung zum christlichen Leben c. 42 und 73*, trans. Georg Holzherr (Zürich, 1982), pp. 220 and 330. See Ambrose Wathen, 'La Regula Benedicti c. 73 et le Vitae patrum', *Benedictina* 28 (1981), pp. 171–97; Aquinata Böckmann, *Perspektiven der Regula Benedicti. Ein Kommentar zum Prolog und den Kapiteln 53, 58, 72 und 73*, Münsterschwarzacher Studien 37 (Münsterschwarzach, 1986), pp. 118–21. Copies of the *Vitae patrum* become very common only in the tenth century, as the libraries at Blaubeueren, Cluny, Monte Cassino, St Gall, and Schaffhausen show; see Gustav Becker, *Catalogi bibliothecarum antiqui* (Bonn, 1895), nos. 22, 24, 69, 71, 74, 76, 77, 132; Wolfgang Milde, *Der Bibliothekskatalog des Klosters Murbach aus dem 9. Jahrhundert. Ausgabe und Untersuchung von Beziehungen zu Cassiodors* Institutiones, Beihefte zum Euphorion 4 (Heidelberg, 1968), no. 255, p. 46; Columba M. Batlle, *Die 'Adhortationes sanctorum patrum' ('Verba seniorum') im lateinischen Mittelalter. Überlieferung, Fortleben und Wirkung*, Beiträge zur Geschichte des alten Mönchtums und des Benediktinerordens 31 (Münster, 1972), pp. 17–30, 71–86, 152–62; Donatella Nebbia-dalla Guarda, 'Les listes médiévales de lectures monastiques. Contribution à la connaissance des anciennes bibliothèques bénédictines', *Revue bénédictine* 102 (1986), pp. 271–326.

[14] Marie-Christine Chartier, 'Art. Grimlaïc', *Dictionnaire d'Histoire et de Géographie ecclésiastiques*, vol. 22 (Paris, 1988), cols. 273f; Jean Heuclin, *Aux origines monastiques de la Gaule du Nord. Ermites et reclus du Ve au XIe siècle* (Lille, 1988), pp. 243–51; Phyllis G. Jestice, *Wayward Monks and the Religious Revolution of the Eleventh Century* (Leiden, New York and Cologne, 1997), pp. 90–127; Karl Suso Frank, 'Grimlaïcus, "Regula solitariorum"', in *Vita Religiosa im Mittelalter. Festschrift für Kaspar Elm zum 70. Geburtstag*, ed. Franz J. Felten and Nikolas Jaspert (Berlin, 1999), pp. 21–35.

[15] Chartier, 'Art. Grimlaïc', col. 273.

[16] *Die deutschen Handschriften der Bayerischen Staatsbibliothek München. Die mittelalterlichen Handschriften aus Cgm 4001–5247*, new ed. Karin Schneider (Wiesbaden, 1996), no. 4884, p. 413. See András Vizkelety, 'Die *Regula solitariorum* des Grimlaïcus deutsch', in *'Fata Libellorum'. Festschrift für Franzjosef Pensel zum 70. Geburtstag*, ed. Rudolf Bentzinger and Ulrich-Dieter Oppitz, Göppinger Arbeiten zur Germanistik 648 (Göppingen, 1999), pp. 325–36; and Otmar Doerr, *Das Institut der Inklusen in Süddeutschland*, Beiträge zur Geschichte des alten Mönchtums und des Benediktinerordens 18 (Münster, 1934), pp. 123–60.

[17] St Gall Stiftsbibliotek, Codex 930, fols. 30r–129r; see Gustav Scherrer, *Verzeichnis der Handschriften der Stiftsbibliothek von St. Gallen* (Halle, 1875) [repr. 1975], no. 930. An edition is currently in preparation by Marc Müntz (Konstanz). On the translation see Gabriela Signori, 'Johannes Hertenstain's Translation (1425) of Grimlaïcus's Rule for the Anchoresses at Steinertobel near St Gall', in *Saints, Scholars, and Politicians. Gender as a Tool in Medieval Studies*, ed. Mathilde van Dijk and Renée Nip, Medieval Church Studies 15 (Turnhout, 2005), pp. 43–63.

spread late medieval German custom of referring to recluses as 'forest brothers' [*Waldbrüder*] and 'forest sisters' [*Waldschwestern*].[18]

Although Grimlaïcus drew on the rules of Basil the Great and St Benedict as well as the *Regula canonicorum*, a text inspired by the Carolingian reforms, he quotes even more frequently from the *Vitae patrum* and *Verba seniorum*, which, like the Rule of St Benedict, he recommends for mealtime reading [*Tischlesung*].[19] Another text from this same period, an 'admonition' written to the recluse Nonsuida, reveals a similarly close relationship to the *Vitae patrum*. Of uncertain origin, this work circulated primarily within German-speaking parts of Europe. It contains numerous formulae of the following type: 'As Antonius says …'; 'The life of the monk Marcus teaches …'; 'Abbot Daniel tells us that …'.[20]

Grimlaïcus made no sharp distinction between coenobitic and eremitic forms of monastic life; he saw them simply as two different versions of the *vita solitaria*.[21] Both monks and anchorites followed the same precept of the Gospel of Matthew 19:21: 'If you would be perfect, go, sell what you possess and give to the poor, and you will have treasure in heaven.'[22] However, Grimlaïcus did recommend that the prospective recluse should first live as a monk among other monks before withdrawing into isolation.[23] This form of life was not suitable for laypersons. Nor should the *inclusus* break off all contact with the former monastic community, but should remain in spiritual contact with it. Complete isolation was in his eyes a source of many dangers. For this reason Grimlaïcus advises the recluse to have at least two or three companions.[24] He counsels moderation in other respects as well. He is not a proponent of strict asceticism. Deep knowledge of scripture is more important for him than other things, since the recluse [*inclusus*] is expected to preach and instruct his pupils.[25] The relevant passage was rendered word for word in Hertenstain's 1425 translation for the female anchorites of Steinertobel. In this regard the *Waldregel* differs fundamentally from other rules composed specifically for women such as the *De Institutione*

---

[18] On the terms *Waldregel*, *Waldschwester*, and *Waldbruder* see Gerold Fußenegger, 'Nikolaus von Kues und die Waldschwestern von Halltal', in *Cusanus Gedächtnisschrift*, ed. Nikolaus Grass (Innsbruck, 1970), pp. 381–456; *Die Beginen und Begarden in der Schweiz*, ed. Cécile Sommer-Ramer, Helvetia Sacra IX/2 (Basel/Frankfurt, 1995), p. 919; Gabriela Signori 'Nikolaus of Flüe, The Physiognomies of a Late Medieval Ascetic', in *The Encroaching Desert. Egyptian Hagiography and the Medieval West*, ed. Mathilde van Dijk and Jitse Dijkstra (Leiden, 2006), pp. 229–55.

[19] Grimlaïcus, 'Regula solitariorum', *PL* 103, col. 633D.

[20] Adalgerus, 'Admonitio ad Nonsuindam reclusam seu Liber de studio virtutum', *PL* 134, cols. 915–38. See. F. J. Worstbrock, 'Art. Adalger', *Die deutsche Literatur des Mittelalters*. Verfasserlexikon, zweite, völlig neu bearbeitete Auflage, vol. 1 (Berlin and New York, 1978), cols. 42f. On manuscript distribution see August Eduard Anspach, *S. Isidori Hispalensis Episcopi Commonitiuncula ad sororem*, Scriptores ecclesiastici hispano-latini. Fasc. IV A (Escurial, 1935), pp. 13–21.

[21] Grimlaïcus, 'Regula solitariorum', col. 578D.

[22] Ibid., col. 579D.

[23] Required for the first time by the seventh Concile of Toldeo (646): *Concilios visigóticos e haipsano-romanos*, ed. José Vives (Madrid, 1963), pp. 255–6.

[24] Grimlaïcus, 'Regula solitariorum', cols. 595C/596B.

[25] Ibid., cols. 599D/601C.

Inclusarum by Aelred of Rievaulx (d. 1167) or the thirteenth-century *Ancrene Wisse*.[26]

A large number of cells were established near Benedictine monasteries and regular canons' priories in the earlier Middle Ages.[27] While this was certainly in keeping with Grimlaïcus's ideas, the fact that a large number of these dwellings were occupied by women was not. The following table is restricted to abbeys with necrologies that name more than five *inclusi* (dated entries increase nearly everywhere during the thirteenth century).

Cells	*Order*	*Men*	*Women*	*Total*
Amtenhausen	OSB (women)	1	14	15
Fischingen	OSB	4	4	8
Hermetswil	OSB (women)	1	9	10
Niederaltaich	OSB	6	11	17
Ottobeuren	OSB	5	9	14
Petershausen	OSB	3	3	6
Roth	Premontré	–	8	8
St Erentrudis	OSB (women)	7	20	27
St Florian	OSA	–	6	6
St Gall	OSB	5	15	20
Schäftlarn	Premontré	–	7	7
Seeon	OSB	2	6	8
Seligental	Cistercian (women)	3	10	13
Weltenburg	OSB	8	3	11
Zwiefalten	OSB	4	7	11[28]

Most of the male recluses had once been monks, as Grimlaïcus recommended. The women, on the other hand, generally came directly from the world.[29] This is true of Liutbirg, Wiborad, 'Margareta contracta' (or Margaret the Lame), Wilbirg, and Dorothea. It is to these recluses that we now turn.

---

[26] Signori, 'Johannes Hertenstain's Translation', pp. 55–7. There are numerous studies dealing with *Ancrene Wisse* and Aelred's *De Institutione Inclusarum*; for an overview of these texts, see Hughes-Edwards's chapter in this volume.

[27] This has been pointed out by Louis Gougaud in his 'Étude sur la réclusion religieuse', *Revue Mabillon* 10 (1923), pp. 26–39 and pp. 77–102; and *Ermites et reclus. Études sur d'anciennes formes de vie religieuse* (Ligugé, 1928); see also Doerr, *Das Institut der Inklusen*, pp. 71–122.

[28] These numbers are not always an accurate record of local anchorites, male or female; some figures include those associated with other monasteries. See Tom Licence, 'Evidence of Recluses in Eleventh-Century England', *Anglo-Saxon England* 36 (2007), pp. 221–34.

[29] Heuclin, *Aux origines monastiques de la Gaule du Nord*, p. 94.

Gabriela Signori

Liutbirg

Liutbirg (d. 865) had spent thirty years of her life enclosed in a cell near the
monastery of Wendhausen, a community of nuns in the vicinity of the city of
Halberstadt. Although her *vita* almost certainly originated in the ninth century, it
was not until the middle of the fifteenth that it was made accessible to a wider public.[30] One of these later copies is found in the *Magnum Legendarium* of Böddeken,
a monastery of regular canons near Paderborn in Westphalia.[31]

Liutbirg was the adoptive daughter of Gisela, a Saxon noblewoman, as Gisela
herself tells her son Bernhard on her deathbed.[32] Initially the hagiographer
directs all attention to the mother, Gisela, the eldest daughter and heiress of the
Saxon noble Hessus.[33] Married to a certain Unwan, Gisela had three children,
the aforementioned Bernhard, Bilihilt, and Hruothilt. The latter two distinguished themselves during their widowhood by founding monasteries, one in
Saxony, the other in Franconia [*Francia*].[34] Gisela met Liutbirg on one of her
'business trips', in the course of which she spent the night at one of the monasteries on her estates. There, she was attended by a 'little virgin' [*virgunculam
quandam*] who, as the hagiographer tells, 'far exceeded the other girls of the
same age both in her stature and in her intellect' [*forma vel ingenio*].[35] When
Gisela inquired about her origin, nobody in the monastery knew anything more
than that she had been born in *Solazburg*. The girl pleased Gisela so much that
she asked her if she wanted to follow her, promising to treat her like her own
child for as long as she remained with her.[36]

Liutbirg – referred to as *virago* from this point onward[37] – proved to be exceedingly virtuous, studied Scripture daily,[38] and demonstrated considerable skill
[*capax ingenii*] in the 'various arts that appertain to women' [*quae mulieribus con-*

---

[30] *Das Leben der Liutbirg. Eine Quelle zur Geschichte der Sachsen in karolingischer Zeit*, ed. Ottokar
Menzel, Deutsches Mittelalter 3 (Leipzig, 1937). The *Vita sanctae Liutbirgae* was rediscovered only in
the fifteenth century, for which see Loren J. Samons II, 'The Vitae Liutbirgae', *Classica et Mediaevalia*
43 (1992), pp. 273–86; Suzanne F. Wemple, 'Late Ninth-Century Saints: Hathmudo and Liutberga', in
The Joy of Learning and the Love of God, ed. E. Rozanne Elder, Cistercian Studies Series 116
(Kalamazoo and Spencer, 1995), pp. 33–47.

[31] Henricus Moretus, 'De magno legendario Bodecensi', *Analecta Bollandiana* 27 (1908), p. 291.

[32] *Das Leben der Liutbirg*, pp. 14–15. A recluse by the name of Haseka (d. 1261) was also commemo-
rated in Böddeken. She had settled near the church of Schermbeck, living off alms and attended to by a
servant [*ministra*] named Bertha. Her five-part biography is remarkably unremarkable; her only
accomplishment seems to have been transforming rancid butter into fresh butter in her servant's presence
on one occasion only.

[33] Hessus had apparently withdrawn into the monastery at Fulda after dividing his estate among his
daughters. In the necrology of Fulda we find the entry *Hessi*, *Bilihilt canonica* and *Benhart comes*; see
Samons II, 'The Vitae Liutbirgae', p. 276.

[34] Wendhausen in Saxony and Karsbach in the Saalegau in Franconia; see Walther Grosse, 'Das Kloster
Wendhausen, sein Stiftergeschlecht und seine Klausnerin', *Sachsen und Anhalt* 16 (1940), pp. 45–76.

[35] *Das Leben der Liutbirg*, pp. 11–12.

[36] Ibid., pp. 11–12.

[37] Claudia Opitz, 'Von der *virago* zur Braut Christi. Jungfräulichkeit und weibliche Libido im späteren
Mittelalter', in *Evatöchter und Bräute Christi. Weiblicher Lebenszusammenhang und Frauenkultur im
Mittelalter* (Weinheim, 1990), pp. 87–103.

[38] *Das Leben der Liutbirg*, p. 13.

veniunt operibus].[39] Shortly before her death Gisela entrusted Liutbirg to her son Bernhard, to whom the hagiographer devotes a short sketch. He had eight children by two wives. The first, named Reginhilda, bore him two sons, Bernhard and Otwin, before dying young. Thereafter he married Helmburg, who bore four sons – Unwan, Adalbert, Asic, and Edira – and two daughters, Gisla and Bilihilt. All the children loved Liutbirg so much that 'she seemed to them more their mother than their nurse' [*genitrix potius quam nutrix*].[40]

Except for Liutbirg's remarkable virtue, nothing at this point in her story points to sainthood. This changes in chapter ten, however. After finishing her household chores, she would spend her nights in prayer. Fasting and vigils robbed her of strength; her face grew pale, and she was reduced to skin and bones. When Bernhard asked if she were ill, people informed him that the reason for her condition lay in her fasting, vigils, and her hazardous barefoot visits to church at night. Bernhard summoned Liutbirg, whom he called 'mother', and reproached her. She had always been a model of virtue and propriety for others, he said, and he could not understand why she was now seeking to end her life. With arguments gathered mainly from the Psalms, Liutbirg not only dismissed Bernhard's reprimand, she convinced him of the rightness of her exercises. In the end she revealed to him her deepest desire, to withdraw from the world and lead the life of a recluse [*vitam solitariam atque seclusam*].[41] To this purpose she petitioned Bishop Theotgrim (or Thiatgrim) of Halberstadt (827–840), who, after carefully considering the matter, agreed. On the appointed day he arrived with numerous priests and blessed Liutbirg's cell [*cellulam mansiunculae*] which, as the hagiographer comments, resembled a shed [*veluti tugurio*].[42] The bishop forbade her to leave the confines of her cell except in an extreme emergency. Then she was walled in. From that moment on she lived in constant prayer, day and night, sustaining herself on bread with salt, herbs, and grasses. Only on Sundays and feast days would she allow herself vegetables and very small fish, occasionally spoiling herself with raspberries or an apple. A small fire burned in her cell, providing light for her work, which she interrupted only for prayer and meditation. If she had any extra time, she used it to instruct her companions [*eas quae sibi aderant*].[43] She was friendly [*affabilis*]

---

[39] Ibid., p. 13. See Ludolf Kuchenbuch, '*Opus feminile*. Das Geschlechterverhältnis im Spiegel von Frauenarbeit im früheren Mittelalter', in *Weibliche Lebensgestaltung im frühen Mittelalter*, ed. Hans-Werner Goetz (Köln, Weimar and Wien, 1991), pp. 139–75, esp. 168–70.

[40] *Das Leben der Liutbirg*, p. 16.

[41] Ibid., p. 21.

[42] Ibid., p. 25.

[43] Ibid., p. 26. Nearly all early *vitae* of female anchorites contain references to their 'counselling', 'teaching', or praying for their visitors. See Henry Mayr-Harting, 'Functions of a twelfth-century recluse', *History* 60 (1975), pp. 337–52; Gabriela Signori, 'Ohnmacht des Körpers – Macht der Sprache. Reklusion als Ordensalternative und Handlungsspielraum für Frauen', in *Frauen zwischen Anpassung und Widerstand. Beiträge zur 5. Schweizerischen Historikerinnentagung* (Zürich, 1990), pp. 25–39; Paulette L'Hermite-Leclercq, 'Les reclus du moyen âge et l'information', *Zeitgeschehen und seine Darstellung*, ed. Christoph Cormeau, Studium universale 20 (Bonn, 1995), pp. 200–20; Anneke B. Mulder-Bakker, 'The Reclusorium as an Informal Centre of Learning', in *Centres of Learning: Learning and Location in Pre-Modern Europe and the Near East*, ed. Jan Willem Drijvers and Alasdair A. MacDonald, Brill's Studies in Intellectual History 61 (Leiden, 1995), pp. 245–54; and 'Lame Margaret of Magdeburg: the Social Function of a Medieval Recluse', *Journal of Medieval History* 22 (1996), pp. 155–69.

to all who came and conversed with her through the small window, sending nobody away. Her possessions amounted to a single garment, vessels for food and drink, and a small bed with a mat.

Liutbirg lived thirty years in her cell near the monastery at Wendhausen. She developed a reputation for prophecy and was widely sought out by abbots and bishops. Among her visitors, admirers and benefactors were Bishop Hemmo (or Haimo) of Halberstadt (840–853) and Ansgar of Bremen (d. 865).[44] Liutbirg died, as her hagiographer tells us at the end of his account, during the reign of Louis the Younger, 'the most famous king of the Franks'. According to Loren J. Samons she died the same year as Ansgar.[45] Despite her *vita*, there is no evidence that she was venerated after her death. This is also true of Paulina, the founder of the monastery of Paulinzella in Thuringia, whose life has been analysed by Camilla Badstübner.[46]

Wiborad

The life of Saint Wiborad (d. 926), who was enclosed in a church near the Benedictine abbey of St Gall a few decades after Liutbirg, presents a rather different case, though her lifestyle choice was similar. Concerning her unusual name her first hagiographer, Ekkehart (d. 973), writes: 'If we transform what Wiborad sounds like in German into Latin, then the result is "women's counsel"' [*nam wiborat teutonica lingua prolatum, si latini sermonis translatione mutetur, concilium mulierum sonat*].[47] New texts were written on the occasion of her canonization in 1047, culminating in a second *vita* from the year 1075, a document as important as Paulina's *vita* for the ecclesiastical reform movement of the high Middle Ages. Before her withdrawal into the solitary life, Wiborad made a pilgrimage to Rome with her brother Hitto. Upon their return to St Gall she advised her brother to enter the monastery, though she herself remained in the world for the time being. At the behest of the bishop of Konstanz she went to live near the church of St George, moving later to St Mang. According to the *Annales Sangallenses maiores*, she became an *inclusa* in the year 916.[48] The later *vita* contains only a terse report: 'And on most holy Pentecost a crowd, praising God, accompanied them [Wiborad and the bishop of Konstanz] as he humbly commended her to God, consecrated her with holy blessings, and shut her up in her cell' [*includens abcessit*].[49] A small community of women quickly formed around her, each woman living in her own enclosure. Among them was the saintly virgin Rachild, Wiborad's spiritual daughter, and a married woman without name.

---

[44] *Das Leben der Liutbirg*, p. 40.
[45] Samons II, 'The Vitae Liutbirgae', pp. 282–3.
[46] Camilla Badstübner-Kizik, *Die Gründungsgeschichte des Klosters Paulinzella und die Lebensbeschreibung der Stifterin Paulina. Sigebotos Vita Paulinae als Denkmal hirsauischer Reformliteratur des 12. Jahrhunderts. Eine reform-, literatur-u. sozialgeschichtliche Untersuchung* (Münster, 1993).
[47] *Vitae Sanctae Wiboradae. Die älteste Lebensbeschreibung der heiligen Wiborada. Einleitung, kritische Edition und Übersetzung*, ed. Walter Berschin, Mitteilungen zur vaterländischen Geschichte 51 (St Gall, 1983), p. 32.
[48] Ibid., p. 2.
[49] Ibid., p. 160.

The feeding of the poor was the centre of Wiborad's life. But she also 'admonished' boys who attended the monastery school and criticized prominent secular figures who stole monastery property and saints' relics.[50] At the window of her cell she had a bell [*tintinnabulum*] that she used to summon her servant [*ministram*].[51] She also performed her own Eucharist.[52] Well into the twelfth century, according to Bärbel Stocker, personal communion was not out of the ordinary among male and female monastic communities that lacked a priest, as well as among recluses.[53]

One day Wiborad foresaw the coming of the 'heathens' (Huns) and her own death as a martyr. She summoned the monk Waldram and asked him to take the people to safety. She also exhorted her brother Hitto to leave his church. Everyone prepared for flight; only Wiborad remained behind. The 'heathens' entered her cell through the roof, stripped her down to her hair shirt and, taking her clothes as booty, struck her dead with an axe.[54] When Hitto returned to St Gall a few days later, he found his sister dead. But her body had been healed of all wounds: the blow from the axe, the frostbite that had disfigured her feet, and the lacerations and bruises caused by the chains she had worn.[55] She appeared to those who stood vigil over her corpse and requested that she be buried in her fetters. Ekkehart concludes his account with various visions and miracles, devoting special attention to the recluse Rachild, her parents and relatives, and Wiborad's brother Hitto.

Much more detailed than Ekkehart's *vita* is the one written by Herimann of St Gall in 1072–76 under commission from the abbot Ulrich.[56] New personages are introduced, including the cautionary figure of the anchorite Cilia, who only had her body enclosed in the cell, not her spirit.[57] The personality of Rachild also emerges more clearly here,[58] and Herimann's dialogue with the hermit Adalrich gives us a fuller picture of life in the cell.[59]

The oldest surviving version of Ekkehart's *vita* is found in the *Stuttgarter Passionale* and dates from the year 1144.[60] The second version, from 1464, comes from the Benedictine abbey of St Ulrich and St Afra. The later *vita* is better attested.[61] Nonetheless, with the exception of Salem, (Heidelberg, Universitätsbibliotek

---

[50] Ibid., p. 58, pp. 68–73.

[51] Ibid., p. 62.

[52] Ibid., p. 64–6: *calicem et patenam uel corporale sed et fanonem cum quo solita es offerre.*

[53] See Bärbel Stocker, 'Die Opfergeräte der heiligen Wiborada von St. Gallen – Eine Frau als Zelebrantin der Eucharistie?', *Freiburger Diözesan-Archiv* 111 (1991), pp. 405–19.

[54] *Vitae Sanctae Wiboradae*, p. 84. See Heuclin, *Aux origines monastiques de la Gaule du Nord*, pp. 227–34.

[55] *Vitae Sanctae Wiboradae*, p. 88.

[56] Ibid., p. 23.

[57] Ibid., pp. 146–53. Cilia is pictured handing Wiborad a purse on the front cover of this present volume.

[58] Ibid., pp. 178–85.

[59] Ibid., pp. 152–7.

[60] Eva Irblich, *Die 'Vitae sanctae Wiboradae'. Ein Heiligenleben des 10. Jahrhunderts als Zeitbild*, Schriften des Vereins für Geschichte des Bodensees und seiner Umgebung 88 (St Gall, 1970), pp. 11–12.

[61] Ibid., p. 13; Rolf Schmidt, *Reichenau und St. Gallen. Ihre literarische Überlieferung zur Zeit des Klosterhumanismus in St. Ulrich und Afra zu Augsburg um 1500*, Vorträge und Forschungen. Sonderband 33 (Sigmaringen, 1985), pp. 77, 161, 169–71.

Sal. IX 21), one of the primary manuscripts of the *vita*, the accounts of Wiborad's life were clearly restricted to St Gall. The eleventh-century Codex 560 in the St Gall Collegiate Library contains a 'trilogy' of the local saints Gallus, Otmar, and Wiborad.[62] Codex Sangallensis 564, from the twelfth century, is a copy or doublet of Codex 560.[63] In Codex 610, which originated in the 1400s and contains marginal notes from the famous St Gall historian, poet, and humanist Joachim Watt, alias Vadian (d. 1551), we also find the *vitae* of Saint Magnus and Saint Notker as well as the *Casus sancti Galli*.[64] Codex 560, compiled by Friedrich Colner (d. 1451),[65] is 492 pages in length and contains the *vitae* of the St Gall saints Gallus, Magnus, Otmar, and Wiborad as well as the *Sprüche der Altväter* ['Sayings of the Old Fathers'],[66] a German version of the *Verba seniorum* that Colner translated at the request of the nuns who lived in seclusion near St George.[67] The last St Gall *inclusa* died in 1509 in Wiborad's cell at the church of St Mang.[68] Most of the other reclusories associated with St Gall were transformed into a *Schwesternhaus* in the course of the fifteenth century.[69]

Caesarius of Heisterbach

In the course of the later Middle Ages, the powerful Benedictine hold over the practice of reclusion was gradually relaxed, and in many places we see the influence of the contemporaneous mendicant ideas. More clearly than ever, life in a solitary cell became merely one of many forms of the religious life, and one chosen ever more exclusively by women.[70] The proliferation of documents during the thirteenth century is remarkable. This is also true of the entries in necrologies.

Caesarius of Heisterbach (d. *c.*1240), long-time prior of the Cistercian monastery at Heisterbach near Königswinter in Westphalia, gives several examples of *inclusae* in his famous *Dialogus miraculorum*, a text intended for the instruction of novices. Caesarius frequently cites the *Vitae patrum*; and excerpts

---

[62] Irblich, *Die 'Vitae sanctae Wiboradae'*, pp. 13–14.

[63] Ibid., pp. 14–16.

[64] Ibid., pp. 16–18.

[65] On Colner see Barbara Christine Stocker, *Friedrich Colner, Schreiber und Übersetzer in St. Gallen 1430–1436 (mit Beigabe der deutschen Wiborada-Vita in dynamischer Edition)*, Göppinger Arbeiten zur Germanistik 619 (Göppingen, 1996), pp. 3–6.

[66] Ibid., pp. 12–16; Irblich, *Die 'Vitae sanctae Wiboradae'*, pp. 18–19.

[67] Anton Näf and René Wetzel, 'Friedrich Kölner in St. Gallen. Übersetzung und Schreibertätigkeit im Dienst von Reform und Seelsorge', in *Mittelalterliche Literatur im Lebenszusammenhang*, ed. Eckart Conrad Lutz, Scrinium Friburgense 8 (Freiburg, 1997), pp. 329–40.

[68] Emil Schlumpf, *Quellen zur Geschichte der Inklusen in der Stadt St. Gallen*, Mitteilungen zur vaterländischen Geschichte 41/2 (St Gall, 1953), p. 19.

[69] *Die Beginen und Begarden in der Schweiz*, ed. Sommer-Ramer, pp. 571–6; *Franziskaner, Klarissen und regulierte Franziskaner-Terziarinnen*, Helvetia Sacra,V/2 (Basel/Frankfurt, 1978), pp. 1086–94; Josef Reck, 'Die Anfänge des Frauenklosters St. Scholastika', *Rorschacher Neujahrblätter* 56 (1966), pp. 87–104; M. W. Lehner, 'Die Schwestern zu St. Lienhart vor der Stadt St. Gallen (1318–1566', *Zeitschrift für Schweizerische Kirchengeschichte* 55 (1961), pp. 191–221 and pp. 275–87.

[70] Patricia J. F. Rosof, 'The Anchoress in the Twelfth and Thirteenth Centuries', in *Medieval Religious Women*, vol. 2: *Peaceweavers*, ed. Lillian Thomas Shank and John A. Nichols, Cistercian Studies Series 72 (Kalamazoo, 1987), pp. 123–44; Ann K. Warren, *Anchorites and Their Patrons in Medieval England* (Berkeley, Los Angeles and London, 1985), p. 20.

from the *Dialogus* were incorporated into the *Vitaspatrum*-complex itself, as in the exemplar of the Cistercian monastery of Erfurt, which dates from the mid-fifteenth century. This manuscript, which contains 351 folios, is currently in the British Library in London (Additional MS 21147).[71] There is also conserved a mid-to-late thirteenth-century florilegium from the regular canon priory at Waldhausen (Austria) containing excerpts from the *Vitaspatrum*, miracles of the Virgin Mary, and exempla from the collection of Stefan of Bourbon and from Caesarius's *Dialogus* (Additional MS 16589).[72] Of similarly hybrid composition is the fifteenth-century omnibus volume Cpl. [818] 143 from the abbey library of Schlägl (Austria). It contains the *Vitaspatrum*, the *Dialogus miraculorum*, excerpts from Jacques de Vitry (d. 1240), the *Disciplina clericalis* of Petrus Alphonsus (d. after 1130) and the *Legenda aurea* of Jacobus de Voragine (d. 1298).[73]

Caesarius of Heisterbach was a great collector of stories and a man who eagerly listened to what was told about noteworthy individuals in the various places he visited.[74] He ordered his material thematically into two parts with a total of ten chapters.[75] In chapter five, devoted to temptations and demons, he tells the story of a recluse of Cologne who, seeking to escape the desires of the flesh, had himself walled up at the church of St Maximus. As a symbol of penitence he bore an iron ring. His former concubine – she wearing a similar ring around her waist – looked after him, provided him with food and drink and other necessities. They died in quick succession. At the behest of his superior the recluse removed his iron ring shortly before his death. That of the woman burst as she lay on her deathbed. This had been witnessed by a large number of honourable women who had kept her company in the last hours of her life, as Caesarius says, who had learned this story from the daughter of the sister of this same priest.[76]

There is a similar account concerning a woman of Liège who had lived for many years with a cleric. After the latter's death, she underwent a change of heart and repented, and had herself shut up in a cell at the church of St Severin. Her remorse was so great that she frequently wept tears of blood. She, too, donned an iron ring, but it burst asunder when she prayed, whereupon she concluded that such fetters were not pleasing to God. She considered having another one made, but first

[71] Batlle, *Die 'Adhortationes sanctorum patrum'*, p. 144.

[72] Ibid., no. 116, p. 100.

[73] Ibid., no. 241, p. 131.

[74] Patrick McGuire, 'Friends and Tales in the Cloister: Oral Sources in Caesarius of Heisterbach's *Dialogus miraculorum*', *Analecta Cisterciensia* 36 (1980), pp. 176–247.

[75] Ludger Tewes, 'Der *Dialogus miraculorum* des Caesarius von Heisterbach: Beobachtungen zum Gliederungs- und Werkcharakter', *Archiv für Kulturgeschichte* 79 (1997), pp. 13–30.

[76] *Caesarii Heisterbacensis monachi ordinis Cisterciensis Dialogus miraculorum*, XI, 27, ed. Joseph Strange, 2 vols. (Köln/Bonn/Brüssel, 1851), p. 293; *Johann Hartliebs Übersetzung des 'Dialogus miraculorum' von Caesarius von Heisterbach aus der einzigen Londoner Handschrift*, ed. Karl Drescher, Deutsche Texte des Mittelalters 33 (Berlin, 1929), p. 344. See Armin Basedow, *Die Inclusen in Deutschland, vornehmlich in der Gegend des Niederrheins um die Wende des 12. und 13. Jahrhunderts, unter besonderer Berücksichtigung des 'Dialogus Miraculorum' des Caesarius von Heisterbach* (Heidelberg, 1895); Johannes Asen, 'Die Klausen in Köln', *Annalen des historischen Vereins für den Niederrhein* 110 (1927), pp. 183–4.

consulted with her confessor on the matter. The priest, recalling the Gospel of Luke 7:48, told her that hers was the same God who had told Mary Magdalene: 'Your sins are forgiven.'[77] For Caesarius of Heisterbach, enclosure and iron rings stand in the service of religious instructions as signs of radical repentance. Most of the *inclusae* presented in the *Dialogus* lived in Cologne or other Westphalian towns, and many of them experienced visions or had the gift of prophecy.[78]

Margareta contracta

Numerous visions are also ascribed to 'Margareta contracta' or Margaret the Lame, an anchorite of Magdeburg.[79] Since her *vita* – written *c*.1260–1270 – has been studied in detail by Anneke Mulder-Baker, here I will restrict myself to a short discussion of its unusual and very informative manuscript history.[80] Thus far, more than ten manuscripts have come to light, the oldest from the Cistercian monastery of Villers-la-Ville in Belgium,[81] the second oldest from the Cistercian convent Ter Kameren near Brussels. The Brussels codex, according to the editor's description, contains the lives of numerous thirteenth-century women, including Lutgard of Tongeren (d. 1246), Christine of St Trond or 'Christina Admirabilis' (d. 1228), Elisabeth of Hungary (d. 1231), and Alice of Schaarbeek (d. 1250).[82] The same is true of another Brussels codex of unknown origins (written *c*.1413) as well as of a manuscript – today in Liège – from the monastery of the Order of the Holy Cross at Huy.[83] The Liège codex also contains the *Liber specialis gratie* of Mechthild of Hackeborn (d. 1299) from the Cistercian convent at Helfta near Eisleben. The *Liber specialis gratie* and the life of Margaret the Lame are also found together in Codex

[77] *Caesarii Heisterbacensis monachi ordinis Cisterciensis Dialogus miraculorum* XI, 29, p. 294; *Johann Hartliebs Übersetzung des 'Dialogus miraculorum'*, p. 346.

[78] *Caesarii Heisterbacensis monachi ordinis Cisterciensis Dialogus miraculorum* IV, 87; V, 46, 47, 50; VI, 5, 18, 31; VII, 29, 49; VIII, 53, 60; IX, 22, 31; XII, 5, 24, 27, 46. Further examples can be found in Caesarius's *Liber octo miraculorum* and in his *Homilies*.

[79] *Die Vita der Margareta contracta, einer Magdeburger Rekluse des 13. Jahrhunderts*, ed. Paul Gerhard Schmidt (Leipzig, 1992); *The Vita of Margaret the Lame, a Thirteenth-Century German Recluse-Mystic, by Friar Johannes O. P. of Magdeburg*, trans. and commentary Gertrud Jaron Lewis and Tilman Lewis (Toronto, 2001).

[80] Anneke B. Mulder-Bakker, 'Lame Margaret of Magdeburg: the Social Function of a Medieval Recluse', *Journal of Medieval History* 22 (1996), pp. 155–69; and 'Monddood maken liet zij zich niet. De kluizenares Kreupele Margriet van Maagdenburg', in *Vrome Vrouwen. Betekenissen van geloof voor vrouwen in de geschiedenes*, ed. Mirjam Cornelis, En tipje van de sluier 10 (Hilversum, 1996), pp. 45–66; and 'De stichtige punten van Kreupele Margriet', *Amsterdamer Beiträge zur älteren Germanistik* 47 (1997), pp. 131–42; see also her *Lives of the Anchoresses. The Rise of the Urban Recluse in Medieval Europe* (Philadelphia, 2005), pp. 148–73. See also Bardo Weiß, *Margareta von Magdeburg. Eine gelähmte Mystikerin des 13. Jahrhunderts* (Paderborn, 1995); Gertrud Jaron Lewis, 'Margareta the Lame and Her Theological Questioning', *Mystics Quarterly* 22 (1996), pp. 133–43.

[81] Berlin, Staatsbibliothek Preußischer Kulturbesitz, Theol. lat. quart. 195, *Die Vita der Margareta contracta*, pp. xv–xvi. See Simone Roisin, *L'hagiographie cistercienne dans le diocèse de Liège au XIIIᵉ siècle*, Recueil de travaux d'histoire et de philologie de l'Université de Louvain, III/27 (Louvain/Brussels, 1947), pp. 23–46.

[82] Brussels, Bibliothèque royale 8609–8620, *Die Vita der Margareta contracta*, p. xvi; Roisin, *L'hagiographie cistercienne*, pp. 49–50 and p. 52.

[83] Liège/Lüttich, Großes Seminar 6 G 4, *Die Vita der Margareta contracta*, p. xvii.

13795 of the Austrian National Library at Vienna, which was compiled in the Augustinian abbey of Böddeken in 1451.[84] Belgian Cistercians cultivated the memory of the Saxon *inclusa* before her *vita* found greater resonance in Westphalia and the lower Rhenish territories in the context of the *Devotio Moderna*.[85] No evidence has survived that she was venerated in Magdeburg itself.

Wilbirg

The *vita* of Saint Wilbirg (d. 1289) is similar to the accounts of the female anchorites in the *Dialogus miraculorum* in the prominent role played by visions and miracles. According to her 'biographer', the monk Einwik of St Florian (d. 1313), an Austrian community of regular canons, Wilbirg was a young woman when she retreated into a cell near the abbey 'so that she would no longer be disturbed in her devotions'.[86] Her parents, 'as is the custom of the wealthy', had given their child into the care of a foster mother. This woman, Alheit, who was very pious, practising strict abstinence and daily mortification of the flesh, became a role-model in every respect for her young charge. After the death of her mother and foster mother, Wilbirg went on a pilgrimage to Compostela together with her friend Mechthild.[87] After their return, Mechthild wished to go on to Rome but Wilbirg refused, and in 1248 she had herself shut up in a cell built where Alheit had lived. There Mechthild served her until her death.[88] Like Alheit, Wilbirg mortified her flesh daily, wore penitential garments and fasted three days a week.[89] She is also said to have worn an iron chain.[90] In this way she lived forty-one years, leaving her cell only once, when Rudolf of Habsburg (d. 1290) threatened the monastery during his conflict with Ottokar of Bohemia (d. 1278). Her *vita* is filled with miracles, visions, and prophecies. She prayed for the dead and gave counsel to the living. We also learn that she became an eager reader after some school boys [*pueri scolares*] taught her how,[91] and that she wrote letters to her friends *propria manu* [with her own hands].[92] Her *vita* survives in four medieval manuscripts, three from St Florian and the fourth from the nearby regular canon priory of Waldhausen,[93] where Wilbirg was also celebrated liturgically.[94] There is a further

---

[84] Ibid., p. xviii.

[85] As McAvoy explains in her introduction to this volume, *Devotio Moderna* or 'modern devotion' refers to a movement towards the regeneration of the spiritual life that began in the Netherlands during the late fourteenth century but whose influence also spread to Germany, France, and parts of Italy.

[86] *Die Vita Wilbirgis des Einwik*, ed. and trans. Lukas Sainitzer, Forschungen zur Geschichte Oberösterreichs 19 (Linz, 1999), p. 185.

[87] Ibid., pp. 180–1.

[88] Ibid., p. 186.

[89] Ibid., pp. 187–8.

[90] Ibid., pp. 216–17.

[91] Ibid., p. 235.

[92] Ibid., p. 238.

[93] Codex British Museum Additional MS 15833 belonged to the monastery at Waldhausen; as previously mentioned, the other three manuscripts came from the abbey of St Florian, including Codex Mellicensis 1831 (298 E 89). See *Die Vita Wilbirgis des Einwik*, pp. 63–83.

[94] Doerr, *Das Institut der Inklusen*, p. 100.

reference to this in the necrology of St Erentrud, a Benedictine abbey on the Nonnberg in Salzburg,[95] but other evidence of veneration is lacking.

Dorothea von Montau

The last recluse to be discussed in detail here was also blessed with the gift of prophecy: Dorothea von Montau (d. 1394), who called herself 'prisoner of Christ'.[96] Dorothea was born of a peasant family in Danzig (Gdańsk). In 1363, according to her *vita*, she was married against her will to a swordmaker, to whom she bore nine children. Eight of them died young. Dorothea's main role-model was Saint Brigitta of Sweden (d. 1373), herself a mother of eight children, and she was present when Brigitta's remains were shown at the church of St Mary in Danzig in May 1374. That she was acquainted with Brigitta's *Revelations* is questionable, however.[97] Like the latter, Dorothea undertook pilgrimages, first to Aachen, then to Rome, after which she had herself shut up in a cell at the cathedral in Marienwerder on 2 May 1393. She died a year later.[98] We know of her life through a 'biography' compiled a year after her death by her confessor, Johannes of Marienwerder (d. 1417),[99] as well as through individual testimonies that Johannes caused to be recorded preliminary to her canonization (the proceedings ran from 1404–6). One of these testimonies was that of her friend Luzia Glogaw (d. 1404), a beguine.[100] Dorothea's daily life, both before and after her inclusion,

---

[95] Ibid., p. 110.

[96] *Vita Dorotheae Montoviensis Johannis Marienwerder*, ed. Hans Westphal with Anneliese Triller, Forschungen und Quellen zur Kirchen- und Kulturgeschichte Ostdeutschlands 1 (Cologne/Graz, 1964); *Des Leben der zeligen frawen Dorothee clewsnerynne in der thumkyrchen czu Marienwerdir des landes czu Prewszen*, ed. Theodor Hirsch, Max Toeppen and Ernst Strehlke, Scriptores Rerum Prussicarum. Die Geschichtsquellen der preußischen Vorzeit 2 (Leipzig, 1863), pp. 257–60. See Elisabeth Schraut, 'Dorothea von Montau: Wahrnehmungsweisen von Kindheit und Eheleben einer spätmittelalterlichen Heiligen', *Religiöse Frauenbewegung und mystische Frömmigkeit im Mittelalter*, ed. Peter Dinzelbacher and Dieter R. Bauer (Cologne/Vienna, 1988), pp. 373–94; Petra Hörner, *Dorothea von Montau. Überlieferung – Interpretation*, Information und Interpretation 7 (Frankfurt/M., 1993), pp. 13–20.

[97] All the German translations are of a later date; see Ulrich Montag, *Das Werk der heiligen Birgitta von Schweden in oberdeutscher Überlieferung*, Münchener Texte und Untersuchungen zur deutschen Literatur des Mittelalters 18 (Munich, 1968); and 'The Reception of St Birgitta in Germany', in *The Translation of the Works of St. Birgitta of Sweden into the Medieval European Vernaculars*, ed. Bridget Morris and Veronica O'Mara, The Medieval Translator 7 (Turnhout, 2000), pp. 106–16.

[98] Parallels to the life of Margery Kempe are noted by Ute Stargardt, 'Whose Life Is This Anyway? Johannes von Marienwerder's Narrative Strategies in the German Vita of Dorothea von Montau', *Michigan Academician* 27 (1994), pp. 39–56; and Liliana Sikorska, 'Internal Exile: Dorothea of Montau's Inward Journey', *Studia Anglica Posnaniensia* 38 (2002), pp. 433–44.

[99] Richard Stachnik, 'Zum Schrifttum über die heilige Dorothea von Montau', in *Dorothea von Montau. Eine preußische Heilige des 14. Jahrhunderts*, ed. Richard Stachnik and Anneliese Triller (Osnabrück, 1976), pp. 59–105.

[100] *Die Akten des Kanonisationsprozesses Dorotheas von Montau von 1394 bis 1521*, ed. Richard Stachnik, Forschungen und Quellen zur Kirchen- und Kulturgeschichte Ostdeutschlands 15 (Cologne/Vienna, 1978), testimony 66, pp. 162–9. On what the Teutonic Knights had to say see Anneliese Triller, 'Die heilige Dorothea von Montau in ihrem Verhältnis zum Deutschen Orden und die Deutschordensmitglieder im Kanonisationsprozeß Dorotheas 1404–1406', in *Von Akkon bis Wien. Studien zur Deutschordensgeschichte vom 13. bis zum 20. Jahrhundert*, ed. Udo Arnold, Quellen und Studien zur Geschichte des Deutschen Ordens 20 (Marburg, 1978), pp. 76–83.

was filled with the kinds of auto-aggressive practices we have seen before. The fifth book of her *vita* contains a rule specially designed for her [*regula in reclusorio observanda*]. In direct speech her Godfather orders:

> In the reclusory [*reclusiorio*], beneath the lower window [*fenestram inferiorem*] through which food and drink may be passed in to you and men may speak, you shall have a glass window [*clausuram vitream*] that can be opened for necessity. A crucifix shall hang in your room so that everyone who visits you gains the impression that this reclusory is a sacred dwelling [*quod hoc reclusorium domus sanctorum sit*] […]. When you enter your cell, you may not offer anyone your hand to receive any gift of money or touch any other without the permission of your father confessor […]. Furthermore, you shall not desire to speak with many people, nor should recluses wish for this community to make much conversation, lest anything be given to them […]. Instead you shall trust Me [i.e., God] completely […]. The Lord spoke further: 'You shall behave exceedingly virtuously, behaving with good morals [*bonis moribus*] and strive assiduously both night and day to please Me, and Me alone. It shall be to you as a wife who has a stern, hard husband who does not allow her to leave the house […]. You shall entrust yourself to your father confessor without reservation, as you have entrusted yourself to Me…[101]

In 1395 Johannes of Marienwerder sent Dorothea's 'biography' to his friend Nikolaus Humilis in Nuremberg, who promptly translated it (and later other of Marienwerder's works) for the Augustinian nuns at the convent in Pillenreuth, a former reclusory.[102] The original missive is lost, though a copy made by a Pillenreuth sister can be found today in the Herzog August Library at Wolfenbüttel. The other works, too, are found in the south: as Werner Williams-Krapp observes, 'only in manuscripts from monasteries closely connected with Pillenreuth'.[103] Dorothea's cult was unable to establish itself in southern Germany, however. Marienwerder's *vita* circulated mainly in Prussia and in 1492 it was printed by the Marienburg goldsmith Jakob Karweiß.[104] The life and miracles of Dorothea of Montau were also included in the *Magnum Legendarium* of the Böddeken brothers, a branch of the manuscript tradition hitherto neglected in the scholarship.[105]

In his *Liber de festis*, Johannes of Marienwerder compiled accounts of the

---

[101] *Des Leben der zeligen Frawen Dorothee*, pp. 286–7; *Vita Dorotheae Montoviensis*, p. 18. See also Ute Stargardt, 'Male Clerical Authority in the Spiritual (Auto)biographies of Medieval Holy Women', in *Women as Protagonists and Poets in the German Middle Ages. An Anthology of Feminist Approaches to Middle High German Literature*, ed. Albrecht Classen, Göppinger Arbeiten zur Germanistik 528 (Göppingen, 1991), pp. 209–38.

[102] Hörner, *Dorothea von Montau*, pp. 49–54.

[103] Werner Williams-Krapp, 'Kultpropaganda für eine Mystikerin. Das Leben der Dorothea von Montau im *Sendbrief* des Nikolaus von Nürnberg', in *Literatur – Geschichte – Literaturgeschichte. Beiträge zur mediävistischen Literaturwissenschaft*, ed. Nine Miedema and Rudolf Suntrup (Frankfurt/M. u.a., 2003), p. 712.

[104] Hörner, *Dorothea von Montau*, pp. 44–8.

[105] Moretus, 'De magno legendario Bodecensi', p. 336.

visions Dorothea experienced at important moments during the liturgical calendar. Unlike the *vitae*, this 'Book of Feasts' is only preserved in two manuscripts from the fifteenth century, one from the Teutonic Knights of Tapiau (Gwardeisk), the other from the church of St Mary in Danzig.[106] Whether and in what form the *Liber de festis* was influenced by the *Revelations* of Bridget of Sweden is a matter requiring further study. In chapter eighty of the *Liber*, which deals with Dorothea's *unio mystica*, Brigitta appears to her friend as a 'god-like creature, that is resembling God more than a human being' [*deiformis, id est plus Deo quam homini similis*] and embraces her.[107]

Conclusion

In the Western Church, recluses were considered the true virtuosi of the ascetic life from the earliest of times, and reclusion was seen as the highest step that could be achieved in the life of a monk. This also remained true in the German-speaking regions and here, as elsewhere, relations between the two institutions – monasticism and reclusion – within a male context were correspondingly close, both in theory and in practice. However, the situation was different for women, as the *vitae* of the women examined above would attest. Most female anchorites came directly from the world without first having 'practised' the solitary life within a monastic community. Furthermore, almost all of those whose lives are recorded had made pilgrimages to distant places (to Rome, Compostela, or the Holy Land) before retreating into the cell. Nonetheless, for the *inclusa*, proximity to the monastic community was a spiritual necessity. Most had their cells at the walls of a monastic church, which meant that they could participate in the liturgical life of the community without being subject to the community's rules. After her death, the monastery kept the memory of the female anchorite alive in written 'biography', liturgical practice, and other forms of veneration. The local nature of her reputation, however, tended to make it difficult for her cult to transcend the walls of the particular community where she had lived and taught. The *vita* of Margareta the Lame is the only exception to this rule among the 'biographies' we have examined here.

The sources tell us that towns begin to replace rural monasteries as focal points of anchoritic life from the thirteenth century. But it is possible that they provide a distorted view of reality. Necrologies from late medieval village churches show us that there were still anchorites of both sexes living in rural locations.[108] From the fourteenth century, our information on urban recluses comes increasingly from wills and other inheritance documents.[109] In Cologne, the largest town in the late

---

[106] Johannes Marienwerder, *Liber de festis magistri Johannis de Marienwerder. Offenbarungen der Dorothea von Montau*, ed. Anneliese Triller, Forschungen und Quellen zur Kirchen- und Kulturgeschichte Ostdeutschlands 25 (Cologne, Weimar and Vienna, 1992), pp. xxx–xi.

[107] Ibid., pp. 135–6.

[108] *Die Beginen und Begarden in der Schweiz*, ed. Sommer-Ramer, pp. 120, 132, 183, 551, 571–7.

[109] Ibid., pp. 316–17 and pp. 330–1

medieval Holy Roman Empire, property transaction records known as *Schreinsbücher* provide evidence for the existence of more than twenty reclusories.[110] Even far smaller towns such as Regensburg could have up to sixteen during the fourteenth century.[111] Unfortunately, we know very little about the individual 'biographies' of these recluses, with one exception: thanks to the writings of Johannes Busch (d. 1479/80), an Augustinian canon in Hildesheim, we are somewhat better informed about the situation in Saxony during the fifteenth century. Acting as representative of the suffragan, Busch personally directed several inclusion ceremonies and the following extract from his chronicle is worth quoting in full here as an illuminating source of information with which to conclude this essay. Besides providing insight into the role of the anchorite's maidservant [*abra*] as providing the indispensable link between cell and society over the centuries, Busch's chronicle shows very clearly that by the late fifteenth century, in this region at least, an anchoritic life without having adopted a *regula* had become all but unthinkable.[112]

Appendix

Johannes Busch, *Liber de reformatione monasterium*, in *Des Augustinerpropstes Iohannes Busch Chronicon Windeshemense und Liber de reformatione monasterium*, ed. Karl Grube, Geschichtsquellen der Provinz Sachsen und angrenzender Gebiete 19 (Halle/S., 1886), Chapter 42, pp. 656–8.

At the request of the auxiliary bishop, who was ill at the time, and at the behest of Bishop Ernst of Hildesheim, I personally shut in the *inclusa* or anchoress at St Nicholas in the eastern part of Hildesheim with due ceremony and in the presence of many people of both sexes. I removed her old, worldly garments, and with them her old person, clothing her anew in the garments of our order.

The anchoress at St Catherine, who was younger, was vested at my behest in a white garment and in a subtle [linen toga] like a nun.[113] But this one here was some sixty years old and an illiterate laywoman, who could not read due to flawed vision. Accordingly, I clothed her in a white garment and a scapular[114] and, as she was to be an anchoress, in a large black veil covering all other garments worn in the manner of our nuns, since all anchoresses in Saxony, both taught and untaught, wear the black veil on their heads, as the anchoress at St Catherine had done.[115]

---

[110] Asen, 'Die Klausen in Köln', pp. 190–201.

[111] Doerr, *Das Institut der Inklusen*, pp. 124 and 160.

[112] See Johannes Heinrich Gebauer, 'Die Fraueneinsiedeleien in der Stadt Hildesheim', *Jahrbuch der Gesellschaft für niedersächsische Kirchengeschichte* 48 (1950), pp. 46–61.

[113] Ibid., p. 655: 'The anchoress or hermitess lives together with her maideservant [*abra*] near the Church of St Katherine's in the eastern part of the city of Hildesheim across from our monastery at Sülte. She was sealed in by Herr Johannes, Bishop of Meißen and representative of the Bishop of Hildesheim, with my subprior in attendance, while I was absent visiting monasteries.'

[114] A loose, sleeveless garment, hanging from the shoulders in front and behind.

[115] Busch also mentions the large black veil in connection with the nuns sent from Dorstadt to Stendal, who, he tells us, had only worn a black cap, not the long veil.

The sister's name is Mya. For thirty years she had been the maidservant of the anchoress who died in this cell, and in that capacity she had to carry food, drink, and other necessities of life on her own shoulders far away from the city. Accordingly, because of her age and for many other reasons, the auxiliary bishop and numerous other clergy did not wish to shut her in. I disagreed, however, and told them that we could not expel from her cell the sister who had served her predecessor for so many years. She had a right to remain there, I said, especially because she had so fervently requested it. In the end all agreed with me and it was decided that I would be the one to shut her in. I replied to them: 'Since the auxiliary bishop, who normally performs this ceremony, is ill, it would be better if the abbot of St Michael does it, since he has a crosier, or the abbot of St Godehard. For I am merely a simple prelate'. To which all responded: 'This sister must adopt the Rule of St Augustine, not the Rule of St Benedict. Therefore it is fitting that you vest her and remain her father; you can better instruct her in the Rule of St Augustine'. In the end, as the bishop of Hildesheim commanded it, I obeyed and complied.

On the day of her vestment she was led to me barefoot before the altar by a pious and wealthy matron, herself barefoot. She lay herself down before the altar steps. I asked her what questions it was customary to ask one who wished to join an order. After her response she removed her old garments and I vested her anew in the manner I have described. Then I gave a short sermon to the priests, clerics, and people, and gave her the Body of Christ at the end of the Mass. Thereupon I led her, still barefoot, to her cell, where along with those in attendance I sang the responsory 'Deliver me, O Lord, from eternal death on that awful day, when the heavens and the earth shall be moved'. 'That day, day of wrath, etc'.[116] The priest must then ask the prospective anchoress: 'Do you desire to be shut in and lead the solitary life for God's sake and do so as long as you shall live?' To which she must answer: 'I do'. And he says: 'Will you be obedient to the bishop and to us as his representative as long as you shall live?' She answers: 'I will'. Thereupon he explains to her what difficulties she will encounter and that she will have to fight against the Devil, and he asks her if she has well considered her decision and is prepared to undertake this manfully [*viriliter*], fighting against this world and her flesh as dead in this world. To which she is to answer: 'For the love of God and her soul and relying upon the prayers of good people, she is prepared for everything, with God's help'. Then the priest, upon his knees, commences the 'Come, Creator blest' [*Veni Creator*] and the versicle 'Send forth' [*Emitte*] and the collect 'O God, Who didst instruct the hearts of the faithful' [*Deus, qui fidelium corda*] and the 'Deeds' [*Actiones*].[117] Then come the petitions, and after the collects 'The kingdom of the world' [*Regnum Mundi*] is sung and after the vestment the Mass of the Holy Spirit. When the credo has been recited, the priest turns to her and says: 'Sister, soon you will have made your vow. Have you well considered your

---

[116] The words are taken from the prayers sung by the choir at the burial of an adult: 'Libera me, Domine, de morte eterna, quando c[a]eli movendi sunt etc. Dies illa, dies ir[a]e ac deinceps.'
[117] These are the beginnings of various prayers recited during the invocation of the Holy Spirit.

decision to make this vow and to fight against the flesh, the world, and the Devil?'
Then he states his approval and gives her the Rule of St Augustine, using the following words: 'Take this Rule. Will you live according to it in this cell until your
death?' She is to say: 'I wish it'. Then she reads her vow. If she is unable to do so,
the deacon or another woman shall do it for her. After the vow the priest says:
'Confirm this, O Lord, etc.' with the five requisite collects. At the end of the Mass
he gives her the Body of Christ. After the Mass he turns to her and pronounces
three collects. Thereupon he places the crucifix on her lap and says: 'Take this
image of the Crucified, whose suffering and death you shall always keep in your
heart'. Then the priest begins with the 'Thou wilt sprinkle' [*Asperges*], leading
her, together with another priest and with the same crucifix, through the cemetery.
Both priests shall wear the alb[118] and sing the responsory 'The kingdom of the
world' [*Regnum Mundi*] and the responsory 'The sinful woman throws herself at
Christ's feet' [*Accessit ad pedes Christi peccatrix*]. Then he leads her to her cell,
along with the crucifix that she shall keep with her in memory of the Passion.
Then the priest says [Psalm 121:8]: 'The Lord will keep your going out and your
coming in from this time forth for evermore'. The choir answers: 'From this time
forth for evermore'. She then falls to the ground in front of her cell, during which
is sung the Psalm 'Out of the depths' [130] with the requiem 'Kyrie eleison,
Christe eleison, kyrie eleison', 'Our Father', 'And lead us not into temptation
[…]',[119] 'The Lord be with you'. And we pray: 'God, in whose mercy reside the
souls of the faithful, forgive the sins of this your handmaiden who rests here in
Christ, so that she is free from all trespasses and has eternal joy with You in
Heaven through Christ, our Lord. Amen. The blessing of God, the almighty Father
and the Son and the Holy Spirit descend upon you and remain with you forever.
Amen'. This is spoken by the priest, who makes the sign of the cross over her
three times. Then he blesses her with five prayers of benediction and five signs of
the cross. Then he blesses her cell with five long prayers. Thereupon the following Psalms are read before the cell: 'Quemadmodum', 'Domine exaudi', 'Laudate
Dominum de coelis', 'Benedictus dominus deus Israel', 'Our Father', 'And lead us
not into temptation', 'In memoria aeterna erat justa', 'Credo videre bona domini',
the requiem, and collects. The anchoress and the whole cell are blessed with holy
water and incense. He leads her inside, closes the doors, and says: 'May she rest
in peace. Amen'.[120] This nun did not promise to live according to the anchoritic
rule, but rather to the Rule of St Augustine, as she had been following the latter
already several years.[121]

---

[118] A liturgical undergarment.
[119] And further: 'A porta inferiore, Domine animam eius.'
[120] Almost all of the prayers are taken from the burial rite.
[121] This, of course, contradicts the introduction.

3 Anchorites in the Italian tradition*

M. Sensi

There is no proper history of the Italian eremitic movement. While there exists an appreciable literature about the 'regular hermits' – those who belonged to an exempt monastic order or to a specific congregation – we know virtually nothing about other religious hermits: those who were professed but who promised obedience to a bishop. In Italy we have only recently begun to study these 'secular' hermits, that is, those without links to any officially recognized religious institutions but who, whether laymen or laywomen, professed simple vows in private. And yet this was a form of religious life that was widespread throughout Europe during the early Middle Ages, as this current volume attests, and that reached its peak with Vatican II, with the acknowledgement of so-called 'consecrated laywomen'.

These secular hermits can be divided into *cenobiti*, who live together; *anacoreti*, who live alone but are tied to a hermitage; *girovaghi*, who refuse the vow of 'stability' and who move freely from one hermitage to another; *rurali* or *dei boschi*, who live in the open countryside, in caves or in hovels, often close to a wood; *urbani*, living in their own houses or in ruined buildings – for the most part keepers, with sacral duties, of the walls, towers, bridges, wells, town-boundaries – and also the hermits, male and female, who look after an oratory, usually a shrine, that is, a *lieu de mémoire*, a place of individual or collective pilgrimage.[1]

---

* I would like to thank Roberta Magnani, for her extremely generous help, and Stephen Penn for advice with Latin.

Translator's note: Given the historical and regional slipperiness of the term 'anchorite', I have used it as a translation only for Sensi's *anacoreti/e*. A number of other terms refer to experiences that might be broadly defined as 'anchoritic', but I have translated these as closely as possible to their Italian equivalents (e.g. recluses, hermits). I have retained some Italian terms for the various kinds of secular hermits (e.g. *incarcerate*, *bizzoche*) because they refer to strictly local phenomena.

[1] On the ambiguity of the terms *eremita/romito*, see B. Nobile, '"Romiti" e vita religiosa nella cronachistica Italiana fra '400 e '500', *Cristianesimo nella storia* 5 (1984), pp. 303–40 (p. 306). On lay hermits in the early Middle Ages, see Ilarius Parisiensis, *Liber tertii ordinis S. Francisci Assisiensis cum appendicibus de chordigeris etc.* (Geneva, Paris, Brussels, 1888), pp. 84–91; G. Penco, 'L'eremitismo irregolare in Italia nei secoli XI–XII', *Benedictina* 32 (1985), pp. 201–21; F. Ferrero, 'Eremitismo individuale', in *Dizionario degli Istituti di Perfezione* III (Rome, 1976), col. 246.

From the Middle Ages to today, diocesan synods in central Italy openly hint at the Church's persistent attempts to take precautions against the secular hermits, requiring them to promise obedience to the diocesan Ordinary, to make vows of poverty and chastity and to follow one of the approved rules.[2] But despite the various efforts to regulate this movement, some canonists maintained that hermits were not obliged to profess religious vows according to a particular rule. Typical here is the *Consilium* given by the canonist Egidio Ghiselini who, in the mid fifteenth century, in answer to the question of whether sanctity could be better achieved by living as a Franciscan tertiary or as a hermit, and which of these two forms of living was the more perfect, replied that what mattered was not subscribing to either the one or the other form of living but rather how one lived one's life.[3] Meanwhile, the life of prayer, austerity and harsh penances – from prolonged mortification of the flesh to ascetic food practices, even to going barefoot in all seasons[4] – so profoundly affected the ordinary people that they came to view these hermits as modern *martyres Christi*, which, *inter alia*, gave rise to a proliferation of local cults, supported by the civic religion, despite the resistance of certain bishops.[5]

The literature

Beginning with a conference held at La Mendola in 1962,[6] scholars in Italy have for some time been studying the male eremitical life, due to the fact that the difficult early stages of the 'Observants' were consistently regarded as having been a more or less prolonged *fuga mundi* [escape from the world].[7] Attention to the female eremitical movement, however, which is recorded throughout the Italian peninsula from late antiquity to the present day, is relatively recent. During the Middle Ages this movement was particularly strong in central Italy, especially in the Duchy of Spoleto, where female hermits went by the names of *incarcerate, recluse, cellane, bizzoche, pinzochere, sorores minores, devote, cristiane*. Like the beguines north of the Alps, these were witnesses to an intense religious

---

[2] See P. Cenci, 'Costituzioni sinodali della diocesi di Gubbio dei secoli XIV–XV', *Archivio per la storia eccl. dell'Umbria* I (1913), pp. 286–379, especially pp. 340ff. and p. 364; M. Sensi, 'Sinodi e visite pastorali in Umbria nel '200, '300, e '400', in *Vescovi e diocesi in Italia dal XIV alla metà del XVI secolo* (Rome, 1990), pp. 337–72 (pp. 367ff).

[3] J. Leclercq, 'Jérôme de Matelica et Aegidius Ghiselini', *Rivista di Storia della Chiesa in Italia* 20 (1966), pp. 9–17, esp. pp. 14–17.

[4] See R. Gregoire, 'L'adage ascetique "nudus nudum Christum sequi"', in *Studi storici in onore di Ottorino Bertolini* I (Pisa, 1972), pp. 395–409.

[5] A. Vauchez, *La sainteté en Occident aux derniers siècles du Moyen Age d'apres les procès de canonisation et les documents hagiographiques* (Rome, 1981), pp. 85 and 117.

[6] Proceedings published as *L'eremitismo in Occidente nei secoli XI e XII* (Milan, 1965). See also *Santità ed eremitismo nella Toscana Medievale*, ed. A. Gianni (Siena, 2000); A. Vauchez (ed.), *Ermites de France et d'Italie (XI–XV siècle)* (Rome, 2003).

[7] See M. Sensi, *Le osservanze francescane nell'Italia centrale* (Rome, 1985) and L. Pellegrini, 'A proposito di eremiti laici d'ispirazione francescana', in *I frati minori e il terzo ordine. Problemi e discussioni storiografiche* (Todi, 1985), pp. 115–42.

life, having many features in common with the Desert Fathers; nevertheless only a few penitential women had a 'literature of their own' and these women largely originate from the ecclesiastical province of Tuscia, and from Umbria.[8]

We have, for example, biographies of Margaret of Cortona (d. 1297) and Angela of Foligno (d. 1309), written with the collaboration of their respective confessors for the edification of the faithful. They were not therefore historical accounts in the modern sense of the word and even less a collection of testimonials to be produced, in the event of each woman's death, in support of their canonization. Clare of Assisi's biography was written immediately after her canonization, by order of Alexander IV, by a Franciscan, possibly Thomas of Celano, while the Vicar General of Spoleto did compose the life of Clare of Montefalco (d. 1308) in preparation for diocesan canonization proceedings. But although the canonization of Clare of Assisi (d. 11 August 1253), called for by Pope Innocent IV (in the bull *Gloriosus Deus*, 18 October 1253), did not encounter any obstacles, that of Clare of Montefalco was hindered by her links with the mendicant world and its protectors, who included the Colonna cardinals and Hubert of Casale. For a great many other holy women things did not go beyond the compilation of their *vitae*: for example, Margaret of Città di Castello, 'the blind woman of Metola' (d. 1320), whose *Legenda* was written in a Dominican milieu by an anonymous friar at the end of the fourteenth century.[9]

These were exceptional women, but for a long time they were understood as singular phenomena by modern scholarship, without any reconstruction of the dense network of connections evidenced in the sources.[10] Venerated as saints or as blessed, they were only the conspicuous manifestations of a vast penitential movement with deep social roots. This constitutes a long-lasting phenomenon, one that has left profound traces in the socio-religious fabric, with important political and economic consequences: political, in so far as various authorities sought to exploit such women for their own ends (as was the case with the canonization of Margaret

---

[8] See Alcantara Mens, OFM Cap., *L'Ombrie italienne et l'Ombrie brabançonne: Deux courants religieux parallèles d'inspiration comune* (Paris, 1967); Anna Benvenuti Papi, *'In castro poenitentiae': Santità e società femminile nell'Italia medievale* (Rome, 1990); Giovanna Casagrande, 'Note su manifestazione di vita comunitaria femminile nel movimento penitenziale in Umbria nei secc. XIII, XIV, XV', in *Prime manifestazioni di vita comunitaria maschile e femminile nel movimento francescano della penitenza (1215–1447)*, ed. R. Pazzelli and L. Temperini (Rome, 1984), pp. 459–79 (p. 463); 'Il fenomeno della reclusione volontaria nel basso medioevo', *Benedictina* 35 (1988), pp. 475–507; and *Religiosità penitenziale e città al tempo dei Comuni* (Rome, 1995); M. Sensi, *Storie di bizzoche tra Umbria e Marche* (Rome, 1995).

[9] See, for example, G. Garampi, *Memorie ecclesiastiche appartenenti all'istoria e al culto della B. Chiara di Rimini* (Rome, 1755); L. Oliger, 'B. Margherita Colonna. Le due vite scritte dal fratello Giovanni Colonna senatore di Roma e da Stefania monaca di S. Silvestro in Capite, testi inediti del secolo XIII', *Lateranum* n. S. 1, 2 (Rome, 1935); *Vita S. Clarae de cruce ordinis eremitarum s. Augustini ex codice Montefalconensi saeculi XIV desumpta*, ed. A. Semenza (Vatican City, 1944); L. Thier and A. Calufetti, *Il libro della beata Angela da Foligno* (Grottaferrata, 1985); M. C. Lungarotti, *Le 'legendae' di Margherita da Città di Castello* (Spoleto, 1994); Iunctae Bevegnatis, *Legenda de vita et miraculis beatae Margaritae de Cortona*, ed. F. Iozzelli (Grottaferrata, 1997).

[10] This is one limitation of the otherwise groundbreaking hagiographies of Lodovico Iacobilli: *Vite de' santi e beati dell'Umbria e di quelli i corpi de' quali riposano in essa provincia*, I–III (Foligno, 1647; 1656; 1661); see also his *Vite de' santi e beati di Foligno et di quelli, i corpi de' quali si riposano in essa città e sua diocese* (Foligno, 1628).

of Cortona);[11] economic, because of the huge numbers who visited their retreats and then their burial places, which became shrines, places of continuous pilgrimage, such as the basilicas *ad corpus* of Clare of Assisi, Clare of Montefalco and Rita of Cascia (d. 1456), to mention only a number of Umbrian shrines that are still visited today by thousands of believers. Crucial in advancing the cult of many of these women – mostly mystics, bound to their city and its concerns[12] – was the civic religion.[13]

To understand the growth of the phenomenon we need only say that the new cult of the 'recluses of St Damian', later known as Clarissans, spread out widely from the Duchy of Spoleto in the thirteenth century. Meanwhile, *incarcerate*, even if *ad tempus* [for a time], like Margaret of Cortona, Clare of Montefalco and Angela of Foligno, inspired spiritual groups that have left their mark on the history of spirituality and mysticism.[14]

However, the women mentioned above are only the tip of the iceberg of a vast penitential movement that between the thirteenth and fifteenth centuries almost certainly involved several thousands of women who, after their initial eremitical experience, were eventually institutionalized under one of the approved rules, founding a regular convent where frequently the eremitical spirit lived on. During the first two of these centuries, in the diocese of Spoleto, for example, there were eighty-five new foundations for women who had gone through the penitential stage. In Perugia there were more than fifty, in Foligno some twenty, as many again in Città di Castello, and some ten in Assisi. Unfortunately, there are no censuses for the convents of the dioceses of Amelia-Terni-Narni, Città della Pieve and Nocera Umbra-Gualdo Tadino.[15] Meanwhile, the number of religious women with voting rights in the chapter meetings of several city monasteries, such as Perugia or Foligno, sometimes exceeded fifty – a veritable army of women. Although not famed for their sanctity or their miracles or for having reached mystical heights, they were nevertheless closely bound to the city and its surroundings, leaving deep-written and material traces. However, my primary focus here is on the female urban anchorites, as well as on the many *bizzocaggi* that sprang up in the city or its sacred perimeter around a charismatic person and under the aegis of the eremitic life. These were women who, via a more or less lengthy route, achieved

[11] F. Cardini, 'Geografia e politica: Margherita da Cortona e le vicende di una città inquieta', *Studi francescani* 76 (1979), pp. 127–36.

[12] See J. Dalarun, 'Parole di *simplices*. Da Celestino V alle sante donne d'Italia tra Duecento e Trecento', in *Aspetti della spiritualità ai tempi di Celestino V* (Casamari, 1993), pp. 27–56.

[13] See Mario Sensi, 'Anchoresses and Penitents in Thirteenth- and Fourteenth-Century Umbria', in *Women and Religion in Medieval and Renaissance Italy*, ed. D. Bornstein and R. Rusconi, trans. M. J. Schneider (Chicago and London, 1996), pp. 56–83.

[14] Garampi, *Memorie ecclesiastiche*, pp. 79–150 (I, *Sopra la religione professata dalla B. Clare e dalle sue compagne*; II, *Sopra l'abito religioso*). A number of academic conferences, as well as the publication of critical editions of the early biographies of women such as these, have now enabled us to re-appraise these women. Garampi, *Memorie ecclesiastiche*, pp. 79–150.

[15] See S. Nessi, 'Appendice storico-documentaria', in Enrico Menestò, *Il processo di canonizzazione di Chiara da Montefalco* (Spoleto, 1991), pp. 533–57; Casagrande, *Religiosità penitenziale*, pp. 231f.; Sensi, *Storie di bizzoche*, pp. 23f and pp. 72ff.

regular status as semireligious – something at that time not allowed by Church law
– and who agreed to live under one of the approved rules, usually the Augustinian
or Benedictine Rule. They did this, however, without binding themselves to the
corresponding male order, and were only subject to the occasional visit of the
diocesan Ordinary or his deputy. Compared to the eremitic movement of the
eleventh century (outlined below) which was, in essence, rural and monastic, this
type of eremitic life was urban in character and, institutionally, it was positioned
midway between the lay and the religious states. This was a movement not of
monastic hermits but of semireligious laypersons who, in order not to have a specific rule, freely adopted the ancient penitential discipline that the Church
imposed on publicly reconciled sinners. In turn, it differs from the contemporary
eremitic movement associated with the mendicant orders, whose institutionalization originated with Francis of Assisi who composed the *Regula pro romitoriis*
[Rule for hermits] for his brethren, conferring on the eremitical life its character
of organized brotherhood where each member is called upon to perform specific
tasks. According to Francis, one person at least must dedicate himself – like Mary
– to the contemplative life, the rest – like Martha – to the active life:

> Let those who wish to live devoutly in the *romitori* [hermitages] be three, or at
> most four. Let two of these act as mothers and let them have two children, or one
> at least. Let the two who act as mothers follow the life of Martha, the other two
> that of Mary. Let those who follow Mary's life have a cloister and in this let each
> have their own cell, in which they pray and sleep [...] and in the cloister where
> they live, do not let them allow anyone to enter or eat there.[16]

Origins of the female penitential movement

Information about female eremiticism in central Italy in the eleventh and twelfth
centuries is scarce, but it was definitely practised. St Peter Damian reports that in
the area around Fabriano, at the beginning of the eleventh century, there were
female hermits without a rule, living communally, who after being petitioned by
St Romualdo granted him their convent up in the mountains.[17] And at the end of
the century (*c*.1092), the female hermit Chelidonia, from Abruzzo, after making a
pilgrimage to Rome, withdrew to a cave in the Simbruini mountains, a few miles
from Subiaco, to live a penitential life.[18] Analogous instances can be found in

---

[16] Francesco d'Assisi, *Del comportamento dei frati negli eremi*, in *Fonti francescane* 136, p. 135.
Additionally, there were hermits brought into the order of the Hermits of St Augustine as a result of the
Magna Unio (1256), for whom Kaspar Elm blazed a trail in his essay, 'Comunità Eremitiche Italiane del
XII e XIII Secol', for which see K. Elm, 'Italienische Eremitengemeinschaften des 12. und 13.
Jahrhunderts. Studien zur Vorgeschichete des Augustiner-Eremitenordens', in *L'eremitismo in Occidente*,
pp. 491–559; see also B. van Luijk, *Gli eremiti neri del Dugento, con particolare riguardo al territorio
pisano e toscano. Origine, sviluppo ed unione* (Pisa, 1968); Vauchez, *Ermites de France et d'Italie*, op.
cit.

[17] Peter Damian, *Vita Beati Romualdi*, 35, ed. G. Tabacco, Fonti per la storia d'Italia 94 (Rome, 1957),
p. 74.

[18] S. Boesch Gajano, 'Terreurs et torments. Formes d'érémitisme en Italie centrale entre le XII.e et le
XIII.e siècle', *Medievales. Langue textes histoire* 28 (1995), pp. 11–23.

Tuscany with Bridget of Fiesole (eleventh century),[19] in the Marche with St Franca (eleventh century), [20] and in Sicily with St Rosalia, a hermit in a grotto (dedicated to St Michael?) on Mount Pellegrino, above Palermo, of which city she became the patron saint (twelfth century).[21]

In contrast to male rural eremitism, which was tolerated, the irregular female movement was vilified in Canon 26 of Lateran II (1139), which referred to 'the damnable and detestable custom of certain women who, while not even living according to the rules of Blessed Benedict, Basil or Augustine, nevertheless desire to pass as nuns in the eyes of the people'.[22]

As stated above, however, the focus of this essay is not on the eremitism arising from monasticism, but on the urban female eremitical movement that began to spread throughout central Italy from the beginning of the thirteenth century. This phenomenon must be seen in the context of that much larger religious movement that by the end of that century had penetrated most of Europe: north of the Alps it was called the Beguine movement, from the name 'beguines' given to the semireligious women of Renania, Alsace and the Low Countries (Flanders and Brabant).[23] In central Italy the movement had various names: *bizzoche, pinzochere* (in Tuscia), *incarcerate, encarcerate* (in the Duchy of Spoleto), *pauperes dominae* (those of St Damian of Assisi),[24] *sorores Minores* in the region of Verona, etc.[25] These were all general terms for devout women, that is, women who wished to live devoutly and chastely, who had in common a life of penance but with vocations that ranged from reclusion to charitable service; they were the 'irregular' hermits of the city, all touched by the ideal of renunciation and mendicant poverty, committed to the adage 'to follow naked the naked Christ'.[26] For the purposes of this present essay, therefore (and in order not to get mired from time to time in making fine distinctions between these multiple forms of female eremitism), I use the generic expression *movimento bizzocale*, which I borrow from Jacques de Vitry's thirteenth-century usage in his *Sermo ad Virgines*, even though other names prevail in the municipal records, not least for the reason that in the follow-

[19] *AASS*, Feb., vol. 1, pp. 243–47; and Benvenuti Papi, *'In castro poenitentiae'*, pp. 326ff.

[20] B. De Gaiffier, 'Hagiographie du Picenum. Vie de S. Elpidius, Passion de Ste Franca', *Analecta Bollandiana* 75 (1957), pp. 288–9; pp. 294–8; also Penco, 'L'eremitismo irregolare', p. 217.

[21] *AASS*, Sept., vol. 2, pp. 273–414, and Benvenuti Papi, *'In castro poenitentiae'*, pp. 324ff.

[22] G. Alberigo, G. L. Dossetti, P. P. Jannou, C. Leonardi and P. Prodi, *Conciliorum oecumeniorum decreta* (Bologna, 1991), p. 203. See further J. B. Valvekens, 'Canonichesse', in *Dizionario degli Istituti di Perfezione* II (Rome, 1975), cols. 24–7, and M. Parisse, 'Canonichesse secolari', ibid., cols. 41–5.

[23] Herbert Grundmann's work on this in *Movimenti religiosi nel Medioevo* (Bologna, 1935) was taken up by Mens in *L'Ombrie italienne*, op. cit. On the analogies between Umbria and Brabant, see further Romana Guarnieri, 'Beghinismo d'oltralpe e bizzochismo italiano tra il secolo XIV e il secolo XV', in *La Beata Angelina da Montegiove e il movimento del terz'Ordine regolare francescano femminile*, ed. Raffaele Pazzelli and Mario Sensi (Rome, 1984), pp. 1–13; Romana Guarnieri, 'La "vita" di Chiara da Montefalco e la pietà brabantina del '200. Prime indagini su un'ipotesi di lavoro', in *S. Chiara da Montefalco e il suo tempo*, ed. Claudio Leonardi and Enrico Menestò (Perugia, 1985), pp. 303–67.

[24] Sensi, *Storie di bizzoche*, pp. xiiif.

[25] G. M. Varanini, 'Per la storia dei Minori a Verona nel Duecento', in *Minoritismo e centri veneti nel Duecento*, ed. G. Cracco (Turin, 1983), pp. 106–9.

[26] See F. Dal Pino, 'Scelte di povertà all'origine dei nuovi ordini religiosi dei secoli XII–XIV', in *La conversione alla povertà nell'Italia dei secoli XII–XIV* (Spoleto, 1991), pp. 53–125 (pp. 91f).

ing two centuries the term *bizzoco* or *bizzoca* refers to those semireligious who were bound to the penitential movement.[27]

The resultant institutions of this heterogeneous world of semireligious women were very varied. In Tuscia, home of the Papal Legate Ugolino Conti di Segni, who became Pope Gregory IX in 1227, the majority of penitential women from the beginning of the thirteenth century were gathered in the Order of St Damian, founded by Cardinal Ugolino,[28] despite his preference for Cistercian monasteries and mixed Hospitaller fraternities.[29] Diverse models of female sanctity thus flourished everywhere, comparable to the beguines, who were called Mothers of the Church by Jacques de Vitry.[30] The aim of this movement, which initially involved the patriciate and the lesser nobility – the ruling classes who were most receptive to the ideals of charity, renunciation and mendicant poverty – and only later the petty bourgeoisie and the common people, was an 'urban' eremitism, based on the Gospel and *imitatio Christi*. Its origins are obscure, so much so that not even its contemporaries could provide satisfactory answers. The canonist John the Spaniard, who studied at Bologna during the mid thirteenth century, declared that he did not know the origins of the movement, acknowledging its spontaneous generation: for him they were '*pinzochere* who only recently arose from the dust' ['biçocare, que de polvere nuperrime surrexerunt'].[31] What Ugolino di Pietro Girardone stated in 1253, during the canonization proceedings of St Clare, is not therefore wholly true: namely, that just as St Francis established the Franciscan Order, so Clare established an order for female anchorites: 'thus this holy virgin Clare [...] was the first in the Order of enclosed women'.[32] Clare did not found the movement of the *incarcerate*, but she did fall under its spell at the *bizzocaggio* of St Angelo di Panzo, a sanctuary modelled on that of St Michael, halfway up Monte Subasio, where she was joined by her sister. There they spent several months together before moving to San Damiano.[33]

This movement was highly innovative compared to both early female monasticism (which had been strongly rooted in the land and in the feudal nobility) and the eremitic movement (which was bound to monasticism). Its innovations were two-fold: on the one hand, its 'urban' character and, on the other, its practice of vicarious atonement, initially confined to an elite but eventually becoming universal. The penitential life adopted by so many young women was emphatically not

---

[27] See Grundmann, *Movimenti religiosi*, p. 374 n. 48; see further p. 317 n. 26.

[28] See M. P. Alberzoni, *Chiara e il papato* (Milan, 1995) and Sensi, *Storie di bizzoche*, pp. 5–9.

[29] For examples, see Sensi, *Storie di bizzoche*, pp. 174–7.

[30] *Vita Mariae Oigniacensis*, in *AASS*, June, vol. 4, pp. 636f.

[31] St John of God, *Liber Poenitentialis* I, ch. 14; see also Iohannes de Deo, Marciana Lat. Cl. III. 34 (2770), 5bc, mentioned in Du Cange (579 s, v, *Pyrocarae*) and Gillis Gerard Meersseman, *Ordo Fraternitatis: Confraternite e pietà dei laici nel medioevo* (Rome, 1977), pp. 390–4 (p. 376 n. 1).

[32] Canonization proceedings of St Clare, *Fonti francescane*, 3117, p. 2375.

[33] Ibid., teste XII, no. 3089, p. 2366; see further *Leggenda di santa Chiara*, in *Fonti francescane*, 3205–6, p. 2416; ibid., nos. 3173–74, p. 2401. On the sanctuary of St Michael in Panzo, see M. Sensi, 'La scelta topotetica delle penitenti fra Due e Trecento nell'Italia centrale', *Collectanea franciscana* 68, 1–2 (1998), pp. 245–75.

about punishing one's own sins, but rather about praising God and atoning for the sins of others – a heroic stance that took Christ as its model and the unity of all Christians as its theological foundation. This was the doctrine of the *corpus mysticum* [mystic body] mentioned by St Paul (1 Cor. 12:12–30). Meanwhile, the strong link between female hermits and the municipality, which recognized their role of suffering for the sins of others, was confirmed by the support they received from the *communitas* which freely granted them their anchorholds; which placed them – though not in a legal sense – within bodies that benefited from public charity; which recommended them to the charity of testators; and finally which intervened against anyone who tried to disturb their peace.[34] Lacking the revolutionary zeal that had characterized the twelfth-century pauperistic movements, these female urban hermits did not wish for anything other than a life of extreme poverty in the service of Christ the Spouse and of poorer brethren; hence the goodwill of the municipal authorities.

Daily Life

Firstly, it must be noted that these penitential women – the vast majority were female urban hermits – were still able to 'live the desert life' among people, by withdrawing into a cell to live alone or in company.[35] One day Christ said to Margaret of Cortona:

> 'You asked me if you could live in the same state of solitude as the Magdalene. Well, I do not command you to live in a desert – deserts are not right for our times – but you may be solitary in your own city, just as though you were living in a boundless desert.'[36]

The same idea is found in the *legenda* of Blessed Umiliana of Cerchi, where urban anchoritism and a monastic life of strict observance are seen as equivalent:

> What did this woman, who lived in continual silence and vigilance over herself, lack of the monastic life? What did she who, in the middle of such a large city, sought and found solitude and a desert, and changed her bedroom into a prison, have less than the holy hermits? What did she have less than the holy sisters of enclosed convents, she whose life was of the harshest, who ate and drank soberly, who refreshed by only a little sleep spent all the night in prayer, and how much grace then can those men and women who see it say she would have received from God, according to what they could understand?[37]

---

[34] G. Antonelli, *Statuti di Spoleto del 1296* (Florence, 1962), p. 63. For further examples, see Sensi, *Storie di bizzoche*, pp. 3–29; pp. 237–56.

[35] See R. Guarnieri, *Donne e chiesa tra mistica e istituzione (secoli XIII–XV)* (Rome, 2004); and D. Stocchetti, 'La fondazione del monastero fiorentino delle murate e la pellegrina Eugenia', *Archivio Italiano per la storia della pietà* 18 (2006), pp. 177–247 (pp. 185ff).

[36] Giunta Bevignati, *Leggenda della vita e dei miracoli di S. Margherita da Cortona* (Vicenza, 1978), p. 39.

[37] *Scrittori di religione del Trecento volgarizzamenti*, III, ed. G. De Luca (Turin, 1977), p. 374.

These places of withdrawal, in common parlance identified as prisons, from which come the epithets *incarcerate, cellane, recluse* and, at Florence, *murate*,[38] but which are defined in the synodal constitutions as *domus* [house] or *cella* [cell], enabled the pursuit of perfection by means of a life of strict penance. They were modest dwellings, *cellae ad penitentiam peragendam* [cells for the pursuit of penance], which made possible the *fuga mundi* (either permanent or *ad tempus*) that typified enclosure, and a life of prayer, fasting and abstinence.[39]

In so far as they were *sub devozione viventes* – that is, having made vows, albeit simple ones – these women wore veils and wool robes that came down to their ankles, secured at the waist with a leather belt, while the penitents who were inspired by Francis of Assisi, even though they were not tertiaries, wore simple robes of cotton or linen (made of a type of fabric known as *gattinello*, which would have been grey), tied round the waist with a cord. The belt and the cord traditionally symbolized chastity, with reference to the Gospels (Luke 12:35) and St Paul (Col. 3:5). According to Simon Fidati, 'The wool shirt is worn for harshness of the body and for unworthiness and to accompany Christ in the harshness he suffered, for virtue, to aid chastity; and also for the memory of the aprons of skin, that is, of the skin given to our first ancestors as punishment for original sin.'[40] Clare of Montefalco, for example, who, after her experience living as a *bizzoca*, had professed the Rule of Augustine whose followers wore the eremitic belt, is represented in the early iconography with the Franciscan cord around her waist, indicating the saint's devotion to Francis of Assisi.[41] We must also not forget that at Rome St Francis met the recluse Prassede, who:

> ... was enclosed in a narrow cell and stayed there nearly forty years; she enjoyed the particular friendship of St Francis. Indeed, the saint received her into his obedience, something that he had not done for any other woman, devoutly granting her the religious habit, namely the cowl and the belt.[42]

Yet, a new order was not spawned by this incident. Rather it was an isolated case, to be understood in the context of the apostolate of the first Franciscans, who with 'the urban hermits shared only a preference for marginality'.[43] For their

[38] D. Stocchetti, 'La fondazione del monastero', pp. 177ff.

[39] See Cenci, 'Costituzioni sinodali', pp. 340f.

[40] Simonis Fidati de Cassia, *L'ordine della vita cristiana, Tractatus de vita Christiana, Epistulae, Laude, Opuscula*; and Johannis de Salerno, *Tractatus de vita et moribus fratris Simonis de Cassia*, ed. W. Eckermann (Rome, 2006), p. 462; S. Basilio Magno, *Parvum Asceticon*, XI, 14–15, in G. Turbessi, *Regole monastiche antiche* (Rome, 1990), p. 175.

[41] Garampi, *Memorie ecclesiastiche*, pp. 145f.; S. Nessi, 'S. Chiara da Montefalco e il francescanesimo', *Miscellanea francescana* 69 (1969), pp. 377–408 (pp. 394f. and Table III); Berengario Donadieu, *Vita Sanctae Clare de Cruce*, ed. A. Semenza (Rome, 1944); *Vita di Chiara da Montefalco*, trans. and ed. R. Sala, notes by S. Nessi (Rome, 1991), pp. 25f.

[42] Tommaso da Celano, *Trattato dei miracoli*, in *Fonti francescane*, 1002, p. 818; Bonaventura da Bagnoregio, *Leggenda maggiore*, in *Fonti francescane* 1020–1255, p. 1004; and S. Di Mattia Spirito, 'Le terziarie dell'osservanza a Viterbo', in *La beata Angelina da Montegiove e il movimento del terz'ordine regolare francescano femminile* (Rome, 1985), pp. 421–35 (pp. 424–46).

[43] L. Pellegrini, 'A proposito di eremiti laici d'ispirazione francescana', in *I Frati Minori e il Terzo Ordine: problemi e discussioni storiografiche*, Convegni del Centro di Studi sulla Spiritualità Medievale XXIII, 17–20 October 1982 (Todi 1985), pp. 115–42 (p. 128).

part, several *recluse* and *pinzochere*, still existing in a simple state of penance without plunging into full Franciscanism, chose to act like paupers, dressing themselves in drab or grey clothes, wearing the cord and even adopting the white wimple that was typical of the Clarissans.[44]

If they went out to attend religious functions or to beg for alms, these women put on drab white clothing (grey if they were Franciscans),[45] and covered their heads with a veil that hid their faces.[46] When St Clare, on the orders of her sister, the principal of the *bizzocaggio*, went with a female companion 'ad mendicandum panem' [begging for bread] through the streets of Montefalco, 'she performed the said activity with great devotion, covering the lower part of her body with a veil, with a cloak over her head, and she wrapped herself in the cloak'.[47] Indoors they usually went barefoot, while in the street they wore clogs, which, from the last quarter of the fourteenth century, were the hallmark of the Observants (hence their name, *zoccolanti*). In comparison, the penitential dress for men was more varied. Some wore a cowl of white hemp sackcloth tied at the waist, without buttons or collar, leaving arms and legs uncovered from the knee down, without any other garments, and in all seasons they went barefoot and bare-headed; others wore a goatskin called a *melota*; others a linen tunic [*colobium*] or a cloak fastened with a cord or with a leather belt, and a hood or a beret on their heads.[48]

About the liturgy of reclusion in the Italian peninsula we know virtually nothing. The clothing ceremony – if he or she were a semireligious – took place not before the bishop but in the presence of an abbot or the local parish priest, according to whether the hermit was a regular or a secular, a practice that lasted right up to Vatican II. From the *vita* of Verdiana of Castelfiorentino, for example, we learn that, on returning from a pilgrimage to Rome, she asked if she could be re-enclosed in the cell that her community had made for her. When the day of her clothing ceremony was fixed, the people were called together and the parish priest, after having received her vow of obedience, 'habitum et velum benedicens, ipsam induit et velavit, suoque canonico, ut eam intromictat, impomit' [blessing the habit and the veil, he dressed and veiled her, and put his canon in charge of her in order that he might lead her in], after which she was accompanied by a procession to her cell and was then walled in.[49]

[44] See Garampi, *Memorie ecclesiastiche*, pp. 145–48 and pp. 224–33.

[45] See Garampi, *Memorie ecclesiastiche*, pp. 148f.

[46] A. Gianni, 'Iconografia delle sante cellane: Verdiana, Giovanna, Umiltà', in *Santità ed eremitismo*, ed. Gianni, pp. 67–90.

[47] Menestò, *Il processo di canonizzazione*, p. 116. See also Jacques de Vitry, *Vita Mariae Oigniacensis*, in *AASS*, Junii, vol. 4, p. 648 n. 45.

[48] By comparison with the women, the men's clothing was very varied: see E. Catoni, 'Dai Padri del deserto ad Agostino: iconografia degli affreschi del chiostro di Lecceto', in *Santità ed eremitismo*, ed. Gianni, pp. 109–30; L. Meiffret, *Saint Antoine ermite en Italie (1340–1540)* (Rome, 2004); D. Russo, *Saint Jérôme en Italie. Étude d'iconographie et de spiritualità, XIII.e–XVI.e siècles* (Paris–Rome, 1987), Plate 2.

[49] *AASS*, Febr., vol. 1, p. 260; A. Benvenuti, 'Velut in sepulchro: cellane e recluse nella tradizione agiografica italiana', in *Culto dei santi, istituzione e classi sociali in età preindustriale*, ed. S. Boesch Gajano and L. Sebastiani (Rome–L'Aquila, 1984), pp. 367–455 (pp. 402–03); see further Benvenuti Papi, '*In castro poenitentiae*', pp. 362–63.

Information about the preferred locales of these penitents and how they controlled and used their environments enables us to understand better the material conditions in which they led their daily life, something crucial for a deeper understanding of their religious and social functions. Their usual dwelling – customarily a place where everything implied the pauperistic injunction 'to follow naked the naked Christ' – might be the penitent's own house, or that of a relative (frequently the case for female anchorites who lived inside the city walls; in this case, they had full authority over their dwelling).[50] One case is that of Giovanna, the widow of the canonist Munaldo of Bettona, a recluse in her own 'prison' situated *'in arcibus'* [within the fortified walls] of Assisi, and who in 1311 made her will, leaving the *reclusorio* to her servant, Cicia of Francescone of Assisi; having become a Franciscan tertiary, Cicia also made her will in 1342 in those same 'fortifications'.[51] Others lived in hermitages with links to a monastery or a convent, or to lay *juspatronato* [right of patronage], or a *dominus* [overlord] or of the *communitas* [community], with contingent rights of *juspatronato*.[52] The anchorholds of Perugia were spread over a very wide area, 'in vinea, in campo, in bonis, in via, extra portam, iusta monasterium' [in vineyards, fields, city-boundaries, streets, outside the gates, by the monastery].[53] Recluses also kept the gates or the towers of a fortified town, like Clare Angolanti of Rimini who, in Urbino where she had gone to look after her sick brother, spent her nights in 'one of the towers, very quiet and appropriate for silence, a most fitting place to pray and to contemplate spiritual things', where 'a lamp burned by night'. Early in the morning, she went begging from door to door; on her return to Rimini, 'inspired by the Holy Spirit', she went to live in a room 'in the old wall of the ancient city, without a roof and open to the air'.[54]

There were also the *religiosae mulieres*, female hermits who lived inside the city walls, who practised poverty and chastity as much as those recluses living inside the sacred perimeter of the town, and if they lived in a community they vowed obedience to the *magistra*, the charismatic leader of the group; and hence their name *devote*, derived from *vovere*, because of the simple vows they professed. Usually, they were self-sufficient or worked with their own hands; some even went begging. In many cases their local community came to their aid: in some municipal statutes these urban hermits figured in the inventory of institutions which periodically became the object of public charity, as they were

---

[50] See *Speculum inclusorum Auctore Anonymo Anglico Saeculi XIV*, ed. L. Oliger, Lateranum, n.s. 4, no. 1 (1938), pp. 63–86 (p. 8); Garampi, *Memorie ecclesiastiche*, pp. 114f.

[51] C. Cenci, *Documentazione di vita assisana (1300–1530)* I (Grottaferrata, 1974), p. 57 and p. 91.

[52] See G. Casagrande, *Documenti inediti sui frati della penitenza a Perugia nei secoli XIII e XIV*, Studi Francescani 74 (1977), pp. 204f.; M. Sensi, 'Gli Ordini mendicanti a Spoleto', in *Il Ducato di Spoleto* (Spoleto, 1983), pp. 429–85 (p. 475 n. 134); P. Bargellini, *I ponti di Florence* (Florence, 1963–1964), pp. 39–49; M. Bacci, *'Pro rimedio animae'. Immagini sacre e pratiche devozionali in Italia centrale (secoli XIII e XIV)* (Pisa, 2000), p. 62; U. Nicolini, 'L'eremitismo francescano nei secoli XIII–XVI', in *Il B. Tomasuccio da Foligno terziario francescano ed i movimenti religiosi popolari umbri nel Trecento*, in *Analecta T.O.R.* 131 (1979), pp. 79–96, repr. in U. Nicolini, *Scritti di Storia* (Naples, 1993), pp. 435–49 (p. 447).

[53] Casagrande, 'Il fenomeno della reclusione', p. 487.

[54] Garampi, *Memorie ecclesiastiche*, p. 19 and p. 25.

considered equal to the mendicant orders; and it was probably the same municipal authorities who asked for the charity of the faithful, calling on testators to remember just how many belonged to the movement.[55] They usually requested a modest sum, which was promptly deposited by the heirs with a suitable procurator who provided for its distribution.[56] Again, this is confirmed by the hagiographic witnesses. Like Clare of Rimini, Clare of Montefalco, when she was still living in a *reclusorio* under the direction of her sister Giovanna, sometimes went out to beg: 'and when she was given alms, she knelt down humbly and with devotion. And if she was not given alms, she nevertheless remained patient, joyful.'[57] Meanwhile St Rosa of Viterbo (d. 1252), a house-penitent who wore grey garments girded with a thin cord, used to go out from her father's house to pray, waving a crucifix – but also 'to take bread to the poor'. Once, when asked by her father what she was hiding in her bosom, she 'opened wide her arms and her bosom was full of multicoloured roses'.[58]

The female urban anchorites, especially those enclosed in *reclusori* – the so-called 'murate vive' ('living immured') – had servants, which allowed them to maintain contact with the outside world. But according to Battista Piergili, a seventeenth-century hagiographer, these *reclusori*

> were not convents of women who lived under a rule, but small houses in the form of a hermitage, where in those times women desirous to serve God used to retire with one or two female companions away from their family homes. These women lived as enclosed women without a particular rule or dress, under the obedience of the bishop and the direction of their confessor. These houses were called *reclusori*, *carceri* and *romitori*.[59]

Piergili also records that there were four of these *reclusori* in the small town of Montefalco towards the end of the thirteenth century: St Caterina del Bottaccio, near the church of the same name; the *reclusorio* of Benedetto which 'a good lady had … built': the *reclusorio* of St Damian, which he built for his daughter Giovanna and which St Clare entered while still a young girl; and the *reclusorio* of the daughters of Feliciano. All of these were *bizzocaggi* that were eventually given institutional status by the diocesan Ordinary, becoming autonomous con-

---

[55] G. Cenci and G. Pensi, *Statuto di Todi del 1275* (Todi, 1897), p. 74 and p. 78; G. Luzzatto, *Gli Statuti del comune di S. Anatolia del 1324 e un frammento degli statuti del comune di Matelica del secolo XIV (1358?)* (Ancona, 1909), p. 41; A. Messini and F. Baldaccini, *Statuta Communis Fulginei*. I, *Statutum Communis Fulginei* (Perugia, 1969), pp. 11–12, p. 142 and pp. 239–40; R. Sassi, 'Incarcerati e incarcerate a Fabriano nei secoli XIII e XIV', *Studia Picena* 25 (1957), pp. 67–85; G. Fabiani, 'Monaci eremiti incarcerati e reclusi in Ascoli nei secoli XIII e XIV', *Studia Picena* 31 (1964), pp. 139–59; Cenci, *Documentazione di vita assisana (1300–1530)* I.

[56] See G. Casagrande, 'Forme di vita religiosa femminile nell'area di Città di Castello nel secolo XIII', in *Il Movimento religioso femminile in Umbria*, ed. R. Rusconi (Florence–Perugia, 1984), pp. 123–57 (p. 149); Casagrande, 'Il fenomeno della reclusione', p. 498.

[57] Menestò, *Il processo di canonizzazione*, p. 116.

[58] E. M. Piacentini, *Santa Rosa da Viterbo* (Viterbo, 1983), p. 151.

[59] B. Piergili, *Vita della B. Chiara detta della Croce da Montefalco dell'ordine di s. Agostino* (Foligno, 1640), p. 4.

vents, which were in the end grouped together due to a lack of nuns.[60] More numerous still were the *reclusori* in cities like Foligno where, in 1370, 62 *incarcerate* lived, dipping to 33 in 1379 and to 22 in 1392, but rising to 54 in 1394;[61] while at Fabriano 21 *carceri* for women were recorded in 1363, dipping in 1367 to 12, with 15 women living in them, but rising in 1372 to 15, with 34 penitents.[62] No different were cities like Perugia, where in 1277 56 sisters and 12 brothers resided,[63] Spoleto[64] and Ascoli Piceno,[65] to name just a few of the places with *reclusori* either concentrated in one ward or far from the town centre, in the environs of the city walls or gates, or in the sacred perimeter 'infra unum miliare' [for a mile around].[66]

We know hardly any biographical details of these women, let alone their names. The exception is Tuscany where, the words of Anna Benvenuti bring a gallery of women brilliantly to life:

> [D]uring the thirteenth and fourteenth centuries almost all the varieties of female experience were represented [in Tuscany], from the conventional convent-based Benedictine Berta of the Alberti, Abbess of Cavriglia, to Blessed Paola of Camaldo in the fourteenth-century [...] to the *cellane* of long-standing tradition [like] Gerardesca and Maria of Pisa, Verdiana of Castelfiorentino, Margaret of Cortona, Giovanna of Signa, Julia of Certaldo, to the domestic penitents of every observance and mendicant guidance.[67]

In the *bizzocaggi* female urban hermits lived communally, while in the *carceri* recluses lived alone, usually with a servant. But a number of coenobitical hermits aspired to pursue the anchoritic way of life, as we know from Berengario Donadieu, the biographer of St Clare of Montefalco: 'in order to do penance more freely, [the saint] ardently desired, if it were possible to do so virtuously, to live as a hermit and to go and live with a holy woman, called Agnes, whom she said lived as a hermit on Monte Cucco'.[68]

We know very little about the life inside these *bizzocaggi* under coenobitic or romitorial direction, since neither rules nor journals are extant, whereas for the enclosed women tied to a monastic institution we can refer to the Rule of Grimlaïcus, a monk living in Lorena (ninth to tenth centuries), to whom several

---

[60] Ibid., p. 5.

[61] M. Sensi, 'Incarcerate e penitenti a Foligno nella prima metà del Trecento', in *I Penitenti di San Francesco nella società del Due e Trecento*, ed. Mariano d'Alatri (Rome, 1977), pp. 291–308.

[62] Sassi, 'Incarcerati e incarcerate a Fabriano', p. 74 and p. 84.

[63] U. Nicolini, 'Ricerche sulla sede di fra Raniero Fasani fuori di Porta Sole a Perugia', in *Bollettino della Deputazione di Storia patria per l'Umbria* 63 (1966), pp. 199–204, repr. in Nicolini, *Scritti di Storia*, pp. 307–19 (p. 318); Casagrande, 'Note su manifestazioni di vita comunitaria femminile', pp. 460–66.

[64] A. Bartoli Langeli, 'I penitenti a Spoleto nel Duecento', in *L'Ordine della penitenza di s. Francesco d'Assisi nel secolo XIII*, ed. O. Schmucki (Rome, 1973), pp. 303–12.

[65] G. Fabiani, 'Monaci, eremiti, incarcerati e reclusi in Ascoli nei secoli XIII e XIV', *Studia Picena* 31 (1964), pp. 139–59.

[66] See J. Dalarun, *Lapsus linguae: La Légende de Claire de Rimini* (Spoleto, 1994), p. 31 and pp. 264f.; Casagrande, *Religiosità penitenziale*, pp. 34–9.

[67] Benvenuti Papi, 'In castro poenitentiae', p. 110; on female recluses, see esp. pp. 119–40; pp. 263–402.

[68] Donadieu, *Vita di Chiara da Montefalco*, p. 27.

other contributors to this volume allude.[69] And for those living in England, we
have rules, guides and literature from the eleventh to the fourteenth centuries,
from the *De Institutione Inclusarum* of Aelred, abbot of the Cistercian monastery
of Rievaulx, composed between 1147 and 1167 for his sister,[70] to the anonymous
Ancrene Wisse, written for three enclosed sisters in the thirteenth century.[71]

Since it would have been quite alien to the nature of these incarcerated men
and women to leave any records of themselves or their lives, information about
the Italian *bizzocale* movement must therefore be gleaned from the hagiographic literature and from ecclesiastical and civil legislation, especially from municipal archives such as notarial records where, in wills and quittances especially,
it is possible to come across penitential women, though often only as bare
records of anonymous people.[72] Hence, we see the difficulty of reconstructing
this page in the history of piety, a page that signals the incursion of the laity into
mysticism and the contemplative life where formerly monks and clerics had
been preeminent.

At the canonization proceedings of Blessed Simon of Collazzone, in Spoleto
in 1252, one of those testifying to his miracles was a certain Sofia of Bartoloneo
da Trevi, a recluse of twenty years, who for fifteen years was confined by paraly-
sis to her *carcere*, unable to move or even to lift food to her mouth, but lovingly
cared for by her female companion Morica. Sofia told the judge how, after asking
for the intercession of Simon the Servant of God, she immediately got up from her
bed and in full view of her companion began to walk. Once the news of the miracle spread, all the people of Trevi ran out to see the miracle: escaping from the
enclosure that she had observed for so many years, she came out of her *carcere*
walking by herself, freely and easily.[73] From the witnesses who testified to the
miraculous event we learn that Sofia used to present herself at the little window
of her *carcere* to listen to anyone who came to ask for her prayers or advice.[74] But
after the illness that confined her to bed, she had to be carried to the window by
her companion – and then cries of grief were heard from outside. Sofia also took
in guests, sheltering in her *carcere* as many as wished to spend the period of Lent
there: this was the testimony of Illuminata di Pietro da Montefalco, who continued to live there as a female recluse.[75] Sister Umile also had a female companion
called Alofita and they lived together at Perugia in the *carcere* of Risiano outside

[69] *PL* 103, cols. 575–664; see also M. Ch. Charter, 'Regula solitariorum', in *Dizionario degli Istituti di Perfezione* VII (Rome, 1983), cols. 1598–1600.

[70] *De Institutione Inclusarum*, ed. H. Talbot, in *Analecta Ordinis Cistercensis* 7 (1951), pp. 167–217.

[71] On English rules, see P. Rouillard, 'Regole per reclusi', in *Dizionario degli Istituti di Perfezione* VII, cols. 1533–6; see also L. Oliger, 'Regulae tres reclusorum et eremitarum Angliae saec. XIII–XIV', *Antonianum* 3 (1928), pp. 170–83. For an edition of the *Regula reclusorum Dubliniensis*, see pp. 151–89; and for an edition of *Speculum Inclusorum*, pp. 63–141.

[72] Sensi, 'Incarcerate e penitenti a Foligno', pp. 291–308.

[73] M. Faloci Pulignani, 'Il beato Simone da Collazzone e il suo processo nel 1252', in *Miscellanea francescana* 12 (1910), pp. 97–132 (p. 124).

[74] See the *vita* of Agnes of Montepulciano by Raymond of Capua, *AASS*, Aprilis, vol. 2, pp. 791–817; and A. Redigonda, 'Agnes Segni da Montepulciano', in *Dizionario Biografico degli Italiani*, I, pp. 438–39.

[75] Pulignani, 'Il beato Simone', p. 124.

the suburb of Porta Sole. Called upon to make a deposition about the flight of a girl called Vicina from her father's house, in response to the accusation that they had fraudulently concealed her in their *carcere*, they claimed that the girl had stood before their *carcere* and had loudly asked to be allowed to enter, at which Sister Umile, moved by pity, had let her in and kept her for a week.[76] The situation in other cities was not dissimilar. At Foligno Angela had a companion, Masazuola (according to the Trivulzian manuscript), who attended to the domestic chores of Blessed Angela, yet who was bound by the same religious and Franciscan aims, even at times acting as an adviser.[77] Another example is 'domina Altruda pauperum' [lady Altrud of the poor] – mentioned by the senator John Colonna in the *vita* of his sister Margarita – who lived at Rome in the second half of the thirteenth century, with a 'a certain religious woman [*religiosa*], a virgin, who lived with her and served her', leading 'for love of Christ' a life of poverty divided between prayer, visits to churches and charitable works.[78] In Rome the phenomenon of the semireligious was striking: in 1320 there were 260 recluses, while there were about 470 women who lived as nuns.[79]

The ascetic regime that held sway in the *carceri* and in the female *bizzocaggi* was the form of living imposed by canon law on publicly reconciled sinners, voluntarily adopted by penitential women. Essentially, it consisted of fasts and abstinence on certain weekdays, in the observance of the canonical hours and, for those who did not impose strict enclosure upon themselves, in daily attendance at mass and in frequent communion – weekly communion was already a sign of fervour – instead of secular festivals and public entertainments. Moreover, several *religiosae mulieres* added particular penances, such as the wearing of sackcloth for flagellation, which up until the eighth century was one of the means of satisfaction permitted by the penitentials as a substitute for fast days imposed for sin,[80] or else they wore iron rings around their necks. Clare of Rimini wore around her neck 'an iron ring and one on each arm and the same round each of her knees'; her shirt, like that of the *loricati* – the famous saints Dominic and William – was 'a breastplate of heavy, rusty iron almost thirty pounds in weight'.[81] The mortification of the body, performed by even the youngest recluses, was accompanied by frequent fasts and by prolonged prayer, with the recitation of the Credo (usually in the reduced *Credoindeo piccolino*) and the Paternoster, and ejaculations accompanied by genuflections. Clare of Montefalco, once she was settled in the *reclusorio* of her sister Giovanna, at the age of six:

> … felt such joy there that, having lost her appetite, in one week she ate only an apple and a piece of bread […]. Once, at the insistence of a female companion,

[76] Nicolini, *Scritti di Storia*, p. 315.

[77] Thier and Calufetti, *Il libro della Beata Angela*, pp. 132, 240f., 264, 320f., 560, 572, etc.

[78] Oliger, 'B. Margherita Colonna', pp. 152–4.

[79] Oliger, 'Regula reclusorum Angliae', pp. 265–6.

[80] Gillis Gerard Meersseman, 'Disciplinati e penitenti nel Duecento', in *Il Movimento dei disciplinati nel settimo centario dal suo inizio (Perugia 1260)* (Perugia, 1962), p. 50.

[81] Garampi, *Memorie ecclesiastiche*, p. 11.

she ate an egg and did great penance for it [...]. If her tongue for a moment ran away with her and violated the silence, she withdrew to a hidden place and did penance for it; in winter, when the temperature was icy, in contrition she punished her body by putting her feet and part of her leg in a bucket of water and stayed there in the ice until she had recited the Paternoster a hundred times [...] when she reached adolescence she began to chastise her body with the curb of austerity [...] the cord that she disciplined herself with was stained as though covered with blood [...] every night she would make a thousand genuflections according to the usual custom, kissing the ground a thousand times and extending her arms in the form of a cross. She did not abandon the canonical hours like the lewd religious, practising special devotions in honour of the blessed Virgin and of many other saints, above all the virgin saints [...] she did not sleep in a bed but prayed assiduously and wished for neither a mattress nor straw for the minimal sleep that she allowed herself [...] she perched on a pole that was set up in her tiny cell or else at the most she laid down on a board to sleep a little [...] rarely and in tiny quantities she ate meat, fish or other foods agreeable to the body, or condiments. She contented herself with taking a little bread and water once a day, usually after nones and often after vespers; she covered the bread-and-water with earth and ashes and then ate it, deeming it delicious like that [...] if at times she took cooked food, she usually ate it without condiments or salt, or else she mixed it with water or made it bland in some other way.[82]

Some of the women who went to live in the sacred perimeter – usually within a mile of the city centre – devoted themselves to contemplation, others to helping in the hospital, performing works of mercy and assisting the most wretched, the ill and the indigent, especially lepers.[83] Archaeological excavations between Umbria and the Marche have revealed double *bizzocaggi* from the end of the twelfth century that served as hospitals: [84] institutions not bound to any of the approved rules and which were active until the middle of the thirteenth century.[85] The fate of these *bizzocaggi* – until now understood as brotherhoods of the Third

---

[82] Donadieu, *Vita di Chiara da Montefalco*, pp. 21ff.; see also Garampi, *Memorie ecclesiastiche*, p. 15.

[83] See S. Saffiotti Bernardi, 'Il monastero di S. Caterina di Cingoli e le sue pergamene', *Studi Maceratesi* 13 (1979), pp. 68–106, especially p. 90; S. Saffiotti Bernardi, 'Esempi di assistenza a Cingoli nel secolo XIII, gli ospedali di Spineto e Buraco', *Studi Maceratesi* 19 (1986), pp. 257–88, especially pp. 275–6.

[84] This research was initiated by Grundmann in 1935. For Italy, see R. Manselli, *Nos qui cum eo fuimus. Contributo alla questione francescana* (Rome, 1980), pp. 218–21; G. De Sandre Gasparini, 'Lebbrosi e lebbrosari tra misericordia e assistenza nei secoli XII–XIII', in *La conversione alla povertà nell'Italia dei secoli XII–XIV* (Spoleto, 1991), pp. 239–68; G. P. Pacini, 'Comunità di poveri nel Veneto: esperienze "religiose" del laicato vicentino dal secolo XII al XIV', in *La conversione alla povertà*, pp. 325–53; see further F. Accrocca, 'Dall'alternanza all'alternativa. Eremo e città nel primo secolo dell'Ordine Francescano: una rivisitazione attraverso gli scritti di san Francesco e le fonti agiografiche', *Via Spiritus* 9 (2002), pp. 7–60.

[85] From the *Anonimo Perugino*, a text about the exploits of the first companions of Francis, in particular brother Leo (d. 1271), we know that this group of penitents was encouraged and organized by St Francis himself and by his first disciples. See L. Di Fonzo, 'L'Anonimo Perugino tra le fonti francescane del secolo XIII: Rapporti letterari e testo critico', *Miscellanea francescana* 72 (1972), pp. 117–483, nos. 147–8.

Order of penitence[86] – was this: ecclesiastical authorities during the thirteenth century were principally concerned with placing the *bizzoche* in nunneries;[87] meanwhile, monasticization of the men is a phenomenon noted from the fourteenth century onwards. The official interventions of the Bishops of Gubbio and Nocera Umbra were crucial to achieving this.[88]

Female hospitallers, hermits and *bizzoche* had in common the desire to do without material goods and to serve others, praying or helping the sick.[89] The *fuga mundi* removed them from society; they took part in religious ceremonies and, very occasionally, in sacred representations of the Passion.[90] Devoted to the infancy of Christ and the Eucharist, but above all to the suffering Christ, the way of life of these penitential women is known to us from their respective biographies. Some of them, in order to imitate closely the suffering Christ, undertook unusual devotions: Clare of Rimini, early one Good Friday morning, enlisted two local layabouts [*ribaldi*] to go with her into the church of St Colomba, where 'when her hands had been twisted and tied behind her with a tight ligature, as she ordered, the layabouts led her with a cord around her throat and tied her to a stone column, as she desired; she remained tied like that until nones on the following Saturday'; once freed, and dressed in white, she visited the churches of the town and its environs, scourging herself along the route 'with bundles of twigs and lashes'.[91]

Other women, contemplating the various stages of the passion, sweated blood and went into ecstasies. Clare of Montefalco:

> ... while still in her adolescence fixed her gaze of meditation so hard on the cruelty of the passion of Christ that she apprehended the greater part of her sensual experiences in terms of his sufferings. When she sat at the table to eat, in her mind she experienced solid food as the sponge, drink as gall and vinegar, the lamp as the eyes of Christ, and related all the other things necessary for the various rites to the Lord's passion. From this incessant meditation she was so joined through compassion to the passion of Christ that rivers of tears were seen flowing from her eyes.[92]

---

[86] For example, G. Pagnani, 'Comunità laiche francescane nell'Appennino umbro–marchigiano', in *L'Ordine della penitenza*, ed. Schmucki, pp. 247–62; F. Allevi, 'Francescani e penitenti a san Ginesio nei secoli XIII e XIV', in *Prime manifestazioni di vita comunitaria*, ed. Pazzelli and Temperini, pp. 543–602.

[87] See Bernardi, 'Il monastero di S. Caterina di Cingoli', especially pp. 89f.; S. Bernardi, 'Esempi di assistenza a Cingoli nel secolo XIII, gli ospedali di Spineto e Buraco', *Studi Maceratesi* 19 (1986), pp. 257–88; on that of Sts Anthony and Bartholomew at Buraco di Camerino, ibid., pp. 275–76; on S. Claudio di Acquaviva, see G. Pagnani, 'Luoghi francescani delle Marche di origine benedettina', in *Aspetti e problemi del monachesimo nelle Marche* (Fabriano, 1982), pp. 135–79 (p. 167); on S. Tommaso, a hospitaller who refused monasticization, see L. Fausti, 'Degli antichi ospedali di Spoleto', *Atti dell'Accademia Spoletina* (1920–2), pp. 80f., pp. 104–11; and Mariano d'Alatri, 'Accuse di eresia a Spoleto e a Narni negli anni 1259 e 1260', *Collectanea franciscana*, 39 (1969), pp. 419–20.

[88] See M. Sarti, *De episcopis eugubinis* (Pesaro, 1755), pp. 185f.

[89] See D. Bornstein and R. Rusconi (eds.), *Mistiche e devote nell' Italia tardomedievale* (Naples, 1992).

[90] Thier and Calufetti, *Il libro della Beata Angela*, p. 278.

[91] Garampi, *Memorie ecclesiastiche*, pp. 44–6 and pp. 234–40.

[92] Donadieu, *Vita di Chiara da Montefalco*, p. 33. See also S. Nessi, 'I processi per la canonizzazione, di s. Chiara da Montefalco (vicende e documenti)', *Bollettino della Deputazione di Storia patria per l'Umbria* 65 (1968), pp. 103–60.

No different was the mystical experience of Margaret of Cortona:

> [T]he Passion of our King and the compassion of the Virgin Mary had so filled the soul of Margaret that there was nothing bitter or hard that she could not bear sweetly and easily [...] towards the ninth hour that soul devoted to God was transported in ecstasy and, having drunk the gall of the passion, she had a vision of the betrayal, of the assault of the Jews; she heard their cries and their fierce counsels as they prepared for the martyrdom of Christ. She saw Christ greeted with the embrace of the betrayal; led away, bound, between torches and lanterns; denied by Peter and abandoned by the Apostles; his face pale. She contemplated him beaten impiously on the Cross, derided, hooded, spat upon, buffeted, his hair pulled, mockingly worshipped. Then she saw in rapid succession the Cross, the nails, the lance, and the hired false witnesses against Christ.[93]

Angela of Foligno's encounter with the Cross 'on which I saw Christ who died for us' happened as she made the first steps of her pilgrimage to Assisi (1295), an episode that marked her conversion.[94] At the eighth step Angela was moved to walk along the way of the Cross, which allowed her to reach the heights of mystical experience by passing through three transformations:

> [T]he first transformation is when one's soul strives to imitate the works of this 'passioned' Man-God, since in these is and was manifested the will of God [...]. The second is when one's soul is united with God and has great feelings and great sweetnesses in God, which can nevertheless be expressed in words and thoughts [...]. The third transformation comes when one's soul in most perfect union is transformed into God and God into the Soul; and it feels and tastes the highest things of God, such that they cannot be expressed in words or thoughts.[95]

This spiritual journey leads finally to the fullness of communion with, and belief in, God, the Greatest Good. Her confessors played a not negligible part in this spiritual adventure: the best known was a Franciscan, her relative and the future redactor of the *Memoriale*, but whose name we do not know.[96] We do know, however, that brother Giunta of Bevignate, another Minorite confessor, composed the *Legenda de Vita et Miraculis Beatae Margharitae de Cortona*, a record of the saint's spiritual life, 'de mandato fratris Iohannis de Castillione, inquisitoris heretice pravitatis' [at the behest of brother John of Castillion, the inquisitor of heretical wickedness].[97] Both friars submitted their manuscripts – evidence for the judicial inquiry into future canonization proceedings – for the approval of the women whose biographies they were writing; but in the absence of any writings by these spiritual guides , it is difficult to establish their precise involvement in the composition of the *vitae*.

---

[93] Bevignati, *Leggenda della vita e dei miracoli*, p. 74.

[94] Thier and Calufetti, *Il libro della Beata Angela*, p. 136.

[95] Ibid., pp. 412–14.

[96] Indicated in the *Liber* with the initial A, usually interpreted as Brother Arnaldo: 'Fra Berardo Arnolti, il "frater scriptor" del Memoriale di Angela?', in *Angela da Foligno terziaria francescana,* ed. Enrico Menestò, (Spoleto, 1992), pp. 127–59.

[97] 'Giunta di Bevignate', in *Dizionario Biografico degli Italiani*, 57 (2001), pp. 65–7.

The duties of solitaries, male and female, were various. Firstly, they prayed and were contemplatives, and those who asked for their prayers did so out of conviction that their prayers would be heard.[98] They prayed in their cells, in church and along the pilgrimage routes, reciting the Paternoster, or repeating ejaculations, meditating on the passion of Christ, and at times were transported in ecstasy, attaining the highest levels of mystical experience.[99] Some of them also agreed to complete pilgrimages of prayer on behalf of others: daily pilgrimages to the rural shrines of the sacred perimeter[100] and occasional pilgrimages to the great Christian shrines.[101] Despite choosing a life of solitude, they still knew how to be part of history, facing the world with serenity and optimism, and with a spirit of total dedication to the people, both high and low, whom they often counselled. One thinks of women of the stature of Clare of Montefalco who knew how to unite contemplation and apostolic activity: she was the adviser of cardinals and peace-broker between the communities of Trevi and Montefalco.[102]

The official interventions

The semireligious life was unquestionably already under way in the first half of the twelfth century, since Canon 26 of Lateran II (1139) deplored the fact that certain 'religious women', even those who followed in spirit the precepts of St Benedict, St Basil or St Augustine, had continued to live freely in their own houses.[103] The Fourth Lateran Council (1215) addressed the problem of the semireligious women in the constitution *Ne nimia religionum diversitas*, which forbade the indiscriminate creation of new orders. From then on, up to the denunciations of the Great Schism and for a further two centuries after that, the female penitential movement was regulated by this constitution, which imposed the choice of one of the already approved rules [*unam de approbatis*] upon any new community.[104] Cardinal Ugolino, later Pope Gregory IX, from the beginning of the thirteenth century channelled most of the penitential movement of central-northern Italy into the Order of St Peter Damian, subjecting it to the jurisdiction of local bishops and putting it under direct control of the Holy

---

[98] In one commentary on the Apocalypse from the Cistercian abbey of Fiastra in the Marche we read that in times of trouble the people went for advice to the 'eremiti in vilibus locis pro Dei amore morantes, et pro ecclesia ne deficiant orantes' [hermits dwelling in poor places for the love of God, and praying that they might not fail on behalf of the Church]: Paris B.N. lat. 627, fol. 82r.

[99] Thier and Calufetti, *Il libro della beata Angela*, pp. 156, 168, 176–8, 182, 486–8, 496–500.

[100] M. Sensi, *Il perdono di Assisi* (Assisi, 2002), pp. 227f., 240f.

[101] Cf. M. Sensi, *Santuari, pellegrini, eremiti nell'Italia centrale*, I (Spoleto, 2003), pp. 87ff. See further Garampi, *Memorie ecclesiastiche*, p. 46; M. Armellini, *La visita alle sette chiese e san Filippo Neri* (Rome, 1894); P. Brezzi, *Storia degli anni santi: da Bonifacio VIII al Giubileo del 2000* (Milan, 1997), pp. 96–7; G. Moneta (ed.), *Viaggio nell'Italia dell'anno santo. Giubileo 2000* (Turin, 1999), pp. 121–3.

[102] Menestò, *Il processo di canonizzazione*, p. 81 and p. 228.

[103] Alberigo et al., *Conciliorum oecumeniorum*, p. 179.

[104] Ibid., p. 242.

See.[105] He did this because of the resistance of both Dominicans and Franciscans to managing the female movement.[106]

There are exceptions: splinter groups from the Franciscan penitential movement who, having escaped the hand of the pontiff and not having entered into the *Ordo sancti Damiani*, were still controlled by the Franciscans. They were part of that complex female Franciscan world to which, in the bulls that appeared between 1241 and 1250, were given the names *discalceatae, chordulariae, sorores minores* and *minoritae* – women who appear to have been searching for a distinctive character of their own outside the orders of Damianites or Clarissans, and who already had experiences of eremitical or itinerant life.[107]

After the death of Gregory IX, and throughout the thirteenth century, the majority of the new communities, almost all with the typical trappings of eremitism, evident from the places they chose for their respective *bizzocaggi* – about a mile outside the city walls – were put into institutions by local bishops. There they remained under the jurisdiction of the diocesan bishop who either personally, or by means of priests who were charged with the *cura monialium*, provided for periodic visits to the convents. The bishop ratified the superior, canonically elected, and managed the concentration of the religious in case the numbers dipped so much that they could no longer live a communal life.[108] Mostly it was not an imposition from above but a request that came from the coenobitic community itself, eager to belong to a structure where they could act as legal subjects, from making deeds of sale to being able to inherit. The Montefalco *reclusorio*, for example, asked the Bishop of Spoleto to profess it in one of the approved rules and he granted it the Augustinian Rule.[109]

Large numbers of *bizzocaggi* were brought under the Benedictine Rule; the exceptions were a few convents placed under the Cistercian Rule and given to the custody of the nearest male abbey,[110] and a few which, even though they had adopted the Augustinian or Benedictine Rule, had obtained, like those of the Damianites, the *protectio b. Petri* or better the *submissio* to the Church of Rome.[111] Undoubtedly, such a request was dictated by a concern to defend their

---

[105] See M. P. Alberzoni, *Chiara e il papato* (Milan, 1995); and 'Chiara e San Damiano tra ordine minoritico e curia papale', in *Chiara claris praeclara: Convivium Assisiense*, 6 (2004), pp. 27–70; and 'Da San Damiano all'Ordine di santa Chiara', in *Gli Ordini mendicanti nel Piceno*, 1, *I francescani dalle origini alla controriforma*, ed. G. Gagliardi (Ascoli Piceno, 2005), pp. 113–35; but see also M. Bartoli, *Chiara d'Assisi* (Rome, 1989), especially pp. 103–28, and Sensi, *Storie di bizzoche*, pp. 5–11.

[106] Meersseman, *Ordo fraternitatis*, p. 376; for the full text see G. Meersseman, *Dossier de l'ordre de la pénitence au XIIIe siècle* (Fribourg, 1982).

[107] C. Gennaro, 'Il francescanesimo femminile nel XIII secolo', *Rivista di storia e letteratura religiosa* 25, 2 (1989), pp. 259–84, especially pp. 281–4. On the Marche, see M. Sensi, 'Clarisse e minorete nei secoli XIII–XV. L'esempio marchigiano', *Atti e memorie. Deputazione di storia patria per le Marche* 103 (1998), pp. 493–522.

[108] Sensi, *Storie di bizzoche*, pp. 49–69, 107–39.

[109] Ibid., pp. 57f.

[110] Sensi, *Storie di bizzoche*, pp. 163ff.; A. Pantoni, 'Monasteri sotto la regola benedettina a Perugia e dintorni', *Benedictina* 8 (1954), pp. 231–56 (pp. 242f); G. Casagrande and P. Monacchia, 'Il monastero di S. Giuliana a Perugia nel secolo XIII', *Benedictina* 28 (1980), pp. 509–71.

[111] Sensi, *Storie di bizzoche*, pp. 76f., p. 104 and p. 113.

own possessions, but also by the need to observe the proper life of a regular. The formula used by the pontiffs was that used by the papal chancellery of the twelfth century, beginning with the defence of the privileges of protection: 'It behoves that papal protection be present to those choosing the religious life, lest perchance an assault of any indiscretion whatsoever [*cuiuslibet temeritatis incursus*] either recall them from their purpose or, because protection is absent, break the sacred strength of religion [*sacre religionis infringat*].' Then the norms of religious life were prescribed according to the Benedictine or Augustinian Rule and a monastic, traditional and patrimonial imprimatur conferred upon the foundation. Their direct dependence on the Apostolic See imposed on the Pope the obligation of special care towards these convents; however, we do not have any records of disciplinary actions taken by the Pope towards these exempt convents.[112]

The question of the female penitential movement was addressed by the Second Council of Lyons (1274). Advisers, duly summoned by the Pope, had isolated this phenomenon as one of the scandals that beset the Church;[113] in order to regulate it, the council issued the constitution *Religionum diversitatem nimiam*, which substantially confirmed the decrees of the Fourth Lateran Council.[114] This made the diocesan Ordinaries more than usually circumspect; they intervened a little bit everywhere in atypical female communities, giving them institutional status with one of the approved rules, usually the Augustinian and less frequently the Benedictine Rule; several communities would have liked to follow the rule of St Clare, but that order was immediately made subject to the Apostolic See.[115] And yet when the waiting-list of young women who intended to become nuns in the Clarissan order was expanding, because the quota of enclosed orders was fixed by canon law and determined by the Apostolic See on the basis of the financial resources of an institution, several diocesan Ordinaries allowed these women, for the most part bound to male spiritual advisers, to live as regulars by dedicating their convent to St Clare and in some cases to follow the same rule as St Clare, while awaiting official approval from the Apostolic See. For example, eight *bizzoche* in Leonessa, a centre in the mountains in the diocese of Spoleto, using the Procurator as a channel, asked the diocesan bishop if they could set up an oratory in honour of St Lucy to make it the canonical seat of their community; and on 13 June 1295 Bishop Francis, under whose jurisdiction fell the building of the oratory, with the privilege *Pios petentium*, recognized it as a monastic community and exempted it from payment of all the episcopal taxes to which the diocesan monasteries were subject. He demanded only an annual tax of a half-measure of wax to offer on St Lucy's day, on the condition that the women would adopt one of the approved rules,

---

[112] See E. Pasztor, 'I papi del Duecento e Trecento di fronte alla religiosità femminile', in *Il movimento religioso femminile in Umbria nei secoli XIII–XV*, ed. Rusconi, pp. 29–65.

[113] Gilberto da Tournai, *Collectio de scandalis Ecclesiae*, ed. A. Stroik, *Archivum franciscanum historicum* 24 (1931), pp. 61–2.

[114] Alberigo et al., *Conciliorum oecumeniorum*, pp. 326–7; see also A. Franchi, *Il concilio II di Lione (1274) secondo la ordinatio concilii generalis Lugduniensis* (Rome, 1965), p. 98 and p. 131.

[115] Sensi, *Storie di bizzoche*, pp. 49ff. and pp. 107ff.

whichever they preferred *quae vobis magis placuerit*. It was understood that these women, once they had built their convent and chosen its rule, would immediately have to submit themselves to an exempt order. The women saw to the building of the convent, after which they chose to live according to the Rule of St Clare, nevertheless without taking the final legal step of seeking the approval of the Apostolic See, as was the practice in Clarissan convents. Such a request was eventually made, but it was only formalized on 6 February 1445, when just three nuns remained in the convent. However, for nearly a century-and-a-half the site was inhabited by religious women who called themselves Clarissans, but who were not answerable to the Apostolic See; Pope Eugene IV, in the bull *Apostolicae Nobis* (21 April 1446), eradicated this anomalous situation and juridically united the community to the Order of Clarissans.[116]

Towards the end of the thirteenth century the eremitic *bizzocale* movement underwent a change under Pope Boniface VIII. Six months after his coronation, in the bull *Saepe Sanctam Ecclesiam* (1 August 1296), he denounced a new heresy, whose adherents – both men and women – contravened ecclesiastical authority: they absolved. Like the Cathars, they conferred the Holy Spirit by way of the laying on of hands; they held assemblies by day and night; they preached; they wore clerical tonsures; they claimed that the prayer of a naked man was more efficacious; they were promiscuous with women; they condemned manual work.[117] The document was very vague: some of the accusations contained within it seemed to refer to the sect which had been identified in Milan at the end of the thirteenth century, around a female visionary called Guglielma la Boema (d. 1279) in whom the Holy Spirit was supposed to be incarnated, and whose followers maintained that the sins of contemporary humanity could be wiped out and that all of them would be redeemed through the intervention of this woman;[118] other accusations, however, seemed directed against the beghards of the Free Spirit;[119] others still seemed to persecute the friars of the *Ordo Apostolorum* of Gerardo Segarelli, an order suppressed by the Second Council of Lyons (1274).[120] Then the following month, in the decretal *Firma cautela* (22 September 1296), the pontiff ordered his bishops to carry out an inquisition of the *bizzochi* and wandering hermits amongst whom there were persons suspected of heresy, who deceived the minds of simple people and led them into error, spreading their poisons over them, poisons that were partly doc-

[116] L. Wadding, *Annales Minorum*, XI, p. 564 n. 184; U. Hüntermann, *Bullarium franciscanum*, n.s. I (1431–55) (Quaracchi, 1929), no. 989, pp. 485–7. On these monasteries, see Sensi, *Storie di bizzoche*, pp. 460–508.

[117] See *Bullarium Romanum ... Taurinensis editio*, IV (Turin, 1859), pp. 134–5 n. 9; *Les registres de Boniface VIII*, ed. G. Digard et al. (Paris, 1907–39), no. 1641.

[118] S. Wessley, 'I guglielmiti del XIII secolo: la salvezza tramite le donne', in *Sante, regine e avventuriere nell'Occidente medievale*, ed. D. Baker (Florence, 1978), pp. 345–61; L. Muraro, *Guglielma e Maifreda, storia di un'eresia femminista* (Milan, 1985).

[119] For Romana Guarnieri, 'this is the first document that alludes to the stark practices that always accompany the accusations against the sect of the Free Spirit': 'Il movimento del libero spirito, testi e documenti', in *Archivio italiano per la storia della pietà* 4 (1965), p. 338.

[120] Honorius IV, *Olim felicis recordationis* (11 March 1286), *Bullarium Romanum*, p. 84; L. Spätling, *De apostolicis, pseudoapostolis, apostolinis* (Monaco, 1947), pp. 114ff.

trinal errors and partly pure lunacy; therefore he invited the bishops to denounce all those solitaries who led suspicious lives.[121]

In addition, the consequences of the decretal *Periculoso*, with which Boniface VIII in 1298 imposed clausura on all female convents of approved orders, were very varied. This universal law of enclosure was then confirmed by the bull *Apostolicae Sedis* (1309): from that date all religiwhere women who had made solemn vows were required to be re-enclosed.[122] With this document it was thought that the female penitential movement could be killed at birth. And yet, the phenomenon of beguines/*bizzoche* continued to survive, resurfacing at the Council of Vienne (1311–12) where – with Gregory X's constitution *Cum de quibusdam mulieribus*, issued at Vienne with the approval of the Council – the beguines who had fallen into the heresy of the Free Spirit were condemned; for the rest, however, the Council Fathers used a tolerant formula: 'we do not intend to prevent those pious women who live honourably in their hospices, with or without a vow of chastity, from doing penance and serving the Lord with the spirit of humility. They will be allowed to do that, following the Lord who inspired them.'[123] Approval did not, however, constitute a recognition of the status of *religiosae*, in so far as these women did not belong to an order of nuns: in fact, they refused the vow of obedience, had their own private means and did not follow an approved rule.

But under the papacy of John XXII the *bizzoche* of central Italy came under further pressure: though tolerant of the beguines north of the Alps,[124] this Pope was intransigent towards the *bizzoche* who had chosen as their rule the *Supra montem*, approved by Nicholas IV in 1289 for the Third Order of secular Franciscans.[125] There were at least three reasons for this position: the fact that the *Supra montem* was a rule for secular laymen and laywomen and not suitable for communal life; the suspicion – a well-founded one – that the regular tertiaries were closely linked to the *Spirituali* movement which the same pontiff had condemned with three constitutions;[126] the appearance in the Vale of Spoleto of the heresy of the so-called Free Spirit, a doctrine widespread throughout Europe, whose leader in Umbria was Bentivenga da Gubbio, called the *apostolo*, with both men and women in his following. The chief tenets of this heresy were: complete refutation of free will and of eternal damnation for all sins and vices; complete passive abandonment to God, without any operation of grace or control of the passions; the sinlessness of those who enjoyed God's charity; indifference towards

---

[121] F. Ehrle, 'Die Spiritualen, ihr Verhältniss zum Franciscanerorden und zu den Fraticellen', *Archiv für Litteratur und Kirchen Geschicthte des Mittelalters* 2 (1886), pp. 156–7.

[122] Text of the Constitution in E. Friedberg, *Corpus juris canonici*, II, *Decretalium collectiones* (Leipzig, 1922), cols. 1054–5; and see J. Leclercq, 'Clausura', in *Dizionario degli Istituti di Perfezione* II (1975), cols. 1166–74, esp. cols. 1170f.

[123] Alberigo et al., *Conciliorum oecumeniorum*, p. 374; J. Lecler, *Vienne. Histoire des Conciles oecumeniques* (Paris, 1964), pp. 159f. and pp. 195–96.

[124] *Bullarium franciscanum*, V, no. 1411, p. 192 (22 November 1320); no. 417, p. 195 (31 December 1320).

[125] See R. Pazzelli and L. Temperini (eds.), *La 'Supra montem' di Niccolò IV (1289): genesi e diffusione di una regola* (Rome, 1988); E. Menestò (ed.), *Niccolò IV: un pontificato tra Oriente e Occidente* (Perugia, 1991).

[126] The constitutions are: *Quorundam exigit* (7 October 1317) (*Bullarium franciscanum*, V, no. 289, pp. 128f); *Sancta romana* (30 December 1317) (*Bullarium franciscanum*, V, no. 297, pp. 134f); *Gloriosam ecclesiam* (23 January 1318) (*Bullarium franciscanum*, V, no. 302, pp. 137f).

the Passion of Christ and the tribulations of one's neighbour. In 1306 he asked Clare of Montefalco, an Augustinian with obedience to a bishop, a series of questions, in an attempt to convert even her to the Free Spirit:

> 'Tell me, Clare, can a priest who in the night has committed the sin of fornication lawfully celebrate mass the following day? [...] Which pleased God more: the virginity of Agnes or the repentance of the Magdalene?'[127]

Two supporters of Bentivenga, both Minorites, used equally aggressive tactics: brother Giovannuccio of Bevagna, a confessor at the convent of Montefalco, and brother James of Coccorone, who arranged the meeting between Sister Clare and brother Bentivenga. The saint, after disproving their every point, denounced them to the ecclesiastical authorities as 'a congregation of the spirit of the worst servitude'.[128]

The monasticization of the female anchorholds and *bizzocaggi* where a coenobitic life was pursued was paralleled, though several decades apart, by the monasticization of male anchorholds and *bizzocaggi* with more than three hermits.[129] Coenobitic hermits who were not following one of the approved rules are corroborated in large or medium-large cities such as Ascoli Piceno, Assisi, Florence, Gualdo Tadino, Gubbio, Matelica, Narni, Perugia, Spoleto-Monteluco, Terni etc., but also in smaller centres, such as Gualdo Cattaneo, Spello, Stroncone etc. Some communities agreed to be taken into convents with the Benedictine or Augustinian Rules.[130] Other coenobitic hermits, hunted down by the condemnations of Boniface VIII, the Council of Vienne and finally John XXII,[131] went underground, managing to survive because of the protection of certain bishops, local noblemen and their communities.[132] This protection is mentioned by one of their charismatic leaders, the Augustinian brother Gentile of Foligno, in a letter sent to Matteuccio of Gubbio soon after the decretal *Ad conditorem* (8 December 1322) with which John XXII declared the doctrine of the poverty of Christ and the Apostles a heresy.[133]

---

[127] Piergili, *Vita della B. Chiara*, pp. 68f.; p. 66.

[128] Menestò, *Il processo di canonizzazione*, nos. 112–16 and 1, 38, 39, 45); L. Oliger, *De secta Spiritus Libertatis in Umbria saec. XIV. Disquisitio et documenta* (Rome, 1983); R. Guarnieri, 'Frères du Libre Esprit', in *Dictionnaire de Spiritualité ascétique et mystique*, V (Paris, 1964), cols. 1241–68; R. Guarnieri, 'Fratelli del Libero Spirito', in *Dizionario degli Istituti di Perfezione* IV (1977), cols. 633–52.

[129] M. Sensi, 'Movimenti di osservanza e ricerca della solitudine: focolai eremitici tra Umbria e Marche nel XV secolo', in *Identités franciscaines à l'âge des réformes*, ed. F. Meyer and L. Viallet (Clermont-Ferrand, 2005), pp. 101–41; see also Sensi, *Storie di bizzoche*, pp. 14ff. and pp. 163ff.

[130] L. Oliger, 'Acta inquisitoris Umbriae fr. Angeli de Assisio contra stigmata s. Francisci negantem. Contra fraticellos aliosque, a. 1361', *Archivum franciscanum historicum* 24 (1931), pp. 63–90; B. Marinelli, 'Santa Maria Novella in Perugia e le origini della Congregazione perugina dell'Ordine di S. Agostino', *Analecta Augustiniana* 55 (1992), pp. 289–327; M. Sensi, 'Agiografia umbra tra Medioevo ed età moderna', in *Santità agiografia*, ed. G. D. Gordini (Turin, 1991), pp. 179f.

[131] On the *bizzochi* condemned by Boniface VIII in the letter *Incrementum catholice* (7 May 1297), see *Bullarium franciscanum*, IV, p. 435, no. 115; and F. Savini, 'Sui flagellanti, sui fraticelli, sui bizzochi nel Teramano durante i secoli xiii e xiv', *Archivio storico italiano* 25 (1905), pp. 82–91 (p. 90).

[132] See L. Oliger, 'Documenta inedita ad historiam fraticellorum spectantia', in *Archivum franciscanum historicum* III–VI (1910–1913), p. 268 and pp. 274f. For the privilege of Bartolomeo Bardi, Bishop of Spoleto, see Sensi, *Le osservanze francescane*, pp. 317–19, and see further pp. 140–2 and pp. 312–13.

[133] See A. Bartoli Langeli, 'Il manifesto francescano di Perugia del 1322. Alle origini dei fraticelli "de opinione"', *Picenum Seraphicum* 11 (1974), pp. 204–61.

The phase of 'open' convents

But these official interventions did not halt the course of the female penitential movement. Rather, by adapting to the times, the phenomenon of reclusion which was characteristic of the thirteenth century – and which, despite everything, continued to survive, though with a reduced number of members, until the beginning of the fifteenth century[134] – was replaced by a new form of urban eremitism: semireligious women called *bizzoche*, living in communities, as, but without being, nuns. The tertiaries were a party to this. Their members – oblates, anchorites and tertiaries living communally, who were assimilated to nuns by the civil legislation[135] – were not subject to the decretal *Pericoloso*, in as much as they were professed with simple vows. Instead they were subject to the constitutions of Pope John, in particular the *Sancta romana*, which should have prevented the birth of the regular tertiaries, encouraging instead convents with obedience to a bishop and those of the Second Order. Instead, the process of enclosure, rigidly controlled by the diocesan bishops, ended up increasing the birth of convents of *juspatronato* out of institutions exempt from ordinary jurisdiction. The convents of *juspatronato*, which from the juridical point of view corresponded to the 'family monasteries' [*Eigenklöster*],[136] in fact constituted a juridical loophole for avoiding the *visita* and the *correctio* of diocesan bishops, to whom *Periculoso* had entrusted the application of the law on enclosure to those women who, having professed religious vows, intended to live in a community. The Roman basilicas of St Peter,[137] St John in Lateran[138] and St Paul Outside the Walls[139] accepted these open convents – basilicas that, in effect, controlled these foundations by periodically sending an inspector from their chapters, but which were tolerant about enclosure.[140] They extended their protection to the convents and even to the abbeys that enjoyed the *libertas romana*: in Umbria, to the abbey of St Peter of Perugia, to which were attached at least four monasteries;[141] to St Maria in Campis at Foligno, to which was attached St Maria of Bethlehem;[142] and even to two convents under the Order of St John of Jerusalem.[143]

The new phase of female piety arose at the beginning of the fifteenth century:

[134] On the recluse Gemma (d. 1439), see Benvenuti Papi, '*In castro poenitentiae*', p. 401.
[135] Luzzatto, *Gli statuti del Comune di S. Anatolia*, pp. 41f.
[136] See B. Kurtscheid, *Historia iuris canonici* (Rome, 1951), pp. 276ff.; W. Kurze, 'Monasteri e nobiltà nella Tuscia altomedievale', in *Atti del V Congresso int. di studi sull'alto medioevo* (Spoleto, 1973), pp. 344–47.
[137] See Pantoni, 'Monasteri sotto la regola benedettina', p. 236; M. Bigaroni, 'I Monasteri benedettini femminili di S. Paolo delle abbadesse, di S. Apollinare in Assisi e S. Maria del Paradiso prima del Concilio di Trento', in *Aspetti di vita benedettina nella storia di Assisi* (Assisi, 1981), pp. 171–231; Sensi, *Le osservanze francescane*, pp. 215–16; Garampi, *Memorie ecclesiastiche*, p. 101 n. c.
[138] Sensi, *Le osservanze francescane*, pp. 212–14; see also Città del Vaticano, Archivio della Basilica Lateransense, Cod. D. II, col. 48 (11 May 1426).
[139] L. Mattei Cerasoli, 'Le chiese di S. Giacomo e di S. Magno in Amelia, appunti storici e documenti', *Bollettino della r. Deputazione di storia patria per l'Umbria*, 30 (1932), pp. 1–92, pp. 57ff. and pp. 71ff.
[140] Sensi, *Storie di bizzoche*, pp. 309–28.
[141] Pantoni, 'Monasteri sotto la regola benedettina', p. 244.
[142] M. Sensi, *S. Maria di Betlem a Foligno, monastero di contemplative agostiniane* (Foligno, 1981).
[143] See F. Tommasi, 'Il monastero femminile di San Bevignate dell'Ordine di San Giovanni Gerosolimitano (secoli XIV–XVI)', in *Templari e ospitalieri in Italia. La chiesa di San Bevignate a Perugia*, ed. M. Roncetti, P. Scarpellini and F. Tommasi (Milan, 1987), pp. 53–78 (pp. 56ff.).

it consisted of the regular Franciscan tertiaries' observance throughout various cities of central Italy, but their form of living was expressly opposed by John XXII. This movement, the result of female religious disquiet of the fourteenth century, had emerged in order to accommodate aristocratic women – for the most part widows – who, whilst following the example of St Clare, had distanced themselves from the Clarissans and whose characteristics at the time were: conspicuous wealth; limited quotas; divided into choral singers, lay convent sisters (without voting rights) and 'serventi' [sisters who served outside the convent], a distinction often made according to the rank and economic class that they came from.[144] Nostalgic for heroic times, these women lived a life of retreat as city hermits, relying on the charity of the faithful rather than on property and free to leave the 'convent' in order to take part in religious functions, to practise the apostolate amongst the needy of body and of spirit, as well as to seek alms. One of the earliest examples was the monastery of St Anna, founded in 1388 at Foligno by Brother Paoluccio Trinci,[145] who in 1368 had founded the regular observance: thus there arose 'experimentally', as an exception to *Sancta romana* and with the approval of the Minister General of the Franciscan Order, a religious family of enclosed women who made simple vows, but who did not fall under the law of enclosure imposed by the constitution *Periculoso*, semireligious women devoted – according to the model that Francis of Assisi gave to his brother hermits – either to the contemplative life or the active life; they were *bizzoche* possessing their own household goods, domestic utensils for eating and some savings, in case of illness,[146] who behaved like urban hermits, leading a mixed life.[147] Because they were from the aristocracy – Angelina, their charismatic leader, was a countess, and the religious women of St Anna, some of whom were of aristocratic lineage, were and still are called 'the Countesses' – they were able to act as apostolates as much among the powerful as amongst the poor. The role of Blessed Angelina was crucial for the establishment of the congregation of Foligno because she obtained initial recognition from Boniface IX, the Roman Pope, a relative of the Trinci, lords of the city. This recognition caused other communities of tertiaries, which in contrast to the monastery of Foligno were still oppressed by the penalties of *Sancta romana*, to ask to federate themselves to it. In the end it was this situation that pushed Pope Martin V in 1428 to approve the congregation of Regular Tertiaries who went by the name of Blessed Angelina; this was done despite the

[144] See J. Leclercq, 'Il monachesimo femminile' in *Il Movimento religioso femminile*, pp. 63–99 (p. 63); M. Del Mar Graña, *Apostolado femenino, clausura y santidad. La obra de Angelina de Monteiove*, in *Enclave di myer … Muyeres que se atrevieron*, ed. I. Gómez-Acebo (Bilbao, 1998), p. 181; M. Sensi, 'Il patrimonio monastico di S. Maria di Vallegloria a Spello', *Bollettino dep. st. patria Umbria* 81 (1986), pp. 77–149.
[145] *La Beata Angelina da Montegiove e il movimento del Terz'Ordine regolare francescano femminile*, ed. Pazzelli and Sensi, op. cit.; A. C. Filannino, *La contessa con gli zoccoli. Angelina da Montegiove nobile, penitente e francescana* (Assisi, 2006).
[146] M. Sensi, 'I monasteri e bizzocaggi dell'osservanza francescana nel XV secolo a Foligno', in *All'ombra della Chiara Luce*, ed. A. Horowski (Rome, 2005), pp. 87–175.
[147] For example, the decoration of the refectory of the monastery of St Anna, Assisi, shows the roles of Mary and Martha by which the tertiaries were known.

Sancta romana, whose sanctions nevertheless remained in force for all the other regular tertiaries living communally. In 1436 Eugenio IV annulled (but only orally) the *Sancta romana*, then it was definitively cancelled in 1487 by Innocent VIII.[148] For his part Sextus IV, in 1480, declared that the three vows made by the brothers and sisters of the Third Order of St Francis living communally, though made as simple, should be considered solemn in all their effects.[149] Therefore the sisters of Foligno remained as tertiaries because they professed the Rule of the Third Order, but at the same time were 'properly considered religious' because the vows they uttered were solemn ones.

This saw the development of single 'open' convents, firmly bound to their respective cities. Meanwhile, the congregation, after less than half a century, entered into crisis for having come into conflict in 1430 with the Minister General of the Franciscan order – whom they refuted – for not belonging either to the First or to the Second Order (obedience to the Constitutions of Pope Martin). This penalized the autonomy of the young congregation and, several years later, brought them into conflict with their confessors. These confessors were observant brothers who, having abandoned the old hermitages, had chosen the *via media* – because of the enclosure imposed on these men. This cost the religious women of Foligno the loss of their spiritual directors. And that was the reason why the regular Franciscan tertiaries and then the Amadeiti took the place of the Observants – until the female tertiaries of Blessed Angelina re-entered the regime of the Observants who, up until the Council of Trent, did not insist emphatically on the need for enclosure.[150]

A similar path, though delayed and without the same success as that of the female Franciscan tertiaries, was followed by the *bizzoche* affiliated to the religious orders, such as the Augustinian *bizzoche*, whose rule was approved by the Roman Pope Boniface IX, on 7 November 1399, in the bull *In sinu Sedis Apostolicae*,[151] and those of the Dominicans, whose rule was approved six years later by the Avignon Pope Innocent VII, with the bull *Sedis Apostolicae* (26 May 1405).[152] Meanwhile, the first community of regular Dominican tertiaries appeared in 1490 at Perugia, under Blessed Colomba da Rieti (d. 1501).[153] Some of these religious women, in the absence of a specific rule that issued from the Holy See, provided their own, as did Blessed Helen Valentinis of

---

[148] *Dudum per* (22 January 1487), *Bullarium franciscanum*, n.s. IV/1, no. 598, p. 266.

[149] *Ad Christi vicarii* (1 December 1480), *Bullarium franciscanum*, n.s. III, no. 1360, p. 681.

[150] See *Biografie antiche della Beata Angelina da Montegiove*, ed. A. Filannino and L. Mattioli (Spoleto, 1996); and Filannino, *La contessa con gli zoccoli*, pp. 63–71.

[151] L. Orsacchi da Empoli, *Bullarium Ordinis Eremitarum Sancti Augustini* (Rome, 1628), p. 54. The Rule was edited in 1479: *Regula fratrum et sororum de poenitentia sacri Ordinis heremitarum beati Augustini* (Rome, 1479). See further B. Rano, 'Agostiniani', in *Dizionario degli Istituti di Perfezione* I (Rome, 1974), cols. 278–381 (p. 380); and Sensi, *Storie di bizzoche*, p. 14, p. 93 and p. 235.

[152] The Dominican *bizzoche* obtained the canonical approval of Innocent VII, in the bull *Sedis apostolicae* (Viterbo, 26 September 1405), *Bullarium Romanum Taur*, IV, pp. 636f. On the Rule composed by Munio di Zamora in 1285 and approved by Innocent VII, see L. A. Redigonda, 'Frati Predicatori', in *Dizionario degli Istituti di Perfezione*, IV (1977), cols. 923–70 (cols. 960–5).

[153] G. Casagrande and E. Menestò, *Una santa, una città* (Perugia and Florence, 1990).

Udine.[154] The same thing happened with the Olivetan oblates of Tor de' Specchi, under the charismatic direction of St Francesca Romana (d. 1440)[155] and, less dramatically, with the tertiaries of the servants of Mary, who were approved by Pope Martin V in 1424.[156]

The phenomenon of urban reclusion underwent a crisis in the fifteenth century with the affirmation of the stages of the observations – designed to reform the old religious orders – and with *Devotio Moderna* – a movement that introduced a new method and spirit – but there were isolated cases of recluses in 1503, in the Basilica of St Peter's in Rome and, in 1507, at Ferrara, where the lady Laura had herself walled into a *celletta* of the cathedral.[157] The foundation of new orders and congregations was, on the one hand, an attempt to annihilate all the semireligious experiences in order to regularize them; on the other hand, it was an attempt to encourage the active life by penalizing, in one sense, the contemplative life which, from the thirteenth century, thanks to urban reclusion, had come within the reach of even laypeople.[158] After a few decades, a new phase for semireligious women began: that of nuns at home and new forms of open convents. In this way the history of the *bizzoche* has continued up until today.[159]

Conclusion

In the hagiographic witnesses, as well as in the Italian municipal documentation, it appears that the urban eremitical movement was a lay penitential movement that involved men and women of all social ranks, unfolding from the thirteenth century to the end of the fifteenth century, with a strong concentration of penitential women in the regions from Romagna to Abruzzo. It only marginally touched other regions. The movement is most strongly attested in Umbria, not only because of the heights of holiness reached by the women there, familiar to all Catholics, but for the quantity of documentary material that has now emerged, largely from research carried out in municipal archives. Tuscany boasts the greater number of recluses with biographies. But we only know about a tiny minority of the women who belonged to the movement, who perhaps numbered several thousands in the course of three centuries: at this point in the research (the Italian phenomenon only began to be studied thirty years ago), we do not know the exact number. It

---

[154] A. Tilatti, 'Le regola delle terziarie agostiniane di Udine (sec. XV)', *Analecta Augustiniana* (1991), pp. 63–79; G. Zarri, *Colomba da Rieti e i movimenti religiosi femminili del suo tempo*, in *Una santa, una città*, ed. Casagrande and Menestò, pp. 89–108; ibid. p. 95.

[155] *Una santa tutta romana. Saggi e ricerche nel VI centenario della nascita di Francesca Bussa dei Ponziani (1384–1984)*, ed. G. Picasso (Monte Oliveto Maggiore, 1984); A. Esposito, *S. Francesca e le comunità religiose femminili a Roma nel secolo XV*, in *Culto dei santi*, ed. Gajano and Sebastiani, pp. 537–62.

[156] The bull given in *Bullarium Romanum Taur.*, IV, pp. 702f. is an exact transcript of that with which Innocent VII, in 1405, approved the constitutions of the Dominican tertiaries.

[157] See G. Zarri, 'Pietà e profezia alle corti padane; le pie consigliere dei principi', in *Il Rinascimento nelle corti padane. Società e cultura* (Bari, 1977), pp. 201–37 (p. 219).

[158] *Speculum inclusorum*, ed. Oliger, p. 7.

[159] Guarnieri, *Donne e chiesa tra mistica e istituzione*, pp. 13–46.

was a heterogeneous movement, ranging from the choice of anchoritism, practised by women 'imprisoned' in cells, to a coenobitic life, led by hermits (largely women) living in communities: these irregular forms of religious life sprang from diverse circumstances – aspiration for the contemplative life together with various socio-religious and economic factors that prevented some women from entering convents, such as widowhood and the capped numbers in regular convents. The movement, made up of semireligious women who had adopted the ancient penitential discipline, drew on the experiences of the Desert Fathers, but with the difference that these modern hermits found solitude in the city or its sacred perimeter.

Loved and protected by the municipal authorities for the sacral service they performed for the community, these women – considered living saints – can be compared to the slightly later phenomenon of 'political' shrines or shrines of civic religion; sought after as advisers, especially at difficult moments in the history of the community, or of the history of ordinary devout people, they in turn allowed themselves to be gently guided by their confessors and spiritual directors, about whom we know very little, not only because of their humility but also because of the secret that they were bound to.

This history is made up of hundreds of tiny fragments with which, given the present state of research, we can only piece together a mosaic of rare beauty: fragments of a history of piety dedicated to Christ the Spouse and to participation in his redemptive works, for the sake of the brothers and sisters in faith of the Church militant as much as the Church purgative.

4 Anchorites in the Spanish tradition

G. Cavero Domínguez

Origins and early expression

It was a relatively common custom among the early Christians of the Spanish Peninsula to retire to secluded places, nearly always for short periods of time, during significant dates within the liturgic calendar. The canons which were intended to fight Priscillian's heresy following the Council of Zaragoza (*c.*380) allude to people leaving their churches for such periods of reclusion during Lent[1] and at Christmas.[2] These customs reveal the beginnings of a practice which would grow stronger over the course of the Middle Ages – the beginning of a flight from the world, a kind of ascesis which also incorporated the world of sex, matrimony and virginity. Also at the end of the fourth century, Bachiarius, an ascetic of Spanish origin who was similarly suspected of being a Priscillianist,[3] recommended to a married woman named Marcella that she retire into the small cell of a monastery because of the lack of a suitable desert.[4] Such a cell should have only one table upon which to read the Holy Scriptures – her only spiritual food. Naturally this would be only a temporary retirement, to be undertaken at Christmas, following which Marcella was to resume her normal activities as the married woman that she was.

This type of temporary reclusion was both eremitic and lay (and attractive to the aristocracy, in particular), both male and female, and not always looked upon favourably by the official Church during this early period. It had a penitential character and people undertook it in an entirely voluntary way, embracing it in response to a drive for a new urban asceticism. However, this kind of reclusion

---

[1] Council of Zaragoza, canon II, *PL* 84, col. 515. Also of interest is the volume *España eremítica*, ed. Abbey of Leyre (Pamplona, 1970), which gathers together articles related to several Spanish regions and late Roman and medieval times.

[2] Council of Zaragoza, canon IV, *PL* 84, col. 515.

[3] M. Marcos, 'Los orígenes del ascetismo y el monacato en Hispania', in *El cristianismo. Aspectos históricos de su origen y difusión en Hispania. Revisiones de historia antigua*, ed. J. Santos and R. Teja, vol. III (Vitoria, 2000), pp. 201–33.

[4] For everything related to Bachiarius and his two letters, as well as other matters dealt with in this and the following paragraphs, see Guido M. Gibert, 'El eremitismo en la Hispania romana', in *España eremítica*, pp. 42–4.

was also often used as a punishment within church milieux, following the tradition of the ancient world.[5]

The letter of Pope Siricius to Himerius, bishop of Tarragona, in 385 speaks about the problems which had arisen in the ascetic world regarding the maintaining of chastity. Any breach of sanctified chastity [*propositus sanctitatis*] resulting in procreation would be severely punished:[6] sexual incontinence was an offence which was punishable by both civil and ecclesiastical law,[7] and the monks and nuns who were convicted of it would be taken away from their communities, locked up in prisons for the rest of their lives, only to return at the time of death. It was an exemplary punishment for a serious misdemeanour. It is interesting in this context to notice that the Latin word used for 'jail' by Pope Siricius is *ergastulum* [a reclusion place], which several authors think must translate as 'the jail of the cell'.[8]

With the arrival of the Germanic peoples, the Spanish anchoritic panorama was expanded. Archaeology has identified a considerable number of caves,[9] sometimes very difficult to characterize chronologically, but certainly used in Visigothic times (sixth to eighth centuries) as places of reclusion. Settlements established in caves and buildings show individual anchoritic occupancy, as well as semi-eremitic (lauratic) and eremitic-communitarian lives. Indeed, some of the Visigothic monasteries had significant anchoritic origins in caves or shelters, like San Millán de Suso, in La Rioja, and San Juan de la Peña, near Jaca, in Huesca. The coexistence of anchoritism, reclusion and eremitism can also be detected in liturgy. The rite described in the *Liber Ordinum*[10] as the 'ordo conversorum conversarumque' [the order of converted men and women] is divided into two parts: first, the tonsure of the priest(s), and in the second part, a prayer and blessing. The latter gives us reasonable grounds to think that there was a predominance of anchorites and recluses in monastic compounds, as two of the

[5] See S. Torallas Tovar and I. Pérez Martín (eds.), *Castigo y reclusión en el mundo antiguo* (Madrid, 2003).

[6] See the original Latin text in *PL* 84, col. 633.

[7] The punishment for sexual incontinence was maintained, though not so strictly, in Visigothic times. When Bishop Potamius confessed his sin of fornication to the assembly of the 10th Council of Toledo in 656, he concluded that he had already been voluntarily enclosed within a jail to do penance and redeem his fault. He had imposed upon himself the penance. See J. Vives, *Concilios visigóticos e hispanorromanos* (Barcelona, 1963), pp. 319–21.

Reclusion as punishment is also to be found in some Visigothic monastic rules. For example, St Fructuosus's rule forbids the monks to eat meat except when they are on a journey or ill; the offence against this rule is punished with reclusion. See J. Campos Ruiz and I. Roca Meliá, *Santos padres españoles II, San Leandro, San Isidoro, San Fructuoso, reglas monásticas de la España visigoda. Los tres libros de las 'Sentencias'* (Madrid, 1971), p. 142.

[8] See, for example, J. M. Torres, 'El término ergastulum en la primera literatura monástica', in *Cristianismo y aculturación en tiempos del Imperio Romano*, ed. A. González Blanco and J. M. Blázquez (Murcia, 1990), pp. 287–90. See also Marcos, 'Los orígenes del ascetismo y el monacato en Hispania', pp. 201–33.

[9] See F. Íñiguez Almech, 'Algunos problemas de las viejas iglesias españolas', in *Cuadernos de trabajos de la escuela española de historia y arquelogía en Roma* VII (1955), pp. 7–100; also A. Azkarate Garai-Olaun, 'El eremitismo de época visigótica. Testimonios arqueológicos', *Codex Aquilarensis*, Cuadernos de investigación del Monasterio de Santa María la Real 5 (1991), pp. 141–79.

[10] M. Férotin (ed.), *Liber Ordinum* (Paris, 1904), pp. 82–6. See also M. C. Díaz y Díaz, 'La vida eremítica en el reino visigodo', in *España eremítica*, pp. 61–2.

invocations and some formulae in the rite cannot be applied to monks, but only to anchorites and recluses.

The most outstanding personality in the intellectual Spanish Visigothic world is St Isidore of Seville (*c*.560–636), who classifies monks into three groups: coenobites, hermits and anchorites.[11] For Isidore the differences between hermits and anchorites are really minimal, to such an extent that some authors think he uses the terms interchangeably.[12]

St Millán,[13] Nanctus,[14] St Fructuosus of Braga[15] and St Valerius of El Bierzo[16] were very popular anchorites and/or hermits. Fructuosus and Valerius were monks, anchorites and recluses,[17] that is to say they underwent different experiences of reclusion during their lifetimes. As recluses [*reclusi*], for example, they retired from their monastic communities and their social groups, but retained contact with society. They practised a kind of strict *anachoresis*, very well known in Eastern monasticism. Valerius (*c*.630–95) is the paradigm of such a combination of these formulae: he retired from the world after an eventful youth and followed the example of the Desert Fathers in search of a contemplative life. Later, he became an unsuccessful monk in the monastery of Compludo and proceeded to lead an eremitic life secluded from the world in a small cell [*ergastulo*] next to a church in the mountains. Later reclusion saw him attached to the monastery of San Pedro de Montes (*in cellulam ... retrusisset* [he withdrew into a small cell]) and, as an exemplary solitary, he prefigures the rules laid down by Grimlaïcus at a later date (as dealt with by Signori in her contribution to this volume). Valerius was a solitary and secluded ascetic, had disciples, devoted himself to the cure of souls and to teaching, copied books, read a lot; but at the same time he was both critical and rebellious.[18]

As Signori also demonstrates, hagiographic models present solitaries and recluses leading exemplary lives and enjoying a popular prestige, devoting themselves to praying, fasting and mortification. But anchoritism and other forms of

---

[11] In fact, he mentions six types of monks, of which three are the best [*optima*]: the first are coenobites [*genus coenobitarum*]; the second hermits [*genus eremitarum*]; and the third anchorites [*genus anachoretarum*] – Isidore of Seville, *De ecclesiasticis officiis*, lib. II, caput XVI (*De monachis*), pars 2–4, in *PL* 83, cols 794–5.

[12] Díaz y Díaz, 'La vida', p. 219.

[13] His *vita* was written by Braulius of Zaragoza, for which see I. Cazzaniga, 'La vita di S. Emiliano. Scritta da Braulione Vescobo di Zaragoza: edizione critica', in *Bolletino del comitato per la preparazione dell'edizione nazionale dei Classici Greci e Latini* (Rome, 1954), pp. 7–44.

[14] Nanctus was an *abbas* who had come from the north of Africa and is highly praised for his anchoritic reclusion in the *Vitae Sanctorum Patrum Emeritensium*, ed. J. Garvin (Washington, 1946), 3–8, p. 158.

[15] M. C. Díaz y Díaz (ed.), *La vida de San Fructuoso de Braga* (Braga, 1974).

[16] Two editions of St Valerius's works were published in the mid twentieth century: R. Fernández Pousa (ed.), *San Valerio (Nuño Valerio), Obras* (Madrid, 1944) and C. Aherne (ed.), *Valerio of Bierzo: an Ascetic of the Late Visigothic Period* (Washington, 1949). The latest edition of his works has been recently published by M. C. Díaz y Díaz, *Valerio del Bierzo. Su persona, su obra*, Colección de Fuentes y estudios de historia leonesa 111 (León, 2006). The following quotations are from this edition.

[17] *Fructuosus ... eremi recessus*: Díaz y Díaz, *Valerio del Bierzo*, p. 218; see also ibid., p. 272, where *eremi* appears again. For anchorites [*anachoretae*], see ibid., pp. 324–7 (*De genere monachorum*, pars 2–3).

[18] He was, for example, critical of the monks of San Pedro de Montes at this time, and on many other occasions; for which see ibid. (*Ordo Quaerimoniae Praefati Discriminis*, nos 22 and 23). He was also rebellious towards his bishop, Isidore; for which see ibid., no. 21.

reclusion did not always attract such people. Valerius himself quotes some examples of wicked recluses devoted to all types of vices. Those people lacked any juridical dependence on the Church and its hierarchy and were practically uncontrollable.[19]

These are some of the reasons why the solitary life sometimes appeared in Visigothic Spain as something people should avoid, a reservation that can be traced both in monastic rules and in the canons of councils which intended to prevent deviations from orthodoxy. When St Leander of Seville (c.540–600), brother of St Isidore, wrote their sister Florentina the letter which would serve her and her community as a rule for their common life, he pointed towards the existence of an urban reclusion practised by women in small cells [*virgines quae in urbibus per cellulis demorantur*] and the risks [*multimoda cura*] involved in it.[20] Leander knew very well the origins and impetus behind the female reclusive life of his day – a desire to keep out of the cloisters, to live away from the world but, at the same time, remain within it. He also perceived such a life as dating back to the times of the Apostles, when it was carried out by the gentiles as a common custom. However, the Jews never practised it.[21]

Like Leander, Isidore was concerned about reclusion but from a different perspective: for him it constituted the highest degree of spiritual perfection. In his rule written for monks, he urges them not to take reclusion hastily. On the one hand, he insists that retiring to a secluded place implies that there is something to hide and that it is community life which can correct vices, whereas reclusion, like vainglory, cannot. On the other hand, sanctity, if it exists, must not be hidden but must be apparent to others as an example.[22]

Council legislation also attempted to support ascetic reclusion as an objective of sanctity. A good example is offered by the 7th Council of Toledo, which took place in 646. One of its decisions determines what the preparation for reclusion should be and expresses the necessity of putting an end to the fact that some people became recluses who were unworthy, wicked and indecorous.[23]

This Visigothic tradition was retained within later Christian monasticism under Muslim law in Andalusia. St Eulogius of Córdoba,[24] writing in the ninth century, equates the flight from the world with another special factor – the yearning for martyrdom. He also considers coenobitism as coexisting alongside other eremitic formulae. Among the several exemplars registered by Eulogius – both male (Servus Dei and Habentius, for example) and some female – Columba is outstanding, offering as she does an example of the confrontation between Islam and Christianity which took place during the period. The case of Columba falls into

---

[19] See ibid. (*Quod de superioribus quaerimoniis residuum sequitur*, no. 3).

[20] Campos and Roca, *Santos padres*, pp. 67–8. Leander knew and followed, to some extent, Caesarius of Arles's *Regula ad virgines*.

[21] See Campos and Roca, *Santos padres*, p. 68.

[22] Ibid., p. 19.

[23] Vives, *Concilios*, p. 255.

[24] Eulogio de Córdoba, *Memoriale sanctorum*, *Documentum martyriale* and *Liber apologeticus martyrum*, also known as *Corpus Scriptorum Muzarabicorum*, ed. Juan Gil (Madrid, 1973). Columba is referred to on pp. 447–52.

traditional hagiographic models. As St Eulogius relates,[25] she was of noble background but fled from matrimony to become an exemplary nun in the cloister. She ate and slept very little, spent endless hours praying and shedding copious tears. When she reached the pinnacle of her monastic life, Columba requested to be walled up so that she could devote herself entirely and only to God and lead an intense, contemplative life. As an authentic *miles Christi* [soldier of Christ], she came out of her cell of reclusion [*claustra in quodam angulo cellula*] only to present herself before the Muslim authorities of Córdoba and tell them that she was a Christian.[26] She challenged them to martyr her – which, obviously, they proceeded to do. Thus, Columba underwent three phases in her enclosed life: firstly, she was a nun, then a recluse and, finally, a martyr.[27] She is also an embodiment of spiritual perfection obtained through ascetic exercise within Christian monasticism – but in an Islamic land.

After the Islamic invasion

Anchoritism and eremitism coexisted with coenobitism in the north of the Iberian Peninsula as monastic life was recovered after the Islamic invasion. Settlements of solitaries, sometimes independent, sometimes within monastic frameworks, were quite common. For example, Genadius, a monk and bishop of Astorga (*c.*909–23) in León, protected anchorites and coenobites alike and brought to life the old monastic site of St Fructuosus in the Valley of Silence in the Bierzo region (San Pedro de Montes). Some solitaries [*fratruum anachoritarum, eremitis*] lived scattered in the same and neighbouring valleys and they were all dependent on the monastery of Santiago de Peñalba [*cenobiale conclave ... monachorum*], where they used to meet on certain occasions.[28]

The later Council of Coyanza (*c.*1055) fostered Benedictine life and monasteries and, as a result, solitaries, both men and women, became quite common under the guidance and protection of the monasteries.[29] For example, Oria (referred to as *emparedada*) shut herself away in the male Benedictine monastery of Santo Domingo de Silos[30] and Constanza (referred to as *reclusa/emparedada*) did the same in the hospital of the Holy Trinity, which she had founded herself and delivered to the said monastery.[31]

---

[25] See ibid., p. 447.

[26] Ibid., p. 449.

[27] In his Latin original, Eulogius uses the verb *retrudo* to indicate Columba's withdrawal into the reclusion of a secluded cell away from the other nuns in the monastery. See ibid., p. 449.

[28] G. Cavero Domínguez, 'Eremitismo y emparedamiento', in *Actas del Congreso El monacato en la diócesis de Astorga durante la Edad Media* (Astorga, 1995), pp. 167–92. See also the testament of St Genadius (920) in G. Cavero Domínguez and E. Martín López, *Colección diplomática de la Catedral de Astorga*, vol. 1 (León, 1999), pp. 73–4.

[29] In this respect, it may be interesting to consult Dom L. Gougaud, 'Étude sur la reclusion religieuse', in *Revue Mabillon* XIII (1923), pp. 26–39 and pp. 77–102.

[30] A. Ruffinatto (ed.), *Vida de Santo Domingo de Silos*, in Gonzalo de Berceo, *Obra completa*, ed. B. Dutton, Emilio Alarcos Llorach and Isabel Uria Maqua (Madrid, 1992), pp. 251–453.

[31] J. González, *Reinado y diplomas de Fernando III* (Córdoba, 1983), vol. II, doc. 39. In August 1218, Ferdinand III, the Castilian king, took Constanza and her hospital at Silos under his protection.

In the first quarter of the twelfth century, Queen Urraca of León and Castile (1109–26) and her second husband, King Alfonso of Aragón and Navarra (1104–34), were embroiled in continuous feuding. Martino, a soldier who fought in these quarrels, probably on Urraca's side, abandoned the world in about 1130 to lead a solitary life as *inclusus/reclusus* next to the church of Santervás de Campos in the present province of Valladolid, where he lived for about thirty years.[32]

Cases of reclusion among the Premonstratensians were quite frequent. The virgin Radegundis (1119–52) was born in Villamayor de Treviño, in the present province of Burgos, to noble and illustrious parents.[33] Fleeing matrimony and moved by the Holy Spirit, Radegundis disguised herself as a pilgrim in order to visit the Holy Places in Palestine. She intended to see for herself the setting where Christ had lived and suffered. She also visited Rome, where she obtained many relics. Back from her pilgrimage and wearing the same livery, she asked to enter the Premonstratensian monastery of San Pablo de Sordillos in the province of Burgos, and later that of San Miguel de Treviño, also in Burgos. She had no footwear, lived on bread and water, prayed and cried. She carried out the most humble chores; her eyes were always turned to the ground and she fled from small talk to concentrate only on conversation with God. After some time, she asked the abbess to lock her up in a small chamber [*como quien se empareda*] inside the monastic church, next to the gate. The cell had a small window [*fenestrella*] through which she could see the altar and follow the divine services as well as confess to her spiritual guide. Radegundis's life as a recluse lasted ten years during which time she underwent mortification, severe fasting, long vigils, prayers and tear-shedding. After such a life it was revealed to her how she would die: she lay down on the floor and, after covering her head in ash, she died.

The later Middle Ages

From the mid-twelfth century, changes can be detected in lay people's religiosity and general behaviour which led to several models of the *vita apostolica* [apostolic life]. *Reclusión* [reclusion] and *emparedamiento* [walling up] became widespread and coexisted alongside eremitism, becoming a phenomenon which was more urban than rural, more female than male, becoming also coexistent with other experiences like beguinage and tertiarism, simple eremitism and *beaterios*.[34] In this context it is interesting to note that, within the Cistercian framework,

[32] L. Fernández Martín, 'Colección diplomática de Santervás de Campos', in *Archivos Leoneses* 64 (1978), pp. 183–214. See also R. Escalona, *Historia del Real Monasterio de Sahagún* (Madrid, 1782), p. 523.

[33] Fr. B. de León, 'La vida de santa Radegundis, canóniga premonstratense y fundación del monasterio de canónigas de Villamayor', in *Chronica General del Orden Blanco, que por otro nombre es llamado de Nuestra Señora de Prémonstré, fundado por el glorioso patriarca San Norberto*, Archivo del monasterio de La Vid, signatura 14 bis.

[34] On the more subtle differences between these terms see, for example, G. Pellizia and G. Rocca, *Dizzionario degli Studi di Perfezione* (Rome, 1983).

Aelred of Rielvaux wrote *de Institutione Inclusarum* for his enclosed sister[35] at the time when reclusion had already become lay and feminine, whereas St Bernard showed his preference for the coenobitic life;[36] and here it is also interesting to highlight the Portuguese groups of walled-up women who founded several Cistercian monasteries, Santa Maria de Cós and San Bento de Cástris.[37]

María García (*c*.1344–1426), a noble woman of Toledo, had been destined by her parents to become a nun in a Benedictine cloister. However, she broke away from that decision to devote herself, together with her governess, to the exercise of poverty in her native city and to perform charitable deeds among her fellow citizens.[38] She chose to make charity the axis of her life whilst at the same time seeking to climb down socially and to practise humility through the exercise of mendicancy. Like many other *mulieres sanctae* or *mulieres religiosae* [holy women or religious women], María followed some evangelical ideals and felt capable of awakening the conscience of the urban society of her time by means of her ascetic extra-monastic option. Religious experiences like this, in their extreme forms, led people to the type of *emparedamiento* which was associated with the anchoritic life. Such individuals had a high spiritual reputation and were sometimes criticized because of their strange social behaviour.

An overview of the geographical distribution of this type of reclusion in Spanish cities, as documented during the twelfth to fifteenth centuries,[39] registers a diffusion of such a lifestyle across cities, towns and villages, and we find people walled up in small cells situated next to churches (cathedrals, collegiate churches, parish churches and chapels),[40] as well as in hospitals, in cemeteries and church-yards,[41] and next to bridges and city walls.[42] Astorga, a small cathedral city in the present province of León, still retains a *celda de emparedamiento* [walling-up cell] between the parish church of St Marta and the chapel of the confraternity of

---

[35] See Aelred de Rielvaux, *La vie de recluse, la prière pastorale*, ed. C. Dumont, Sources Chrétiennes 76 (Paris, 1961).

[36] See 'Epistola CXV' in *Obras Completas de San Bernardo* (Madrid, 1990), vol. VII, p. 437; and 'Epistola CDIV', in ibid., vol. VII, p. 404.

[37] See L. M. Rêpas, 'Os mosteiros cistercienses femininos em Portugal: a herança medieval. Fundações e fundadores', in *Fundadores, fundaciones y espacios de vida conventual. Nuevas aportaciones al monacato femenino*, ed. M. I. Viforcos Marinas and M. D. Campos Sánchez-Bordona (León, 2005), pp. 51–78.

[38] Biblioteca de El Escorial, MS C-III.3, fols 252–64. Her life is also recorded by J. de Sigüenza, *Historia de la orden de San Jerónimo*, re-edited by F. J. Campos, 2 vols (Valladolid, 2000), vol. 2, pp. 629–37.

[39] G. Cavero Domínguez, 'Fuentes para el estudio del emparedamiento en la España medieval', *Revue Mabillon* 17 (2006), pp. 105–26.

[40] The cathedral of Cuenca and the collegiate church of Belmonte are two outstanding examples. They are cited in A. López de Atalaya Albadalejo, 'Una reivindicación necesaria: algunas noticias indirectas relativas a emparedadas conquenses', *Cuenca* 35 (1990), pp. 27–34.

[41] There was a *casa de emparedadas* inside the church of San Pedro de Artajona, which people could enter through the churchyard. It was called Magdalen House and is described in J. M. Jimeno Jurío, 'Artajona. Monjas emparedadas', *Cuadernos de Etnología y Etnografía de Navarra* 29 (1997), pp. 67–75.

[42] There was a reclusion cell between the church of St Gil and one of the towers in the wall of the city of Burgos. See 'Castilla y León /1 Burgos, Palencia, Valladolid, Soria, Segovia y Ávila', in *La España Gótica*, ed. J. Sureda Pons (Madrid, 1989), pp. 143–9.

St Esteban.[43] It is very near to the cathedral and on *El Camino de Santiago* [the Way to Santiago], which is still one of the busiest streets in town. The cell is quite small and it has one door and two windows: one of the windows gives on to the street, the other to the church itself. The small window has a solid grille and there is a Latin inscription above it: *Memor esto juditii mei, sic enim erit et tuum. Mihi heri et tibi hodie* [Remember my doom, since it will be yours too. Yesterday was my day, today is yours].[44] This window connected the *emparedada* with the outer world, with her fellow citizens, and she was given material food through it. At the other end of the cell, the other window (now blocked off) connected the recluse with the inner life; it allowed her to follow the church liturgy and therefore provided her access to spiritual food. The cell door is in the inner wall of the chapel of St Stephen and would have been blocked off after the recluse entered.

Generally one walled-up person was allocated to each cell, sometimes assisted by a servant or governess. But on other occasions enclosure was undertaken by small groups of people (between three and six) in a collective way. For example, there were *casas de emparedamiento/emparedadas* [reclusion houses] at Santa María de Rebolleda, in Burgos,[45] and San Juan de la Palma, in Seville.[46] Individual and collective anchorholds were scattered through urban centres and their surroundings. These were cells situated in busy places: the recluses living there operated as spiritual reminders for their fellow citizens.

The success of such reclusion was extraordinary, judging by how it spread in many cities. For example, Pamplona, in the north of Spain and the capital city of the kingdom of Navarra, had as many as 100 *reclusas*.[47] Seville, in southern Spain and in the kingdom of Castile,[48] registered one *emparedada* per parish church – about thirty in all. Reclusion (*reclusion/emparedamiento*) was protected by both the monarchy[49] and the different social sectors alike.[50] Recluses were classified as

[43] G. Cavero Domínguez, 'Emparedamiento en Astorga', *Yermo* XVI, 1–2 (1978), pp. 21–44.

[44] The Latin text is taken from Ecclesiasticus 38:22. The inscription can be dated from the late fifteenth or early sixteenth century. The cell was occupied during the later Middle Ages, as is recorded in the documentation of the Astorgan confraternities. The construction of the chapel of St Esteban was started in 1304.

[45] Archivo General de Simancas, Registro General del Sello, 1490, f. 151, dated 27 May 1489.

[46] See J. M. Miura Andrades, 'Formas de vida religiosa femenina en la Andalucía medieval. Emparedadas y beatas', in *Religiosidad femenina: expectativas y realidades (siglos VIII–XVIII)*, ed. M. M. Graña Cid and A. Muñoz Fernández (Madrid, 1991), pp. 139–64.

[47] Archivo Catedralicio de Pamplona 14 (Catalogue 1218), Testament of Sancho Miguel de Sansoain, dated 25 March, 1335.

[48] Andrades, 'Formas de vida religiosa', p. 144. It refers to the early sixteenth century.

[49] Kings' testaments: Teobaldo II of Navarra, 1270, published as *Colección Diplomática de los Reyes de la Dinastía de Champaña, 2, Teobaldo II (1253–1270)* by R. García Arancón (San Sebastián, 1985), pp. 175–81; tax exemptions: Juan II of Castile and the Catholic Kings, as recorded in M. A. de Orellana, *Tratado histórico-apologético de las mujeres emparedadas* (Valencia, 1887), p. 23.

[50] A. Rucquoi's research on the city of Valladolid in the Middle Ages reveals the interest of Valladolid's inhabitants in *emparedamiento* [reclusion]. After studying bequests relating to the period between 1370 and 1480 the author draws the conclusion that 68.8% of the testaments (77 in total) contain bequests intended for anchorites. Such a high percentage is only outnumbered by the convent of the Holy Trinity and that of the Merced and exceeds that of other significant convents such as St Benedict's as well as the mendicants – the Franciscans and Clares. A. Rucquoi, *Valladolid en la Edad Media. El mundo abreviado*, 2 vols (Valladolid, 1987), vol. II, p. 311.

belonging to the needy – those individuals and organizations entitled to receive the benefit of charity, which included hospitals (especially those for lepers),[51] confraternities, pilgrims, beggars and institutions of religious or municipal character (mendicants, churches, captives).[52]

The person becoming an *emparedada* was locked up in a cell, ostensibly buried alive, to live as (in Catalonian) a *reclosa*, immersed in prayer and meditation, as the example of Elisabet Cifre (detailed below) indicates.[53] I have not discovered any reclusion ceremonials in Spain along the lines of the ones extant in England, but the scant details which do remain suggest that the veil and blessing were granted by an ecclesiastical person when the reclusion was guided by a confessor or a spiritual director, that is, when it remained under church control – whether episcopal or monastic. However, it was also common that enclosure was undertaken in a totally independent way. In this sense, anchoritic enclosure could be a temporary or permanent experience, the latter being the more common. Nor was age of any consequence: we can find evidence for both young and adult women who might be maidens or widows. Social class was not important either: anchoritic women were drawn from the nobility, the bourgeoisie and the lower classes.

The anchoritic lifestyle

This kind of ascesis, deemed to be so special, was intended to combine active and contemplative lifestyles:

a) *Emparedadas* and/or *reclusas* did jobs, even in relationship with people from the outside. These jobs were mainly associated with teaching,[54] textiles[55] and social work – for hospitals and charities, for example.[56] They practised charity as

---

[51] Testament of Leonor de Guzmán, issued in 1441, for which see J. L. Carriazo Rubio, *Los testamentos de la Casa de Arcos (1374–1530)* (Seville, 2003), p. 135.

[52] Testament of María Fernández de Gijón, daughter of a member of the chapter of the Oviedo Cathedral, for which see S. Beltrán Suárez, 'Emparedadas en Oviedo', *Anuario de Estudios Medievales* 15 (1985), pp. 467–71.

[53] See E. Botinas i Montero, J. Cabalerio i Manzanedo and M. À. Duran i Vinyeta (eds), *Les beguines* (Barcelona, 2002), p. 97.

[54] Ibid., p. 54 and p. 156. This activity occurred mainly amongst beguines. In some cities, like Palma de Mallorca, there were teaching centres for the education of the daughters of important families, as in the case of Puig de Pollença. In the first part of the sixteenth century Elisabet Cifre, a beguine, managed the Casa de Crianza in Palma de Mallorca, intended primarily for education.

[55] Andrades, 'Formas de vida religiosa', p. 154. This concerns the testament of Juan de Santa María in 1488.

[56] María de Toledo (*c*.1437), a married woman, widow and Franciscan tertiary, was also a mystic and visionary. She was walled up only for one year and then channelled all her activities into helping the poor at the hospital of the Misericordia in Toledo. See L. de Yanguas, *Breve catálogo de los siervos de Dios, así religiosos como religiosas y de la Tercera Orden que han fallecido con singular opinión y fama de mui virtuosos en la Santa provincia de Castilla de la reglar observancia de Nuestro Seráfico Padre San Francisco desde el año de 1465 asta el de 1687* (Rome, 1684), Archivo de la Curia General de la OFM, MS C/12. See also A. Muñoz Fernández, *Beatas y santas neocastellanas: ambivalencia de la religión, correctoras del poder (ss. XIV–XVII)* (Madrid, 1994).

a manifestation of God's love, and on some occasions they begged, above all as a symbol of humility.

But they were also advisors, counsellors, mystics, visionaries and prophets. In the early thirteenth century, for example, Diego García, Chancellor of Castile and a relation of St Dominic of Guzmán,[57] wrote an ascetic work under the title *Planeta*. This cleric had studied theology in Paris, and while in that city he also took advantage of opportunities to experience other activities such as pilgrimage. On one pilgrimage he paid a visit to a virgin called Gerois. Diego was shocked by the four special gifts she possessed. The first was that she wore a hair shirt made of hedgehog skin. Her second gift – continuous fasting – showed that she could do without eating and drinking. The third gift was particularly amazing for Diego: a lamp outside Gerois's cell turned itself on and off without human control. Moreover, the boundaries between heaven and earth were different in her cell: angels visited Gerois's cell to envelop her with their chants while divine services were held – this was her fourth gift. The first two gifts are, of course, characteristic of the late medieval penitential forms associated with eremitism and reclusion based on activities which had originated in ancient anchoritism and with those who retired to the wilderness, as discussed at the start of this chapter.[58]

Gaining access to the spiritual world, receiving advice or getting to know the future were some of the reasons an individual might visit a recluse, visits which often seem to have been linked to pilgrimages or other journeys. Pedro de Luna, the future antipope Benedict XIII, learned that he would be pope after visiting a holy recluse when he was a student at Montpellier, for example.[59] On occasion,

---

[57] Diego García, *Planeta (Obra ascética del Siglo XIII)*, ed., intro. and notes M. Alonso (Madrid, 1943), pp. 108ff.

[58] Leonor de Urgel was a member of the lineage-house of Urgel. She retired to the wilderness in a place near Poblet, in the province of Tarragona. She built there a hermitage dedicated to St John the Baptist: 'donde, a imitación de aquellos antiguos anacoretas, hizo muy áspera y penitente vida: su vestido era cilicio, y con ser aquella tierra muy fría de natural, siempre anduvo descalza; su comida fue un continuo ayuno y abstinencia: el cilicio ordinario era de asperísimas cerdas, además de tres círculos de hierro que traía, el uno ceñido y los dos a las piernas, y tomaba disciplina con una cadena de hierro llena de punzas de lo mismo.' [where, imitating those ancient anchorites, she led a very hard, penitent life: her dress was cilice, and, though that was a very cold land, she was always barefoot; her food was always continuous fasting and abstinence; her cilice was of very rough bristles; besides she wore three iron circles, one on her waist and the other two on her legs; and she disciplined herself with an iron chain full of spikes also of iron]. The Spanish quotation has been taken from Botinas i Montero et al. (eds), *Les beguines*, p. 51, which refers, in its turn, to D. Monfar y Sors, *Historia de los Condes de Urgel*, ed. J. Eusebio Monfort , 2 vols (Barcelona, 1853), vol. II, pp. 259–60.

[59] As the editors of Martín de Alpartil's biography of Padro de Luna point out: 'Martín de Alpartil inicia su biografía de Benedicto XIII con una anécdota significativa: el futuro vicario de Cristo, en su etapa de estudiante en Montpellier, había conversado en diversas ocasiones con una mujer santa reclusa. En una ocasión Pedro Martínez de Luna iba con el hermano Fernando, prior de los Predicadores de Burgos, y con Pedro Garcés de Cariñena, y los tres se acercaron a hablar con ella. Interrogaron a la reclusa sobre el porvenir de Pedro Martínez de Luna, y la mujer santa dijo que llegaría a ser un altísimo prelado de la Iglesia; al demandarle mayor precisión, vaticinó que ciertamente sería papa.' [Martín de Alpartil commences his biography of Benedict XIII with a significant anecdote: the future Vicar of Christ, at his student stage in Montpellier, had conversed on several occasions with a holy recluse woman. On one occasion, Pedro Martínez de Luna was walking with Friar Fernando, Prior of the Preachers in Burgos, and with Pedro Garcés de Cariñena, and the three of them came up to talk to her. They questioned the woman

recluses learned by means of their visions what had happened to people of their acquaintance, and they frequently enjoyed the company of other saints and holy virgins; they also received premonitions about precise facts or even regarding their own death. As we have seen, the *vitae* of the holy women quite often register some of their visions as a demonstration of and evidence for their holiness. Mystic Elisabet Cifre's prophecies, which originated in visions and divine revelations received whilst in ecstasy, refer to her social milieu – specifically to the prediction of the death of her relations and acquaintances, and also to Palma de Mallorca, her home city. She foretold it would suffer three tribulations: 'guerra, fam e morbo' [war, famine and illness]. She also foresaw other kinds of events, such as Emperor Charles V's expedition to Algiers, which she predicted would end badly.[60]

b) When a person became a recluse he/she took a step into his or her grave, and doing penance had to be one of his/her most cherished activities. Recluses wore hair shirts, flogged themselves, fasted frequently and suffered manifold privations. The objective of all these sacrifices was to expiate faults – theirs and other people's – and seek sanctity by reaching perfection: they believed in the redeeming value of suffering, which would propel them towards everlasting life.[61]

c) Recluses devoted a significant part of their lives to praying and meditation. Their favourite meditation topic was Christ's passion. Prayer was also more valuable if they had the gift of tears.[62]

Walled-up women committed themselves to working on behalf of the people around them. Their seeking of ascetic heights should be able to influence their fellow citizens. As P. L'Hermite-Leclercq has pointed out in the context of French anchoritism, a recluse is a 'fonctionnaire de la prière et de la pénitence' [a functionary of prayer and penance],[63] praying and undertaking penance for both the living and the dead.

In the late Middle Ages the spirit of women leading honest lives and prepared to pray for the community was put to good use again.[64] In 1412, the ordinance of the Navarran council of Olite provided that a recluse [*seror reclusa*] should pray

---

about the future of Pedro Martínez de Luna, and the holy woman answered that he would become a very high prelate in the Church; when asking her to be more precise, she predicted that he would certainly be a pope.] Martín de Alpartil, *Cronica actitatorum temporibus Benedicti Pape XIII*, ed. and trans. A. Sesma and M. M. Agudo (Zaragoza, 1994), p. 3.

[60] See G. Mora, *La vida y revelaciones de sor Helisabet Cifra* (Palma de Mallorca, 1944).

[61] See T. Vinyoles and E. Varela, 'Religiosidad y moral social en la práctica diaria de las mujeres de los últimos siglos medievales', in *Religiosidad femenina*, ed. Graña and Muñoz, pp. 41–60 (p. 52).

[62] See Mora, *Sor Helisabet Cifra*, pp. 120–1.

[63] See P. L'Hermite-Leclercq, 'Le reclus dans la ville au bas Moyen Âge', *Journal des Savants* (juillet–decembre 1988), p. 248.

[64] P. L'Hermite-Leclercq, *L'Église et les femmes dans l'Occident Chrétien des origines à la fin du Moyen Âge* (Turnhout, 1997), especially pp. 377–9, where she mentions the case of 'La recluse, officier municipal préposé à la prière (1517)' [the recluse, a municipal officer predisposed to prayer] in Carmes de Limoges. There are also abundant references in her essay, 'Le reclus dans la ville', p. 245.

continuously to God for the lives and health of both present and future inhabitants of that town and was accordingly maintained by the council. There was, therefore, a type of pact forged between the authorities and the person wishing to become a recluse.[65] In this case, the reclusory was attached to the chapel of St Brígida (Bridget)[66] and the walled-up person (here referred to as *seror*) was seen to be in the service of the community. St Brígida evokes a model widespread amongst female anchorites and beguines all over Europe in the fifteenth century – Bridget of Sweden, whose worship spread widely in Europe, especially in the territories of the Crown of Aragon, as a result of Italian influence.[67] The Olite recluse's job, in the service of the council, was to pray and do penance for the community,[68] and the same was also true of other cases beyond the Pyrenees. Eustaquio Muñoz, a member of the chapter in the cathedral of Cuenca at the beginning of the sixteenth century, considered that the prayers of a recluse allowed God to tolerate people's sins and thus deferred the penalty they deserved. In addition, he believed their prayers sought the good of all, along with the happy state of the monarchy.[69]

Prayers were particularly directed at a specific moment, that is to say the most transcendental moment in the medieval world – the moment of death: it was in the prayers *pro anima* [for the soul] at the last moments of a person's's life and *pro defunctis* [for the dead] that the intercession of *mulieres religiosae* seems to have been most potent. For example, Sister Vicença, a recluse in Barcelona in the fifteenth century, received quite substantial bequests for her role as mediator at the time of death: she recited psalms, conducted prayers and commended the person's soul to God.[70] Indeed, many contemporary bequests express the commission of prayers with the specific requirement that the recluse should pray to God so that he would direct the soul to heaven,[71] as the words of

[65] 'Que debe ser mantenida una seror reclusa que continuamente ruegue a Dios por la vida y salut de todas las gentes que viven et moran a present et en el tiempo advenir en la dita vila, la cual dita seror debe ser mantenida a espensas del dito concello.' [Let there be a recluse 'seror' that continuously prays to God for the life and health of the people who live at present and will live in the future in the said town. This said 'seror' must be maintained at the expense of the said council.] R. Ciervide Martinena, *Registro del Concejo de Olite (1224–1537)* (Pamplona, 1974), p. 251.

[66] J. Goñi Gaztambide, *Historia eclesiástica de Estella,* vol. II: *Las órdenes religiosas (1131–1990)* (Pamplona, 1990), p. 393.

[67] On the Swedish saint, see V. Almazán, *Santa Brígida de Suecia: peregrina, política, mística, escritora* (Santiago de Compostela, 2000).

[68] P. L'Hermite-Leclercq, 'Reclus et recluses dans le sud-ouest de la France', in *La femme dans la vie religieuse du Languedoc (s.XIII–XIV)* (Paris, 1988), p. 288.

[69] Orellana, *Tratado,* p. 23.

[70] 'Aquesta funció de mitjanceres en la mort, que esdevingué amb freqüència una de llurs principals activitats, els donà, com diu J. C. Schmitt, una funció social que, no solament les justificava, sinó que les convertia fins i tot en indispensables.' [This function of mediators at the time of death, which frequently became one of their main activities, granted them, as J. C. Schmeitt says, a social function which not only justified them but made them even indispensable.] Botinas i Montero et al. (eds), *Les beguines,* p. 97.

[71] See, for example, the testament of Juan Martínez, a shopkeeper from Astorga, in 1361. It contains a bequest for the recluses in the city and its surroundings: 'et por esta alimosna que sean tenidas de rogar a Dios por mi alma et de aquellos a que yo soe tenido' [and by means of these alms let them feel obliged to pray to God for my soul and the souls of those for whom I am obliged to pray]. Archivo monástico de Santa Clara de Astorga, scroll II–42, published in G. Cavero Domínguez, *Catálogo del monasterio de Santa Clara* (León, 1992), doc. 95, p. 56.

Alonso de Madrigal, bishop of Avila, testify.[72] At the last moment prayers such as these were imperative for the dying person to enter paradise, even people like a bishop.

Oración de la Emparedada ['Prayer of a Walled-up Woman']

Walling-up thus became an efficient means for requesting spiritual insurance in all sectors of late medieval Spanish society. It was within this context (between orthodoxy and heterodoxy) that the well-known 'Prayer of a Walled-up Woman' [*Oración de la Emparedada*] appeared. Juan Carrasco, the recent editor of the copy found in the Biblioteca de Barcarrota,[73] considers that the prayer was part of a book of hours from Italy. It was passed on to Castile and Portugal, where it became widespread. This prayer was already known as early as the fifteenth century at least. It was so popular that a copy was found among the books of Queen María of Aragón in 1485,[74] and it is also quoted in contemporary literature.[75] This type of religiosity, with repetitive prayers intended for an immediate and specific purpose, was common in the late Middle Ages.[76]

The central theme of this prayer is Christ's passion and it was allegedly transmitted by him to a Roman walled-up woman who had requested from her cell that Christ reveal to her how many wounds he had received. Christ answered her question, telling her that he had received 6,676 wounds in all, adding how powerful the prayer would be.[77] What this anecdote really brings to the fore is how powerful *emparedadas* in Spain were as spiritual mediators at the time. It also accounts for the fact that kings, noblemen and the bourgeoisie considered them to be among those souls which could get closest to God and the Virgin Mary with their prayers. It also reflects the custom among medieval people of quantifying prayers, giving them a specific equivalence, a capacity to erase faults.

García de Enterría argues that these sorts of prayers eventually shifted towards spells ('se deslizan hacia el conjuro'),[78] as a consequence of which this one ended up in the *Index* of forbidden books, having been considered useful for getting rid of illnesses, protection against sudden death and any other kind of similar ills. The benefits and indulgences attributed to it and its miracle-working character gave it

---

[72] See A. López de Atalaya Albadalejo, 'Una reivindicación necesaria', p. 28 n. 3.

[73] See J. M. Carrasco González, (ed.), *La muy devota oración de la emparedada*, Col. La Biblioteca de Barcarrota 2 (Badajoz, 1997), with a preliminary study by M. C. García de Enterría. See also the recent study by A. L-F. Askins, 'Notes on Three Prayers in Late 15th Century Portuguese (the *Oração da Empardeada*, the *Oração de S. Leão, Papa*, and the *Justo Juiz*): Text History and Inquisitorial Interdictions', *Península, Revista de Estudios Ibéricos* 4 (2007), pp. 235–66; and '*La Oração da Empardeada*. Introduzione, trascrizione e note a cura di Arlindo Castanho', *Artifara* 7 (enero-diciembre 2007), pp. 1–13.

[74] Carrasco González, *La muy devota*, p. xi.

[75] Ibid., pp. xiii–xiv, where García de Enterría refers to *El Lazarillo de Tormes*.

[76] For example, the prayers known as 'Plegarias de Santa Brígida', which deal with the topic of Christ's passion. They were supposed to guarantee that those who recited them would get to know the day and time of their death.

[77] See Carrasco González, *La muy devota*, pp. 29–30.

[78] *La Oração da Empardeada*, ed. García de Enterría, pp. xxv–xxvii.

popularity and diffusion, of course – one of the primary reasons why so many people bought it and prayed it and commissioned others to pray it.

Anchoritism and institutional control

As mentioned earlier, penitential reclusion and its derivatives were performed freely and quite often without the control of church authorities. Such recluses were certainly closely affiliated with mendicants and bishops but there was no complete control wielded by the Church, although it did attempt to do so via diocesan synods after detecting some deviations from orthodoxy. The first of the controlling provisions came at the end of the Middle Ages in southern Spain,[79] precisely where some deviations had been detected, as in the case of Mayor de Medina, a very well-known noble woman who entered the Sevillan anchorhold of St Bartolomé when she was already a widow. After some time, she abandoned her *emparedamiento* and married again.[80]

In the late Middle Ages the evolution of female anchoritic enclosure, as well as other seams of female spirituality,[81] was marked by Cisneros's (1436–1517) reformation and Tridentine regulations. Both insisted on the spiritual and, above all, juridical submission of recluses to their Ordinary. This brought about deep change: the Church, which had been somewhat permissive towards these late medieval expressions of reclusion, began to exert far stricter control over them, particularly if they were female. As a result, the Church began to prefer the cloister as the appropriate location for an expression of female spirituality. The diocesan synod held in Valencia in 1566 is a remarkable example of this posture. Its regulations stipulated that no more recluses [*emparedadas*] must be accepted; those existing must be visited by the Ordinary; masses must not be celebrated in their anchorholds except *in articulo mortis* [at the moment of death].[82]

---

[79] 'Hemos sabido que en las iglesias de esta ciudad, como en toda nuestra diócesis, hay muchos emparedamientos en los cuales hasta ahora no se ha guardado el encerramiento debido, lo cual trae mal ejemplo y podría ser causa de daño para las conciencias de algunos emparedados o de otras personas; por ello, queriendo poner remedio, mandamos que, de aquí en adelante, estén encerradas, por manera que ni ellos salgan fuera ni otra persona, varón ni hembra, de cualquier estado o condición que sea, entre dentro sin nuestra licencia.' [We have learned that in the churches of this city, as well as in all our diocese, there are a lot of *emparedamientos* in which there has not been due retirement, which is a bad example and might be harmful to the conscience of some walled-up people and any others. Therefore, to remedy this situation, we command that from now they must be walled up, so that they cannot come out nor any other person, man or woman, whatever their condition might be, enter there without our permission.] See J. Sánchez Herrero, 'La iglesia andaluza en la Baja Edad Media, siglos XIII al XV', in *Actas del I Coloquio de Historia de Andalucía. Andalucía Medieval* (Córdoba, 1982), p. 321. The same thing seems to have happened in other countries, like Italy, where, for example, in 1303, Francesco, bishop of Gubbio, issued synodal provisions to regulate the situation of the *incarcerate* in his diocese. A. Benvenuti Papi, '*Velut in sepulcro*: cellane e recluse nella Tradizione agiografica italiana', in *Culto dei santi, istituzioni e clasi sociali in età preindustriale*, ed. S. Boesch Gajano and M. L. Sebastiani (L'Aquila-Rome, 1984), pp. 365–456 (pp. 370–1 and p. 435 n. 25).

[80] See Andrades, 'Formas de vida', p. 149.

[81] In this respect, see the comments by C. Segura Graíño, 'La religiosidad de las mujeres en el medievo castellano', in *Santes, Monges I Fetilleres. Espiritualitat femenina medieval, Revista d'Història Medieval* 2 (1991), pp. 51–62 (p. 61).

[82] See Orellana, *Tratado*, p. 25.

Evangelical simplicity, the meditation on Christ's suffering, the exercise of charitable works put into practice by recluses as a means of reaching sanctity now had to fall under the full control of the corresponding bishops in order to prevent all kinds of deviations. Let us remember how the walled-up woman's prayer ended up in the *Index* of forbidden texts. Certainly, instances of 'false' mysticism and the Inquisition[83] show how frequent deviations became in the sixteenth century, to the extent that walling up was once more used as a punishment. For example, Magdalena de la Cruz, a nun from the nunnery of St Isabel in Córdoba, was convicted of being friends with the Devil and sentenced by the Holy Office to 'emparedamiento y cárcel perpetua en público y notorio auto' [to be walled up and jailed for life in a public judicial decree].[84]

The term 'reclusion' (synonymous with the Spanish *emparedamiento*), underwent a shift in its meaning during the course of the Middle Ages, as Hermite-Leclercq also points out elsewhere in this volume.[85] Originally referring to voluntary anchoritic enclosure, it eventually left the religious field to become associated again with punishment, part of the legal and juridical lexicon, as it had been prior to what we refer to as the Middle Ages, when, as discussed previously, the Church channelled and reformulated penitential reclusion into the institutional monastic framework.

Spanish anchoritism: two lives

I will conclude this essay by examining in some detail the lives of two of Spain's most prominent female anchorites, one a monastic recluse, the other lay and urban.

The monastic recluse: Oria

Oria can be said to be representative of the recluse who sought the metaphorical desert as this desire was expressed in female Iberian anchoritism, functioning as it did under the guidance of male monasticism and fluctuating between the coenobitic and the lay worlds in the central centuries of the Middle Ages.

Oria's life was recorded by a clergyman named Gonzalo de Berceo. Berceo wrote poetry, and his source of information as far as Oria is concerned was a *vita*, now lost, written by a monk called Munio, who was Oria's spiritual guide. Munio wrote his *vita* in the monastery of San Millán in the eleventh century.[86] Berceo,

---

[83] See M. Palacios Alcalde, 'Las beatas ante la Inquisición', *Hispania Sacra* 40 (1988), pp. 107–31; and M. L. Giordano, 'Entre violencia i persuasió. El control inquisitorial de la riligiositat femenina a l'Espanya del segle XVI', in *Dones i Monaquisme. Vida religiosa femenina a l'Etat Mitjana*, *L'Avenç, Història, cultura, pensament* 255 (febrer 2001), pp. 66–73.

[84] J. Imirizaldu, *Monjas y beatas embaucadoras* (Madrid, 1977), p. 34. The author records the 'Carta de Luis de Zapata en que se Menciona a Magdalena de la Cruz'.

[85] P. L'Hermite-Leclercq, 'La reclusion volontaire au Moyen Âge: une institution religieuse spécialement féminine', in *La condición de la mujer en la Edad Media*, Coloquio Hispano-Francés (Madrid, 1986), pp. 135–54 (pp. 144–5).

[86] This Oria is a different person from the one mentioned in the first part of this essay (p. 95). The place where this present Oria became a recluse was a Benedictine monastery called San Millán de la Cogolla, situated in the province of La Rioja, which was first in the kingdom of Navarra and then in the kingdom of Castile. This monastery was made up of two compounds: Suso (upper) and Yuso (lower). It is in the former that Oria was walled up.

the clergyman-poet, wrote his *Poema de Santa Oria* in the thirteenth century[87] at the time when walling-up was already popular among Iberian urban recluses, nearly always as an ascetic life free from monastic and regular restrictions. However, since the original *vita* by Munio is lost, there is no way of knowing how much there is of literary creation and of hagiographical transmission in Berceo's work. But, even allowing for that, the reading of his poem can adequately convey the Iberian atmosphere of monastic reclusion in the eleventh to thirteenth centuries.

Oria was born in Villavelayo to good Christian parents, García and Amuña. The *vita* follows a very common hagiographic pattern, which insists that the subject always sought good against evil, both in private life and in social behaviour. García's and Amuña's relationship with God had become closer when, on asking him for a child, he had granted them a daughter, whom they would dedicate to the divine service. Whilst she was still a child, Oria's conduct was impeccable and she stood out amongst her peers for her humility, which fostered an early reclusive desire – so early, in fact, that, as the poem highlights periphrastically,[88] she must have been of the age when she was changing her teeth, that is, about nine years old, between childhood and adolescence.[89]

Oria entered the monastery of San Millán, wore black and was walled up in a small cell. Berceo tells us how she was ready to do penance, fasting and wearing a hair shirt in order to deserve God's reward. She mortified her flesh to keep away the Devil's temptations. She practised the virtues of charity, patience and humility. Fame of her lifestyle spread and invoked the admiration of the people living in the surrounding areas. This, however, did not turn her into someone vain or incite her to waste time in small talk. On the contrary, she spent her time praying and reciting the psalms, and in particular she went on with her life of mortification. Her reclusion was extremely strict: she did not have much contact with the outer world through the window of her cell and her prayers moved God to turn her into a visionary.

The main features of Oria's life are to be found in the introductory part of the *Poem*. This introduction functions like a preamble to contextualize the issues dealt with in the poem itself. Berceo was interested in a precise aspect of Oria's life – that is to say her visions. This aspect also strongly attracted the attention of Berceo's contemporaries; indeed the other essays included in this volume all attest to the many other female anchorites, lay sisters and beguines from the thirteenth century onwards who lived surrounded by their visions. And it was clerics who tended to register these visions, or else, in the case of Julian of Norwich in England, the visionary herself seems to have written her own experiences.

During the time that she was walled up, Oria experienced three visions, which started at the age of twenty-five, when she had been a recluse for many years and

---

[87] *Poema de Santa Oria*, ed. Uría Maqua, in Gonzalo de Berceo, *Obra completa*, ed. Dutton et al., vol. I. pp. 491–551.

[88] Ibid., p. 502, comments to verse 19.

[89] A. Muñoz Fernández, 'Oria de Villavelayo, la reclusión femenina y el movimiento religioso femenino castellano (siglos XII–XVI)', *Arenal. Revista de historia de las mujeres* 5-1 (1988), pp. 47–67.

was 'full of holiness' [*plena de sanctidat*]. Usually they occurred when the vision-ary was sleeping or ill. About her three visions Oria remembers the time, the day (together with its patron saint) and the month. The first vision is extensively nar-rated and transports Oria to the other world; the second, brief and premonitory, shows the Virgin Mary visiting her in her cell; the third, short and interrupted, transports the recluse to Mount Olivet. The poet registers the dates of the three visions and toys with the festivals upon or near which the visions took place and also with the number three: the first vision occurred three days after Christmas; the second, on the third night before the feast of St Saturnine; the third is not dis-tanced in time from the second since it heralds Oria's illness and death. Her visions are always associated with sleep, tiredness, illness or somnolence. It is dif-ficult to draw a line between sleep and a vision.

As stated, Oria's first vision occurs on 27 December, the feast of St Eugenia, a martyr who died in Rome in 258. Oria was following her *passio* in the liturgy after matins. During the vision, Christ sends three young female martyrs,[90] who had consecrated their souls to God from their childhood, to guide the recluse. These are St Agatha of Catania, St Cecilia and St Eulalia of Mérida. The three martyrs come down to Oria's cell in the form of doves and talk to her as if she were a partner of theirs, saving the distance between this and the other world.

The recluse enters paradise after climbing up a long ladder – Jacob's ladder – which leads her to the top of the Tree of Life. On this heavenly route Oria travels back to the past rather than into the future and, as she is asking questions of her guides, she is interested in finding out what has happened to people with whom she has been acquainted. She is shown the throne God has prepared for her, a lav-ishly ornamented throne which is described in detail. When she sees her seat vacant, she refuses to leave heaven, as it would be like a 'return from gold to slag' [*del oro tornar a la scoria*]. But Christ replies to her that she must finish her time of being walled up, her hard life on earth and her catharsis. Oria is promised heav-en and the menace of hell is kept away. She must, however, be returned to her cell to finish her experience as a recluse. Her three guides climb down the ladder to lay her soul back in her body, and this is the end of their mission.

Back in her cell, the recluse tries very hard to lead an ascetic life with fasting, mortification and prayers. About eleven months later she has her second vision, on 27 November, the feast day of the martyred St Saturnine of Toulouse; and fre-quently using this type of precision, the poet registers a second feast, that of St Andrew, on 30 November. Now Oria is visited by another three virgins whose names are not revealed but who are equal in quality, goodness, age and aspect. She is sleeping on the floor when the three virgins announce to her that she is going to be visited by St Mary, which is why she is laid on a rich bed. The Virgin Mary promises her that she will leave human poverty to gain heavenly riches after her death. For the time being, the reward she receives from the Virgin is her embrace.

---

[90] For an analysis of the virgins who appear in Berceo's work, it may be useful to consult J. A. Ruiz Domínguez, 'Pecadoras y santas en el mundo de Gonzalo de Berceo', in *Las Mujeres en el Cristianismo Medieval*, ed. A. Muñoz Fernández (Madrid, 1987), pp. 54–8.

The recluse talks to her and asks her for a signal that she is really St Mary and not a dream or a product of her imagination – doubt is part of the behaviour shown by medieval visionaries. The signal given to her by the Virgin is premonitory of Oria's illness and death, which will take place very shortly. At this point her second vision ends abruptly – there is no goodbye from the Virgin's retinue as there is within other visions in the poem, the scene being incomplete because of the loss of one of the manuscript's folios.[91] On waking up, Oria comes back to 'real' life.

Oria's third vision arrives among dreams and suffering and it is unclear when exactly it occured.[92] Because she is described as being very ill, she is surrounded by many people praying, among them her mother and Munio, her confessor, and also the whole monastic community of San Millán. Before the many people present there praying on earth, heaven opens its doors to receive Oria, who is transported to Mount Olivet. As she is delirious, she utters confusing things which the people fail to understand. Therefore Amuña urges Munio to go into Oria's cell and shake her body to make sure whether she is dead or alive, which he does. Oria awakes and reproaches them for interrupting her vision but when Munio begins to ask her about the content of her vision, she recovers her spirits and narrates how she had been carried to Mount Olivet, a good place, with many trees and flowers, where people wearing elegant clothes had received her singing *lauds*. When her confessor asks her if she would like to recover her vision, Oria answers affirmatively, upon which point she dies.

Hers was an announced death, which occurred on the feast day of St Leander. Her mother was at her side, as were Abbot Peter and the whole community of San Millán de Suso. It was a ritualistic death which happened at a peaceful moment: we are, for example, told how she put her hands up in the air and crossed herself on her chest before dying. The abbot and the monks then took her body to bury it near the church in a place similar to her anchoritic cell – a cave. Her body, dressed in the habit of the order, was accompanied by monks and hermits praying the psalms. Her remains were laid on a hard flagstone, like the hard, cold floor of the cell on which she had usually slept.

After the death of her daughter, Amuña decided to lock herself up too, seeking sanctification through mortification and the hard ascesis of reclusion. God rewarded her in her cell with visions in which she was in contact with her daughter, whom she could embrace and ask questions. We are told that Oria's answers were comforting and encouraging.

The Urban Recluse: Brígida Terrera

My second example of Iberian female anchoritism is Brígida Terrera, an urban anchorite who was born into a bourgeois family consisting of gentleman Francisco

---

[91] Uría indicates that the missing folio CIX may have stated 'the Virgin's goodbye and Oria's awakening, which the other visions in the poem share'. It would explain why the poem passes from her vision directly to her illness. *Poema de Santa Oria*, ed. Maqua, p. 532.

[92] 'The loss of folio CIX also affects the third vision, in which the heading indicating its month, date and time when it occurs is missing. Besides, there is a lack of transition between the second and third visions.' Ibid., p. 534.

Terré, her father, and Ángela, her mother; there were also two brothers, Bernardo and Jaime.[93] Her birth occurred in Barcelona (in the Crown of Aragón at the time) at the end of the fourteenth century or the beginning of the fifteenth, and her name evokes that of St Bridget of Sweden, who was well known in fifteenth-century Catalonia.

In about 1418 Brígida decided to become a recluse in the service of God. Her decision seems to have originated in an enclosed house for women called Santa Margarita, which existed from the mid fourteenth century in Barcelona next to a hospital for lepers. The recluses living there were called 'Margaridoyes', a name derived from Margarita, the hospital's patron saint. It was this community which Brígida entered to lead a life not as a nun, but adhering instead to the late medieval strain of lay spirituality associated with poverty and the love of God. According to her own choice, she carried out her reclusion aided by a servant. She followed the way indicated by her predecessors in the *resclusatge*. Its founder, whose name is unknown, was a maiden from Barcelona who, inspired by the Holy Spirit, had used her inheritance more than a hundred years previously to found an anchorhold where she could live as a recluse. Brígida confessed that another recluse called Sancha had also exerted a deep influence on her. Before becoming a recluse at Santa Margarita, Sancha had been a companion of St Bridget of Sweden, an association which had lent her a special attractiveness for the monarchy and her contemporary Catalonian society.

Having such antecedents and models, Brígida chose to lead a combination of a contemplative and active life: she would retire from the world to devote herself to the service of God but also to be in the service of society, mainly of the sick. It is hardly surprising then that it was lepers who comprised the main focus of her attentions. Lepers and recluses were two groups who shared some similarities. A leper had to keep to his leprosarium and was isolated from the society where he had once carried out his activities.[94] Likewise, the recluse was confined to her cell, having abandoned the outside world; at the same time, however, she remained part of it, went on being intrinsic to the life of the city.

In 1426 Brígida received from a public notary her share of her parents' inheritance, not a dowry – which is why she could dispose of a sum of 4,000 *sueldos* and an annual pension of 36 *libras*. This inheritance was used by Brígida to sustain her reclusory, which had initially been individual but now became collective. She tells us that she had been thirty years in her anchorhold, as 'an unworthy and useless servant of Jesus Christ' [*indigna e inutil servidora de Jhesu Xrist*] when she requested from the 'Council of the Hundred' of Barcelona to be protected and allowed to receive alms and bequests. In this way, Brígida establishes that she and her companions did not have any juridical dependence on the Church.

The extant sources suggest that the recluses of Santa Margarita devoted them-

---

[93] The sources are diverse and frequently indirect. Some of them, however, can be consulted in Botinas et al. (eds), *Les beguines*. Both the Old and New Testaments contain some of these ideas regarding the exclusion of lepers from society. See particularly pp. 151–69.

[94] Both the Old and New Testaments contain some of these ideas regarding the exclusion of lepers from society. See Leviticus 13:45–6 and Luke 8:1–4, for example.

selves to the care of lepers and, sometimes, to teaching poor girls. But certainly what they got from these activities, together with Brígida's inheritance, seems not to have been enough to maintain their reclusory. Brígida's inheritance, though, was essential, particularly after her mother, already a widow, became a member of the community and its administrator. Brígida died in about 1471 after a long life. Her body was buried in the chapel of the hospital itself. After her demise, the members of Santa Margarita ended up in several monastic orders as a means of regularizing their existence.

Conclusion

These two examples of Iberian female reclusion taken from the later period offer an insight into how the phenomenon developed from its earliest stages to its demise. In late Roman times, *fuga mundi* – that is, leaving the world in search of retirement and solitude – was already an ascetic practice very attractive to the Christian aristocracy. It was a kind of experience which, in its most radical form, led to temporary reclusion, whether penitential or punitive.

During Germanic times, particularly during the Visigothic kingdom, the existence of a special 'indigenous' type of monasticism which alternated coenobitic with eremitic practices was relatively common in Iberia alongside feminine urban reclusion, to which Leander of Seville was not sympathetic. Both penitential and punitive reclusion may have been associated with coenobitic and eremitic lives: Valerius of El Bierzo was successively a monk and a hermit. As a solitary, he confined himself to a type of isolated hut, which he built himself in the style of the solitaries whom Grimlaïcus later regulated. These formulae continued to be practised among the Christians who lived under Muslim rule, sometimes endorsed with the sign of martyrdom: the type of monasticism described by Eulogius of Córdoba, for example, includes some cases of isolation and reclusion – as in the cases of Columba and Servus Dei.

This late Roman and Visigothic ascetic reality was projected into the Middle Ages, together with problems derived from the various terms for spaces of reclusion (caves, *ergastula*, cells) and formulae of reclusion (*inclusi, reclusi*) which seem to have echoed different realities but were connected in some way. They were all experiences that evolved both within monastic enclosure and outside it.

There was an intense 'benedictinization' (with a full symbiosis between coenobitism and eremitism) in the Iberian milieu as monasticism was regularized and the Christian space advanced at the expense of Muslim rule. This atmosphere provided a base for the development of reclusion, both voluntary and penitential, masculine and feminine – but especially monastic – between the tenth and twelfth centuries, as in the cases of Oria and Radegundis.

The big change started with the awakening of the urban world, the new formulae of spirituality and the changes in mentality – but particularly with the arrival of the Mendicants. The rapid and broad development of the new Roman language, Castilian, brought along a variety of vernacular terms. *Emparedamiento* [walling-up] was the new term for reclusion or enclosure. The Latin expression *inclusa intra parietes* ceded now to *emparedada* [walled-up woman] and the same was also the case for men: *emparedado* [walled-up man].

Reclusion now became especially urban. It was practised in cells situated in the busiest streets, at city gates, on or next to bridges, next to and within city walls, abutting churches, graveyards and hospitals. There were individual and communal anchorholds which enjoyed the protection of kings and queens, nobles, councils, private citizens, and churchmen and lay people alike. There were *emparedadas* who worked, advised people, prayed for the community and were mystics and visionaries. Some of them were honest women who did not accept the cloisters though sometimes they ended up within them. There were *emparedadas* who lived independently of the ecclesiastical hierarchy and others who lived protected by it. As for the *emparedamientos*, some had personal objectives (the search for salvation, personal purification) and others had social aims – the benefit of a social group, the council, the town itself and its citizens. Their popularity is shown in the *Oración de la Emparedada*, mentioned above, which was widespread in the late Middle Ages and ended up in the list of the banned books in the *Index*. Finally, due to the deviations and the lack of control over these people, which had deepened from the end of the fifteenth century, the post-Tridentine Church attempted to control reclusion and returned to the concept of reclusion as punishment.

5 Anchoritism in medieval France[*]

P. L'Hermite-Leclercq

Jesus said: 'And he that taketh not up his cross, and followeth me, is not worthy of me. He that findeth his life, shall lose it: and he that shall lose his life for me, shall find it' (Matthew 10:38–9). During his lifetime he attracted disciples who gave up everything for him. But how might this precept be followed after the Resurrection? There were various responses: martyrs embraced death with courage, goading the executioner, while the Egyptian and Syrian Fathers went into the desert, like St Antony, and soon formed the first monastic communities. Hermits and monks vowed to become 'dead to the world', whose prince is the Devil (John 12:31). Crucified with Christ, they were freed of all ties from before their baptism which, in the words of St Paul, had made new men of them (Ephesians 4:24). Some chose to live alone, whilst others forged between them spiritual bonds which had nothing to do with the ordinary ties of blood, family connections and life within society. The 'true family' of the Gospels (Mark 3:31–5) is in fact completely different, for it demands 'self-renunciation' in pursuit of what is beyond – that is, eternal life. It is in fact a premature death in exchange for Life, and the same rationale applies to the anchoritic life. Is that life worthier than the hermit life, or less so? This may be a matter of debate among theoreticians of the religious life but, for some at least, the state of solitary enclosure is the most glorious of all: 'The epithet "recluse" surpasses all other religious epithets'[1] – and the danger of losing oneself and of scandalizing one's fellows is evidently balanced by these sublime ambitions. The rediscovery of Aristotle's works provided a further argument that 'Man alone is either an animal or God'.[2] Paphnutius imprisoned the prostitute Thaïs in solitary confinement, sealing the door, so that she might expiate her life of sin and earn grace in the eyes of the

[*] Translator's note: the French terms *reclus*, *réclusion*, *se reclure*, *reclusoir* do not all have exact or comfortable equivalents in English and have had to be translated in various ways according to the context.

[1] 'Super omnia religiosorum nomina magnum est nomen reclusi', ed. Livarius Oliger, in 'Regula reclusorum angliae et Quaestiones res de vita solitaria. Saec. XIII–XIVe' ('Walter's Rule'), *Antonianum* 9 (1934), pp. 37–84 (p. 71).

[2] See, for example, Denys le Chartreux [Denys the Carthusian], 'De vita inclusarum', in *Opera omnia*, vol. 38 (Tournai, 1909), p. 394.

Saviour.[3] With these points in mind, we can embark on our task in this essay. First we need to grasp the difference between the various types of religious *status* which have endured down the centuries in the search for salvation. Next, and most importantly, we need to understand what relationships may develop between an elite capable of such renunciation and the rest, the ordinary flock of the *Ecclesia* who continue to perpetuate society in the normal way. Whether those whom the English-language tradition calls *anchorites*[4] (the type of recluse focused on by Hughes-Edwards elsewhere in this volume), or those known on the Continent by the various terms *reclusus, inclusus, muratus, incarceratus, Klausner, empierré, emparerada* amongst others (as enumerated by Mulder-Bakker, Signori, Sensi and Cavero), or whether they had previously been priests, monks or nuns, or laypeople, their change of state sets them apart. In the region now called France, at least, they must not be confused with priests, with regular or secular canons, with coenobites or even the old-style hermits and anchorites who lived out their vocation in the countryside.[5] Anchorites, whether male or female, are now defined by their choice of a life separate from their fellows, that separation made concrete not by spatial distance but by walls which mark their solemn and definitive enclosure at the heart of a community. Ironically, by this choice, anchorites challenge the often-evoked precept in Ecclesiastes 4:10, 'woe to him that is alone, for when he falleth, he hath none to lift him up.' In this essay, therefore, it will be useful to begin with a few remarks on methodology, then to trace the evolution of the phenomenon, before finally going beyond the narrow religious perspective to consider anthropological and sociological aspects of the subject.

The kind of solitary confinement which concerns us here is a freely chosen type of religious life, as opposed to its present-day connotations: today it belongs to the judicial system, forming part of a scale of penalties, the severity of the sentence being underlined by the fact that life-imprisonment has replaced the death

---

[3] *PL* 73, col. 661. The *Vitae Patrum* transmitted to Western Europe a tradition which was undoubtedly the blueprint for the anchoritic life in the Middle Ages. This is attested by the *vita* of Abraham of Quiduna in Syria, who is said to have converted Edessa to Christianity (*PL* 73, cols 283–92, cols 651–60). He rejected the world and marriage and hid himself away in a cell. When his friends and relatives found him, he persuaded them to let him stay there and he then enacted the founding gesture: 'They went away and he closed up the entrance to the cell; shutting himself up inside, he left only a tiny aperture to serve as a window, through which on an appointed day he received his food.' Abraham had a niece, Marie, whose father died when she was seven years old. Abraham ordered her to be enclosed in an adjoining cell, connected to his by means of a narrow opening. He taught her the Psalms and educated her. They lived together in a state of abstinence and moral perfection for twenty years. But a monk who regularly visited the anchorhold fell in love with her and one day she opened her window, came out and joined him. He 'polluted' her and she lived a life of debauchery for several years. Abraham persuaded her to come back to him and expiate her sins through penitence in the anchorhold to which she returned. Her story was copied repeatedly, especially in manuscripts produced from the eleventh century onwards.

[4] As Liz Herbert McAvoy points out in her introduction to this volume, the etymology of the term 'anchorite' is Greek and denotes a retreating movement: the anchorite parts company by moving away, but the medieval interpretation gave it a new, spiritual dimension. It compared *chor* with *cor, cordis*: thus 'anchorite' was related to *Sursum corda*, 'Lift up your hearts!' Other interpretations were *chorus, -i*, the heavenly choir, or *ancora, -ae*, the anchor which prevents the ship from drifting. On all this see my article 'La réclusion féminine au Moyen Âge: une institution religieuse spécialement féminine', in *La condición de la mujer en la Edad Media* (Madrid, 1986), pp. 135–54 (p. 149).

[5] On this see, for example, Abbé Sainsaulieu, *Les ermites français* (Paris, 1974).

penalty in some countries. Since this kind of vocation responds to aspirations fostered by Christian values, it is inconceivable, therefore, that it should not be embodied in the framework of the Church. We must therefore trace how this institution first appeared and spread, how it was brought under clerical control, how it evolved until it gradually disappeared in the modern period. It will not be enough to conclude, for example, that the phenomenon has 'served out its term' or that it disappeared under pressure of Reform imposed by authority, or even that the new values stemming from the Renaissance or from the gradual process of de-Christianisation are responsible for the drying up of vocations and for converting anchorholds into vestries or schools. We must take care to avoid *a priori* reductionism, for solitary enclosure as the expression of religious feeling is not a simple or ahistorical phenomenon. For this study I shall draw on every kind of available source from within the field of religious belief and beyond, everything that can shed light on the political background, in both the broad and narrow senses of the word, for the anchorite has a particular place in the *polis* and is embedded within a set of religious as well as economic, social and cultural circumstances.[6] Nor must we fall into the trap of relying on only the most prestigious documents, whether intended for edifying the reader (as in the case of hagiography) or prescriptive (such as conciliary legislation, statutes of synods, rules for anchorites, letters of direction, or *exempla*). In France there is a great variety of extant sources which allow us to distinguish the heroic or the exemplary from the everyday practice of the enclosed life. They include chronicles, obituaries, cartularies, notarial registers recording bequests to anchorites,[7] even specifications for building anchorholds. In addition, there are anchorites' wills, royal charters and accounts, records of proceedings and parish accounts, not to mention the contributions of archaeology,[8] place-name studies,[9] iconographical and literary sources.[10] Sources are far more plentiful in the later Middle Ages, but does chance alone account for their survival? Apparently not: we must first assess fully the main changes which occurred at the turn of the second millennium. A chronological approach should allow us to tease out the constants and variants down the centuries.

In France[11] the 'matter of Egypt' is attested very early. It was this material

---

[6] For example, when Charles V had a female anchorite from La Rochelle brought to Paris and installed there, it was certainly because he approved of this way of life, but also undoubtedly because he expected that this would bring symbolic benefit to his capital city (see p. 120 below).

[7] In 1199, for example, the countess of Montferrand, wife of the count of Clermont in the Auvergne, made a bequest to two female anchorites at Clermont, to three at Brioude, to one each at Montrognon, Champeix, Auzat and Saint-Germain, and to two at Orival and at Saint-Fliaz. On these locations, see my article, 'Le reclus dans la ville au bas Moyen-Âge', *Journal des Savants* (July–Dec. 1988), pp. 219–62.

[8] See P. L'Hermite-Leclercq, 'La réclusion volontaire au Moyen Âge: aspects topographiques et archéologiques', *Publications du CAHMER* 1 (1988), pp. 92–100. Epitaphs, often engraved on lead tablets found during archaeological excavations, are a particularly valuable source.

[9] Many place-names recall the existence of an anchorite or recluse: rue de la recluse, pont du reclus, localities called Le Reclus, La Reclusière and so on. See further my article referred to above, n. 7.

[10] See n. 34 below.

[11] Here defined as France within its present-day borders.

which first claimed hermits, including female ones like Mary of Egypt[12] and recluses like John of Lycopolis (who one day entered a cave and blocked the entrance with a rock)[13] as founders of both the first groupings of anchorite cells and of the first monasteries, for men and for women. The lives of the Desert Fathers had always fostered a nostalgic view of these largely mythical origins. John Cassian, for example, had lived in Egypt before founding the monasteries of Saint-Victor at Marseilles in *c.*415. The vitality of this tradition is also reflected in the work of Gregory of Tours, the great chronicler of the Merovingian period, who mentions several anchorites, male rather than female,[14] notably the figure of young Anatole, enclosed at twelve years of age, *famulus* [servant] of a merchant who tried but failed to dissuade him.[15] He lived in a vaulted crypt at the corner of which was a cell, enclosed by stone walls and so tiny that a man could scarcely stand up in it. There he stayed for eight years, eating and drinking very little, before going mad. He had to be carried to the tomb of St Martin at Tours in hope of a miracle. In most cases Gregory tells us nothing of the precise circumstances of the enclosing of an anchorite. He sometimes mentions the individual's previous *status*,[16] but he makes no reference to a bishop or even a priest going in for enclosure. Many of the individuals mentioned are saints such as Monegund,[17] Cybard of Angoulême, Leobard of Marmoutier,[18] or Hospitius who had himself enclosed

---

[12] This saint's name is conserved in corrupt form in the former parish church of La Jussienne in Paris which, with its anchorite, maintained the anchoritic tradition. On this see P. L'Hermite-Leclercq, 'Les reclus Parisiens au bas Moyen Âge', in *Villes et sociétés urbaines au Moyen Âge* (Paris, 1994), pp. 223–31.

[13] For this and other similar examples, see J.-M. Besse, *Les Moines d'Orient Antérieurs au Concile de Chalcédoine* (Paris–Poitiers, 1900), pp. 36–43. This action inevitably recalls the image of Christ's tomb, a wish to flee the secular world and to be crucified with him.

[14] Nevertheless, there were female anchorites, as witnessed by the *vita* of Bruno, archbishop of Cologne (d. 965), who, after a religious service, had several female hermits shut away, either singly or in twos [*alibi singulos, alii binos inclusit*] in anchorholds of monastic or other churches. On this see Ruotgerus, *Vita Brunonis*, *PL* 154, col. 964.

[15] *PL* 71, *Hist. Franc.*, cols 473–4.

[16] For example, ibid., p. 396. Radegund enclosed, at her own request, a nun from her monastery at Poitiers. She led the virgin there by the hand, in a torch-lit procession, to the singing of psalms. The nun embraced each sister then was shut in [*obstructo editu per quem ingressa fuerat*].

[17] Born at Chartres, she had married and had two daughters who died, leaving her inconsolable. She became an anchorite with her husband's assent. The cell which she had prepared had one tiny window [*fenestellula*] and a little garden adjoining the side-wall of St Martin's basilica at Tours. Although she had a serving maid, she made her own bread of barley flour mixed with wet ashes. She performed many miracles. Her anchorhold attracted young girls whom the saint supervised, and this soon led to the foundation of the abbey of Saint-Pierre-le-Puellier (see Hermite-Ledercq, 'Les reclus Parisiens', op. cit, n. 12, above). The anchorhold evolved into a monastery in response to strong demand, which allowed the Church to control it more easily. This often occurred; see, for example, *AASS*, Julii, vol. 2, pp. 309–16.

[18] *PL* 71, *Vitae patrum*, cols 1092–5. He was under the supervision of Gregory of Tours, who states that he was of humble birth but had been to school. Being convinced of the absolute vanity of the world, after the death of his parents, who would have wished him to perpetuate the family line, he finally became an anchorite near the monastery of Marmoutier. He enlarged his cell by cutting away the rock with a pick-axe and spent his life in fasting, prayer, reading and meditating on the Scripture. The bishop spoke to him about the *Vitae Patrum*, Cassian's *Institutiones* and the discipline which anchorites should observe. He prayed for all and performed many miracles by prescribing his own saliva. A servant took care of his needs. Gregory was glad to note that he cut his hair and beard regularly. An oratory was dedicated to him and his name was invoked to cure fevers.

in a tower at Villefranche near Nice, in a hair-shirt, iron fetters and heavy chains. He foretold the arrival of the Lombard invaders, who, on entering the town, gained access to the anchorite through the roof. In his humility he told them he was a dangerous criminal.[19] The anchorites' motives are rarely given, but we may suppose that love of God and consciousness of being an unworthy sinner were sufficient.[20] Apart from Gregory's chronicle, if we cast our net further, to cover hagiographic sources in particular, we gain the impression that many kinds and conditions of people might become anchorites, people of either sex, of any age, social status or level of education. They could be bishops, abbots, archdeacons,[21] nuns, or lay virgins fleeing imminent marriage.[22] Their activities as anchorites were equally varied. Most lived a life of prayer and mortification. Some remained at the service of others. Hardouin (d. 811),[23] a priest who was enclosed near the oratory of St Saturninus at Saint-Wandrille, copied manuscripts for the monastery and taught the young to write and do arithmetic. At the end of the tenth century Humbert, an anchorite at Verdun, gave instruction to two nuns through the window.[24]

This type of narrative gives prominence to the sacrificial aspect of anchoritism as a life-choice. Ermelinde (d. 595), following St Paul's exhortation (Romans 12:1), offered herself as a living sacrifice, *hostia viva*.[25] There are cases, however, where enclosure seems to have been neither definitive nor stable. Thus Humbert, the anchorite of Verdun, moved cell, whilst Junian (d. 587) lived as an anchorite before becoming abbot of Mairé in Poitou.[26] These sources point to a number of facts. Solitary enclosure was not unusual, and individuals, whose cases are very varied, sought to emulate the prestigious examples of the desert anchorites, with their fierce love of solitude and penitence and with God as their only partner; in the end this revival of the earlier model provided the peoples of Gaul with a class of saintly ascetics who, in parallel with other kinds such as bishop-saints or founders of religious houses, undoubtedly helped to spread Christianity in a world still itself very closed off. But more than that, perhaps, it brought communities together around local patrons, holy men who contributed to the sacralisation of towns. Taken as a whole, conversions to the anchoritic life certainly preceded and went beyond all attempts by the Church to channel and regulate it. Here we may, in fact, identify a particular and constant characteristic of this form of religious life. Because anchorites, like hermits, are solitary, they cannot

---

[19] *AASS*, Maii, vol. 5, pp. 41–2.

[20] For example, a woman asked to become an anchorite in order to expiate the crime of having calumniated St Radegund (*PL* 71, cols 519–20).

[21] For example, Einold of Toul, in the tenth century, for which see *MGH, Script.*, IV, p. 345.

[22] For example, Hiltrude, from the ranks of the aristocracy, fled from her prospective husband and took refuge with the bishop of Cambrai from whom she took the veil. Her parents agreed to her adopting the religious life, and she had a cell built near the chapel of the monastery of Liessies in Hainaut, which her parents had founded in 751 and where her brother was the abbot (*AASS*, Sept. vol. 7, pp. 488–506).

[23] *MGH, Script.*, II, p. 292.

[24] Ibid., IV, p. 343.

[25] *AASS*, Oct., vol. 12, pp. 842–72. Ermelinde was of noble birth, and pledged her virginity when she was very young; it was also said of her, '*holocaustum proprium corpus offerens*' [offering her own body [as] burnt offering].

[26] J. Mabillon, *Acta Sanctorum Ordinis Sancti Benedicti* (Paris, 1672), saec. I, pp. 307–19.

be seen as an institution except in a purely abstract sense, forming an aggregate of unique cases. It is far easier to impose rules on monastic groups than on a collection of individuals passionately in love with God, some of them antisocial, a loose cannon of the faith, and scattered geographically. This can be confirmed by looking at the demands set out by the Church in the course of councils held during this period and by looking at Grimlaïcus's rule for anchorites, the only one we have from the early Middle Ages.[27] This second type of source will enable us to make a crucial point in terms of methodology, namely that individual initiative precedes rule-making and, above all, that there is a substantial gap between a practice which is anarchical in the strict sense and the Church's attempts to unpick this practice and then to impose its own theoretical framework upon it.

It is not possible here to list all the prescriptions laid down by all the councils of the first millennium, but it so happens that there are several early examples from Gaul. Their message is very different from that of the chronicles. Three church councils, held at Vannes in 463, at Agde in 506 and at Orleans in 511,[28] passed and set down the following rules on anchoritism:

1. They relate only to men.[29]
2. Only monks who have already proved themselves in their community may become anchorites.
3. The abbot's authorisation is required.
4. The place of enclosure must be within the curtilage of the monastery and the anchorite subject to his abbot.

Note how cautious were the bishops, who would regularly maintain that solitude is dangerous. This type of life is out of the question for non-monks and for women – even those in religious orders – and candidates must first harden themselves alongside their brothers in religion. The profession of monasticism being a preliminary requirement, the anchorite remains constrained by the vow of obedience, and the power to make decisions remains with his spiritual father. We should also note that these canon laws were confirmed by Act 12 of the great Carolingian council held at Frankfurt in 794[30] and incorporated much later in Gratian's *Decretum* of *c*.1140. The hierarchy of merit between the anchorite and the monk can be put down to the prestige of the Rule of St Benedict which defined the roles of the anchoritic life and of enclosure more generally. The coenobitic life was aimed at beginners; later, after preparative training in the monastery, some elite

---

[27] Grimlaïcus's text, written specifically for the male recluse, is also examined briefly by Signori in her essay in this present volume.

[28] For details see Giovanni Domenico Mansi, *Sacrorum conciliorum amplissima collectio* (Florence and Venice, 1758–98), vol. 7, col. 954, c.7 ; vol. 8, col. 331, c. 38 ; and vol. 8, col. 355, c. 22, respectively.

[29] These synods never mention nuns.

[30] *MGH, Leges*, I (Capitularia Regum Francorum), p. 75, canon 12: 'Ut reclusi non fiant nisi quos ante episcopus provinciae atque abbas comprobaverint, et secundum eorum dispositionem in reclusionis loco ingrediantur' [Let recluses not be made unless the provincial bishop and the abbot have approved them, and after their arrangement let them enter into the place of reclusion].

monks might consider solitude.[31] The anchoritic life was thus a pinnacle of excellence. The Rule of St Benedict was imposed on all monasteries in the Carolingian empire. The reasoning advanced by the monk Grimlaïcus, probably in the climate of religious reorganization at the beginning of the ninth century, responds to the same preoccupations but is far more precise.[32] And it is all the more important for its long-lasting influence.

The argument can be summed up as follows. The anchorite should be a monk who has undergone training in the 'army of brothers' (col. 579) before becoming a desert trooper. He must not distance himself too far from his brothers. It is the bishop who encloses him by sealing his door but he is not removed from his community, which remains responsible for him materially and spiritually (col. 594). He is not to be enclosed alone but with one or two other monks in communicating cells so that he must still exercise patience and love. He is not vowed purely to contemplation. It is indeed God whom he seeks [*Deo vacant*, col. 611] but a *vita otiose* [life of leisure] even if *spiritualis* [spiritual] is out of the question: the anchorite retains his responsibilities to others. He must be useful, serving in word and deed by preaching 'to bishops, to priests or else to the solitary' (col. 601), and by pointing out the errors of Jews and heretics (col. 609). This retreat [*retrusio*] into what Grimlaïcus describes as a prison [*carcer*] is accompanied by ascetic practices. However, the *afflictio carnis* [torment of the flesh] is not an end in itself but a means of freeing the soul by subduing the senses: the anchorite's vocation should not cause him to turn in on himself but lead him to greater charity. There are known examples of anchorites who adhere to these 'norms' such as Sigebert, a monk of Saint-Denis.[33]

So far in this history, however, we have not come across many women, but then St Benedict did not write a rule for the 'other sex' and it is certainly thanks to his influence that neither Grimlaïcus's rule nor ecclesiastical law applies to female religious. So what was it that changed in the second millennium?

From the tenth and eleventh centuries onwards, the plethora of sources of information on anchorites in France cannot be explained solely by chance survival, or by the spread of writing. If we come across so much evidence for anchorites, this must surely be due to major changes of all kinds – political, social, economic, religious and cultural – coming into play. The West was no longer

---

[31] A minimum age of thirty years is often suggested, for which see Edmond Martène, *Commentarius in regulam S. P. Benedicti* (Paris, 1690), pp. 44–5 and p. 60, citing among others Jerome and Isidore of Seville.

[32] This long rule was published in *PL* 103, cols 575–644. The numbers in brackets, included here in my main text, refer to columns of the *PL*.

[33] See Dom Michel Félibien, *Histoire de l'abbaye de Saint-Denys en France* (Paris, 1706), p. 38: 'C'était un moine du nombre de ceux qui, poussés du désir d'une plus haute perfection, se faisaient quelquefois, avec la permission de leur abbé, sans sortir du lieu de leur engagement, comme une seconde solitude plus étroite que la première, où ils vivaient séparés de leurs frères.' [He was one of those monks who, driven by a desire for the highest perfection, sometimes, with their abbot's permission, and without leaving the place to which they had committed themselves, embraced a second solitude, more restricting than the first, where they lived apart from their brothers.] Faced with the Lombard threat, Gregory III had persuaded Charles Martel to send some trusted men to Italy to report on the situation: Sigebert was one of the appointees, along with the abbot of Corbie.

under siege – the Normans and Hungarians had become Christian and settled, albeit as conquering powers. The structure of feudal societies, the development of agriculture and commerce and the expansion of towns were coupled with potent changes in religious feeling, the questioning of old-style monasticism – the so-called 'crisis of coenobitism' – and the search for new models of life closer to the *vita apostolica* [apostolic life] which became part of the general context of ecclesiastical reform. It also gave rise both to an increasing number of new religious orders and to the flowering of a new form of eremitic life of which solitary enclosure was one variety. Unfortunately, even if we can establish the existence of anchorites in a particular area, all too often we have no information about their numbers, sex, age, previous status (whether cleric, monk, or layperson), marital and social status (whether orphan or virgin, repudiated wife[34] or widow(er), rich or poor), exactly where they lived[35] or the institution which provided their material and spiritual support. Let us start with some hypothetical situations which it will be useful to keep in mind if we are to understand the practical reality of anchoritism as an institution:

1. An anchorite, who enjoys economic independence, establishes her/his place of enclosure.
2. A specific individual, or an institution or body, owns a suitable place or has one built, recruits a tenant and makes a commitment to support her/him.

Let us consider each of these cases. The anchorite may have the means to set her/himself up and support her/himself. This presupposes a combination of many factors: ownership of a piece of land, no matter how tiny the dwelling may be, the ability to pay its construction costs, no matter how basic it may be, and furnish it, having enough assets to ensure lifelong subsistence and to pay a servant to deliver the essentials regularly: such as food, if public charity is not enough, clothes, water for washing, and firewood, but also to remove excrement etc. Even more importantly, because it is a matter of a religious *propositum* [purpose] first and foremost, arrangements must made be to ensure spiritual assistance. Ideally, the anchorite will be a priest, and thus virtually self-sufficient with regard to the sacraments, though he will need to have a consecrated altar. He will also need a priest himself to receive the sacraments of penitence or extreme unction. Gone are the

---

[34] Here special mention might be made of the wives of priests after the ecumenical synods of 1123 and 1139 following the Gregorian reform, which forbade marriage to those in orders from subdeacon upwards and forced married priests, on pain of loss of benefice, to expel their wives and children from the diocese. It is interesting here to observe the literary response to such situations. A romance written in Walloon-Picard dialect c. 1250, *Le roi Flore et la belle Jeanne* (published in Monmerqué and F. Michel, *Le Théâtre français au Moyen Âge* [Paris, 1839]) relates how king Flore loved his first wife deeply; she possessed all the virtues but sadly was barren. The barons persuaded him to repudiate her (pp. 423–4). Flore intended to send her back to her parents, but what was the abandoned wife's reaction? She went to see a hermit, her confessor, who advised resignation. She then suggested that she become an anchorite beside him and under his direction, but he persuaded her to enter a monastery. Yet by this period, marriage had nonetheless become indissoluble, at least in principle. My thanks to F. Lesaint for bringing this document to my attention.

[35] A significant percentage of anchorites, both male and female, left to become enclosed elsewhere, often a very long way away, as mentioned below.

days when it was acceptable for hermits in the desert to live with no liturgical framework or, like St Benedict, not know the date of Easter for that year. A lay person of either sex would of course be subject to far greater limitations. A very high proportion of anchorholds were attached to churches,[36] in which case some form of direct communication would be needed so that the anchorite could take part in the services, have access to a confessor who could hear confession, converse and pass communion. If, as many sources attest, the anchorite's cell was in a secular location – such as a perimeter wall or a town gateway, a bridge, street, crossroads, leper-house or hospital[37] – a small annexe to the tiny dwelling would have to be provided, with an altar where a priest could come to say mass and give the sacraments to the anchorite.

Let us now consider the second hypothesis, where the impulse to build the anchorhold comes not from the candidate for enclosure but from another individual or from a civil or religious body. This is what Charles V undertook for two female anchorites.[38] He had some land set aside at La Grange-Saint-Eloi to accommodate Marguerite, a pious girl who was at that time an anchorite at Saint-Paul. The reason for her move is not known. An even more interesting case is the conversion of a 'fine oratory built of wood' at Saint-Merry to accommodate Guillemette. She was an anchorite at La Rochelle, the fame of whose piety had even reached Paris. Even if we cannot identify exactly when and where a place of enclosure was established, it is often possible to tell by whose authority it was set up, who owned it and who was the patron of the benefice. In Lyons, where there were eleven anchorholds, each under the direct authority of the Church, seven were owned by the four great chapters of the town, three by two abbeys and one by a church.[39] Here the anchorite held an ecclesiastical benefice no different from any other: he was appointed and inducted by the religious institution under whose jurisdiction he came. The situation in most southern French towns was quite different. In both Nîmes and Limoges the anchorhold belonged to the town, which had had it built and maintained it, invited applicants when there was a vacancy and made its own enquiries about their morality, leaving only a very limited role for the religious authorities in the induction. We find that the consuls* regularly looked after the tenants, their clothes, their linctus when they had a cough and the

---

[36] Where the anchorite's cell adjoined a church, it seems to have been most frequently situated at the northern end and/or in the cemetery, at the chevet and opened onto the choir via a tiny opening through which the altar could be seen. But there is evidence of other anchorholds as part of the church porch, a part of the architecture which often disappeared after the Middle Ages, or in one of the towers, as at Saint-Omer, or even in the basement, in a crypt close to the relics. On this see L'Hermite-Leclercq, 'La réclusion volontaire', op.cit.

[37] To our list could be added the case of large, central graveyards such as the Cimetière des Innocents at Paris, where the dead from most of the parish churches of Paris were buried, since the latter lacked the space. On the anchorhold at the Innocents', home to many generations of anchorites, see L'Hermite-Leclercq, 'Les reclus Parisiens au bas Moyen Âge', op. cit.

[38] For more details and bibliographical references, see L'Hermite-Leclercq, 'Le reclus dans la ville au bas Moyen-Âge', op. cit.

[39] Ibid., p. 240; a map of the anchorholds in Lyons can be found on p. 259.

* Translator's note: *consul* was a title applied to municipal magistrates or officials in southern French towns.

shroud when they died.[40] We should also bear in mind that, as in the first millennium, some anchorholds eventually became separate monasteries. The Cistercian abbey, appropriately called Le Reclus, in the diocese of Troyes was founded in 1142 on the site of a chapel near which the anchorite Hugues de Broyes had settled.[41]

But who became an anchorite? Did the Church, while insisting on keeping to the theory that only experienced monks might embrace this mode of life, not know what went on in practice? This can no longer be maintained, for several reasons. Firstly, demand was very strong, and came from all walks of life. Secondly, the papacy, from the launch of its great reform movement in the eleventh century, wanted to impose order on the whole of Christian society, lay as well as clerical, at every level in the hierarchy. These demands forced anchoritism to adapt, and the consequences of this are clear. Anchoritism as an institution becomes both more structured and more diverse; it becomes a feature of the geography of the later Middle Ages and far easier to 'read' than the eremitic life. Anchorites are found in towns and villages, and the vast majority of them are lay or female. These three characteristics – urban, lay and increasingly female – are attested everywhere and are easily explained, especially as regards feminization. It is true that the Church's distrust of the solitary life never abates entirely, especially with regard to women, perpetually 'the weaker sex'.[42] This can be observed within the monastic world. In the Carthusian Order, founded in 1084 with a semi-eremitical rule, each monk was accommodated in a single cell where he ate, slept, prayed and worked alone, and communal life was strictly limited. But when, bit by bit, the order came to accept a female wing, it asserted that women were not strong enough to cope with solitary confinement and so a dormitory and refectory were provided for them.[43] The pressure for enclosure was so great that the tide could not be held back.

It is impossible to establish firm numbers. As we have seen, all too often the documentary sources mention the existence of anchorites but without giving details. Where details are given, there are considerable variations. The choice of this way of life may stem from a variety of motives. Of course some would have religious reasons: a burning desire to vow oneself to God, to preserve one's virginity or to avoid a second marriage in order to prepare for death in a state of chastity, prayer and asceticism,[44] or even a conviction that becoming an anchorite

[40] See the examples cited in my article, 'Reclus et recluses dans le sud-ouest de la France', in *La Femme dans la vie religieuse du Languedoc (XIII–XIVe s.)*, *Cahiers de Fanjeaux* 23 (1988), pp. 281–98.

[41] See A. Longnon, *Obituaires de la Province de Sens*, vol. IV, *Diocèses de Meaux et Troyes* (Paris, 1923), p. 334.

[42] Two dangers connected with the *fragilitas sexus* [fragile sex] must be identified. Women hermits who lived out in the countryside were more vulnerable to the elements, wild animals and to male prowlers: this was often stressed. But in the clerical way of thinking the main risk which women ran was an inner one, linked to their weakness in the face of temptation – as the rule of Aelred of Rievaulx, discussed by Hughes-Edwards elsewhere in this volume, attests.

[43] Similarly the statutes of the Beguines state that they should never remain alone, on which see P. L'Hermite-Leclercq, *Le monachisme féminin dans la société de son temps* (Paris, 1989), p. 292.

[44] Saint Adjuteur (d. 1131), son of a lord from Vermont who had gone on crusade to Palestine with 200 men, was captured by the Saracens. On his return he first became a monk at the abbey of Tiron in the diocese of Chartres but later became an anchorite near Vernon. His cult is attested in the dioceses of Rouen, Évreux and Chartres. See Abbé Pavy, *Les recluseries* (Lyon, 1875), p. 142.

was the only way to expiate a grave sin and to have hope of forgiveness,[45] or in order to repay a debt for a saint's protection.[46]

Thus we find both sexes, all age groups and social classes amongst the many anchorites,[47] and from now on markedly more women than men. Another feature which often emerges when the anchorite's geographic origins are known, is that many moved from elsewhere. The reasons for this are often unclear. Hugues, archbishop of Lyons, took the trouble to write to the bishop of Arras to inform him of the death of Emma, *apud nobis reclusa* [a recluse near us], and to ask him to remember her in his prayers for she 'was a daughter of your Church, as she very often reminded me'.[48] In other cases, self-imposed exile is motivated by a classic desire for penitence in the centuries-old tradition of the Irish missionaries (and touched upon by Anna McHugh in her essay in this volume).[49] An unpublished example, that of the female anchorite of the church of Saint-Père at Melun, is typical.[50] She is said to have lived in Chartres and to have had extensive social connections. Once she was widowed and freed from the conjugal yoke, she became an anchorite not far away near the monastery of Saint-Chéron where she lived for seven years practising contrition and mortifying the flesh. One day, however, an angel warned her that she was still too much a prisoner of the world and no-one fighting in God's service in such circumstances could be saved. The angel ordered her to leave her shelter and become an anchorite at Melun, on the Seine upstream from Paris. She

[45] A nun seduced by a knight had a vision of him in hell: she became an anchorite as a penance, as recounted in Caesarius of Heisterbach, *Libri VIII miraculorum*, ed. A. Meister (Rome, 1901), lib.1, p. 44. One of the most enigmatic cases is that of St Druon (*AASS*, Aprilis, vol. 2, pp. 443–5). Born in Artois, he was a shepherd near Valenciennes, an obsessive pilgrim (he went to Rome nine times), and an anchorite for forty-five years, dying in 1186. What emerges most clearly from his late, rhapsodic *vita*, containing very few dates, is that he was overcome by remorse for having caused his mother's death at his birth and for being the posthumous son of his father. Here sexuality and death are linked in a paradigmatic way. In the end this unstable, anti-social *pauper*, imprisoned in his distress, became an anchorite, shut up next to the church of Sebourg, near Valenciennes in Hainaut.

[46] Such was the case of the cowherd Pierre of whom the *Legenda Aurea* [*Golden Legend*] of Jacobus de Voragine relates that he had dared to plough on the Feast of St Mary Magdalene and was immediately punished: his oxen were struck by lightning and he himself so badly burned that his leg became detached from his body. He dragged himself as far as the church and supplicated the Virgin Mary. Once healed, he became an anchorite. For the French translation see Jacobus de Voragine, *Légende dorée*, ed. and trans. J.-B. M. Roze, vol. 2 (Paris, 1967), pp. 85–6.

[47] In the eleventh century, for example, Leo, abbot of Fondi and bishop of Gaeta, ended his days in the abbey of Aurillac in a cellar *sub crypta quadam* [under a certain crypt], for which see Jean Mabillon, 'Breve chronicon Auriliacensis abbatiae', *Vetera Analecta* (new edn, Paris, 1723), p. 350.

[48] Stephan Baluze, *Miscellanea*, ed. J. Mansi, vol. 2 (Lucca, 1761), epistle 21, p. 140.

[49] In the seventh century, for example, St Didier, the bishop of Cahors, was a friend of St Arnan who came originally from Ireland or Scotland [*ex genere Scotorum*] and had been enclosed below the level of the basilica; he was buried in this vault [*in ipso specu*]. St Didier would send him food which he in turn gave to the poor (*MGH, Script.*, VI, p. 589). Only brief mention can be made here of the well-known case of Eve (d. *c*.1125), the nun of Wilton who went off to become an anchorite near a monk of Vendôme at Angers. The *Liber Confortatorius* which was dedicated to her by the monk Goscelin de Saint-Bertin will be discussed elsewhere.

[50] This story is found in the *Récit des miracles* of St Liesne (MS BN 12690, fol. 224r–v), one of the two patrons of Melun, written by a monk of the Benedictine abbey of Saint-Père de Melun in 1136. The female anchorite was dead by the time of writing. The narrative in which she figures can be dated to *c*.1100. I am preparing an edition of and commentary on this compilation which was thought to have been lost.

obeyed. The cell [*teguriolum*], which she had built at her own expense, was undoubtedly very basic and no doubt conformed to the usual model. It opened onto the church, for she could hear cries coming up from the crypt, where miracles took place near the tomb of the saint to whom the church was dedicated.

But there were plenty of other reasons for becoming an anchorite, first and foremost of which involved economic and/or social factors. A letter survives to the consuls of Saint-Flour in the Auvergne from a woman of Le Puy who, having heard that their anchorhold was vacant, begged the town magistrate to let her occupy it. She argued that her mother had already lived there, she herself was a widow and had no means of support.[51] It should not be forgotten, either, that many women with a religious vocation were fleeing marriage, or were orphans or widows, or had been abandoned and were unable to enter a monastery because a dowry was more or less essential and, in any case, there were never enough places.[52] The ecclesiastical authorities were thus forced to reconsider the question of this type of religious life and manage it as best they might. In any case it was out of the question that they should maintain the fiction that it was an elitist way of life open only to experienced male monks. Hence two types of definitive documents were drawn up: rules for anchorites and rituals for their enclosure when that was done by bishops.

No rule (or 'guide', as they tend to be referred to within the English tradition) for anchorites has survived from France.[53] I will not, therefore, resort to those from other countries dating from the twelfth to fifteenth centuries, since these are dealt with by other contributors within this volume. I will, however, examine whether they corroborate conclusions drawn from attested practice. Be it Aelred of Rievaulx's *De Institutione Inclusarum,* or the anonymous *Ancrene Wisse* (both of which are examined by Hughes-Edwards in her own essay included here), or other surviving guidance texts from England,[54] or the last of the great treatises of this kind, *De Vita Inclusarum* by Denys the Carthusian (d. 1471),[55] all are aimed at women who are not nuns in regular orders.[56] They had, therefore, to be suitable for applicants from all levels of society who were often uneducated. How many of them knew about these guidance texts? It is impossible to judge, but the great majority of anchorites probably followed a few pieces of advice given by the priest, monk or other cleric who took them under his wing. Conciliary legislation

---

[51] I have given the text of her supplication on p. 252 of my article, 'Le reclus dans la ville au bas Moyen-Âge', op. cit.

[52] Although there were many new foundations during the eleventh and twelfth centuries in both France and England, there were not enough of them and a *numerus clausus* is often mentioned: L'Hermite-Leclercq, *Le monachisme féminin*, p. 247.

[53] Many letters of direction to individual female anchorites survive but they are obviously not of comparable interest.

[54] A good many of these were published by Livarius Oliger, including that referred to in n. 1 and others published in *Antonianum* 3 (1938), pp. 151–90, pp. 299–322; *Antonianum* 9 (1934), pp. 27–84, pp. 243–368; and *Lateranum, nov. ser.* (1938), pp. 9–12.

[55] See n. 2 above.

[56] The nuns who became anchorites, whether they were Benedictines or belonged to one of the new orders (monastic or canonical like the Cistercian or Carthusian nuns, and so on), continued to follow the rule and customs of their monastery and were still subject to their community.

from after 1000 AD often recalls that only the bishop can take the necessary steps for the enclosure of an anchorite. Rituals preserved in old pontificals categorise these as a specific *ordo*. In France, that of the church of Soissons survives.[57] The *Ordo ad reclusum faciendum* [Order for undertaking reclusion] took place before the anchorite, male or female, who remained prostrate on the ground throughout the ceremony. It began with litanies and penitential psalms, following which the bishop or abbot,[58] dressed in alb and stole, said the mass for the dead,[59] before the postulant was led in procession to the anchorhold. The bishop went in alone to bless the cell and after many prayers and blessings, he led the anchorite in and went out again.[60] The most interesting point here is that the tone of this ceremony is unique, quite different from the blessing of hermits, for it borrows from the funeral rite and is also related to the late medieval ceremony for the exclusion of lepers – who were likewise dead to the world.[61] Two points must be made here. This rite was never incorporated into the Roman pontifical. Thus the highest authority of the Church, the bishop of Rome, seems never to have taken part in this symbolic putting to death. Nowadays the greatest authorities[62] on the long history of the Catholic liturgy evidently find it hard to accept the rationale of all those bishops in the past who asked the angels to carry this living-dead person to heaven forthwith. Contemporary liturgists have, of course, given consideration to the theological questions raised by such a ritual. For the anchorite is not, in fact, dead.

---

[57] On this, see Edmund Martène, *De antiquis ritibus Ecclesiae*, vol. 2 (Antwerp, 1773), p. 178, and A. E. Poquet, *Rituale seu mandatum insignis Ecclesiae Suessionensis* (Paris, 1856), pp. 261–4. The bishop was Nevelon de Chérisy, who was consecrated in 1176, not Nevelon II (d. 1262) as Martène thought. Two other unpublished rituals will be examined elsewhere.

[58] In the traditional instance of the monk, it was not a requirement that the bishop should officiate.

[59] 'Expleta letania, tanquam pro mortuo celebretur missa, eo semper jacente prostrate'. [Having completed the litany, as if celebrating the Mass for the Dead, he remains lying prostrate].

[60] Here it is not expected that the anchorite should receive Extreme Unction in advance, nor that his grave should be dug in the cell, nor that the bishop, before leaving, should pronounce absolution over the anchorite who is to live there. Nonetheless, the practice of anchorites digging their own graves did exist. Matthew Rader in his well-known *Ordo inclusorum* published in *Bavaria sancta* (München, 1704), 3, 118, provided for this. See also Oliger, 'Regula reclusorum', ch. 15: 'Qu'il prépare sa propre tombe ... Qu'elle soit toujours ouverte afin que nuit et jour il puisse voir vers où il s'avance ...' [Let him prepare his own grave ... It should be left open so that day and night he may see where he will be going]. One of the thirteenth-century English guides, *Ancrene Wisse*, records the same practice at the end of Part 2: 'ha schulden schrapien euche dei þe eorðe up of hare put þet ha schulen rotien in' [she should scrape up each day the earth out of her grave in which she shall rot]. *Ancrene Wisse: A Corrected Version of the Text in Cambridge Corpus Christi College, MS 402 with Variants from other Manuscripts*, ed. Bella Millett, EETS 325, 2 vols (Oxford, 2005), vol. 1, p. 46.

[61] On this aspect see L'Hermite-Leclercq, 'La réclusion féminine au Moyen Âge', op. cit.

[62] See M. Righetti, *Storia liturgica*, 4 vols (2nd edn, Milan, 1966), vol. 4, p. 484. It is significant that the author only refers to this liturgy in an unexpected place: in the chapter on the consecration of virgins. He states (my translation and my emphasis): 'Bien *heureusement* notre pontifical n'a pas admis certains rituels *étranges* du bas Moyen Âge qui mettaient au second plan l'aspect de la consécration et faisaient prévaloir un autre aspect, celui de la *mort mystique* de la professe, *enterrée vivante*, avec cercueil, drap mortuaire et sonnerie du glas' [*Happily* our pontifical has not included certain *strange* late medieval rituals which put the consecration aspect in second place and gave prominence to another aspect, the *mystical death* of the professed nun, who is buried alive, with coffin, pall and tolling of the passing-bell'] and he adds in a note: 'ce *macabre* rituel fut imité des rituels des XIIe–XIIIe siècles consacrés aux *reclus, enterrés vivants*' [this *macabre* ritual was imitated by those rituals of the twelfth and thirteenth centuries devoted to *anchorites, who were buried alive*].

The die is not cast. To push the metaphor 'dead to the world' further – to the extent of making it visible and legible by acting it out – has no real sense because the anchorite exists, as we have seen, in a state between two deaths, which could last for decades.

It is now time to consider how this type of enclosed life might have been viewed by contemporaries. In this I shall confine myself to a few remarks. First, what do we know about those concerned? Even where there is the most evidence, we do not know if they lived out a colourless half-life in a state of melancholy or in the promised mystical exaltation.[63] But, in many cases it seems clear that this mode of existence gave anchorites dignity and authority, as well as a sense of usefulness. There is every reason to suppose that they were usually fully integrated into the urban community. There are very many indications that they were invested with responsibility for public penitence and prayer – that is to say, they were invested with a formal role. Sacrificing their freedom seems to imply sanctity, which would attract offerings and bequests. In wills, anchorites are often mentioned in conjunction with lepers and hospital patients. In return they take on a symbolic responsibility for security and for material and spiritual prosperity,[64] such as helping individuals to whom they administer advice, comfort and reproof. They attract God's blessing: even taking into account the usual hagiographic hyperbole, it is probably no exaggeration to say that, as an anchorite, St Hildeburge (d. *c.*1115) had a satisfying end to her life and was widely venerated.[65]

Descended from a noble family in Île-de-France, Hildeburge was married in her teens to a husband who was certainly far older than she, and bore him three sons. Her husband, already elderly and unwell, became a monk and died. Hildeburge's sons stressed – or made a pretext of – the difficulty of remaining chaste for a woman who was still young, and decided to marry her against her will to a local knight in order to avoid any scandal. The wedding was prepared but Providence, which sometimes deigns to help women to remove themselves from sexual commerce and the laws of nature, intervened. The saint fell from a ladder leading to the tower and broke her pelvis. Nothing more was said about marriage and henceforth she had freedom of choice. She managed to have herself accepted by the monks of Saint-Martin at Pontoise and had a cell built on the north side of the church. Thereafter she devoted her life to the service of the community, in prayer and strict penitence to subdue the flesh. The abbot provided her with an anchorite's habit. She gave the monastery the wealth at her disposal and put pressure on her sons to be equally generous. Humble and obedient, she became a maternal figure to the monks and looked after their clothes. They buried her in the church, a monk wrote her *vita* and her name was added to the list of saints.

Canon law had ruled that the choice of the anchoritic life was irreversible, but that did not mean it could not be left if God so willed it. In those circumstances only the Pope could relieve the anchorite's vow. St Colette (d. 1447) had lived for

---

[63] Some documents, which cannot be discussed here, tell of serious crises of doubt or suicide attempts.

[64] See my article, 'La reclus dans la ville', pp. 248–50.

[65] Mabillon, *Acta S. O. S. B.*, saec. VI, pp. 832–35.

a time in several monasteries before spending four years as an anchorite at Corbie in Picardy. She then heard Christ's call, commanding her to go and reform the Poor Clares, and Benedict XIII gave her his blessing.[66] This instance confirms that, in some special cases, anchorites formed spiritual networks extending from one town, or even region, to another, even without direct contact between them. Thus, a female anchorite from Avignon told the Franciscan Henri de la Baume that he should do something for a female mystic at Corbie – this was Colette – and Henri went off to Picardy instead of setting sail for the Holy Land. From then on he stayed with the saintly reformer. This *vita* and others like it suggest that certain anchorites were already pure in spirit,[67] could read others' hearts, prophesied and worked miracles.[68]

It is now time to assess the strength and unique nature of the individual and collective mind-set from which anchoritism as a religious life-choice derives, and pinpoint what distinguishes it from eremitism. The anchorhold fits perfectly into what E. Konigson calls 'une scénographie à la fois mythique et sociale de la ville médiévale' [both a mythic and a social scenography of the medieval town].[69] Let us start with the elaboration of the dyad anchorite/anchorhold, a living being inconceivable without its shell. In the symbolism of this *status* everything revolves dizzyingly around paired antonyms: inside/outside, dead/alive, enclosed/free, narrow/infinite, earth/heaven, putrefaction/glorious resurrection. The contrast with the hermit could not be greater. The hermit withdraws from and breaks with the world; he returns to nature, wanders in the *saltus* [forest] and becomes invisible. He distances himself in the 'horizontal' plane, and his project is self-centred. He takes his epithet from a geographical formation, *eremos* – the wilderness; it is not the specific spot where he sleeps, eats or prays which gives him his title, but unpopulated, empty, harsh space. He embodies the *salutem in fuga* [salvation in flight]. Moreover, the *ordo* which solemnises his vocation is not a collective one. The community is not involved, and he is not accompanied by a procession. The bishop does no more than he would for pilgrims, which is to bless the *private* attributes such as scrip and bell. The anchorite – the French term *reclus* is a past participle used substantivally – is defined by the step that s/he has decided to take: s/he has been immured but by men and among people. Furthermore, the ceremony of enclosure is collective, solemnizing a contract between the two parties, just as with prisoners today (but with the important difference that prisoners are not imprisoned voluntarily and their primary concern is about being released). The

---

[66] On this, see my article 'Les reclus du Moyen Âge et l'information', in *Zeitgeschehen und seine Darstellung im Mittelalter*, ed. Ch. Cormeau (Bonn, 1995), pp. 200–20 (p. 213).

[67] See, for example, the female anchorite who neither ate nor drank for years and 'from whose natural organs nothing came out': Jacques de Vitry, *Historia Occidentalis*, ed. J. F. Hinnebush (Freiburg, 1972), pp. 87–8.

[68] The female anchorites of Angers and Trélazé acted as proxy miracle-workers for St Girard (d. 1123), monk and founder, who himself became an anchorite near the monastic church of Saint-Aubin at Angers, where, in irons, he embraced a true *martyrium* [martyrdom]. The female anchorites took scraps of fruit which he left and they performed cures by applying them to the affected parts of the sick who came to them for help: *AASS*, Nov., vol. 2, pp. 491–509.

[69] Elie Konigson, *L'espace théâtral médiéval* (Paris, 1975), p. 107.

anchorite has chosen the *salus domi* [salvation of the cell] for the salvation of self and the urban community which takes her/him into its bosom. Thus the anchorite has become part of an advanced economy with a third sector, the service sector. The town feeds and looks after the anchorite, who, quite literally incorporated in the minuscule dwelling, transmutes material services into spiritual ones. Of course the anchorhold is first and foremost a material reality, just as prison is for the prisoner, and in this respect we might say that it becomes part of a transitive discourse: an anchorhold is built, people walk past it, and the anchorite lives in it. But, at the same time, it evidently becomes the vehicle of a myth, primarily because its inhabitant can no longer leave it. What sets the anchorhold apart from ordinary dwellings are three characteristic architectural elements of the 'container' within which the anchorite represents the 'content'. First the walls, the only boundary between the anchorite and other people, symbolize the break with them: these walls 'speak' of her/him and for her/him. Then there is the door[70] whose peculiarity is that it no longer plays its usual role. Like the anchorite himself, it has a life-sentence which turns the anchorhold into a kind of impermeable shell: to one side, a tiny window which barely opens onto the outside and which the rules recommend should be closed with dark curtains; this is the only outlet to the secular world and thus an Achilles' heel, a place of necessary exchange, fraught with all sorts of danger or, conversely, a rich source of divine grace. Then there is the interior: the anchorite is imprisoned, immobilized – *affixus* [fixed] like Christ. Here an array of images present themselves: the combination of shadows, silence, secrecy, both a fruitful tomb and a matrix, the oyster-shell where the pearl of eternal Life will develop. There may also be terrifying beasts – associated with shadows and death – and, associated with the Devil, toads and snakes which the anchorite must overcome. Everything in the anchorhold encourages the anchorite to restrict both spirit and eyes to a vertical movement and discourages lateral movement towards the world and sin. At the anchorite's feet lie the grave and death; above is heaven. S/he prostrates her/himself and her/his prayer ascends. Nearby stands a bed, however spartan, rich in sublimation, a metaphor for the nuptial bed, placed in the intimacy of the cell for the ineffable embrace of the soul and its creator – especially that of the female anchorite with Christ – a polarity which was, no doubt, a factor in the feminization of the institution.[71] In this confusion – continually maintained both by the theory of this practice and by the liturgy –

---

[70] I shall return elsewhere to the obsession with the *ostium* [door] which the faithful are advised to close upon themselves in order to find God, and which crops up repeatedly in the Bible. Two key quotations will suffice: 'Come, my people, enter thou into thy chambers and shut thy doors about thee' (Isaiah 26:20), picked up again in Matthew 6:6: 'Enter into thy closet, and when thou hast shut thy door, pray to thy Father, which is in secret'.

[71] On the special connections between women as givers of life and anchoritism, see my article 'La réclusion féminine au Moyen Âge', op. cit. I have again addressed this question in 'La femme à la fenestrelle du reclusoir', in *La femme au Moyen Âge*, ed. J. Heuclin and M. Rouche (Maubeuge, 1990), pp. 49–68; 'La femme, la recluse et la mort', in *Muerte, religiosidad y cultura popular siglos XIII–XVIII*, ed. E. Sarrano Martin (Zaragoza, 1994), pp. 151–62. On Aelred of Rievaulx's analysis of the links between female anchoritism and death as fertilisation, see my article 'Aelred de Rievaulx, la recluse et la mort d'après le *Vita inclusarum*', published in English translation in *Cistercian Studies* 34, 2 (1999), pp.183–201.

between death-to-the-world and actual death, it is clear that the anchorite, like the hermit, has broken all those horizontal ties which attach each human being to several discrete groups: those of family, wedlock, friendship, occupation, confraternity, parish, town and nation. None of these are reconstructed, in contrast to the case of monks, who become part of a new *familia*, spiritual instead of natural. This is the point where the similarity between hermit and anchorite ends, for the hermit remains solitary, without social responsibility, whereas the anchorite might be said to represent a double paradox. The asocial nature of being dead-alive, of being between two deaths, depends upon human society without which the anchorite will 'really' die; but, better still, it recreates social capital. Far from being egotistical acts, depriving oneself of freedom and becoming dead to the world are undertaken for collective advantage. In the medieval imagination, therefore, the anchorhold has much in common with the reliquary which also encloses a living corpse possessing a *virtus* [miraculous power]. The analogy can be taken further, for the anchorite's tiny window recalls the aperture in reliquaries which allows devotees to pass their hands through to touch the saint's coffin, and the anchorite, whether silent or singing hymns, glimpsed unseen, embodies the sacrificial victim of a sacred place known to all and which surrounds what we might perhaps call a death pregnant with the promise of life, a literal euthanasia, for the benefit of all. Hence, we see the newly elected magistrates of southern French towns going in procession to greet the anchorite, the only municipal official appointed for life, raising a toast at the anchorhold window; or the anchorites of Lyons taking their place in the rituals of beating the bounds,[72] and on the route of processions; or, again, at Chambéry, the anchorites, in exceptional circumstances, coming out for important public events and processing, dressed in the town's livery.[73]

This, of course, is the idealized image. But there is another, extremely negative one too. As mentioned earlier, reservations were raised from the beginning about anchorites who, to use the telling phrase coined by bishop Burchard of Worms, constituted an *ordo mortuorum* [order of death]. However, the barriers of the learned, set up during the first millennium, were too weak, given how widespread the phenomenon was. A substantial file of criticism can be assembled from the writings of certain bishops, abbots and theoreticians of the religious life – such as St Bernard, Peter the Venerable, Aelred or Gerson, to mention but a few – and only a brief synopsis can be given here. The starting point is an observation that the apparently heroic aspect of the anchorite's commitment spontaneously brings prestige, gratitude and influence, whilst her/his solitary situation *per se* allows her/him to avoid all discipline and regulation.[74] Indeed, the living dead might even enjoy themselves in the tomb! At best, an anchorite may betray trust, at worst s/he

---

[72] Beating the bounds was a widespread practice whereby the community or its representatives would walk the boundaries of the parish to share and preserve the knowledge of where these boundaries lay and to pray for their protection.

[73] For these aspects I refer the reader to my earlier studies and to my recent article: 'La réclusion dans le milieu urbain français au Moyen Âge', *Ermites de France et d'Italie (XI–XVe siècle)*, ed. A. Vauchez, Coll. de l'École française de Rome 313 (Rome, 2003), pp. 155–73.

[74] To some extent the hermit avoids these temptations because he is self-sufficient, whilst the enclosed anchorite is totally dependent on others, even if s/he has private means.

is dangerous. Specialists who question the anchorite's motives deplore the fact that an anchoritic life may often be chosen for negative reasons, especially the – inadmissible – calculation that this will ensure s/he will 'lack for nothing' and be sheltered from life's difficulties.[75] Then there are all the imaginable ways of straying from the path: avoiding work, doing as one pleases, cultivating idleness,[76] letting the mind wander. Unseen behind a curtain, the anchorite does what s/he likes, eats and sleeps when s/he chooses![77] This caricatured image of the anchorite, discernible particularly clearly in the guidance texts, presents the anchorhold as a broth which boils up and spreads all the worldly vices, a *prostibulum* [brothel], a seat of gossip if not of heresy, a storehouse where riches pile up. The bad anchorite is a hypocrite, a procurer, a miser, a sensualist, a lazybones; or s/he may be arrogant, seeking the crowd's veneration by passing her/himself off as a saint, a prophet or a miracle-worker in order to bring people to the window.[78] In practice, some anchorites apparently leave their place of enclosure without the sanction of the church hierarchy. We know of some female anchorites who ask to leave their cell to 'keep up with the secular world',[79] sometimes for reasons unknown, but sometimes because they can no longer cope with their solitude. It is even more surprising that the specified penalty for behaviour considered scandalous is that s/he is to be dismissed by the anchorhold's patron![80] Even though such cases may not be plentiful, those attested do seem to justify the clerical misgivings, however. Not only does this kind of anchorite prove false to the penitential vocation, s/he

[75] For example, Hugh of Saint-Victor, *Expos. in Reg. b. Augustini*, PL 176, col. 887: 'Many in fact enter religion not so much for the salvation of their souls but because of the needs of the body.' Even in Augustine's day monastic life could be dictated by material concerns: see, for example, *Reg. S. Augustini*, PL 32, col. 1379, where he sums up this attitude thus: 'Those who lacked possessions in the secular world, let them not seek them in the monastery!' The rules of the second millennium also reflect this: see Oliger, 'Regula reclusorum', op. cit., n. 1, ch. 10. They castigate those who became anchorites because they are afraid of having nothing to live on.

[76] This fear of settling into indolence seems to be the worst of the temptations which threaten the anchorite, according to the late twelfth-century nun Herrade of Landsberg. Depicting the heavenly Ladder leading to the crown of glory, with God's hand emerging from the clouds, she arranged the various *status* in order of merit: those nearest to heaven are the hermit and anchorite, followed by the monk, the cleric and the layperson. All of them, harassed by demons right up until their last moments, run the risk of giving way to the enticements of the world and of falling into the gaping jaws of Leviathan. It is striking to note which objects of desire she associates with each state. The hermit is preoccupied with his means of subsistence, his garden plot. The anchorite does not have this worry, but he misses his very comfortable bed, so he is penalized for letting himself give way to what Gaston Bachelard has called the 'reveries of rest' (*Earth and Reveries of Rest: Essay on Images of Intimacy* (Dallas, 2000)). The fat monk, holding a huge eel, sighs for the pleasures of the table; the cleric cannot prevent himself thinking of his sweetheart, and the knight and his wife are unable to drag themselves away from the whole gamut of pleasures of worldly existence, their castle, arms, horses, and so on. On this, see G. Cames (ed.), *Allégories et symboles dans l'*Hortus deliciarum (Leiden, 1971), plate 18.

[77] This is one of the fears of Hugh of Saint-Victor, for which see n. 75 above.

[78] To cite one example, Peter the Venerable's vehement criticism in his letter to an anchorite called Gilbert: 'The minute the anchorite opens his narrow window crowds of people rush to receive oracles. The divine prophet considers each case, discusses each and gives a response to each. The wide doorway may have been blocked, but what cannot reach him that way can get through the narrow opening of his little window' (PL 189, *Epist.*, I, 20, col. 93).

[79] L'Hermite-Leclercq, 'La réclusion féminine', p. 142. Unfortunately the statement is given without any comment or qualification.

[80] M.-C. Guigue, *Les recluseries de Lyon* (Lyons, 1887), p. 17.

also deceives those who, unbidden, look to her/him for the altruism of voluntary death and devotion to collective prayer.[81] Can this anchorite, then, still take part in the sacralisation of the town? Could the anchorites be the converse of St Paul's example of the Christian: 'And they that are Christ's, have crucified their flesh, with the vices and concupiscences' (Galatians 5:24)? Might s/he not instead bring down divine thunderbolts by profaning the anchoritic life? And if these risks are permanent, should the institution itself be allowed to continue?

For centuries anchoritism furnished the proof, by and large very positive, of what Pierre Bourdieu has called the 'dialectique de l'expérience intime et de l'image sociale' [dialectic of private experience and social image].[82] On the threshold of the modern period, there was a gradual shift from one type of society, in which the structures and system of representation both gave rise to and welcomed individual vocations, 'digesting' them to make them collective, to another model which rejects this choice of religious life and refuses to take responsibility for it. Why should this happen? Was it because of a lack of vocation or because such vocation no longer struck a chord? We have to weigh up this new dialectic and the force the opposing arguments advanced against bringing back a thousand-year-old institution – that solitary enclosure would now be considered too demanding for human beings, that it would be unhealthy, inhuman, archaic and harmful to the image of the Church as an institution, or that it would serve no purpose or even pose a danger to the social system. Once it disappeared from the domain of religion, permanent solitary confinement moved into the legal domain, where it is defined as a physical penalty with loss of civil rights. Nonetheless, hermits, and those who call themselves 'anchorites', still exist today.

---

[81] P. L'Hermite-Leclercq, 'La mauvaise prière du reclus hypocrite', in *Prier au Moyen Âge*, ed. N. Bériou, Jacques Berlioz and Jean Longère (Turnhout, 1991), pp. 108–9.

[82] Pierre Bourdieu, 'Genèse et structure du champ religieux', *Revue française de sociologie* 12 (1971), pp. 295–334 (p. 317).

6 Anchoritism: the English tradition[1]

Mari Hughes-Edwards

Studies on English anchoritism

Medieval English anchoritism is currently paradigmatic in the field of Anglophone anchoritic scholarship. Whilst this volume seeks to qualify its critical supremacy through direct comparison of the anchoritism of England with that of wider medieval Europe, it does not seek to do so at the expense of English expressions of the vocation. Knowing more about wider European anchoritism can only serve to strengthen current understandings of English anchoritic culture. Accordingly, this chapter reinforces the very real importance of English anchoritic spirituality and acknowledges its continued significance in the context of the study of medieval spirituality as a whole. It offers an overview of the history, expression and popularity of anchoritism in England, detailing the local, social and ecclesiastical attitudes which helped sustain it. It defines English anchoritism in the context of eremitism and problematizes the terminology of solitude. It concludes with a case-study of the fourteenth-century female contemplative anchorite Julian of Norwich, a recluse intimately connected with the literary and spiritual worlds of her day, whose contemplative treatise, *A Revelation of Love*, has had an important impact on our perceptions of anchoritic spirituality.

Any contemporary exploration of English anchoritism owes a considerable debt to the century of English anchoritic scholarship that has preceded it. As McAvoy points out in her introduction to this volume, three survey works on English anchoritism have been produced since 1900: Rotha Mary Clay's *The Hermits and Anchorites of England* (1914), Francis Darwin's *The English Mediaeval Recluse* (1944) and Ann K. Warren's *Anchorites and Their Patrons in Medieval England* (1985).[2] Clay's comprehensive and exhaustive work in particular has paved the way for *every* subsequent study of English anchoritism, especially for Warren's, which relies, in part, on Clay's data. Since every post-Warren study of anchoritism has, to a greater or lesser extent, relied on her work, and

---

[1] I am grateful to Dr J. W. Binns and Dr E. A. Jones for their comments on early drafts of this chapter.
[2] Rotha Mary Clay, *The Hermits and Anchorites of England* (London, 1914); F. D. S. Darwin, *The English Mediaeval Recluse* (London, 1954); and Ann K. Warren, *Anchorites and their Patrons in Medieval England* (Berkeley, Los Angeles and London, 1985).

through that work on Clay, it is to Clay ultimately that the scholarship of English anchoritism continues to return. In this context, it is impossible to overstate her importance in the field. Her exploration of the vocation is founded on readings of wills, ecclesiastical and court documents, ceremonies of enclosure and the *Victoria County Histories*, although these were only in their early stages of production at the time. E. A. Jones writes that:

> [Clay's] biggest debts ... were to the nineteenth-century county historians who came before the *VCH*, national and local record series and her correspondents: she seems to have sent out letters to all the librarians and archivists in the land ... she also drew on hagiographical sources, perhaps less critically than we would today.[3]

Unsurprisingly, Clay's methodology is somewhat outmoded by today's standards. She relies heavily on readings of extant anchoritic guidance writings, interpreting them factually as evidence of practice rather than as evidence of ideology, and reading them as prescriptive rather than persuasive texts (all tendencies echoed by Darwin, and, although to a markedly lesser extent, also by Warren). Recent anchoritic scholarship has shown that these guides are normative texts, revelatory of medieval cultural anxieties, and reflective not necessarily of practice but of the normative ideological framework which perpetuated the vocation and which was itself shaped and sustained by wider medieval spiritual and cultural change.[4] Nonetheless, Clay's volume, if approached circumspectly, remains a vital source of information about solitaries and sites – a monumental study which has never been eclipsed – and her tabulated list of cells is of crucial importance to our present understanding of English anchoritism, although England does seem to have had a more extensive anchoritic community than Clay envisaged. She herself realized the continual need for revisions of her original lists, beginning a process before her death in 1961 which Basil Cottle continued until his own in 1994, and which Jones has since assumed. Cottle and Jones have thus far found evidence of far greater numbers of English recluses than those cited by Clay and Warren.[5] Jones's recent publication of updated lists for medieval Bedfordshire, Hertfordshire and Huntingdonshire, when combined, feature fifty solitaries, compared with Clay's twenty-four, although this important new data does not necessarily imply that radical differences in anchoritism's gendered, geographical or chronological tendencies will

---

[3] Conclusions communicated in personal correspondence with Jones on 14 June 2004.
[4] See my forthcoming monograph, *The Ideology of Medieval English Anchoritism* (Cardiff, 2010), which explores the normative ideology of English anchoritic guidance writing from c.1080 to c.1450 in tandem with wider medieval spiritual and cultural change. See also *Rhetoric of the Anchorhold: Space, Place and Body within the Discourses of Enclosure*, ed. Liz Herbert McAvoy (Cardiff, 2008), and *Anchorites, Wombs and Tombs: Intersections of Gender and Enclosure in the Middle Ages*, ed. Liz Herbert McAvoy and Mari Hughes-Edwards (Cardiff, 2005).
[5] For Clay's tabulated list of cells see *Hermits and Anchorites*, Appendix C, pp. 205–65. See also her later pamphlet: Rotha Mary Clay, 'Further Studies on Medieval Recluses', *Journal of the British Archaeological Association* 16 (1953), pp. 74–86.

become apparent, or that radical alteration in current conceptions of English anchoritism will be required.[6]

Francis Darwin's slim volume on anchoritism has been rather overlooked in critical terms. Published in between Clay's study and Warren's, and certainly outdated in its discourse, his opening chapter, 'Some Misconceptions', nonetheless draws clear attention to the acceptably social aspects of anchoritism.[7] He also focuses on ceremonies of enclosure in new and significant detail. Yet it is Warren's larger and later survey of anchoritism that dominates the field in much the same way as Clay's. Chiefly an exploration of the financial support framework that enabled the perpetuation of the English vocation, it relies heavily on testamentary data and ecclesiastical and court documents, and classifies anchoritic patrons into four groups: royal, aristocratic and gentry, merchant and the laity, and clerical. Warren's readings of guidance literature tend chiefly to be explored as evidence of practice, although she does make more of these texts as potentially ideological constructed entities than does Clay and she also explores later medieval anchoritic guidance in greater detail.

Defining English anchoritism

An anchorite, in modern critical conception, is regarded as distinct from a hermit. Both solitaries seek comparative isolation in which to foster their connection with God and to develop their interior spirituality. Both, to a greater or lesser extent, also seek paradoxically, through intercessionary spiritual acts, to foster their connection with the community which surrounds and supports them. Yet, whereas a hermit's location is potentially mobile, an anchorite is understood as bound to one geographical position for the term of her natural life.[8] It is potentially the difference then in the geographical location of a given solitary that dictates the quality of her solitude, something Clay acknowledged in the very structure of the first seven chapters of her volume (which is separated according to seven different geographically shaped experiences of solitude).[9] Anchorholds were built in diverse locations – adjoining churches, religious foundations, hospitals and even castles – but their incumbents were nonetheless bound to that single location in a way in which the hermit was not. Clay writes: 'There were, indeed, two distinct classes of solitaries: the *anchorite*, enclosed within four walls, and the *hermit* who went out of his cell and mingled with

---

[6] Jones's new findings so far are detailed in E. A. Jones, 'Christina of Markyate and the *Hermits and Anchorites of England*', in *Christina of Markyate: A Twelfth-Century Holy Woman*, ed. Samuel Fanous and Henrietta Leyser (London and New York, 2005), pp. 229–50; 'The Hermits and Anchorites of Oxfordshire', *Oxoniensia* 63 (1998), pp. 51–77; and 'Rotha Clay's *Hermits and Anchorites of England*', *Monastic Research Bulletin* 3 (1997), pp. 46–8.

[7] See for example Darwin, *English Mediaeval Recluse*, pp. 1–8, pp. 8–20 and pp. 20–42 respectively.

[8] This chapter uses the female as the default anchoritic gender where it is unspecified by a given text, since current evidence suggests that female anchorites outnumbered their male counterparts throughout the Middle Ages. See footnote 40 below for more information on the statistical breakdown of English anchoritism.

[9] These are: islands and fens; forests and hillsides; caves; sea-coasts; highways and bridges; towns; churches and cloisters. See Clay's list of contents, *Hermits and Anchorites*, p. ix.

his fellow-men.'[10] Warren points to a legalistic distinction: 'Once they [anchorites] entered the cell they could not retreat. Solitary by choice, they became solitary by law and in this way distinct from hermits.'[11] Here it is the legal vow of permanent fixity which sets one kind of solitary apart from the other.

Yet this rigid differentiation between hermit and anchorite was not of necessity medieval, and was certainly not acknowledged by the pre-medieval Church. As several of the other contributors to this present volume also point out, St Benedict (*c*.480–*c*.550) in his influential Rule, synonymizes anchorites and hermits, regarding them as similarly spiritually sophisticated and inspired in their shared adherence to the ideals of the Desert Fathers and Mothers (the ancient solitaries including St Anthony, St Paul and St Mary the Egyptian whose isolation greatly inspired both types of medieval recluse). Benedict writes:

> ... Anchorites or Hermits: ... after long probation in a monastery ... go out well armed from the ranks of the community to the solitary combat of the desert ... with no help save from God, to fight single-handed against the vices of the flesh and their own evil thoughts.[12]

Warren emphasizes the fluidity of early reclusive solitude, specifically that of these fourth-century desert solitaries who:

> belonged to that time when hermit and anchorite were one in meaning. To be [either] ... was to withdraw (*anachōrein*) to the desert (*eremus*) ... [to] live quite alone or with a group of like-minded solitaries. The recluse was *anachoreta* or *eremita* interchangeably.[13]

Jones also recognizes the early Christian synonymity of reclusive terminology as:

> general in the West until around the end of the first millennium. Thereafter ... the two terms are applied ... to two increasingly clearly demarcated forms of the solitary life ... 'Anchorite' ... begins to refer ... specifically to one who is strictly enclosed (effectively incarcerated) in a 'cell' or 'anchorhold'.[14]

Warren similarly argues:

> During the Middle Ages ... the word *anchorite* became more restricted in use ... The anchorite was *inclusus/inclusa* or *reclusus/reclusa*, enclosed and stable ... the hermit remained free.[15]

---

[10] Clay, *Hermits and Anchorites*, pp. xvi–xvii.

[11] Warren, *Anchorites and their Patrons*, p. 7.

[12] Taken from an online translation of the Benedictine Rule by Leonard J. Doyle entitled *The Rule of St Benedict* http://www.osb.org/rb/text/rbejms1.html#1 (last accessed 08.02.09). The original Latin for this can be consulted online via the hypertext Latin version of the Benedictine Rule entitled *Sancti Benedicti Regula* created by Intratext http://www.intratext.com/X/LAT0011.HTM (last accessed 08.02.09).

[13] Warren, *Anchorites and their Patrons*, p. 8.

[14] E. A. Jones, 'Anchorites and Hermits in Historical Context', in *Approaching Medieval English Anchoritic and Mystical Texts*, ed. Dee Dyas, Valerie Edden and Roger Ellis (Cambridge, 2005), pp. 3–19 (pp. 7–8). See also his 'Langland and Hermits', *Yearbook of Langland Studies* 11 (1997), pp. 67–86, for information on the etymology of eremitism.

[15] Warren, *Anchorites and their Patrons*, p. 8.

Yet it is possible that, certainly in the earlier part of the medieval period, these two states of medieval solitude at times shared the same kind of fluidity, porousness and reciprocity that was experienced by the desert matriarchs and patriarchs, and which was envisaged by St Benedict.[16] The vocations of hermit and anchorite may not always have been mutually exclusive. Three women at Kilburn in Middlesex (c.1130) may have experienced this kind of eremitic fusion. They are described as anchorites by those modern scholars who have worked on anchoritism – for example, by Clay and Warren – but elsewhere as female hermits 'living communally' – for example, by the archaeologist Roberta Gilchrist and in the recent collection *Christina of Markyate: A Twelfth-Century Holy Woman*.[17] Were lives such as these eremitic or anchoritic in practice? They seem at once to have been both and neither. Or rather, the modern distinction between the two states, influenced by the increasing rigidity of the later Middle Ages, struggles to comprehend a life like theirs in the spirit in which it was actually lived. The case of Christina of Markyate (c.1096–c.1160) provides another example of potential eremitic porousness. She experiences, so her extraordinary Latin *Life* tells us, both anchoritic enclosure and eremitic freedom in her search for spiritual fulfilment and stays with not one, but two recluses during her period of enforced anchoritism whilst in flight from an unwanted marriage. She ends as abbess of one of the most important coenobitic communities, founded for her in Markyate, not far from St Albans. Jones writes that even in her own lifetime:

> Christina seems to have been difficult to classify … all approached her with a particular set of preconceptions, but came away from the encounter having had those assumptions challenged and in many cases confounded.[18]

Jones, in his work on revising Clay's lists of solitaries, seems intuitively sympathetic to the problematics of the classification of solitude in his rejection of her process of classification by site, and his adoption instead of classification by solitary, which can allow for the difficulty of making the distinction between anchorite and hermit in situations like that of the Kilburn women and Christina.[19] Widening the definition of anchoritism to include hermitic experiences of solitude need not imply a total breakdown of anchoritic ideals, or suggest that stricter

---

[16] Eremitism and monasticism also intersected strongly at this time, as Henrietta Leyser argues in her excellent overview of the more fluid kinds of solitude experienced by hermits in the high Middle Ages: *Hermits and the New Monasticism: A Study of Religious Communities in Western Europe 1000–1150* (London, 1984). See especially pp. 4–8.

[17] Warren, *Anchorites and their Patrons*, p. 33, records the existence of the sisters' threefold anchorhold as part of an exploration of double-occupancy anchorholds without an acknowledgement of the potential duality of their solitude. Roberta Gilchrist records them as one of a number of communal hermit groups 'regularised into nunneries' in the case of Kilburn by 1139 in *Contemplation and Action: The Other Monasticism* (London and New York, 1995), p. 175. See also *Christina of Markyate*, ed. Fanous and Leyser, which references Kilburn at p. 40, p. 42 and p. 51, and which, as a volume, discusses Christina's porous experience of solitude. On Christina see also Diane Watt, *Medieval Women's Writing* (Cambridge, 2007), pp. 19–39.

[18] Jones, 'Christina of Markyate and the *Hermits and Anchorites of England*', p. 237. See also pp. 232–3 and p. 235.

[19] Ibid., p. 232.

forms of anchoritic enclosure were not in operation at the same time as these more porous groups existed, as other essays in this volume clearly demonstrate. A metaphorical widening of the anchorhold is needed, so that conceptions of early anchoritism can include arrangements that contradict the image of the space-deprived recluse, locked down in her narrow, single-occupancy cell.

Anchoritic guidance writing

An ideological reading of the anchoritic guidance-writing tradition implies the concurrent and continued importance to the English anchoritic ideal of comparative solitude within one fixed location. Current data suggests that thirteen anchoritic guides are extant, some composed in Latin and some in the vernacular, for both male and female English anchorites. The earliest of these is Goscelin of St Bertin's *Liber Confortatorius*, written for the recluse Eve *c*.1080.[20] The latest is possibly *The Myrour of Recluses*, a fifteenth-century vernacular translation (*c*.1450) of the fourteenth-century Latin guide written for male recluses, *Speculum Inclusorum* (*c*.1349–*c*.82),[21] although many of the later medieval guides are, at present, difficult to date with certainty.[22] Often taking the form of a letter from one male writer to a recluse, or group of recluses, anchoritic guidance texts vary in size from short epistles to extensive, intricately subdivided works. They seek to accustom their recluses to the demands of their enclosure and to assist them in their comparative rejection of society.[23] As such, they are rich sources of spiritual ideology rather than of historical practice. They address, amongst other things, the extent to which a recluse should interact socially and they try, persuasively, to direct the nature of anchoritic spirituality and to regulate its orthodoxy. We cannot know how many English recluses actually used a guide. Some may have used several whilst others used none. However, there was clearly a perceived need for this kind of literature in England, which inspired the regular creation of new guides and, significantly, the translation and revision of existing ones, from the early Middle Ages onwards. To date, much scholarly attention has focused on high medieval guides at the expense of their later medieval

---

[20] C. H. Talbot, 'The *Liber confortatorius* of Goscelin of Saint Bertin', *Analecta monastica, Studia anselmiana* fasc. 37 (Rome, 1955), pp. 1–117. See also its recent translation, with an excellent introduction: Goscelin of St Bertin, *The Book of Encouragement and Consolation (Liber Confortatorius)*, ed. and trans. Monica Otter (Cambridge, 2004).

[21] For editions of both see P. L. Oliger (ed.), 'Speculum Inclusorum', *Lateranum*, n.s. 4 (1938), pp. 1–148; and Marta Powell Harley (ed.), *The Myrour of Recluses* (London, Ontario, 1995). Jones is currently working on a new parallel-text edition of *Speculum*.

[22] Although Warren imposes a chronology on the guides, which she calls rules (see 'Appendix Two' of *Anchorites and their Patrons*, pp. 294–8), in reality their dating should be approached with caution. Even the precise number of guides is difficult to establish since variants of some exist, notably of *Ancrene Wisse* but also of *Speculum Inclusorum*. Some revisions of existing guides may be better classed as different guides, where new material or textual omission has altered them significantly.

[23] Their categorization as guides rather than rules stresses their non-prescriptive nature. Linda Georgianna has argued this persuasively for *Ancrene Wisse* in her *The Solitary Self: Individuality in the Ancrene Wisse* (Cambridge, Mass. and London, 1981), pp. 30–1 and pp. 8–32, but this chapter proposes that this term be applied to every anchoritic guide.

counterparts.[24] Of the earlier guides, *Ancrene Wisse* has undoubtedly commanded the most scholarly attention. The original text of this high medieval guide,
probably written between 1216 and 1230,[25] is lost but seventeen manuscripts in
French, Latin and the vernacular, are extant which contain material from the lost
original, sometimes reworked or with added revisions.[26] Of its vernacular texts,
that which is found in MS Cambridge Corpus Christi College 402 (*c*.1224–25) is
perhaps the best known, and is the only text of the guide which refers to itself by
this title, which is generally translated as 'guide for anchoresses'. In it, mention is
made of a new, extended reclusive group, expanded from what seems to have been
its original audience of three sisters:[27]

> You are the anchoresses of England, so many together – twenty now or more [. . .]
> among whom is most peace, most unity and [. . .] agreement in a united life

---

[24] New and forthcoming critical work seeks to redress this balance. See, for example, Liz Herbert
McAvoy, '"Neb ... sumdeal ilich wummon & neddre is behinden": Reading the Monstrous in the
Anchoritic Text', in *The Medieval Mystical Tradition in England. Exeter Symposium VII*, ed. E. A. Jones
(Cambridge, 2004), pp. 51–68; see also her 'Gender, Rhetoric and Space in the *Speculum Inclusorum*,
Letter to a Bury Recluse and the strange case of Christina Carpenter', in *Rhetoric of the Anchorhold*, pp.
111–26; Mari Hughes-Edwards, '"How good it is to be alone"? Sociability, Solitude and Medieval
English Anchoritism' (forthcoming, *Mystics Quarterly*, 2009/10); and E. A. Jones, 'A New Look into the
Speculum Inclusorum', in *The Medieval Mystical Tradition: England, Ireland and Wales. Exeter
Symposium VI*, ed. Marion Glasscoe (Cambridge, 1999), pp. 123–47.

[25] Bella Millett, whose work on this guide has contributed in fundamental terms to our understanding of
high medieval English anchoritic theology and ideology as a whole, proposes a composition date 'at some
point between about 1216 and 1230, probably in the later 1220s'; see Bella Millett, '*Ancrene Wisse* and the
Book of Hours', in *Writing Religious Women: Female Spiritual and Textual Practices in Late-Medieval
England*, ed. Denis Renevey and Christiania Whitehead (Cardiff, 2000), pp. 21–40 (pp. 25–6). A comprehensive survey of critical work on the origins and dating of the different texts of *Ancrene Wisse* is found in
Millett's annotated bibliography, *Ancrene Wisse, The Katherine Group and the Wooing Group: Annotated
Bibliographies of Old and Middle English Literature*, vol. 2 (Cambridge, 1996), pp. 6–17, and in Millett's
critical edition of *Ancrene Wisse*, vol. 2, pp. 305–28 (see n. 26 below for full details of that text).

[26] Of the editions of *Ancrene Wisse* available, the most recent is Millett's critical edition: *Ancrene Wisse:
A Corrected Edition of the Text in Cambridge, Corpus Christi College, MS 402, with Variants from Other
Manuscripts*, vol. 1, EETS o.s. 325 (Oxford, 2005) and vol. 2, EETS o.s. 326 (Oxford, 2006). Vol. 1
includes the 'Preface', 'Textual Introduction', the edited text and the *apparatus criticus*; vol. 2 includes
the 'General Introduction', the 'Textual Commentary' and the Bibliography, Glossary and Index. Both
volumes draw on the uncompleted edition of the guide by E. J. Dobson, and the Glossary and Additional
Notes are by Richard Dance. All quotations from *Ancrene Wisse* in this chapter are taken from this edition but, in line with the policy of this volume, will appear in the footnotes. Other editions include: J. R.
R. Tolkien (ed.), *Ancrene Wisse, MS. Corpus Christi College Cambridge 402*, EETS o.s. 249 (London,
1962), and R. Hasenfratz (ed.), *Ancrene Wisse* (Kalamazoo, 2000), available online via the *TEAMS
Middle English Texts* webpage at http://www.lib.rochester.edu/camelot/teams/hasenfratz.htm (last
accessed 08.02.09). Translations of *Ancrene Wisse* include: Bella Millett (trans.), *Ancrene Wisse/Guide
for Anchoresses: A Translation* (Exeter, 2009); Ann Savage and Nicholas Watson (trans.), *Anchoritic
Spirituality: 'Ancrene Wisse' and Associated Works* (New York and Mahwah, 1991); and Hugh White
(trans.), *Ancrene Wisse: Guide for Anchoresses* (London, 1993). All references to *Ancrene Wisse* in the
main body of this chapter are from White's translation of the Corpus Text.

[27] We know little for certain about this original audience, despite speculation, beyond a potential reference to them in the text of *Ancrene Wisse* extant in MS BL Cotton Nero A.xiv which refers to their well-
born status, their blood-sisterhood, their secure patronage arrangements and their youthful anchoritic
renouncement of the world. See Mabel Day (ed.), *The English Text of the Ancrene Riwle, Edited from
Cotton MS. Nero A.xiv*, EETS o.s. 225 (1952), p. 85 and for a translation of this vernacular passage see
J. Morton (ed.), *The Ancren Riwle: A Treatise on the Rules and Duties of Monastic Life* (London, 1853),
p. 193.

according to one rule [. . .] all turned in one direction [. . .] as though you were
a community of London or Oxford, of Shrewsbury or of Chester, where all are
one with a common manner [. . .] so that your community begins to spread
towards the end of England. You are, as it were, the motherhouse of which they
are begotten.[28]

That this group is much bigger than the original tripartite sisterhood does not
imply a marked increase in the number of shared anchorholds in England, and the
Corpus text does not imply the existence of a 'convent' of female anchorites. The
Ancrene Wisse author is clear that this is a virtual community, not a literal one. He
writes *as though they were* a community. Millett notes the importance of this:

> The revisions continue to assume an anchoritic rather than a communal life   ...
> [it remains] a virtual cloister ... the women ... are not ... recapitulating a twelfth-
> century pattern of progression ... from anchoritism to cenobitism ... *Ancrene
> Wisse* ... reveals [an] ... ambivalent ... even antagonistic, attitude to traditional
> monasticism.[29]

This passage then, as part of the guide's ideological discussion of the importance
of enclosure, sets up the rhetorical notion of a community-in-separateness; a community-in-solitude.[30] Joined together metaphorically, this anchoritic community is
ideologically united, their spirituality mediated through a shared commitment to
the ideals of enclosure and solitude.

An earlier anchoritic guide on which *Ancrene Wisse* draws is Aelred of
Rievaulx's *De Institutione Inclusarum* (*c*.1160–2), written for his enclosed sister.[31] It is possible, although unproven, that his sister had attracted other would-
be solitaries to her, since Aelred implies that he writes partly for them in his
declaration: 'it was not for yourself alone that you wished me to write this rule,
but also for the young girls who, on your advice, are eager to embrace a life
like yours'.[32] It is by no means certain that his sister's cell formed the focal

---

[28] White, *Ancrene Wisse*, p. 119. In Millett's critical edition this reads: '3e beoð þe ancren of Englond,
swa feole togederes (twenti nuðe oðer ma [...]) þet meast grið is among, meast annesse ant [...] some-
treadnesse of anred lif efter a riwle, [...] alle iturnt anesweis [...] as þah 3e weren an cuuent of Lundene
ant of Oxnefort, of Schreobsburi, oðer of Chester, þear-as alle beoð an wið an imeane manere [...] swa
þet ower cuuent biginneð to spreaden toward Englondes ende. 3e beoð as þe moder-hus þet heo beoð of
istreonet.' Millett (ed.), *Ancrene Wisse*, pp. 96–7.

[29] Bella Millett, '*Ancrene Wisse* and the Life of Perfection', *Leeds Studies in English* 33 (2002), pp. 53–76
(p. 58).

[30] See Cate Gunn, *Ancrene Wisse: Pastoral Literature to Vernacular Spirituality* (Cardiff, 2007) for an in-
depth discussion of the rhetorical techniques of *Ancrene Wisse*.

[31] The original Latin text of *De Institutione* was composed between 1160 and 1162 by Aelred, then abbot
of the Cistercian foundation at Rievaulx. The original letter has been lost and the earliest complete text
is found in the thirteenth-century MS BL Cotton Nero A.iii. It has been edited by C. H. Talbot in *Analecta
Sacrae Ordinis Cisterciensis* vii (1951), pp. 167–217, and in *Aelredi Rievallensis Opera Omnia: I Opera
Ascetica, Corpus Christianorum Continuatio Mediaevalis* I (Turnhout, 1971), pp. 637–82. It has been
translated by M. P. MacPherson in *Aelred of Rievaulx: Treatises and Pastoral Prayer* (Kalamazoo, 1971),
pp. 40–102. All quotations in the main body of this chapter will be taken from this translation, with corresponding references to the Latin original given in the footnotes.

[32] MacPherson, *Aelred of Rievaulx*, p. 52. For the Latin version of this quotation see Talbot (ed.), *Aelredi
Rievallensis*, p. 642.

point of a literal, rather than virtual, community-in-solitude like that of Christina of Markyate, or even of an ideological community like that of *Ancrene Wisse*, and little information exists about this recluse and her companions, beyond veiled internal references in the guide itself.[33]

The tenor and tone of later medieval anchoritic guidance writing can often be quite different from earlier guidance. More frequently emotive and affective, the later guides focus on the recluse's contemplative experience with the same emphasis that their earlier counterparts gave to ascetic practice.[34] They encourage, for the most part, a greater level of acceptable social interaction in their recluses, but nonetheless are firm in their belief that anchoritism enables a particularly strong spiritual practice to develop because of its comparative solitude. Consequently, the anchorhold and the outside world are still juxtaposed in the later texts, one at the expense of the other, as in earlier guidance writing. Richard Rolle (c.1290–1349) in his guide *The Form of Living* (c.1348) argues: 'If we be about to hide vs fro speche or preisynge of þe world, God wol shewe vs to his praysynge and oure ioy.'[35] Rolle believes that social interaction, in so far as it is in tension with anchoritic enclosure, is in tension with a meaningful relationship with God: 'The state þat þou art in, þat is solitude, þat is most able of al othre to reuelaciouns of þe Holy Goste.'[36] Yet Walter Hilton (c.1343–96), author of the guide extant in Book I of his *The Scale of Perfection* (c.1384–6), displays more ambivalence about anchoritism, characterizing it as one of the best, not *the* best of spiritual lives to lead. He is also more ambivalent about the need to maintain comparative social distance from the community, although he does still admire the vocation's relative solitude. He departs radically from the high medieval anchoritic ideal in his recommendation that the recluse allow herself to be interrupted by a visitor:

> be soone redi with a good wille [...] though thou be in preiere or in devocioun, that thee thenketh looth for to breeke of, for thee thenketh thou schuldest not leve God for mannys speche, me thenketh it is not so in this caas; for yif thou be wise, thou schal not leve God, but thou schal fynde Hym and have Hym and see Him in thyn evene Cristene as wel as in praiere.[37]

---

[33] See C. H. Talbot (ed. and trans.), *The Life of Christina of Markyate, A Twelfth Century Recluse* (Oxford, 1959), pp. 144–5. For information about the surprisingly varied and social functions of some of the solitaries who were nearly contemporary to Christina and also to Aelred's sister, see H. Mayr-Harting, 'Functions of a Twelfth-Century Recluse', *History: The Journal of the Historical Association* 60 (1975), pp. 337–52.

[34] For a detailed account of the development of anchoritic ascetic practice from the high-medieval to the late-medieval period see Mari Hughes-Edwards, 'Hedgehog Skins and Hairshirts: The Changing Role of Asceticism in the Anchoritic Ideal', *Mystics Quarterly* 28 (2002), pp. 6–25.

[35] The text of *The Form of Living* quoted in this chapter is from S. J. Ogilvie-Thompson (ed.), *Richard Rolle: Prose and Verse from MS Longleat 29 and Related Manuscripts*, EETS o.s. 293 (1988), pp. 3–25 (p. 5).

[36] Ogilvie-Thompson (ed.), *Richard Rolle*, p. 6.

[37] The text of *The Scale of Perfection* quoted in this chapter is taken from Thomas Bestul (ed.), *Walter Hilton: The Scale of Perfection* (Kalamazoo, 2000), here at p. 124. This text is also available online via the *TEAMS Middle English Texts* webpage at http://www.lib.rochester.edu/camelot/teams/hilfr1.htm (last accessed 08.02.09).

Anchorites could not, of course, exist without the tacit and explicit approval of the society they sought, comparatively, to reject. Warren concludes:

> The medieval Englishman who passed by the cell of the anchorite was more than a passive observer. He was part of a network of support that enabled the anchorite to exist and persist ... [the recluse's] choice implied a culture in consonance with his views, one that both sanctioned [it] and also encouraged it by responding to its demands.[38]

Locating English anchoritism

Currently the statistical picture concerning English anchoritic numbers, gendered differentials and geographical locations remains largely that of Warren, who proposed, on the basis of the evidence available to her in 1985, that it was 'a wide-ranging and far-reaching religious phenomenon: many anchorites all over the country ... Not one in every parish, but in many.'[39] She argues for the recorded existence of at least 780 English recluses on 601 sites, proposing that the vocation reached its zenith in the fourteenth century, and that more English women than men were enclosed at every stage of the period.[40] Anchorites, in geographic terms, have been located in all but four counties of medieval England: Buckinghamshire, Rutland, Cumberland and Westmorland, although it is possible Jones's revisions of Clay will alter this picture. Whilst some counties evidenced strong anchoritic identities in all periods, some demonstrated strong links at times but lost their anchoritic identities. In this context, Warren notes high levels of anchoritism in Oxfordshire, Sussex, Worcestershire and Hampshire during the twelfth and thirteenth centuries, which seem to have diminished thereafter; and in Yorkshire, where it was on the wane by the last quarter of the fifteenth century, having been strongly prevalent there throughout the thirteenth and fourteenth centuries. In the counties of Lincolnshire and Middlesex (including London), however, where anchoritism had been slow to establish itself, it remained active throughout the period, and the same was true for Norfolk.[41]

What began as a largely rural expression of spirituality did remain an important rural phenomenon. Warren represents the twelfth-century situation in terms of a village to city/town ratio of 69:14, and the numbers of rural anchorholds remained strong until the sixteenth century.[42] Nonetheless, the number of urban

[38] Warren, *Anchorites and their Patrons*, p. 15.

[39] Ibid., p. 18. Millett, drawing on the similar arguments of Brenda Bolton, Warren and Patricia Rosof, also argues this in '*Ancrene Wisse* and the Life of Perfection', p. 55.

[40] Warren's tabulated evidence is at *Anchorites and their Patrons*, p. 20. She writes: 'In the twelfth century there is a ratio of about five women to three men; in the thirteenth century, about four to one; in the fourteenth century, about five to two; in the fifteenth, about five to three again; and in the sixteenth, about three to two' (*Anchorites and their Patrons*, p. 19). A total of 414 solitaries are known to Warren to have been female, in contrast to 201 known males and 165 indeterminates (whose gender is not currently recoverable because recluses are sometimes referred to simply as *anachorita* in the records). See Jones, 'Anchorites and Hermits in Historical Context', p. 9, for more on indeterminates.

[41] Warren, *Anchorites and their Patrons*, p. 36.

[42] Ibid., p. 37.

English anchorholds, in tandem with the wider European trend identified in the previous essays, steadily increased until the sixteenth century as anchoritism became an important urban phenomenon; as Gilchrist argues, anchorholds became 'an integral element of the ecclesiastical topography of medieval towns'.[43]

Becoming an anchorite

Although anchoritism predated coenobitism, the vocation never constituted an organized religious order in itself and this potentially made it difficult for the medieval Church to regulate it with any rigid form of institutionalized control. The author of *Ancrene Wisse*, in his construction of the ideology of enclosure and the Religious life, gives the following advice to enable his recluses to combat pressure on this issue:

> If any ignorant person asks you of what order you are, as some do, you tell me [. . .] answer 'Of St James's' [. . .] He says what religion is and what right order is: *Religio munda et immaculata apud Deum et Patrem hec est: uisitare pupillos et uiduas in necessitate sua, et immaculatum se custodire ab hoc seculo* [. . .] Herein is religion, not in the wide hood, or in the black cape, or in the white surplice, or in the grey cowl.[44]

In practice, anchorites could certainly come from the coenobitic life and, indeed, it was exactly this kind of solitary that St Benedict anticipated in his Rule: an individual whose former life in community could function as a kind of religious probation and who could consequently make a more reliable recluse. Coenobitic recruits could continue in their obedience to their religious order after enclosure, particularly if the cell were attached to the conventual house, but in general, once a recluse was enclosed, obligations to her old order would potentially cease (with the permission of both her superior and bishop). It was more common for female anchorites to relinquish their previous identity completely, as Warren has argued, although male anchorites who had formerly been priests could maintain both their old and new identities concurrently.[45]

In some respects anchoritism was a great leveller. In theory, successful candidates could come from any social sphere if they had the support of a patron and were deemed suitable by ecclesiastical authorities. Even the servants of anchorites, potentially rendered quasi-anchoritic themselves by their association

---

[43] For a general overview of the process of medieval urbanization see, N. Baker and R. Holt, *Urban Growth and the Medieval Church: Gloucester and Worcester* (Aldershot, 2004); D. Nicholas, *Urban Europe, 1100–1700* (Basingstoke, 2003); and R. Holt and G. Rosser (eds.), *The English Medieval Town: a Reader in English Urban History 1200–1540* (London, 1990). For Gilchrist see *Contemplation and Action*, p. 183.

[44] White (ed. and trans.), *Ancrene Wisse*, pp. 4–5. In Millet (ed), *Ancrene Wisse*, this reads: '3ef ei unweote easkeð ow of hwet ordre 3e beon— as summe doð, [3]e telleð me [...] ondswerieð: of Sein Iames [...] He sei[ðhwet] is religiun, hwuch is riht ordre. *Religio munda et immaculata apud Deum et Patrem hec est: visitare pupillos et viduas in necessitate sua, et immaculatum se custodire ab hoc seculo* [...] Her-in is religiun, nawt i þe wide hod ne i þe blake cape, ne i þe hwite rochet ne i þe greie cuuel' (pp. 3–4).

[45] Warren, *Anchorites and their Patrons*, pp. 24–5.

with the anchorhold, were able, in some cases, to assume ownership of the cell after the death of their master or mistress.[46] Within the English tradition and elsewhere, as this volume attests, the largest group of female anchorites was drawn from the lay community. Both unmarried women and widows were enclosed, and Warren even documents the case of a married couple, the Cheynes, who both became recluses in the fifteenth century.[47] It was for the lay recluse that the writers of anchoritic guidance felt most concern, for life in the medieval home, however hard it might be, could not necessarily prepare the recluse for the harsh realities of life inside the anchorhold. Some writers, notably the *Speculum* author, recommend a period of probation, although this is not a common guidance-writing recommendation.[48]

The archaeology of anchoritism

Limited archaeological work is being done on what little remains in material terms of the medieval English anchorhold. Consequently, it is hard to build up a consistent picture of the interior of a 'typical' anchorhold.[49] The cell was customarily built as a lean-to structure adjoining the northern (less hospitable) side of a religious building, and commonly sited in the churchyard, its geographical placement concurrently symbolic of both the anchorite's dependence on God and on the Church, and of her permanent removal from the world. The image of a recluse who had withdrawn from the world, buried alive, a living corpse in the darkness of an anchor-grave, surrounded day and night by real corpses, was deeply affective, particularly for high medieval anchoritic guidance writers.[50] In this context, Gilchrist's theory of 'material culture' can usefully be applied to the anchorhold to convey the ways in which the architectural significance of a building can reinforce and perpetuate its metaphorical and spiritual purpose.[51] The material culture of the anchorhold, its penitential location and the metaphorical significance that gives rise to, reinforces its spiritual significances, codifying the meanings of the spirituality enacted within it. The anchorhold functions, for those within and without it, as an extended metaphorical symbol of the piety which gave rise to its spatial construction.

---

[46] See Warren, *Anchorites and their Patrons*, p. 26.

[47] Emma Cheyne's lay background clearly did not prevent her from either becoming, or remaining, an anchorite for some years. See ibid., *Anchorites and their Patrons*, p. 27.

[48] Oliger, 'Speculum Inclusorum', pp. 73–4; and Powell Harley (ed.), *The Myrour of Recluses*, pp. 9–10.

[49] Potential new anchorholds are still coming to light, however, and they deserve full archaeological investigation. See for example the uninvestigated case of a lean-to structure colloquially known as 'The Sacristy' at the Church of St Mary and All Saints, Willingham, Cambridgeshire, documented on the website *The Case for an Anchorhold* by Jeremy Lander, Freeland Rees Roberts Architects in collaboration with Randolph and Laura Miles. For which, see http://www.willinghamchurch.org/Lander/Lander.htm (last accessed 08.02.09). In addition, Michelle M. Sauer has created an extensive photographic database of extant English anchorholds and their traces, with a view to publication.

[50] See Gilchrist, *Contemplation and Action*, p. 190, on the graveyard and the anchorhold.

[51] See especially ibid., pp. 1–7, for an explanation of material culture.

Anchorites rarely owned their own cells, and customarily rented them. If insufficient funds were available to support a new recluse when a previous incumbent died, some bishops ordered the destruction of their cells.[52] More were destroyed during the Reformation, and of those that survived many are now in disrepair, or are commonly used for storage or as vestries. Some common elements of the English anchorhold are implied by both architectural and written sources (for example records which detail structural repairs). Cells were commonly one- or two-roomed structures (although exceptions did exist), often featured a door to the outside world which could be literally or symbolically blocked, and could feature a squint which opened onto the church and through which an altar might be glimpsed, and a window or windows on the outer, and sometimes on the inner, walls. Yet a consideration of the anchorhold's two archaeological extremes implies a material culture intentionally as individualized as the spirituality of its incumbent. The most extensive surviving cell is undoubtedly that of Chester-le-Street in County Durham, notable for its four rooms.[53] Jones also notes another spacious anchorhold at Chichester cathedral which measured 8.7 × 7.2m.[54] Some cells even had gardens, for example that of Emma Scherman of York.[55] At the other extreme, however, lies the spatial privation of the anchorhold at Compton in Surrey. A cell which housed male recluses from the late twelfth to the early fourteenth centuries, its proportions measured, in the words of Jones, '2.04 × 1.31 m – the dimensions of a moderately sized lift'.[56] Although it is almost impossible to generalize due to the deliberately individualized nature of the vocation, it is likely that the architectural arrangements of most anchorites knew neither the potential anguish of Compton's spatial severity nor the comparative comfort of Emma Scherman's garden. The further erosion of architectural evidence by ecclesiastical rebuilding and renovation, however, brings with it the increased improbability of recovering detailed information.

Enclosure and support

Although the enclosure of recluses without proper licences, without adequate financial support, without a ceremony of enclosure and in some cases without episcopal permission is recorded, anchoritism was a vocation in which the bishop's support was vital.[57] Clay writes that he was 'by virtue of his office, the

---

[52] Warren, *Anchorites and their Patrons*, pp. 20–1, records such action on the part of Robert Bingham, bishop of Salisbury from 1228–46.

[53] Clay, *Hermits and Anchorites*, p. 185.

[54] Jones, 'Anchorites and Hermits in Historical Context', p. 12.

[55] See Warren, *Anchorites and their Patrons*, p. 31, p. 50 and p. 78. In the latter case, the York anchorite Emma Scherman was granted a garden *refrigerum aeris recaptando* [for the sake of taking fresh air]. She was also granted permission to leave her cell once a year to visit churches 'and other pious places' without having to seek special permission from the bishop each time.

[56] Jones, 'Anchorites and Hermits in Historical Context', p. 12.

[57] See Clay, *Hermits and Anchorites*, p. 91 and Warren, *Anchorites and their Patrons*, p. 56, pp. 58–62, pp. 74–5 and p. 83, amongst which the curious case of 'St Michael on the Mount Without', Bristol, is particularly vivid: an anchorite was enclosed (in 1237) without securing the permission of the established patron of the anchorhold, Tewkesbury Abbey.

guardian of every solitary in his diocese'.[58] This was a grave legal and spiritual responsibility, and one which was taken seriously, as the creation of the fifteenth-century *Provinciale* (a collection of provincial statutes which reflects the relationship between bishops and recluse) by the canon lawyer William Lyndwood demonstrates.[59] The relationship between recluse and bishop had, Warren argues, a five-fold significance, involving him in: 1) investigating the suitability of the candidate; 2) examining her financial support; 3) examining the suitability of the anchorhold; 4) performing the rite of enclosure;[60] 5) supervising the recluse in order to ensure orthodoxy and spiritual success, which was the lengthiest part of his charge.[61]

Anchoritic enclosure was a permanent undertaking which could, in theory, only end with death. The extant ceremonies of enclosure within the English tradition certainly reinforce this,[62] for in some of them the graveyard setting of the anchorhold becomes a liturgical reality when the corpse-like candidate is given the sacrament of Extreme Unction, is sprinkled with dust and is processed into the anchorhold to the sound of the same prayers and psalms that would have accompanied the dead body into the graveyard.[63] Jones argues that the evocation of death is far from metaphorical:

> The lengthy rubrics to the Chichele *ordo* – which is the most developed of the extant *ordines* – include detailed consideration of the prerequisites for an enclosure ceremony [including the readying] ... in the reclusory [of] 'a grave of the length of a man and a foot and a half in depth.'[64]

Enclosure represented a considerable financial outlay on the part of society. If an individual entered the anchorhold while still young, their enclosure could be of some duration. Norman Tanner suggests that the Norwich recluse Elizabeth Scott was enclosed for thirty years at St Julian's, Conisford, while at nearby Carrow

---

[58] Clay, *Hermits and Anchorites*, p. 93.

[59] W. Lyndwood, *Provinciale (seu Constitutiones Angliae)* (Oxford, 1679). Jones discusses Lyndwood in 'Hermits and Anchorites in Historical Context', pp. 9–10, as does Warren, *Anchorites and their Patrons*, pp. 88–91.

[60] Many recluses would have gone through a ceremony, or rite, of enclosure, certainly by the later part of the high medieval period. The bishop was meant to perform this rite, although he could send a deputy. The earliest extant ceremony of enclosure, detailing the final moments of an anchorite's life in the outside world and providing a rite of passage for entrance into the anchorhold, is found in a twelfth-century pontifical, and the latest in a printed sixteenth-century manual. For a detailed account of these extant documents, of the bishop's role in these rites and of the ceremony of enclosure itself, see E. A. Jones, 'Ceremonies, of Enclosure: Rite, Rhetoric and Reality', in *Rhetoric of the Anchorhold*, ed. McAvoy, pp. 34–49. See also Darwin's chapter 'Four Forms of Enclosure', in *English Mediaeval Recluse*, pp. 71–8.

[61] Warren, *Anchorites and their Patrons*, pp. 53–91.

[62] Housed in English and Welsh libraries there are fourteen such pontificals which contain an *ordo* for anchoritic enclosure, although three of these are of Continental provenance. On this see Jones, 'Ceremonies of Enclosure', p. 35–6.

[63] Darwin, *English Mediaeval Recluse*, pp. 71–8, gives detail on the liturgical resonances between enclosure and burial. See also Jones, 'Ceremonies of Enclosure', pp. 42–4.

[64] Jones, 'Ceremonies of Enclosure', p. 42. The Chichele *ordo* is to be found in Cambridge, Trinity College, MS B. XI. 9, fols 98v–99r. See ibid., p. 36.

Priory, Julian Lampett may have passed fifty years in solitude.[65] Such anchorites clearly required long-term financial support. The patronage and the financial arrangements that powered English anchoritism were therefore many and varied, and are as important to the vocation's perpetuation as are the spiritual guidance writings written for its adherents. Acquiring anchoritic funding appears to have been difficult for all but the wealthiest of candidates who had the finances to pursue their ambitions.[66] The less wealthy were forced to acquire sustenance from a combination of different sources, and not all would-be recluses were successful at gathering support. Of those who were, some supported themselves through part-time employment, such as needlework or copying, or (if male) through continuing in the priesthood despite their enclosure. This alone would not have provided sufficient money on which to subsist, and such work could potentially have impacted upon their vocational professionalism, a problem with which many anchoritic guidance writers concerned themselves.[67] Aelred, for example, warns against allowing work to draw the recluse back into the community, condemning those recluses who 'Are yet so eager to make money [. . .] that they could well be mistaken for châtelaines rather than anchoresses'.[68]

Other, less problematic, sources of external funding open to anchorites included almsgiving (arbitrary or regularized); pensions from lay, ecclesiastical individuals or from religious orders; bequests (as one-off payments or a regular income); anniversary arrangements and indulgences; corrodies (a fixed share in the common goods of a religious house); and some recluses were granted 'royal rate' pensions (one penny per day in the twelfth and thirteenth centuries) by the king and members of the aristocratic classes and the episcopy.[69] The percentage of wills which mention recluses is relatively small and they typically document small individual bequests made to recluses on an individual or geographical basis, but very rarely life-time donations. Endowed cells carried their own scheme of financial support tied to the longevity of the site itself, not to the life-span of a particular anchorite, and this often afforded the greatest measure of security for the medieval recluse.[70]

Extant letters, court documents and bishop's registers report the problems of unstable anchoritic patronage arrangements. Some could, and did, break down, and in such a context the recluse was extremely vulnerable for her geographical fixity limited her ability to save herself. A total breakdown of support could potentially mean the death of the recluse unless the bishop stepped in. Warren records the case, in 1281, of one 'aging anchoress who had partially supported herself in

---

[65] Norman P. Tanner, *The Church in Late-Medieval Norwich, 1370–1532* (Toronto, 1984), p. 60.

[66] Warren, *Anchorites and their Patrons*, p. 42.

[67] See ibid., pp. 42–3, for more information on self-support.

[68] MacPherson, *Aelred of Rievalux*, p. 47. The Latin original can be found in Talbot (ed.), *Aelredi Rievallensis*, p. 639.

[69] See Warren's detailed exploration of the financial arrangements of recluses, particularly pp. 41–52 of *Anchorites and their Patrons*. Warren's analysis of wills documents the advantages and disadvantages of the analysis of testamentary data. See *Anchorites and their Patrons*, pp. 190–5.

[70] Ibid., p. 46.

her younger days [who] was found ill and in want in her cell at Blyth, Nottinghamshire'. She was rescued ultimately by the Archbishop of York, William Wickwane.[71] Legal action was instigated by some anchorites who found themselves in this situation, for example in the case of Miliana, who sued the Prior of Hardham in 1279.[72] She lost this action but other recluses were successful in theirs.[73]

Anchoritic sociability

The image of an enclosed woman taking on a representative of the might of the patriarchal Church in a legal battle over money is very different from the submissively entombed solitary imaged in high medieval guidance writing and in the ceremonies of enclosure. The agenda and rhetorical purpose of the documents in which these very contrasting images of anchoritism are revealed are of course also very different. The guides and rites offer us glimpses of high medieval anchoritic ideals, ideals which shift and change as the medieval period progresses. Legal documentation affords an image of recluses rendered socially interactive by necessity. Yet all such depictions of anchoritism provide equally valid glimpses of the English vocation.

Guidance writings, wills, ecclesiastical documents and letters suggest that anchorites had a recognized and acceptable social function in addition to a solitary one. Even the ideological texts suggest that total solitude was not only impossible but undesirable. In order to live and in order to thrive spiritually the recluse had to see those who brought her food, money, fuel, confession and the Eucharist, and it is the central paradox of anchoritism that social interaction is needed to perpetuate its comparative solitude. Total solitude was regarded as psychologically unwise by those who supervised the spirituality of the anchorites in their charge. Yet the ideal of comparative solitude seems to have remained crucial to anchoritism in England as it is reflected in anchoritic guidance writing, and there is no evidence to suggest that solitude and geographical fixity did not motivate and characterize anchoritic enclosure *as an ideal* right up to Henry VIII's dissolution of the monasteries in the sixteenth century. Nonetheless, recluses do seem to have interacted with those who served them and with those who came to them for advice. They may even, as shall be explored later in this chapter's focus on Julian of Norwich, have interacted with prestigious guilds and the upper echelons of medieval society. Yet these same historical sources, not just the guides, also vivify the space, the silence and the creativity of the possibilities that comparative freedom from social interaction will bring the recluse. In essence then, the sources which document the English anchoritic life (of which anchoritic guides with their ideological stress on the vital nature of solitude are only a part) suggest that, although the social function of a recluse cannot be ignored, withdrawal from the world

---

[71] Warren, *Anchorites and their Patrons*, p. 74.

[72] Ibid., pp. 44–5.

[73] For example, the recluse of St James, Colchester, successfully sued the abbot of St Osyth's in 1272. See ibid., p. 73 and see also *Curia regis 1201–03*, p. 205, and pp. 255–6.

dominates and motivates the ideology which is intended to shape the anchorite's desire for a solitude achieved through geographical fixity. That ideological motivation appears to remain constant as a shaping force brought to bear upon anchoritism throughout the Middle Ages.

Some English anchorites were intimately involved in the spiritual and literary worlds of their day, despite their comparative physical liminality. Individual recluses inspired the creation of specific anchoritic guides and thereby shaped the guidance-writing tradition, including Aelred's sister, and Margaret Kirkby, for whom Rolle composed *The Form of Living*. Anchorites also inspired wider textual production. The Carmelite Richard Misyn translated Richard Rolle's *De Emendatione Vitae* into English from its original Latin, renaming it the *Mendynge of Lyfe*, apparently at the behest of the recluse Margaret Heslington of St Margaret's Church, Walmgate (herself a member of York's powerful Corpus Christi Guild). A translation of Rolle's more famous contemplative text, the *Incendium Amoris*, or *Fyer of Lufe*, is also included in the three extant manuscripts in which this text appears (dated 1434).[74] Anchoritic guides highlight the importance of education, reading and reflection to their constructions of anchoritic ideology in references to recluses who own and loan books, and to a potential network of literate solitaries as virtual community.[75] Known anchoritic book-loaners and owners include Margery Pensax of St Botulph's, Bishopsgate, and Kathryn Mann, anchorite of the Dominican Friary, Norwich, who was placed in potential danger when she was suspected of receiving Tyndale's New Testament from Thomas Bilney prior to his execution for heresy in 1531.[76] Anchorite scribes, translators and authors included John Lacy, a Blackfriar at Newcastle-upon-Tyne, Northumberland (*c*.1407–34), John Dygoun, a Carthusian anchorite at Sheen, Surrey (1438–44), Simon Appulby, a secular at All Hallows-on-the-Wall, London (*c*. 1513–32) who wrote *The Fruit of Redempcyon*, a popular 1514 translation of a series of affective meditations on Christ's life taken from the anonymous Latin text *Meditationes de vita et beneficiis Jesu Christi, siue gratiarum actiones*.[77]

Julian of Norwich

The most famous anchoritic author within the English tradition is undoubtedly Julian of Norwich (*c*.1342– after 1416), anchorite of St Julian's Church in Norwich: an extraordinary recluse enclosed in an extraordinary city. Marion

---

[74] For more information on Carmelites and anchorites and on Misyn and Margaret see Johan Bergstrom-Allen's MPhil. thesis: '*Heremitam et ordinis carmelitarum*: A Study of the vernacular theological literature produced by medieval English whitefriars, particularly Richard Misyn, O. Carm.' at http://www.carmelite.org/jnbba/thesis.htm (last accessed 08.02.09).

[75] White (ed. and trans.), *Ancrene Wisse*, p. 116; Millett (ed.), *Ancrene Wisse*, p. 94.

[76] For references to Mann's friendship with Bilney (who exonerated Mann before his execution) see Clay, *Hermits and Anchorites*, pp. 184–5; Clay, 'Further Studies', pp. 78–9; and Warren, *Anchorites and their Patrons*, p. 287.

[77] Clay, *Hermits and Anchorites*, pp. 167–82. See Mary C. Erler, 'A London Anchorite, Simon Appulby: His *Fruyte of Redempcyon* and its Milieu', *Viator: Medieval and Renaissance Studies* 29 (1998), pp. 227–39.

Glasscoe argues that Julian's '"story" is one of the most remarkable ... of the Middle Ages'.[78] Tanner writes: 'Norwich was ... remarkably religious ... [possibly] Europe's *most* religious city ... premised ... on ... intensity of religion ... irrespective of ... size.'[79] This is a bold claim, but there is no denying the city's peculiar sanctity. Prominent in the development of medieval English spirituality as a whole, Norwich was possibly unique in its links with the Continent and the Low Countries through trade which, Tanner argues, gave its spirituality, in line with London, an important European dimension. It was one of the three great English urban centres which fostered anchoritism, alongside York and London.[80] Current data suggests that Norwich supported up to thirty-five recluses at its height, to York's ten and London's twelve. Jones argues that 'Julian [is] ... part of a renaissance in the solitary life in late medieval Norwich, for which Clay found more hermits and anchorites than for any other English town.'[81]

Julian's text, the complex theological treatise *A Revelation of Love*, is an account of sixteen specific visions, variously called 'showings' or 'revelations', made to her during a period of severe illness in May 1373, when she was thirty years of age. It is extant in two versions: the Short Text, extant in a single copy in the mid-fifteenth-century MS BL Additional 37790 (also called 'the Amherst Manuscript') and the Long Text, extant in three complete manuscripts and two manuscripts which contain textual redactions, none of which is earlier than the seventeenth century. In addition there is a 1670 printed edition of the Long Text by Father Hugh (Serenus) Cressy.[82] The relationship of the Short Text to the Long has been evaluated convincingly by Nicholas Watson who argues that the former was written in the mid 1380s rather than immediately after the visions themselves, while the Long Text may have been crafted from the late 1380s until Julian's death after 1416.[83] It may have been crafted, then, while she was enclosed in her anchorhold, which, according to testamentary evidence, she entered in or around 1393.[84]

At the heart of both versions of Julian's text is the image of the bleeding Christ, and hers is a narrative that focuses particularly on wider constructions of the suffering body. Hers is a graphic depiction of Christ's divinity through sorrow, which

---

[78] Marion Glasscoe, *English Medieval Mystics: Games of Faith* (London, 1993), p. 215.

[79] Norman Tanner, 'Religious Practice', in *Medieval Norwich*, ed. C. Rawcliffe and R. Wilson (London and New York, 2004), pp. 137–57 (pp. 137–8).

[80] For a discussion of how medieval Norwich may have affected Julian's anchoritic spirituality and her writing, see Alexandra Barratt, '"No such sitting": Julian Tropes the Trinity', in *A Companion to Julian of Norwich*, ed. Liz Herbert McAvoy (Cambridge, 2008), pp. 42–63; and Cate Gunn, '" A recluse atte Norwyche": Images of Medieval Norwich and Julian's *Revelations*', in ibid., pp. 32–41.

[81] Jones, 'Anchorites and Hermits in Historical Context', p. 10.

[82] The text quoted in this chapter is taken from *A Revelation of Love* in *The Writings of Julian of Norwich: A Vision Showed to a Devout Woman and A Revelation of Love*, ed. Nicholas Watson and Jacqueline Jenkins (Turnhout, 2006), pp. 123–381. See also *Julian of Norwich: A Book of Showings*, ed. E. Colledge and J. Walsh (Toronto, 1978), pp. 1–10, for useful detail on the manuscript traditions of Julian's text.

[83] Nicholas Watson, 'The Composition of Julian of Norwich's Revelation of Love', *Speculum* 68 (1993), pp. 637–83 (p. 663).

[84] Translations of the bequests made to Julian during the course of her enclosure can be found in *Writings of Julian of Norwich*, ed. Watson and Jenkins, pp. 431–5.

focuses with particular violence upon the bodily sufferings of his passion. She describes in detail 'his holy flesh and [. . .] his precious bloud, his holy passion, his dereworthy death and worshipful wounds'.[85] Her vision of the crucifixion achieves an almost cinematically visual intensity:[86]

> The grete droppes of blode felle downe fro under the garlonde like pellottes, sem-
> ing as it had comen oute of the veines. And in the coming oute they were browne
> rede for the blode was full thicke. And [. . .] bright rede [. . .] the bleding contin-
> ued tille many thinges were sene and understonded [. . .] they were like to the
> scale of hering, in the spreding of the forehede. [87]

The broken body represents for Julian the ultimate symbol of Christ's humanity; his pose is one of defeat, of human fallibility. Man reaches out to humankind from the cross, God and Man united in Christ's willingness to embrace mortality.

The irony of Julian of Norwich for the scholar of anchoritism is that, although she is the best-known English recluse of modern times, she is known chiefly as an author not an anchorite;[88] very little is known about her as an individual. She could certainly have made her text more personal had she wished to and had she thought it important for an understanding of her spiritual insights. Glasscoe argues: 'Julian tells us all she thinks needs to be known about her circumstances in order to clarify the implications of her visionary experience.'[89] We know from the text itself that she prayed for illness, so that she might learn from suffering like Christ, that she desired a visual experience of the Passion and that she wished to experience, in Glasscoe's words: 'the ... pain involved in the knowledge of, and sorrow for, sin, the suffering involved in love, and a will totally subsumed in a desire for God – what she calls three wounds ... of contrition, compassion and longing'.[90] We can tell that she was educated from the intellectual incisiveness with which she communicates her complex theology, despite her own textual protestations to the contrary, protestations which are clearly (whether deliberate-

---

[85] *Revelation of Love*, 6: 9–11, p. 143.

[86] For a discussion of Julian and cinematography see Elizabeth Robertson, 'Julian of Norwich's "Modernist Style" and the Creation of Audience', in *A Companion to Julian of Norwich*, ed. McAvoy, pp. 139–53. In turn, Robertson's analysis has been influenced by that of Barry Windeatt in 'The Art of Mystical Loving: Julian of Norwich', in *The Medieval Mystical Tradition in England: Exeter Symposium I*, ed. Marion Glasscoe (Exeter, 1980), pp. 55–71.

[87] *Revelation of Love*, 7: 10–20, p. 147. For more information on Julian's embodiment imagery see Liz Herbert McAvoy, '"For we be doubel of God's making": Writing, Gender and the Body in Julian of Norwich', in *A Companion to Julian of Norwich*, ed. McAvoy, pp. 166–80 ; G. M. Jantzen, *Julian of Norwich: Mystic and Theologian* (New York, 1987), especially pp. 74–89, 'Her Visions'; G. Brandolino, 'The "Chiefe and Principal Mene": Julian of Norwich's Redefining of the Body in *A Revelation of Love*', *Mystics Quarterly* 22 (1996), pp. 102–10; F. C. Bauerschmidt, 'Seeing Jesus: Julian of Norwich and the Text of Christ's Body', *Journal of Medieval and Early Modern Studies* 27 (1997), pp. 189–214.

[88] Arguably the states of author and anchorite are difficult to separate, but the point is that Julian *as anchorite* is largely absent from her text (although, for a useful discussion of how Julian's anchoritic enclosure may have influenced the spatial metaphors within her text, see Laura Saetveit Miles, 'Space and Enclosure in Julian of Norwich's *A Revelation of Love*', in *A Companion to Julian of Norwich*, ed. McAvoy, pp. 154–65.

[89] Glasscoe, *English Medieval Mystics*, p. 215.

[90] Ibid., p. 216.

ly or not) part of the 'modesty topos' within which the medieval female writer often operated. It does not seem from Julian's descriptions of the sick-room and (in the first and shorter text) the presence within it of her mother,[91] that she had already been enclosed as an anchorite by 1373. It is possible that enclosure came much later, in the mid 1390s, when Julian would have been middle-aged.[92] Much, therefore, has been suggested about the life she may have lived prior to her visions and prior to her enclosure: she has been cast variously as Benedictine nun, lay-woman of gentle birth, and wife and mother who lost her family to the plague (motherhood is certainly a dominant theme of her writing, although by itself this is not enough to prove such an assertion).[93] Liz Herbert McAvoy writes:

> some contemporary scholars have ... attempt[ed] to reconstruct a life for Julian out of a mixture of circumstantial evidence, social context and raw speculation ... some ... raise ... interesting possibilities and questions ... nevertheless, they should be used with ... caution.[94]

However, she reminds us that these new ideas have 'encouraged the examination of Julian's writing as ... the product of a woman with far more worldly and secular experiences than [has been] hitherto considered'.[95] We do know for certain, however, that bequests were made to Julian in some fourteenth- and fifteenth-century wills (as part of her own individualized anchoritic patronage arrangements), which indicate that she was held in significant esteem by her contemporaries.[96] Another source which corroborates this is the narrative of Margery Kempe (c.1373–c.1438), an altogether more unruly laywoman, not a recluse, who nonetheless constructs herself as living 'in devocyon of holy medytacyon of hy contemplacyon and of wonderful spechys and dalyawns whech owr Lord spak and dalyid to hyr sowle'.[97] Although the mother of fourteen children, with a spouse still living, she constructs herself as a contemplative gifted with spiritual visions of Jesus, a contemplative who travels in accordance with God's will. Significantly, she seeks spiritual approbation from anchorites, placing their authority below only that of 'worshepful clerkys',[98] and it is in this context that we must read her account of meeting Julian, for her faith in the contemplative expertise of

---

[91] In her second, reworked and developed version of her text, Julian eradicates all references to her mother, along with other autobiographical material.

[92] McAvoy, *Authority and the Female Body in the Writings of Julian of Norwich and Margery Kempe* (Cambridge, 2004), p. 69.

[93] On these respective points of view, see *Writings of Julian of Norwich*, ed. Watson and Jenkins, p. 4; 'Julian of Norwich and the Holy Spirit: "Our Good Lorde"', Alexandra Barratt, *Mystics Quarterly* 28 (2002), pp. 78–84; Benedicta Ward, 'Julian the Solitary', in *Julian Reconsidered*, ed. Kenneth Leech and Benedicta Ward (Oxford, 1988), pp. 11–35.

[94] McAvoy, '"And thou, to whom this Booke Shall Come": Julian of Norwich and her Audience, Past, Present and Future', in *Approaching Medieval English Anchoritic and Mystical Texts*, ed. Dee Dyas, Valerie Edden and Robert Ellis (Cambridge, 2006), pp. 101–15 (p. 102, n. 6).

[95] McAvoy, *Authority and the Female Body*, p. 68.

[96] See above, n. 84.

[97] Margery Kempe, *The Book of Margery Kempe*, ed. Lynn Staley (Kalamazoo, 1996), p. 18.

[98] Ibid., p. 18. Margery tells us that God urges her to reveal her contemplative experiences to 'the ankyr at the Frer Prechowrys' (p. 31), and he becomes one of her spiritual advisors.

anchorites is crucial to it. Kempe writes of the 'wondirful revelacyons whech sche schewyd to the ankres [Julian] to wetyn yf ther wer any deceyte in hem, for the ankres was expert in swech thyngys and good cownsel cowd gevyn'.[99] Although the exact circulation of Julian's text in the Middle Ages is uncertain, if, indeed, it was circulated at all, Kempe's *Book* implies that Julian is sufficiently well known to be sought out and valued by her contemporaries as a contemplative spiritual authority. In her recognition of Julian's spiritual power, Kempe implies medieval society's respect for the anchoritic contemplative, even as she concurrently seeks to validate the contemplative experiences of the laity. Kempe was by no means admitted to the presence of every recluse whose company she sought,[100] but her narrative suggests that the desirous laity had the potential to gain restricted access to anchorites as figures of respected wisdom, and this echoes Hilton's unusual advice about welcoming the interruptions of the laity as a spiritual gift.[101] In this context Jonathan Hughes recognizes fourteenth- and fifteenth-century recluses as 'influential members of lay society who communicated ... their experiences of the contemplative life, and ... suggested that laymen could aspire towards these same experiences'.[102] Felicity Riddy has identified an important sense of orality in Julian's prose style which she links specifically to the kinds of interactions Julian might, as recluse, have had with the laity generally, and with Margery in particular, casting them both as members of a virtual textual community:

> Belonging to this [community] ... allows Julian to construct a self whose femininity is its strength. Unlike ... Kempe, she occupies without strain a marginal cultural space, embracing its confines, rather than struggling against them.[103]

The anchorhold, in this context, supplies this remarkable author and anchorite with what McAvoy has called 'a paradoxical freedom for self-definition, self-expression and spiritual development which was unlikely to be available to them [female anchorites] if they remained in the world'.[104]

Conclusion

Jones points out that 'all of the ... authors comprising the canon of the "Middle English Mystics" were closely associated with solitary vocations, either as practitioners themselves or in composing works for an anchoritic or eremitic

---

[99] Kempe, *Book*, p. 54.

[100] She describes being sent away by a York anchorite because of her dangerous reputation. See ibid., p. 120.

[101] See p. 139, above.

[102] Jonathan Hughes, *Pastors and Visionaries: Religion and Secular Life in Late-Medieval Yorkshire* (Woodbridge, 1988), p. 78.

[103] Felicity Riddy, 'Women talking about the things of God: A late medieval sub-culture', *Women and Literature in Britain, 1150–1500*, ed. Carole Meale, pp. 104–28 (pp. 111–12). See also Anne Savage, 'From Anchorhold to Cell of Self-Knowledge: Points along a History of the Human Body', in *Rhetoric of the Anchorhold*, ed. McAvoy, pp. 157–72.

[104] McAvoy, *Authority and the Female Body*, p. 70.

audience'.[105] Julian, and other anchoritic writers such as Simon Appulby, and indeed hermit writers such as Rolle and Hilton, represent the creative potential of the English solitary vocation. Their writings imply that anchoritic spirituality did not just reflect medieval spiritual thought, but had the potential to shape it. Their texts imply that English anchorites were far from marginal, despite their ideological desire for seclusion and despite their comparative solitude. This chapter has shown that many, often disparate, sources vivify quite different, sometimes even contradictory, perceptions of the English anchoritic life in operation concurrently in medieval England. Many imply that anchorites were not entirely cut off from society, but that they did attempt, in England at least, *as much as was possible*, to withdraw from it. Many imply that English anchoritism was accorded considerable spiritual authority and respect. In the case of Julian and other reclusive writers, their comparative solitude may have given them the space to continue to wrestle intellectually with the sinfulness of the world in ways that informed that world's spirituality despite their relative liminality. That Julian's text is today so well known, that she was acknowledged by her contemporaries as a spiritual authority and that yet, as an anchorite and as an individual, she remains largely a mystery, is in fact testimony to the successful living-out of a sometimes paradoxical vocation. Despite her great fame, Julian joins the ranks of those nameless, faceless recluses who, in the words of George Eliot, 'lived faithfully a hidden life, and rest in unvisited tombs'.[106] In this context, it is entirely right that, in the words of Jones, 'behind the names, dates and place-names ... lie ... lives of ... richness and complexity that even ultra-violet light will not bring back'.[107] The anchoritic guidance writers understood and encouraged their recluses in the comparative seclusion which facilitated their spiritual fulfilment and led to their continued anonymity, for as Rolle explains in *The Form of Living*:

> I haue loved for to sit, for no penaunce ne for no fantasie þat I wold men spake of me ne for no such þynge, bot only for I knewe þat I loved God more, and langer lested with me confort of loue, þan goynge or standynge or knelynge. For syttynge am I in most reste, and my hert most vpward.[108]

---

[105] Jones, 'Anchorites and Hermits in Historical Context', p.3.

[106] George Eliot, *Middlemarch* (Edinburgh and London, n.d.), p. 621.

[107] Jones, 'Christina of Markyate and the *Hermits and Anchorites of England*', p. 237.

[108] Ogilvie-Thompson (ed.), *Richard Rolle*, pp. 23–4.

7 Anchorites in late medieval Ireland*

Colmán Ó Clabaigh OSB

Introduction

Interest in the eremitical and anchoritic life is enjoying something of a revival at present. Nor is this interest entirely academic: in Ireland at least five individuals have made profession as hermits since this category of religious life was again recognized in the 1983 *Code of Canon Law* of the Roman Catholic Church.[1] The life of the anchorite or recluse attracts fewer active practitioners but remains a temporary or permanent vocational option for monks and nuns belonging to the Camaldolese Benedictine tradition. At present one Camaldolese monk is living as a permanent recluse in the monastery of Monte Corona in Italy and Sister Nazarena Crotta, the last female Camaldolese anchorite, died in Rome in 1990.[2]

If the practitioners of the solitary life are relatively few, this is more than compensated for by the high numbers of scholars prepared to cross land and ocean to lecture on stability and enclosure at academic conferences, a fact reflected in the wide range of relatively recent learned publications on anchoritic themes. As a number of the other contributors also note, the pioneering studies of Rotha Mary

*This essay is dedicated to Norman Tanner SJ. I am grateful to Dr Bernadette Williams for commenting on an earlier draft and to my confreres Anthony Keane, Senan Furlong, Cyprian Love, William Fennelly, Luke Macnamara and Luke Beckett for their assistance. I am also grateful to Mr Conleth Manning, Dr Tomás Ó Carragáin and Lord Henry Mountcharles for arranging access to sites at Cashel, Fore and Slane.

Research for this article was carried out while holding a postdoctoral research fellowship from the Irish Research Council for the Humanities and Social Sciences under the auspices of the UCD Mícheál Ó Cléirigh Institute.

[1] 'Besides institutes of consecrated life, the Church recognizes the life of hermits and anchorites, in which Christ's faithful withdraw further from the world and devote their lives to the praise of God and the salvation of the world through the silence of solitude and through constant prayer and penance.' *The Code of Canon Law* (London, 1983), no. 603:1.

[2] For the legislation governing contemporary Camaldolese anchoritism see the *Constitutions and Declarations of the Camaldolese Congregation of the Order of St Benedict* (Rome, 1985), nos. 105–6. Two monks of the Camaldolese Hermitage at Big Sur in California recently died in reclusion: Brother Anthony Barabe (1914–2004) and Father Joseph Diemer (1918–2005). For an account of the last female Camaldolese anchorite see Thomas Matus, *Nazarena: an American Anchoress* (Mahwah, New Jersey, 1998). Her cell is now a place of pilgrimage. I am grateful to Father Robert Hale OSB Cam., New Camaldoli Hermitage, Big Sur for generously responding to my queries on this topic.

Clay and of Ann K. Warren continue to be touchstones for the study of medieval English anchoritism.[3] Their conclusions have subsequently been qualified and developed by scholars such as Liz Herbert McAvoy, Mari Hughes-Edwards, Henry Mayr-Harting, Edward A. Jones, Bella Millett and Norman Tanner. The work of North American and European scholars such as Anna Benvenuti Papi, Susannah Chewning, Robert Hasenfratz, Paulette L'Hermite-Leclercq, Michelle Sauer and the other contributors to this present volume has provided important reassessments of the social significance, educational role and gendered experience of anchorites. Anneke Mulder-Bakker in particular has emphasized how largely male (and frequently clerical) scholarship has hitherto failed to recognize how the anchoritic life acted as a vehicle for female spiritual authority.[4] The application of feminist, gender and queer theory as analytical categories has also resulted in many interesting perspectives.[5] Similarly the adoption of anthropological concepts such as 'liminality' and 'communitas' has helped clarify the paradoxical manner in which medieval anchorites were central to the communities on whose margins they existed.[6] The publication of a volume of medieval English anchoritic writings in the *Classics of Western Spirituality* series, as well as recent critical editions of the writings of Julian of Norwich indicate that the subject retains the interest of theologians and literary theorists.[7] As the contributors to this volume demonstrate, all this combines to produce an impressive array of hermeneutical frameworks within which to interpret the data of medieval European anchoritism.

The state of affairs in Ireland stands in stark contrast to this and to date the late medieval anchoritic and eremitical tradition has not attracted sustained scholarly attention.[8] This is in part attributable to the scarcity of material on which to base such a survey.[9] The poverty of the medieval Irish church meant that it produced fewer records than its sister institutions elsewhere and the subsequent upheavals of Irish history meant that even fewer of these sources have survived. Of the thirty-two dioceses that constituted the medieval Irish church, substantial archives survive only for the primatial see of Armagh, with a smaller amount of material surviving for Dublin, Kilkenny and other centres.[10] Nor has archaeology con-

---

[3] Rotha Mary Clay, *The Hermits and Anchorites of England* (London, 1914); Ann K. Warren, *Anchorites and their Patrons in Medieval England* (Berkeley, Los Angeles and London, 1985).

[4] Anneke B. Mulder-Bakker, *Lives of the Anchoresses: the Rise of the Urban Recluse in Medieval Europe* (Philadelphia, 2005). See particularly her foreword to *Anchorites, Wombs and Tombs: Intersections of Gender and Enclosure in the Middle Ages*, ed. Liz Herbert McAvoy and Mari Hughes-Edwards (Cardiff, 2005), pp. 1–5.

[5] Ibid.

[6] Victor W. Turner, *The Ritual Process: Structure and Anti-Structure* (Chicago, 1969); Peter Brown, 'The Rise and Function of the Holy Man in Late Antiquity', *Journal of Roman Studies* 61 (1971), pp. 80–101.

[7] Ann Savage and Nicholas Watson (eds), *Anchoritic Spirituality: Ancrene Wisse and Associated Works* (New York, 1991).

[8] Diane Hall, *Women and the Church in Medieval Ireland c.1140–1540* (Dublin, 2003), pp. 186–7 is the only recent treatment of the phenomenon.

[9] For a comprehensive guide to the surviving sources and the challenges they pose see Philomena Connolly, *Medieval Record Sources* (Dublin, 2002).

[10] Ibid., pp. 38–49.

tributed much to the discussion, with only one anchorhold being the subject of a modern excavation.[11] Establishing the basic data therefore remains the primary goal and this preliminary survey relies heavily on the work of English and Continental scholars to interpret the surviving Irish evidence coherently. These caveats notwithstanding, sufficient material survives to indicate that hermits and anchorites were familiar figures on the religious landscape of late medieval Ireland, and their experiences, lifestyle and influence were comparable to their counterparts abroad.

The Irish eremitical tradition

That the monastic and ascetic life exercised a great attraction for the first Irish Christians is evident from the earliest Christian text to survive from Ireland: the *Confessio* of St Patrick. In it he speaks of numerous monks and nuns recruited from among his high-ranking converts.[12] Early Irish monastic sites, such as the remote island sanctuaries of Skellig Michael off the coast of Co. Kerry or Inishmurray in Sligo Bay, provide spectacular if largely undocumented testimony to the eremitical zeal of early Irish monasticism.[13] The origins of monasticism in the Egyptian desert were well known in the early Irish church and can be traced in the literature and art of the period. In particular, the *Dialogues* and the *Conferences* of John Cassian were seminal texts in early Irish monasticism, disseminating the monastic ideals of the Desert Fathers and influencing the most notable Irish contribution to medieval pastoral theology, the *Pentitentials*.[14] The figures of the hermit saints Paul and Anthony frequently appear on the great High Crosses of the ninth and tenth centuries.[15] While the somewhat romantic view that hermits were responsible for some of the most beautiful lyric poetry in Old Irish has been comprehensively dismissed by Donnchadh Ó Corráin, monastic ideals and ascetic literature did influence early Irish vernacular literature.[16] In like manner the traditional identification of anchorites as expressions of ecclesiastical reform, particularly in the context of the eighth- and ninth-century *Céli*

---

[11] Miriam Clyne, 'Archaeological Investigations at Holy Trinity Abbey, Lough Key, Co Roscommon', *Proceedings of the Royal Irish Academy*, 105c (2005), pp. 23–98. Even here the purpose of the structure is uncertain. Given its position, abutting the north-eastern corner of the church, it could have functioned as an anchorhold. A female anchorite is known to have died in the monastery in 1436 and the excavation revealed three burials, one of which was that of a woman. Clyne describes it as a sacristy.

[12] Ludwig Bieler, *Libri Epistolarum Sancti Patricii Episcopi* (Dublin, 1993), p. 81.

[13] Walter Horn, Jenny White Marshall, Grellan D. Rourke, *The Forgotten Hermitage of Skellig Michael* (Berkeley, 1990); J. O'Sullivan and Tomás Ó Carragáin, *Inishmurray: Monks and Pilgrims in an Atlantic Landscape* (Cork, 2008).

[14] Thomas O'Loughlin, *Celtic Theology: Humanity, World and God in Early Irish Writings* (London, 2000), pp. 48–67; Uinseann Ó Maídín, *The Celtic Monk* (Kalamazoo, 1996).

[15] Eamonn Ó Carragáin, 'The Meeting of Saint Paul and Saint Anthony: Visual and Literary Uses of a Eucharistic Motif', in *Keimelia*, ed. Gearóid Mac Niocaill and Patrick F. Wallace (Galway, 1988), pp. 1–58.

[16] Donnchadh Ó Corráin, 'Early Irish hermit poetry?', in *Sages, Saints and Storytellers: Celtic Studies in Honour of Professor James Carney*, ed. Donnchadh Ó Corráin, Liam Breatnach and Kim McCone (Maynooth, 1989), pp. 251–67; Thomas Owen Clancy and Gilbert Márkus, *Iona: the Earliest Poetry of a Celtic Monastery* (Edinburgh, 1995), pp. 211–22.

Dé movement, has also recently been called into question.[17] The ambiguity of
the term *anchorite* in Ireland is illustrated by the career of Feidlimid Mac
Crimthainn, king of Cashel in Munster from 820 to 847, who was described in
his obit in the *Annals of Ulster* as 'the best of the Irish, a scribe and an
anchorite'. These encomia notwithstanding his other activities cast him, in
Follett's phrase, as 'the scourge of the ninth-century church, seizing, sacking
and profaning religious houses as far north as Clonmacnois'.[18] Though the
anchorite (the *dísertach* or *déorad Dé*) was a familiar figure in early Irish
monasticism, what that individual's role in the Irish church was before the
reforms of the twelfth century remains a complex and contested question and
one beyond the scope of this essay.

The eleventh and twelfth centuries witnessed various attempts at ecclesiastical
reform and renewal across Europe. In the context of monasticism, these found a
variety of expressions, but with each having a desire to return to an austere observance of its particular way of life, whether based on the Rule of St Benedict or that
of St Augustine. Some monastic reformers began their religious lives as hermits
and even when their foundations adopted a more coenobitic regime, they continued to reflect eremitical values: withdrawal, silence, recollection, abstinence and
frugality.[19] The impulse towards reform was also felt in Ireland and in Irish centres abroad. On the Continent a number of Irish Benedictine monasteries were
established in the eleventh and twelfth centuries with those in German-speaking
territories forming the congregation of St James, or the *Schottenklöster*.[20] In
Ireland itself a series of reforming synods in the first half of the twelfth century
attempted to regulate and re-order diocesan church structures.[21] In tandem with
these an effort was made to restore Irish monasticism by introducing reformed
religious orders from England and the Continent, most notably the Cistercian
monks and Augustinian canons. Both orders experienced rapid expansion: by
1250 thirty-four Cistercian houses and 122 Augustinian foundations had been
established in Ireland. The Benedictine monks and Victorine and
Premonstratensian canons enjoyed a more modest growth, while the Carthusians,
the most austere of the reformed orders, made only one Irish foundation, in 1252,

---

[17] For the traditional view see Kathleen Hughes, *The Church in Early Irish Society* (London, 1966), pp.
173–93; and Peter O'Dwyer, *Céli Dé* (2nd edn., Dublin, 1981). For a critique of this position see Colmán
Etchingham, *Church Organisation in Ireland AD 650–1000* (Maynooth, 1999), pp. 319–62. The most
recent and comprehensive treatment of the subject is Westley Follett, *Céli Dé in Ireland* (Woodbridge,
2006).

[18] Follett, *Céli Dé*, pp. 17–18.

[19] Giles Constable, 'Eremiticial Forms of Monastic life', in *Instituzioni monastiche e instituzioni canonicali in Occidente (1123–1215)* (Milan, 1980), pp. 239–64; Henrietta Leyser, *Hermits and the New
Monasticism* (London, 1984).

[20] Dagmar Ó Riain-Raedel, 'Irish Benedictine Monasteries on the Continent', in *The Irish Benedictines:
A History*, ed. Martin Browne OSB and Colmán Ó Clabaigh OSB (Dublin, 2005), pp. 25–63.

[21] Aubrey Gwynn, *The Irish Church in the Eleventh and Twelfth Centuries* (Dublin, 1992); John Watt,
The Church in Medieval Ireland (2nd edn., Dublin 1998), pp. 1–27, pp. 229–36. Martin Holland, 'Dublin
and the Reform of the Irish Church in the Eleventh and Twelfth Centuries', *Peritia: Journal of the
Medieval Academy of Ireland* 14 (2000), pp. 111–60.

which had been abandoned before 1341.[22] Approximately seventy foundations were made for the female branches of these Continental orders, with houses of Augustinian canonesses predominating. These female foundations tended to be much smaller and less well endowed than their male counterparts and are poorly represented in the historical record.[23]

In Ireland, as elsewhere in Europe, each of these orders facilitated the anchoritic and eremitical aspirations of individual members.[24] The Irish Benedictine monastery of St James at Regensburg in Bavaria originated in the group of disciples that gathered around the pilgrim and anchorite Marianus Scottus (Muredach Mac Robartaigh) (d. 1088) and the literature associated with the movement contains numerous references to the presence of recluses in the community.[25] The earliest account of the pilgrimage to the island sanctuary of St Patrick's Purgatory in Lough Derg, Co. Donegal, contains a reference to an Augustinian canon living as a hermit.[26] In 1227 the English abbot Stephen of Lexington, conducting a tempestuous visitation of the Irish Cistercian monasteries, permitted Brothers Isaac and James, monks of Holy Cross Abbey, Co. Tipperary, and their companion Flan, a *conversus* or laybrother, 'to transfer to the solitary and eremitical life' [*ad vitam solitariam et heremiticam se transferre*].[27]

The Anglo-Norman presence in Ireland after 1169 had a number of significant consequences for the Irish church. It led to an Anglicization of the Irish episcopate and the adoption, to varying degrees, of English liturgical and administrative practices. It also fomented ethnic tension between the Gaelic population and the newcomers that found expression in long-running and occasionally violent disputes over the control of dioceses, monasteries and religious orders.[28] As demonstrated below, these increased contacts with England in the

---

[22] Aubrey Gwynn and R. Neville Hadcock, *Medieval Religious Houses: Ireland* (Dublin, 1970 [repr. Dublin, 1988]), pp. 114–44, p. 145, pp. 146–200, pp. 201–7; Marie Therese Flanagan, 'St Mary's Abbey, Louth and the Introduction of the Arroasian Observance into Ireland', *Clogher Record* 10, no. 2 (1980), pp. 223–34; Sarah Preston, 'The Canons Regular of St Augustine in Medieval Ireland: An Overview', (unpublished PhD thesis, University of Dublin, 1996); Stuart Kinsella (ed.), *Augustinians at Christ Church* (Dublin, 2000); Hugh Bernard Feiss, 'The *Ordo* of St Victor in Ireland', *Ordo Canonicus*, Seria Altera N.4 (1988), pp. 56–87; Dom Andrew Gray, 'Kinaleghin: a Forgotten Irish Charterhouse of the Thirteenth Century', *Journal of the Royal Society of Antiquaries of Ireland* 89 (1959), pp. 35–58.

[23] Gwynn and Hadcock, *Medieval Religious Houses*, pp. 307–26. The definitive work on medieval Irish nuns is Hall, *Women and the Church*, pp. 63–206.

[24] On this aspect of religious orders see the various articles in *L'eremitismo in occidente nei secoli XI e XII* (Milan, 1965).

[25] Ó Riain-Raedel, 'Irish Benedictine Monasteries', pp. 34–42.

[26] Robert Easting (ed.), *St Patrick's Purgatory*, EETS 298 (Oxford, 1991), p. 125. For the context of this phenomenon see Ludo Milis, 'L'évolution de l'érémitisme au canonicat régulier dans la première moité du douzième siècle: transition ou trahison?', in *Instituzioni monastiche e instituzioni canonicali*, pp. 223–38.

[27] Bruno Greisser (ed.), 'Registrum Epistolarum Stephani de Lexinton', *Analecta Sacri Ordinis Cisterciensis* 2 (1946), pp. 1–118 (p. 27). For the background to the dispute see Barry O'Dwyer, 'The Problem of Reform in the Irish Cistercian Monasteries and the Attempted Solution of Stephen of Lexington in 1228', *Journal of Ecclesiastical History* 15 (1964), pp. 186–91. See also Jean Leclercq, 'L'érémitisme et les Cisterciens', in *L'eremitismo in Occidente nei secoli XI e XII*, pp. 573–6.

[28] John A. Watt, *The Church and the Two Nations in Medieval Ireland* (Cambridge, 1970).

twelfth and thirteenth centuries led to the circulation in Ireland of English anchoritic rules and related literature.

In Ireland, as elsewhere in Europe, the revival of coenobitic monasticism was paralleled by individuals becoming hermits and anchorites on their own initiative. Here it becomes necessary to clarify terms.[29] Before the twelfth century the words 'hermit' or 'anchorite' were used almost interchangeably for practitioners of a solitary ascetic life in Ireland. In both instances it was presumed that, following the teaching of John Cassian, the candidate had passed first through a period of preparation by living the communal or coenobitic life in a monastery. As Follett notes: 'Among Hiberno-Latin writers the term anchorite seems to have been used most often to designate a religious not living in complete isolation but in semi-reclusion near a coenobitical community.'[30] After the twelfth century, and particularly in the towns and districts of the Anglo-Norman colony, the term anchorite was increasingly reserved for recluses (*reclusus/a*; *inclusus/a*), individuals who pursued a solitary ascetic vocation enclosed in a cell or anchorhold, generally adjacent to a church. The *Dublin Rule,* which dates to the first half of the thirteenth century, illustrates this development in its fanciful etymology of the word *anachorita*:

> This name 'anchorite' is Greek and is understood as 'one who lifts up his heart'. Therefore every servant of Christ ought to lift up his heart, so that it may abide among heavenly things and not wander among earthly things. Holding the heart raised up to God: the name of this (i.e. this term) took its origin from the holy fathers of old, the life of whom is told in the book which is called the *Vitas Patrum*. Some of these live in the desert, some in caves, some having been enclosed [*inclusi*] beside the church, separated from all, having cast behind all worldly things, holding their hearts raised up to God.

> [Hoc nomen anachorita grecum est et interpretatur cor elevans sursum. Ita et debet omnis Christi servus cor suum sursum elevare, ut inter celestia moretur, et non inter terrena vagetur, vel cor habens erectum ad Deum; huiusmodi nomen ex patribus olim sanctis sumpsit excordium (*recte* exordium), de quorum vita, in liber (*recte* libro) qui dicitur Vitas Patrum insita, narratur. Horum quiddam habitant in deserto, quidam in speluncis, quiddam iuxta ecclesiam inclusi ab omnibus segregati, omnibus mundanis retropositis, corda habentes erecta ad Deum.][31]

Though the author recognizes that the term *anchorite* can be applied to those who follow the eremitical life in the desert or in caves, the anchorites for whom his legislation is intended are those 'enclosed beside the church'.

---

[29] Jean Leclercq, 'Eremus et eremita, pour l'histoire du vocabulaire de la vie solitaire', *Collectanea ordinis Cisterciensium reformatorum* 25 (1963), pp. 8–30. But see E. A. Jones, 'Langland and Hermits', in *The Yearbook of Langland Studies* 11, ed. John A. Alford and Andrew Galloway (Asheville, 1997), pp. 67–86 (p. 71) for an important qualification of Leclercq's position.

[30] Follett, *Céli Dé*, pp. 26–7.

[31] Livarius Oliger (ed.), 'Regulae tres reclusorum et eremitarium Angliae saec. XIII–XIV', *Antonianum* 3 (1928), pp. 151–90. Reference at p. 175 (my translation).

The hermit's vocation was also a solitary one, formalized by liturgical rite and the donning of a distinctive religious habit.[32] Unlike the anchorite, however, the hermit was not bound to strict enclosure but retained freedom of movement. While living on the margins of society hermits often supported themselves by repairing roads and bridges or maintaining beacons, social services for which their contemporaries were willing to bestow alms and bequests. In this respect it may be significant that the Carmelite friars, who arrived in Ireland before 1272, were charged with the maintenance of the bridge at their first foundation of Leighlinbridge, Co. Carlow. The Carmelites originated as hermits in Palestine and the eremitical tradition remained a potent influence in the order.[33]

Men of low social standing, often illiterate, particularly favoured the eremitical vocation and in England various rules for hermits survive from the fourteenth and fifteenth centuries. These were simple texts, often in the vernacular, committing the candidate to an ascetic and (generally) celibate lifestyle with a commitment to a cycle of regular prayer and a modified form of the Divine Office. The most widespread of these English rules were the *regula eremitarum* (often erroneously attributed to Richard Rolle), the rule of St Paul (the first hermit) and other texts variously ascribed to Pope Celestine V and Pope Linus.[34] Nothing of this nature survives for late medieval Ireland and references to hermits in either Gaelic or Anglo-Irish sources are remarkably few. In September 1455 hermits were included in the list of Gaelic friars, nuns, clerics, beggars and other undesirables who were forbidden to enter the royal city of Dublin.[35] In 1533 William Dyllon, a hermit [*heremita*], made a deposition concerning the lands of the Dean of St Patrick's Cathedral, Dublin, at Clondalkin.[36] While the documentary sources are relatively few, the evidence of folklore, hagiography and archaeology indicates that caves, rock shelters and island sites associated with early Irish saints were intermittently occupied by hermits throughout the later Middle Ages.[37] The most spectacular example of this is the site known as St Kevin's Bed in the valley of Glendalough, Co. Wicklow. Situated on a cliff-face ten metres above the south shore of the upper lake in the valley, it is accessible only by boat. It consists of a rock-cut chamber measuring two metres in depth and ninety centimetres in height, and it may originally have been a Bronze Age mine. As a hermitage and place of religious retreat it is associated both with St Kevin (d. 618), the founder of Glendalough, and with St Laurence O'Toole (Lorcán Ua Tuathail), a twelfth-century abbot of the community and reforming archbishop of Dublin from

[32] A text of the Office for the Benediction of Hermits from a sixteenth-century English pontifical is given in Clay, *Hermits and Anchorites*, pp. 199–202.

[33] Peter O'Dwyer, *The Irish Carmelites* (Dublin, 1988), pp. 3–4; Johan Bergström-Allen, 'The Whitefriars Return to Carmel', in *Anchorites, Wombs and Tombs*, ed. McAvoy and Hughes-Edwards, pp. 77–91.

[34] Virginia Davis, 'The Rule of St Paul, the First Hermit, in Late Medieval England', in *Monks, Hermits and the Ascetic Tradition*, ed. W. J. Sheils, Studies in Church History 22 (Oxford, 1985), pp. 203–14.

[35] J. T. Gilbert, *Calendar of Ancient Records of Dublin* 1 (Dublin, 1889), p. 287.

[36] Newport B. White (ed.), *The Dignatis Decani of St Patrick's Cathedral Dublin* (Dublin, 1957), p. 123. I am grateful to Professor Raymond Gillespie for this reference.

[37] Conleth Manning, 'Rock Shelters and Caves associated with Irish Saints', in *Above and Beyond: Essays in Memory of Leo Swan*, ed. Tom Condit and Christiaan Corlett (Bray, 2005), pp. 109–20.

1162.[38] The latter's Latin *vita*, commissioned by the Augustinian Canons of Eu in Normandy, where he died on 14 November 1180, records that he regularly spent periods of forty days on retreat in the cave, even after he became archbishop.[39]

The longevity of the eremitical tradition and the awe with which hermits' spiritual power was regarded is given, literally, graphic expression in Captain John Baxter's 1603 'Map of the North-West parts of Ireland'. Beside the depiction of the island of Inishmurray, the cartographer has noted:

> In this islande there dwelleth a holye man called Scanlon of whom the contrie people holde a superstitious opinion that if he be angry with any one and doe turne the speckled stones uppon them, which he kepeth for that use, they shall dye within that yeare.[40]

The 'speckled stones' – cross-marked sea stones used for maledictions and imprecations – are still preserved at the site.

A further expression of the esteem in which the vocation was held comes from Edward Bletso's curious poem lamenting the death of Owen O'Hara, governor of Carrickfergus, in a racing accident in 1622. The poem takes the form of a dialogue on the fragility of human existence between the characters Viator and Heremita, and concludes with a ringing endorsement of the solitary life:

Viator:

> Holy father, though my learning
> Unsufficient is to answere,
> Yet in my corrupt discerninge
> You are blessed by my censure.
> Above the primum mobile,
> Thou whordest thy wealth celestiall,
> And despist base trash ignoble,
> Vile, inconstant & terrestiall.
> Tis not wealth nor worldly glory,
> Bewty, strength, or wit to know
> All earths pride is transitory
> Fayre in sight but is not so.
> [...]

Heremita:

> Since the world doth nought delight thee,
> Learne with me therto to dy
> Let its fickleness incite thee.

Viator:

> So I shall, farewell vanity.[41]

---

[38] Ibid., pp. 110–14.

[39] Charles Plummer (ed.), 'Vie et miracles de S. Laurent, archevêque de Dublin', *Analecta Bollandiana* 33 (1914), pp. 121–86 (pp. 141–2).

[40] O'Sullivan and Ó Carragáin, *Inishmurray*, p. 23. I am grateful to Mr Michael Gibbons for first alerting me to this reference and to Dr Tomás Ó Carragáin for discussing it with me.

[41] Edward Bletso, 'Dialogus inter Viatorem & Heremitam', in *Verse in English from Tudor and Stuart Ireland*, ed. Andrew Carpenter (Cork, 2003), pp. 152–3.

Anchorites in late medieval Ireland

Evidence for the existence of anchorites in late medieval Ireland is only slightly more abundant than for hermits and conforms to the analytical categories employed by Warren in her analysis of the English sources. The surviving material consists of episcopal legislation concerning anchorites; liturgical material relating to the rite of enclosure; anchoritic rules of life; evidence for support by benefactors; and references to anchorites in contemporary literature. Given the paucity of surviving Irish material, the recent discovery by Dr Donna Thornton of a dossier of anchoritic material in St Patrick's College, Maynooth MS RB 201 is of particular significance.[42] The material in the codex was transcribed in 1627 by Dr Thomas Arthur, a Limerick-born physician, from exemplars preserved in the library at Drogheda, Co. Louth, of James Ussher (d. 1656), the scholarly archbishop of Armagh.[43] These consist of several medieval Irish saints' *vitae* and a copy of the twelfth-century treatise *De statu ecclesiae* of Gilbert of Limerick. The anchoritic material includes what appears to be a previously unknown rule for recluses, an abbreviated version of the enclosure rite and an anchorite's profession formula dating to 1401. It is possible that the anchoritic material was preserved among the muniments of Ussher's medieval predecessors as archbishops of Armagh and that it represents the norms by which the anchoritic life in the diocese was regulated.[44]

Bishops and anchorites

The legal responsibility for anchorites was vested in the bishop of the diocese. As Warren notes in an English context, his obligations to his charges were fivefold.[45] Either he or his delegate had first to establish the credentials and suitability of the candidate for the life; he then determined whether the candidate had sufficient financial resources to sustain him or her and might assist in finding a suitable anchorhold. Only then did he or his delegate perform the rite of enclosure. His final obligation was to supervise and support the anchorite for the duration of his or her lifetime, offering counsel and correction as required and occasionally intervening to secure support or alleviate distress.

No examples of preliminary investigations survive in any of the extant Irish sources. However, an interesting and illustrative account of the experience of one female Irish anchorite's experience survives in an English episcopal register. In 1447 Christine Holby, a former Augustinian canoness of Kildare, sought enclo-

---

[42] St Patrick's College, Maynooth MS RB 201, pp. 233–40. I am grateful to Dr Thornton for generously drawing this material to my attention. An edition and translation is in progress.

[43] Donna Thornton, 'The Lives of St Carthage of Lismore' (unpublished PhD thesis, University College Cork, 2002), pp. 43–4 and pp. 54–5.

[44] St Peter's church in Drogheda functioned as the pro-cathedral for the archdiocese of Armagh for much of the Middle Ages. In 1335 a bequest was left to the female anchorite attached to the church of St Laurence in Drogheda. See Charles McNeill and A. J. Otway-Ruthven, *Dowdall Deeds* (Dublin, 1960), p. 53.

[45] Warren, *Anchorites*, pp. 92–124; Clay, *Hermits and Anchorites*, pp. 193–8.

sure as an anchorite in the churchyard of St Leonard in Exeter, having fled from her convent in Ireland after it had been attacked by the Irish. The bishop of the diocese, Edmund Lacy, commissioned the precentor of the cathedral, Walter Collys, to examine her to see

> that Satan had not transformed himself into an angel of light [*in lucis angelum*] to seduce her [and to] ensure that she has sure and certain sustenance [*secura et certa sustentacione*] to sustain her and who will bestow it and sustain it until the end of her life, and of how much and of what things this manner of dowry [*huius-modi dotacio*] ought to consist, so that we and our successors in this place shall never be burdened by this conclusion.[46]

While it is clear from elsewhere in the document that Lacy approved of the anchoritic life and was supportive of her petition, he was also mindful of not imposing a burden on his successors. Holby was obviously able to satisfy Precentor Collys as a later document in the register indicates that she had duly been enclosed.

The rite of enclosure

As the ceremony of enclosure was generally reserved to a bishop or other prelate, the text of the rite is normally found in the *Pontificale*, the service book containing texts of ceremonies such as priestly ordination, the consecration or reconciliation of a church and other liturgical rites that only a bishop could perform. Only one such *Pontificale* survives from medieval Ireland, Trinity College Dublin MS 99, a late fourteenth-century manuscript from either Italy or Avignon, which was used in the diocese of Meath. It has suffered the loss of several quires and individual leaves and is badly water-stained. Much of the surviving material is also out of sequence as a result of subsequent rebinding. The section containing the texts of blessings and consecrations of individuals includes the texts for the benediction of an abbot, the profession of a nun and the consecration of a widow as a vowess. It is possible that the rite for enclosing an anchorite was among the other texts now missing from this section.[47]

The principal features of the enclosure ceremony can be reconstructed from English pontificals and complementary Irish material.[48] The rite of enclosure contained elements of the funeral liturgy as well as that of religious profession. During Mass the candidate, holding a candle, made profession of the religious vows to the bishop or his delegate, promising to remain in the anchorhold, devoting themselves to prayer and penance. This was accompanied by the singing of the

---

[46] G. R. Dunstan (ed.), *Register of Edmund Lacy, Bishop of Exeter 1420–1455*, Canterbury and York Society 60–3 (1963–71), vol. ii, pp. 394–5; Warren, *Anchorites*, p. 74 and p. 269.
[47] TCD MS 99, ff. 120v–141v. See also Marvin L. Colker, *Trinity College Library, Dublin: Descriptive Catalogue of the Medieval and Renaissance Latin Manuscripts*, 2 vols (Dublin, 1991), vol. 1, pp. 198–201.
[48] For a comprehensive analysis of the various elements of the rite of enclosure see E. A. Jones, 'Ceremonies of Enclosure: Rite, Rhetoric and Reality', in *Rhetoric of the Anchorhold: Space, Place and Body within the Discourses of Enclosure*, ed. Liz Herbert McAvoy (Cardiff, 2008), pp. 34–49.

litany of the saints and after communion the prayers for the dying were recited and the anchorite sprinkled with clay. The bishop then entered the adjacent anchorhold and blessed it, sometimes consecrating an internal altar for the celebration of Mass if the anchorite was a priest. After this the anchorite took possession and the bishop or his delegate sealed the door.

An abbreviated form of the rite is found in Maynooth MS RB 201. It makes no reference to Mass, but it describes the procession to the anchorhold, the blessing of the cell and its occupant, and gives the *incipits* of the various collects and prayers recited during the ceremony:

> At the entrance of an anchorite a procession is made by the bishop or abbot or prior and after they come to the anchorhold let him be led by the major prelates before the altar and let them say the seven penitential psalms. After the psalms let the prelate say the prayers *Salvum fac servum tuum. Deus meus sperantem in te. Mitte ei Domine auxilium de sancto, et de Syon tuere eum. Esto ei Domine turris fortitudinis, a facie inimici. Nihil proficiat inimicus in eo. Et filius iniquitatis non apponat nocere ei. Domine exaudi est et clamoretur*, etc.
>
> Let us pray: Bless O Lord this bridal chamber and this your servant J. living in it and may he remain in your love with fasting, prayers and vigils and may he day by day build up the clergy and people of God by leading a pure and religious life until the end of his life. Amen.[49]

The Maynooth manuscript also gives the text of the short formula of profession by which the anchorite committed him/herself to the new calling:

> I, J., make profession to Almighty God and to the Blessed Mary, ever virgin and to all the saints whose feast is celebrated today in the church of God and of the rule constituted by the saints and fathers in the year of the Lord, 1401.[50]

> [Ego J professionem do omnipotenti Deo et beatae Mariae semper virgini et omnibus sanctis qicorum festa hodie aguntur in ecclesia Dei et regulae a sanctis patribus constitutae anno Domini milessimo quadragentessimos primo 1401 Finis.]

Further evidence for knowledge of the rite of enclosure comes from the accounts of the medieval pilgrimage to the island shrine of the Cave of St Patrick's Purgatory in Lough Derg, Co. Donegal. Here the Knight Owein, a twelfth-century Welshman, had a vision of heaven and the underworld, and his graphic account, compiled *c*.1185 by the Cistercian monk Henry of Saltrey, circulated widely throughout medieval Europe. The shrine's subsequent fame drew pilgrims from throughout the British Isles and from as far afield as Catalonia and Hungary.[51] The twenty-eight surviving accounts of the pilgrimage dating from the twelfth to the sixteenth centuries indicate that the ritual performed before admitting a pilgrim to

---

[49] St Patrick's College, Maynooth MS RB 201, ff. 239–40 (my translation).
[50] Ibid.
[51] Michael Haren and Yolande de Pontfarcy, *The Medieval Pilgrimage to St Patrick's Purgatory* (Enniskillen, 1988).

the cave was adapted from the rite of enclosure. The most detailed account is that of Knight Owein himself.[52] Before the pilgrim was admitted to the island he had to secure the permission of the bishop of the diocese who interrogated him about his resolve, warning him of the many dangers faced by those who entered the cave. This possibly represents an adaptation of the requirement of securing episcopal licence before being enclosed. On the pilgrim's arrival at the Purgatory the prior of the Augustinian canons who administered the shrine again attempted to dissuade him, but if he proved adamant in his desire, then:

> The prior summons the neighbouring clergy and in the morning during the cele-bration of Mass the penitent is strengthened by Holy Communion and sprinkled with holy water blessed at the same ceremony. Then he is led to the door of the purgatory accompanied by procession and litany. As the prior opens the door in front of everyone he warns him again against the attack of the demon and of the many people lost in the pit. If, however, the penitent is firm in his intention, after receiving benediction from all the priests, he commends himself to the prayers of all, impresses the sign of the cross on his forehead and enters. The prior imme-diately bolts the door.[53]

Support, supervision and patronage

Very little remains in any surviving Irish episcopal or synodal *acta* to illustrate an Irish bishop's ongoing supervisory role in relation to anchorites.[54] This is in marked contrast to England where the episcopal registers clearly demonstrate his role as supervisor, corrector and supporter. A common expression of such support was the granting of indulgences to those who gave alms to an anchorite and here the Irish sources are a little more forthcoming. In May 1406 Archbishop Nicholas Fleming of Armagh granted forty days of indulgence to those of his subjects who, having confessed their sins, gave alms to the proctor of Sir Eustace Roch, a priest-anchorite 'of praiseworthy life and honest conversation' [*vite laudabilis et conver-sationis honeste*] enclosed [*sit inclusus*] in the chapel of St Mary and Sts Peter and Paul in St Doolagh's church in Dublin.[55] Over a century later, in July 1508, Octavian de Palatio, Fleming's successor as archbishop of Armagh, granted an indulgence of forty days to those who supported Friar Meylerus Bratnagh, an Observant Franciscan friar who, despite being old and blind, henceforth proposed to adopt a stricter religious discipline by becoming an anchorite [*anachoreticam ... vitam*] in a cell adjacent to the cathedral at Cashel, Co. Tipperary.[56] In both instances the length of indulgence was forty days, or a quarantine, the standard

---

[52] Easting (ed.), *St Patrick's Purgatory*, pp. 121–54.

[53] Ibid., pp. 125–6. Translation in Haren and de Pontfarcy, *The Medieval Pilgrimage*, p. 11.

[54] Gerald Bray (ed.), *Records of Convocation XVI: Ireland 1101–1690* (Woodbridge, 2006).

[55] Brendan Smith (ed.), *The Register of Nicholas Fleming, Archbishop of Armagh 1404–1416* (Dublin, 2003), pp. 7–8.

[56] Mario Alberto Sughi (ed.), *Registrum Octaviani*, 2 vols (Dublin, 1999), vol. 1, p. 30; vol. 2, pp. 123–4. Contributors were to be in the state of grace to benefit from the indulgence and the archbishop noted that Friar Meylerus had undertaken this project with the support of his superiors.

length granted for donations to charitable causes. The reference to the proctor of Sir Eustace Roch indicates that third parties solicited support for anchorites. That the archbishops of Armagh issued these indulgences for anchorites located in other dioceses indicates that these proctors ranged widely in their quest for alms. The use of proctors and indulgences to garner support for medieval English hermits and anchorites is well attested and, as shown below, there is evidence for the practice in Ireland in the late seventeenth century.[57]

In Ireland, as elsewhere in Europe, anchorites depended entirely for their sustenance on the support of a network of patrons and benefactors. This reliance brought them into contact with a wide cross-section of society and created strong bonds of mutual dependence, affection and spiritual relationship.[58] In an age where prayer was a valued and negotiable commodity, anchorites enjoyed a high status within their communities and frequently featured as recipients of alms and beneficiaries of wills. The making of testaments and wills became more common in Europe from the twelfth century, and a number of Irish examples survive from the thirteenth century onwards.[59] The estate of the deceased was generally divided into three portions after the discharge of outstanding debts. Of these one third was reserved for *pro anima* purposes, the various charitable and religious legacies that were held to benefit the soul after death, and bequests to anchorites generally occur in this category. Fewer than 120 wills survive from late medieval Ireland, mostly emanating from the towns of the Anglo-Irish colony and containing very few bequests to anchorites.

The earliest record of a bequest to an Irish recluse occurs in 1275 when Katherine, wife of John le Grant, left a legacy to the female anchorite of St Paul's chapel in Dublin and to her servant, Petronilla.[60] In 1306 John de Wnynchedon, a wealthy Cork merchant, left bequests of forty pence each to the male anchorites [*incluso*] enclosed in the city's churches of the Holy Trinity and of St Brigid. He also left forty pence to the male anchorite [*incluso*] of St Finbarr's Cave [*de antro Sti Finbarri*], the title of the monastery of Augustinian canons that occupied the reputed site of the city's patron saint's place of retreat.[61] In 1326 Robert de Moenes, a wealthy citizen of Dublin, left bequests to a female recluse at St Paul's chapel and to two male anchorites at other churches in the city.[62] The only reference to an anchorite in the important commercial port town of Drogheda occurs in 1335 when Richard Tanner bequeathed forty pence to the female anchorite

---

[57] Warren, *Anchorites*, p. 81, n. 70; Jones, 'Langland and Hermits', pp. 67–86 (p. 77). I am grateful to Dr Jones for advice on this point.

[58] Mulder-Bakker, *Lives of the Anchoresses*, pp. 1–23.

[59] See the important article by Margaret Murphy, 'The High Cost of Dying: an Analysis of *Pro Anima* Bequests in Medieval Dublin', in *The Church and Wealth, Studies in Church History* 24 (1987), pp. 111–22.

[60] M. J. McEnery and Raymond Refaussé, *Christ Church Deeds* (Dublin, 2001), no. 106, p. 54.

[61] Denis O'Sullivan (ed.), 'The Testament of John de Wynchedon of Cork', *Journal of the Cork Historical and Archaeological Society* 59 (1956), pp. 75–88 (p. 78 and p. 79). O'Sullivan's translation of *incluso* as 'to the priest living in retirement' is misleading. See also Manning, 'Rock Shelters and Caves', p. 114.

[62] Trinity College, Dublin MS 1207/85–26. Cited by Hall, *Women and the Church*, pp. 186–7.

enclosed by the church of St Laurence.[63] Similarly, the only reference to an anchorite in the western sea port of Galway occurs in the 1420 will of John Oge Blake, a member of one of the fourteen families or 'tribes' who dominated the city's affairs; he bequeathed a measure of corn and a vat of butter to Fergal the anchorite [*Fergallo anchorite*].[64] Curiously, the only register of wills to survive from medieval Dublin contains no references or bequests to anchorites. The register contains seventy-four wills proved during the pontificates of Archbishops Michael Tregury (1449–71) and John Walton (1472–84) and perhaps indicates that the life had fallen into desuetude in the capital in the latter part of the fifteenth century.[65] This is all the more remarkable in light of the contemporary revival of the reclusive life in Gaelic and Gaelicized parts of the country.

In England the crown and aristocratic patrons constituted a mainstay of many anchorites' support networks.[66] This support could include patronage of an anchorhold, a regular payment of alms, whether in cash or in kind, or a one-off benefaction in response to specific needs. Between 1270 and 1281 the Irish Exchequer rolls record an annual grant of a robe and a daily stipend of one and a half pence by King Henry III to the female anchorite [*inclusa*] of the church of St Mary del Dam in Dublin.[67] This church was adjacent to Dublin Castle, the seat of royal government in Ireland, and to the Irish Exchequer, which proximity may account for the patronage.

The evidence for Irish aristocratic patronage of recluses is likewise scanty. In 1512 the Baron of Slane, Christopher Fleming and his wife, Elizabeth Stuckley, restored the anchorholds at St Erc's hermitage on their demesne at Slane, Co. Meath, for the use of Father Malachy O'Byren and Brother Donagh O'Byrne, both recluses and Franciscan Tertiaries.[68] Though much of the fabric that currently survives at the site dates to this restoration, the hermitage is first mentioned in a deed of 1344.[69] Writing *c.*1618, Friar Donatus Mooney, the Franciscan Minister Provincial, records the tradition that one of the early barons of Slane, also a Franciscan tertiary, had been enclosed as an *inclusus* there [*se perpetuo inclusit in quadam caverna*].[70] Mooney also records an incident from *c.*1496 in which the saintly anchorite [*anachoreta devotus*] of Lismore in Co. Waterford had a vision of the soul of a Gaelic chieftain ascending to heaven while celebrating Mass in the presence of the earl of Kildare.[71] While this does not indicate that the earl was his

[63] McNeill and Otway-Ruthven, *Dowdall Deeds*, pp. 53–4.

[64] Roderic O'Flaherty, *A Chorographical Description of West or H-Iar Connaught*, ed. James Hardiman (Dublin, 1846), pp. 198–201 (p. 200).

[65] TCD MS 552; Henry F. Berry, *Register of Wills and Inventories of the Diocese of Dublin in the Time of Archbishops Tregury and Walton 1457–1483* (Dublin, 1898).

[66] Warren, *Anchorites*, pp. 127–221.

[67] Philomena Connolly (ed.), *Irish Exchequer Payments*, vol. 1, 1270–1326 (Dublin, 1998), pp. 2, 6, 12, 17, 22, 25, 29, 37, 46, 50, 54, 60, 61, 66.

[68] Gwynn and Hadcock, *Medieval Religious Houses*, pp. 274–5.

[69] James Mills and M. J. McEnery, *Calendar of the Gormanstown Register* (Dublin, 1916), pp. 55–6. I am grateful to Dr Charles Smith for this reference.

[70] Brendan Jennings (ed.), 'Donatus Moneyus, De Provincia Hiberniae S. Francisci', *Analecta Hibernica* vi (1934), pp. 12–138 (p. 104).

[71] Ibid., p. 62.

patron, it does demonstrate the regard with which the anchorite was held and the access to elite social groups that this afforded him.

Rents and other income from properties were another important source of support for recluses. In September 1234 Margaret, daughter of Richard Gillemichelle of Dublin, donated a substantial annuity to the Augustinian nuns of St Mary de Hogges in the city for the good of her soul and that of Sir Alexander, the priest-anchorite of St Clement's chapel on the outskirts of the city.[72] Sir Alexander appears to have been her brother and had his own property portfolio from which c.1230 he had granted an annuity of two shillings to the Augustinian canons of the city's All Hallows priory for the welfare of his soul and that of his sister Margaret. This annuity derived from rents accruing from a property in the suburbs of which, presumably, he had hitherto been the beneficiary.[73] At its dissolution in 1540 St Mary's Cistercian abbey in Dublin possessed a parcel of three acres of pasture adjacent to the monastery, known as the 'Ankerest Parke'. It is likely that this provided an income for an anchorite resident in the house.[74] Although rents provided a degree of financial security for the recluse, such involvements in temporal affairs also brought their own hazards. In 1300 the anchorite Roesia de Naungles was forced to bring Adam of Trym to court for non-payment of a debt. The nature of the debt is not stated and the anchorite, who appears to have been based in Dublin, was represented by James le Whyte, an attorney.[75]

As an act of charity religious houses occasionally undertook the support of an anchorite.[76] In addition to the three recluses mentioned above, Robert de Moenes also left bequests to two women described as Minorite sisters [*sororibus minoribus*] in his 1326 will. This term was normally used to describe Franciscan or Poor Clare nuns but as no such community existed in Dublin at this date it may refer to female anchorites attached to the city's Franciscan friary.[77] In 1436, the *Annals of Connacht* record the death of the anchoress Gormlaith at Holy Trinity Abbey, a house of Premonstatensian canons situated on Trinity Island in Loch Key, Co. Roscommon.[78] The Augustinian nuns of Grace Dieu near Dublin supported the anchorite Felicia in their chapel at Ballymadun at an unspecified date in either the fourteenth or fifteenth century.[79] Occasionally these arrangements did not end felicitously, as the nuns of St Mary de Hogges in Dublin discovered when they had go to court to evict the anchorite Maria from their church at Aghade and the grange of Kilselli near Dublin.[80]

---

[72] H. S. Sweetman (ed.), *Calendar of Documents Relating to Ireland*, vol. 1, 1171–1251 (London, 1875), no. 2210, pp. 327–8.

[73] Richard Butler (ed.), *Registrum Prioratus Omnium Sanctorum Juxta Dublin* (Dublin, 1845), p. 49.

[74] Newport B. White (ed.), *Extents of Irish Monastic Possessions 1540–1541* (Dublin, 1943), p. 1.

[75] James Mills (ed.), *Calendar of the Justiciary Rolls: Ireland, 1295–1303* (Dublin, 1905), p. 313; Hall, *Women and the Church*, p. 186.

[76] For the English evidence see Warren, *Anchorites*, pp. 265–79.

[77] Hall, *Women and the Church*, pp. 186–7.

[78] A. Martin Freeman, *Annála Connacht: The Annals of Connacht* (Dublin, 1944), p. 479.

[79] Meryn Archdall, *Monasticon Hibernicum* (Dublin, 1786), pp. 131, pp. 216–17. Diane Hall gives an alternative date of 1308 in *Women and the Church*, p. 187, n. 182.

[80] Hall, *Women and the Church*, p. 187.

Lifestyle and rules of life

In addition to supporting recluses, religious communities occasionally permitted their own members to embrace the anchoritic life. In these cases the adoption of an anchorite's rule was unnecessary and the candidate passed from the communal to the solitary life relatively smoothly, though religious superiors did occasionally offer advice on the new lifestyle.[81] This transition was in keeping with the Rule of St Benedict, which saw the coenobitic life as preparing the anchorite for the 'single combat of the desert' and presumably determined the process by which the three Cistercian monks of Holy Cross described above became hermits in 1227.[82] Such anchorites remained under the jurisdiction of their religious superiors and continued to be supported by their communities, often occupying cells within the monastic enclosure. This also meant that they did not come under the jurisdiction of the diocesan bishop.[83] In 1508 the Cistercian abbot John Orun sought burial near the tomb of the anchorite Richard Grace [*quondam reclusum*] in the church of St Mary's abbey in Dublin.[84] Grace appears to have been a member of the community who adopted the anchoritic life and was evidently held in high esteem by his erstwhile confreres.

Occasionally the process went in reverse and individuals made the transition from the solitary to the coenobitic life. In England and elsewhere this generally occurred when disciples gathered around a hermit or anchorite.[85] In 1297 Agnes of Hereford, formerly a recluse in Cork, sought permission to establish a house for herself and her nuns at Clonboly in the city. Despite misgivings about the loss of income that endowing the foundation would incur, the local aristocracy supported her petition as there was 'no other house of nuns where knights and other free men may have their daughters brought up and maintained'.[86] Here the social and educational requirements of a social elite appear to have outweighed an individual's desire for solitude. This incident also provides a unique example of an (ex-)anchorite fulfilling a social and educational role in medieval Ireland. Though often frowned on by legislators, the female anchorite as educator was an important and widespread phenomenon in England and on the Continent.[87]

The remarkable second flowering of mendicant life in the Gaelic territories of Ireland in the fifteenth and sixteenth centuries also inspired a revival of the soli-

---

[81] Antonia Gransden, 'The Reply of a Fourteenth-Century Abbot of Bury St. Edmunds to a Man's Petition to be a Recluse', *English Historical Review* 75 (1960), pp. 464–7.

[82] Timothy Fry (ed.), *RB 1980: The Rule of St Benedict* (Collegeville, 1981), ch. I, p. 169.

[83] Warren, *Anchorites*, pp. 68–71.

[84] John T. Gilbert (ed.), *Chartularies of St Mary's Abbey Dublin*, 2 vols (London, 1884), vol. 1, p. 382; vol. 2, p. xxiv.

[85] Jane Herbert, 'The Transformation of Hermitages into Augustinian Priories in Twelfth-Century England', in *Monks, Hermits and the Ascetic Tradition*, ed. Sheils, pp. 131–46.

[86] James Mills (ed.), *Calendar of the Justiciary Rolls: Ireland, 1295–1303* (Dublin, 1905), p. 313; Hall, *Women and the Church*, p. 155.

[87] Anneke Mulder-Bakker, 'The Reclusorium as an Informal Centre of Learning', in *Centres of Learning: Learning and Location in Pre-Modern Europe and the Near East*, ed. J. W. Drijvers and A. A. MacDonald (Leiden, 1995), pp. 246–54.

tary life.[88] Friar Meylerus Brathnach, the anchorite of Cashel granted an indulgence in 1506, was a member of the austere Franciscan Observant reform movement. Architectural evidence discussed below suggests the presence of anchorites at some of the reformed Franciscan and Dominican foundations in the west of Ireland in the late fifteenth and sixteenth centuries. The Observants' pastoral activities led to a quickening of devotion among their lay followers, with their promotion of the Third Order (or Tertiary) rule being particularly effective. From the ranks of these lay tertiaries a new form of religious life emerged, that of the Third Order Regular or Regular Tertiaries. Their order consisted of members, generally men, living the vowed life in community as professed religious.[89] In addition, as has been shown in the case of St Erc's Hermitage at Slane, the Third Order rule was also adopted as a basis for anchoritic living.

In general, however, the peculiar needs of the anchorite were not well catered for by coenobitic legislation and from the ninth century, rules catering specifically for anchorites began to appear in Europe and England.[90] The earliest evidence for the circulation of this type of literature in Ireland is found in Trinity College Dublin MS 97, a late thirteenth- to early fourteenth-century manuscript from the Victorine Abbey of St Thomas in the suburbs in Dublin. Along with a martyrology, the Augustinian rule and Victorine legislation, the codex contains the earliest Irish copies of the rules of St Benedict and St Francis and is a unique witness to the various expressions of religious life found in the city at the turn of the fourteenth century. It also contains two texts addressed to male practitioners of the anchoritic life, originally composed in England.[91] These are the *Dublin Rule* and a set of admonitions on the anchoritic life addressed to Hugo, an anchorite, by Robert, a priest. [92] The *Dublin Rule* consists of a prologue and twenty-four chapters and is an interesting and, at times, amusing mixture of the spiritual and the mundane. It draws from the Rule of St Benedict, the *Regula solitariorum* of Grimlaïcus, Aelred's *De Institutione Inclusarum* and *Ancrene Wisse*, and was compiled sometime between 1220 and 1312, probably in the first half of the thirteenth century. It also has close verbal and thematic similarities with the anchorites' rule contained in British Library MS Vitellus E. IX, ff. 39–53 and with the recently discovered *Rule of Godwin of Salisbury*. Whereas the admonitions are found as an appendix to the *Dublin Rule*, they are an earlier composition, consisting principally of a treatise on the Eucharist compiled between 1140 and 1215.

Although much of the *Dublin Rule* is concerned with the practicalities of the

---

[88] Colmán N. Ó Clabaigh OSB, *The Franciscans in Ireland, 1400–1534* (Dublin, 2002).

[89] Ibid., pp. 80–105. Between 1426 and 1527 forty-seven houses were established for these tertiaries, of which forty-six were for Franciscan Tertiaries and one for Dominicans.

[90] Warren, *Anchorites*, pp. 92–124; pp. 294–8.

[91] Marvin L. Colker, *Trinity College Library, Dublin: Descriptive Catalogue of the Medieval and Renaissance Latin Manuscripts*, 2 vols (Dublin, 1991), vol. 1, pp. 183–95.

[92] Oliger (ed.), 'Regulae tres', pp. 151–90. See also Livarius Oliger, 'Regula Reclusorum Angliae et Quaestiones Tres de Vita Solitaria Saec. xiii–xiv', *Antonianum* 9 (1934), p. 37, n. 1, for the relationship between the *Dublin Rule* and the rule in British Library MS Vitellius E. IX.

reclusive life, the prologue contains a very beautiful meditation on the Christian vocation to praise and worship God:

> What is more natural for all creatures of God than that they should love their God and Father above all? He acts in accordance with nature who loves God above all, He who is called wisdom, the highest good. Where is wealth, where is beauty, where is light, where is fortitude, where is health, where is plenitude, where is delight, where is glory, where is joy, where is the fullness of goodness, where is rest, where is any good unless with God?

> [Quid naturalius omnibus Dei creaturis, quam Deum suum ut patrem super omnia diligant? Naturaliter enim agit qui Deum super omnia diligit, qui sapientia, summum bonum dicitur. Ubi sunt divitie, ubi pulcritudo, ubi lumen, ubi est fortitudo, ubi salus, ubi plenitudo, ubi letitia, ubi Gloria, ubi gaudium, ubi plenitudo bonitatis, ubi requies, ubi aliquid boni nisi cum Domino?][93]

The first chapter urges the anchorite to have Job as his model, bearing patiently with poverty and infirmity if this is his lot. The second urges attention to the 'daily bread' of Divine doctrine before dealing at length with what must have been an occasional temptation: the abuse of alcohol. Considerable attention is devoted to the maintenance of silence and the avoiding of gossip, scandal and detraction. The anchorite's voice was not to be heard raised in laughter or coming from the window of his cell.[94] He was not to have too many servants, to be avaricious or to use his cell for inappropriate secular activities or for storing valuables.[95] Other sections were dedicated to the spiritual and liturgical aspects of the life. He was to receive communion each Sunday, having prepared appropriately by confessing his sins.[96] The hours of the Divine Office were to be celebrated at the appropriate times, and from the feast of All Saints (1 November) until Easter he was to rise at midnight to recite Vigils. The Office of the Virgin Mary was also recited and the *Dirige* or Matins from the Office of the Dead was said after the midday meal during the summer, unless it was a feast-day. Each day the recluse was instructed to recite the seven penitential psalms and the litany of the saints, to pray for his servants and benefactors. If the anchorite was illiterate he substituted multiple recitations of the *Pater noster* for the psalmody.[97] The final chapter was devoted to the seasons and manner of fasting, and the anchorite was urged, if possible, to abstain from all inebriating drink, though this was not imposed by the rule [*sed hoc non ponimus ad regulam*]. The anchorite's habit was to be black, white or grey in colour and he was not to wear linen underclothing unless seriously ill.[98]

The anchorite's rule contained in Maynooth MS RB 201 consists of a prologue and twenty-eight chapters and runs to approximately 370 lines of text. A colophon

---

[93] Oliger (ed.), 'Regulae tres', p. 171 (my translation).
[94] Ibid., chs iv, v, x.
[95] Ibid., chs xiv, xvii.
[96] Ibid., ch. vi.
[97] Ibid., chs xviii, xix, xii.
[98] Ibid., ch. xxiv.

attributes its compilation to Canon Godwin of Salisbury who may be identical with the early twelfth-century writer whose *Meditationes* are preserved in Oxford Bodleian MS Digby 96.[99] Though it bears close verbal and thematic similarities to the *Dublin Rule*, it is a more extensive, better structured and more developed document, as a comparison of both texts' prohibition on the storage of valuables in the anchorhold demonstrates:

> Do not accept the custody of gold or silver or the money of any man in your dwelling, for you are not the custodians of money but men of prayer [*oratores pro salute*] for the well being of all the churches. One and the same rule is enjoined on both monk and anchorite [*monachis quam anchoritis*]; that they have neither money nor possessions save only to love God as they have promised. Remember Ananias and Saphira who, by retaining money, broke the apostolic rule and immediately perished. Moreover they are not servants of God who guard money. For the reward of men of the world they make a dragon's treasury [*thesaurum Draconis*] out of the bridal chamber of Christ. Anchorites should not guard their own money or their food or their drink in their bridal chamber [*in suo thalamo*] but all these things must be handed over to their servants or to any other good people for guarding; otherwise they are not anchorites but evil hypocrites [*non sunt anchoritae sed mali hypochritae*].[100]

In contrast, the Dublin rule's prohibition is not as comprehensive:

> You must not accept the money of another, or clothing or any precious thing into your custody, lest you suddenly die [*ne subito moriaris*]. For there is one rule for monks and for anchorites, namely they do not guard the money of another. Remember always Ananias and Saphira who lied to Peter, the prince of the apostles, and broke the rule and immediately died. O beloved, they are not anchorites who guard anything for gain and who make a vile treasury of the dragon [*vilem tesaurum draconis*] out of the bridal chamber of Christ [*ex thalamo Christi*]. Therefore we beseech you that you guard your heart from all errors of such sort [*ab omnibus huiusmodi erroribus*] and turn over to your servant all that you have.[101]

Eremitical literature

One of the chief attractions of the English eremitical tradition is the remarkable body of vernacular literature that its practitioners produced in the thirteenth and fourteenth centuries. Fourteenth-century works such as the anonymous *Cloud of Unknowing*, Richard Rolle's *Fire of Love* and Julian of Norwich's *Revelations* are as significant for literary and linguistic reasons as for their religious and theolog-

---

[99] Richard Sharpe, *A Handlist of the Latin Writers of Great Britain and Ireland before 1540* (Turnhout, 1997), p. 151. I have not had the opportunity to ascertain what relation, if any, exists between the rule and the *Meditationes*, but the latter text appears to be a much longer work.

[100] St Patrick's College, Maynooth MS RB 201, f. 237.

[101] Oliger (ed.), 'Regulae tres', pp. 179–80.

ical content. Yet even in England these 'literary recluses' were very much a minority and the vast majority of recluses made little impact on the world of letters. Their Irish counterparts made none.

The solitary life did, however, give rise to a distinctive body of literature designed for a broader readership and there is evidence that this circulated in late medieval Ireland. Reference has already been made to the influence of John Cassian in the early Irish church, and the popularity of the Fathers (and Mothers) of the Egyptian desert continued throughout the later Middle Ages. By 1491 the Franciscan library in Youghal, Co. Cork, possessed a copy of one of the most popular works of this genre, the *Vitas Patrum* or the *Lives of the Desert Fathers*, and both the *Dublin Rule* and the *Rule of Godwin of Salisbury* refer to it.[102] Another copy of this work, translated into Irish, was listed in the 1526 catalogue of the earl of Kildare.[103] Contemporary English eremitical literature also circulated in Ireland. In 1491 the Youghal friars possessed an unidentified work of Richard Rolle, the hermit of Hampole in England, and a copy of one of his works was held by the Augustinian canons of Llanthony Secunda in their cell at Duleek, Co. Meath.[104] A more literary approach to the solitary life occurs in William Langland's fourteenth-century masterpiece *Piers Plowman*. Part satire, part Christian allegory, part vision or dream poem, this text circulated widely in late medieval England and hermits and anchorites, false or true, play a prominent role in the three versions of the work.[105] Evidence of its circulation in Ireland comes from Bodleian MS Douce 104, the linguistic, codicological and internal evidence of which indicates it was written in Dublin in 1427. The codex contains a version of the C-text of the poem. In addition to being the only known copy of the work to exist outside of England, it is also unique on account of the seventy-two detailed marginal illustrations that accompany the text.[106]

However, the most striking example of the impact of anchorites on popular consciousness comes from an incident recounted in the *Liber Exemplorum*, a collection of anecdotes for the use of preachers, compiled by an English member of the Irish Franciscan province c.1275. Treating the subject of confession, the story relates how:

> A certain woman, who was more devoted than many to prayers, almsgiving and other good practices, always, for shame, concealed one sin which she had committed in the flower of her youth. When it came to pass that she was sick unto death an almost infinite number of demons gathered beside the cell of an anchorite [*habitaculum anachorite*] who dwelt in that town. Amongst them one presided like a judge demanding of each what they were doing. One arose and said that tomorrow he would have the soul of a dying woman who was renowned by men for her holiness. Saying that she had one sin that she had never confessed:

---

[102] Ó Clabaigh, *Franciscans in Ireland*, p. 136 and p. 162.

[103] Gearóid Mac Niocaill, *Crown Surveys of Lands 1540–41 with the Kildare Rental begun in 1518* (Dublin, 1992), p. 356.

[104] 'Ricardus Heremita in uno volumine', in Ó Clabaigh, *Franciscans in Ireland*, p. 112 and p. 166.

[105] Jones, 'Langland and Hermits', op. cit.

[106] Derek Pearsall and Kathleen Scott (eds), *Piers Plowman: A Facsimile of Bodleian Library, Oxford, MS Douce 104* (Cambridge, 1992).

'And I' he said, 'when she wants to confess, block her mouth [*os eius obstruo*] so that she may not show the sin to the priest.' And he named the sin. Truly, the anchorite heard everything. In the morning the anchorite sent for the priest and made known to him everything he had seen and heard. On the advice of the anchorite the priest went to the woman and spoke to her about confession. But she did not want to intimate anything to him about this sin. The priest however, seeing her so near damnation, could dissimulate no longer and he said to her, 'Is there not some sin which you committed in your youth and which you have not revealed to me in confession?' Hearing this the woman confessed her sin and with a continual flow of tears washed away that sin [*continuo lacrimarum profluvio peccatam illud abluebat*] until she gave up her spirit. That very night, for a second time other demons congregated in the same place as before and the presiding demon demanded the soul promised him. And in reply the one who made the promise said that she had already been confessed (as they say) and through this her soul was borne off to heaven [*animam eius ab angelis in celum delatam esse*] before God by the angels. Behold how great is the power of penance and confession by which a sinner can be thus snatched from the devil.[107]

In addition to emphasizing the necessity of confession, this exemplum illustrates a number of perceptions of the anchoritic life. At the most basic level it demonstrates that late thirteenth-century Irish congregations were familiar with anchorites. The recluse's ability to hear demons and his dwelling in a churchyard highlight his position as a liminal figure, conducting a spiritual warfare on behalf of the community on the twilight frontier of the visible and invisible worlds. Finally, his ability to summon the priest to advise him how to proceed gives some indication of his authority in spiritual matters.

Anchorholds

The anchoritic calling and peculiar lifestyle gave rise to a distinctive religious architecture: the *reclusorium*, a structure which allowed anchorites to pursue their radically separate vocation while remaining at the heart of a community.[108] As was the case elsewhere, in Ireland these structures took a variety of forms and in many cases constitute the only indication of the presence of an anchorite. Tomás Ó Carragáin has recently suggested that the chambers above the vaults in twelfth-century Hiberno-Romanesque churches such as Cormac's Chapel in Cashel and St Kevin's Kitchen at Glendalough may have functioned as anchorholds.[109] Architectural features in a number of fifteenth-century mendicant foundations in the West of Ireland also suggest the presence of recluses. The Franciscan Tertiary

---

[107] A. G. Little (ed.), *Liber exemplorum ad usum praedicantium saeculo xiii compositus a quondam fratre minore Anglico de provincia Hiberniae* (Aberdeen, 1918), p. 57.

[108] For a survey of the English evidence see Roberta Gilchrist, *Contemplation and Action: The Other Monasticism* (London and New York, 1995), pp. 157–208.

[109] Tomás Ó Carragáin, *Churches in Early Medieval Ireland. Architecture, Ritual and Social Memory* (New Haven and London, 2010).

foundations at Rosserk in Co. Mayo and Court in Co. Sligo and the Observant Franciscan house at Moyne in Co. Mayo have curious cells embedded in the walls of the transepts of the friary church. Each is equipped with a doorframe, a squint looking on to the altar in the adjoining chapel and a narrow external window. Their dimensions are extremely confined and it is hard to envisage what other function they could have fulfilled other than some form of penitential or anchoritic one. Other mendicant foundations such as the Augustinian priory at Adare and the Dominican priory at Kilmallock, both in Co. Limerick, have first-floor cells above stone-vaulted sacristies to the north of the chancel equipped with hagioscopes overlooking the high altar. These may have been used by members of the community who had adopted the anchoritic life. The Franciscan friary at Ennis in Co. Clare also has a cell in this position, equipped with a fireplace. It is equally possible, however, that these cells functioned as another well-documented medieval monastic phenomenon – the house prison.

The *reclusorium* normally abutted a church and was equipped with a small window or squint through which the anchorite could watch Mass and liturgical offices being celebrated in the chancel or transept. Another small window, generally set in an external wall, allowed the recluse to conduct necessary business with servants and benefactors and to offer counsel and conversation to visitors. The only written reference to this type of arrangement in Ireland occurs in Donatus Mooney's account of the anchorite baron of Slane noted above. In cases where the anchorite was a priest it was not necessary for him to have a line of vision on an altar as he could celebrate Mass himself. Certainly the free-standing fifteenth-century anchorhold in Fore, Co. Westmeath, discussed below, could only have been occupied by a priest-anchorite and both its known occupants in the seventeenth century were priests.

Writing in the early seventeenth century Bishop David Rothe of Ossory noted that his diocese once hosted a large number of anchorites. The foundations of an anchorhold abutting the north wall of the chancel in St Canice's Cathedral in Kilkenny (the episcopal see of Ossory) were discovered in the mid-nineteenth century and the effigies of two vowesses that survive in the cathedral may represent various of its occupants.[110] At Kilfane church in Co. Kilkenny (also in Ossory diocese) the tower abutting the north wall of the chancel seems to have fulfilled a dual purpose with the ground floor functioning as an anchorhold, complete with squint, altar and tomb recess, while the upper stories, accessed at first-floor level, functioned as a residence for the priest.[111] Nothing survives of the anchorite's cell recorded by Rothe at Freshford in the diocese. References in seventeenth-century sources suggest the presence of anchorites' cells at the Dominican priory in Galway and at Youghal in Co. Cork where the occupant maintained a beacon for passing ships.[112]

---

[110] Cited in James Graves and John G. Augustus Prim, *The History, Architecture and Antiquities of the Cathedral Church of St Canice, Kilkenny* (Dublin, 1857), pp. 68–71. I am grateful to Mr John Bradley for this reference.

[111] I am grateful to Mr Conleth Manning for discussing the architectural elements of this site with me.

[112] Canon Hayman, *Memorials of Youghal, Ecclesiastical and Civil* (Youghal, 1879), p. 30.

Case study: the anchorites of Fore

The fortuitous survivals of an anchorhold at Fore in Co. Westmeath and of a number of texts relating to its late medieval and early modern occupants coalesce to give a remarkably comprehensive picture of the anchoritic experience in Ireland and provide a fitting case study with which to conclude this survey. This evidence also demonstrates the extent to which the experience of Irish anchorites was similar to their English, Scottish and Continental counterparts.

The village of Fore is situated in a picturesque valley in the rural heartland of Co. Westmeath. Between the eighth and seventeenth centuries its remote location proved particularly attractive to various expressions of the monastic life. An early Christian monastery was established at Fore c.730 by St Féichín, a Sligo-born ascetic who had previously established foundations on High Island and Omey Island off the coast of Connemara. Though the community flourished until the twelfth century and its abbots and bishops were frequently mentioned in the Irish annals, the twelfth-century St Féichín's church constitutes the principal physical remains of this early foundation. Following the Anglo-Norman invasion of Ireland in 1169 the kingdom of Meath was granted to Hugh de Lacy (d. 1186) by Henry II. De Lacy established a motte-and-bailey castle in the valley and a Benedictine monastery on the site of the early foundation sometime before 1185.[113] The new priory was a dependency of the abbey of St Taurin at Evreux in Normandy, a fact reflected in its unusual twin dedication to Sts Taurin and Féichín. The new foundation was well endowed with lands and tithes and its impressive remains, heavily remodelled in the fifteenth century, are the most extensive of all medieval Benedictine foundations in Ireland.[114] In addition a parish church dedicated to the Virgin Mary was also established in the village.

The anchorite's cell at Fore is a freestanding structure situated on a terrace to the south of St Féichín's church. Originally constructed in the fifteenth century it was remodelled in the seventeenth century and again in the nineteenth to serve as a mausoleum for the Grenville-Nugent family.[115] In its current form it presents as a small, two-storey, fifteenth-century tower with a nineteenth-century extension. Its original configuration was that of a small chancel and nave chapel with a single first-floor chamber over the chancel, accessed through a spiral staircase in the north-east angle. This chamber functioned as the residence for the priest-anchorite; it contains a fireplace and garderobe and is lit by four windows, three of which give a view of the surrounding countryside while the fourth opens into the nave. Architectural evidence notwithstanding, the earliest reference to an anchorite at Fore occurs in an inquisition of 1614, which found that a parcel of

[113] See Rory Masterson's articles, 'The Alien Priory of Fore, Co. Westmeath, in the Middle Ages', *Archivium Hibernicum* 53 (1999), pp. 73–9; 'The Church and the Anglo-Norman Colonisation of Ireland: A Case Study of the Priory of Fore', *Ríocht na Midhe* xi (2000), pp. 58–70; and 'The early Anglo-Norman colonisation of Fore, Co. Westmeath', *Ríocht na Midhe* xiii (2002), pp. 44–60.

[114] Colmán Ó Clabaigh, 'The Benedictines in Medieval Ireland', in *The Irish Benedictines: a History*, ed. Martin Browne OSB and Colmán Ó Clabaigh OSB (Dublin, 2005), pp. 79–121 (pp. 100–4).

[115] Harold Leask, *Fore, Co. Westmeath* (Dublin, n.d.), p. 17.

land called Ankersland had formerly belonged to the Benedictine priory.[116] The cell was occupied in the early seventeenth century by a priest-anchorite called Patrick Beglan, described *c*.1622 as 'a pernicious fellow exercising ecclesiastical jurisdiction'. He appears to have been a person of considerable influence and standing among the Catholic population of Meath:

> On the Friday of Easter week, 1624, in the vicinity of the home of the earl of Westmeath, two diocesan ordinaries, together with several priests, presided over a large crowd who went to visit the anchorite living at Fore, about seven miles from the Nugent residence.[117]

Beglan's grave-slab survives, mounted on the south wall of the chancel: he is depicted as a hooded figure in a pleated habit reaching to his shins. Though Beglan has often been described as the last occupant of the cell, it was again in use in 1682 when Sir Henry Piers, a local Protestant landowner, left a remarkable description of it and its occupant. Despite its late date, his account demonstrates that many of the features and support structures characteristic of late medieval anchoritism continued to operate well into the seventeenth century:

> Foure, an antient corporation, sending two burgesses to parliament, seated on the north side of the hill or rising ground, which interposeth between it and Lough-Lene before-mentioned ... But if this town were not a mart of learning, surely it was of devotion, there being no less than the ruins of three parish churches, more by two than the greatest and best town of our county hath, one monastery, one church or cell of an anchorite, the sole of the religious of this kind in Ireland. This religious person at his entry maketh a vow never to go out of doors all his life after, and accordingly here he remains pent up all his days, every day of which he says mass in his chapel, which also is part of, nay almost all his dwelling house, for there is no more house, but a very small castle, wherein a man can hardly stretch himself at length, if he laid down on the floor, nor is there any passage into the castle but thro' the chapel. He hath servants that attend on him at his call in an out-house, but none lyeth within the church but himself. He is said by the natives, who hold him in great veneration for his sanctity, every day to dig, or rather scrape, for he useth no tools but his nails, a portion of his grave; being esteemed of so great holiness, as if purity and sanctity were entailed on his cell, he is constantly visited by these of the Romish religion, who aim at being esteemed more devout than the ordinary amongst them; every visitant at his departure leaveth his offering or (as they phrase it) devotion on his altar; but he relieth not on this only for a maintenance, but hath those to bring him in their devotion whose devotions are not so fervent as to invite them to do the office in person; these are called his proctors, who range all the countries in Ireland to beg for him, whom they call the holy man in the

---

[116] Masterson, 'The Church and Anglo-Norman Colonisation', p. 63.

[117] R. Hunter (ed.), 'Catholicism in Meath *c*.1622', *Collectanea Hibernica* 14 (1971), pp. 7–12; Falkland to Conway, 19 April 1624, PRO SP/63/238/42, *Calendar of State Papers relating to Ireland, 1615–25*, p. 482. I am grateful to Dr Brian MacCuarta SJ, for both these references.

stone: corn, eggs, geese, turkies, hens, sheep, money and what not; nothing comes amiss, and nowhere do they fail altogether, but something is had, insomuch that if his proctors deal honestly, nay if they return him but a tenth part of what is given him, he may doubtless fare as well as any priest of them all; the only recreation that this poor prisoner is capable of, is to walk on his terras built over the cell wherein he lies, if he may be said to walk, who cannot in one line stretch forth his legs four times.[118]

Here, a century and a half after the last recluses had been expelled from their cells in England, we see an Irish anchorite in his characteristic, paradoxical position: simultaneously on the margins and at the heart of his community, sustained in solitary state and spiritual significance by a wide network of social relationships.

---

[118] Henry Piers, *A Chorographical Description of the County of West-Meath* (1682 [reprinted 1981]), pp. 63–4.

8 Anchorites in medieval Scotland

Anna McHugh

Introduction

The problem of medieval Scottish anchoritism evokes the conspiracy theorist's paradigm of the absence of evidence versus the evidence of absence. Although the medieval Scottish church as a whole has been well studied, forms of personal devotion, especially the various manifestations of the eremitical life, have not. Monsignor David McRoberts' essay of 1965 on the hermits of medieval Scotland remains the only study of the eremitical phenomenon, and this focuses on hermits rather than anchorites.[1] Ian Cowan, arguably the twentieth century's leading authority on the medieval Scottish church, did not discuss either hermits or anchorites in his two standard works on the subject, *The Medieval Church in Scotland* and *Medieval Religious Houses in Scotland*. In the early twentieth century, Bishop John Dowden's work *The Medieval Church in Scotland: its Constitution, Organisation, and Law* covered most aspects of the medieval church except that of the eremitical or contemplative life as lived by the laity.[2] Apart from Mgr McRoberts' comprehensive article, we are left with little scholarship of the anchoritic phenomenon and virtually no primary evidence (except what the Royal

---

[1] David McRoberts, 'Hermits in Medieval Scotland', *Innes Review* 26 (1965), pp. 199–216; much of Mgr McRoberts' original research into Scottish hermits is included in this essay. I am greatly indebted to Dr Sally Mapstone for drawing this article to my attention, as well as for her comments on the Loretto shrine at Musselburgh. I am also indebted to Mr Thomas FitzPatrick for his learned comments on the hermitages and minor ecclesiastical sites of Scotland.

[2] Ian B. Cowan, *The Medieval Church in Scotland*, ed. James Kirk (Edinburgh, 1995). Dowden's work is *The Medieval Church in Scotland: Its Constitution, Organisation, and Law* (Glasgow, 1910). Other significant works on the medieval Scottish church include: Ian B. Cowan and David E. Easson, *Medieval Religious Houses in Scotland, with an Appendix on the Houses in the Isle of Man* (London, 1976); Alan Macquarrie, 'Early Christian Religious Houses in Scotland: Foundation and Function', in *Pastoral Care Before the Parish*, ed. John Blair and Richard Sharpe (Leicester, 1992), pp. 110–36; James Kirk (ed.), *The Church in the Highlands* (Edinburgh, 1998); James Kirk (ed.), *Humanism and Reform: The Church in Europe, England, and Scotland 1400–1643: Essays in Honour of James K. Cameron* (Oxford, 1991); Andrew D. M. Barrell, *The Papacy, Scotland and Northern England 1342–1378* (Cambridge, 1995); R. Barrie Dobson (ed.), *The Church, Politics, and Patronage in the Fifteenth Century* (Gloucester, 1984); Barbara E. Crawford (ed.), *Church, Chronicle, and Learning in Medieval and Early Renaissance Scotland: Essays presented to Donald Watt on the occasion of the completion of the publication of Bower's Scotichronicon* (Edinburgh, 1999); Peter Yeoman, *Pilgrimage in Medieval Scotland* (London, 1999).

Commission on the Ancient and Historical Monuments of Scotland databases provide in the way of archaeological evidence).[3] There is nothing to compare with Rotha Mary Clay's exhaustive study of hermits and anchorites in medieval England;[4] there are no known works of anchoritic instruction or authorship in Scotland; the two pontificals which survive from the Middle Ages do not contain a ceremony of enclosure.[5] We are thus left somewhat adrift in our search for Scottish anchorites, and must therefore speculate as best we can about the existence and nature of Scottish anchoritism, and consider why there is so little evidence of a phenomenon which was so widespread throughout the rest of Europe.

Literature overview and the absence of evidence

McRoberts' study of medieval Scottish eremitism begins with certain assumptions which should be examined by this newer attempt to explain the absence of anchoritism. His statement that 'in general, the customs and ideas of medieval Scotsmen probably differed little from those of contemporary Europe' encapsulates both ends of the problem of this absent anchoritism.[6] On the one hand, McRoberts is probably correct that, in general, things, including the anchoritic phenomenon, differed little – the rest of Scotland's religious and cultural aspect was not so radically different from the remainder of Christian Europe to warrant any other assumption. Yet, the fact that we only assume, and, because of the almost complete dearth of records of anchorites, we cannot know, suggests that there was something different about the way Scottish anchorites were integrated into the community and the record-making paradigm. This dearth of records is in itself, however, not enough to challenge McRoberts' assertion that 'we can be sure that this way of life was widespread also in the kingdom of Scotland', but it certainly provides grounds to examine it closely.[7]

At this point it is perhaps prudent to note that neither McRoberts, nor indeed Clay, makes a real qualitative distinction between hermits and anchorites. In many cases the term 'chapel', so often used to describe both the eremitical and enclosed dwelling, misleads researchers and clouds analysis, which might explain the apparent presence of hermits and the absence of anchorites.[8] Certainly, as Hughes-Edwards points out earlier in this volume, Clay does acknowledge the distinction between the two, and includes both an Office for the Enclosing of Anchorites and

---

[3] These databases, of which *Canmore* is the most useful, may be searched at www.rcahms.gov.uk and in person at the John Sinclair House in Edinburgh.

[4] Rotha Mary Clay, *The Hermits and Anchorites of England* (London, 1914).

[5] For details of these pontificals, see David McRoberts, *Catalogue of Scottish Medieval Liturgical Books and Fragments* (Glasgow, 1953). For further details on medieval Scottish literary holdings in general, see John Durkan and Anthony Ross, *Early Scottish Libraries* (Glasgow, 1961); and John Higgit (ed.), *Scottish Libraries* (London, 2006).

[6] McRoberts, 'Hermits', p. 199.

[7] Ibid., p. 199.

[8] For an illustration of the complexities of defining the medieval Scottish chapel see Cosmo Innes and James B. Brichan (eds), *Origines Parochiales Scotiae. The Antiquities, Ecclesiastical and Territorial, of the Parishes of Scotland* (Edinburgh, 1851–5).

an Office for the Benediction of Hermits,[9] but this distinction is not followed up by an analysis of the distinct context which produced anchorites, or the circumstances which nurtured their vocation, and is largely followed by McRoberts. McRoberts lists only one anchorite in his essay, compared to some thirty-odd hermits, and like Clay, does not suggest why, in 1516, there is only 'ane woman callit Helena Grant, ane anarcadell [*sic* for *ancarsadell*] inclosit in the Grenesyid' compared to some thirty male hermits.[10] Anchoritism must have been known in medieval Scotland, but there are some pertinent reasons why it may not have assumed the proportions it reached in England or the Continent. The first of these is the practical consideration of population size: England is generally regarded as having a population ratio to that of Scotland of around 5:1. Despite war and disease, the population of medieval England remained relatively constant, mirrored by Scotland, a fifth her size. T. M. Cooper's estimation of Scotland's population in 1300 is around 400,000, with the majority of the mainland population settled in the Lowlands.[11] With such a small population, it would be unfeasible to allow many fertile women to abstain not only from childbearing but from labour to support the rest of the population.[12] We are therefore looking to numbers of anchorites which are considerably fewer than those of England, perhaps even fewer than one-fifth of the number recorded for the south of Britain. This assumption seems confirmed by the number of men by comparison who were involved in the eremitical life – which, in Scotland, seemed inevitably to include some form of public service such as maintaining a ford, bridge or lighthouse, or even acting as clerk and advisor to a patron.[13] That the eremitical life was accept-

---

[9] Clay, *Hermits and Anchorites*, Appendices A and B.

[10] McRoberts, 'Hermits', p. 214. The reference is from T. Thomson (ed.), *A Diurnal of Remarkable Occurents that have passed within Scotland since the death of King James IV till 1575* (Edinburgh, 1833), p. 6. On the religious life of women in medieval Scotland, see David E. Easson, 'The Nunneries of Medieval Scotland', *Transactions of the Scottish Ecclesiological Society* 13 (1940), pp. 22–38; R. Andrew McDonald, 'The Foundation and Patronage of Nunneries by Native Elites in Twelfth- and Early Thirteenth-Century Scotland', and Audrey-Beth Fitch, 'Power Through Purity: The Virgin Martyrs and Women's Salvation in Pre-reformation Scotland', both in *Women in Scotland c.1100–c.1750*, ed. Elizabeth Ewan and Maureen M. Meikle (East Linton, 1999), pp. 3–15 and pp. 16–29 respectively. Christina Harrington's *Women in a Celtic Church: Ireland 450–1150* (Oxford, 2002) includes Scottish material. For the problem of the general occlusion of women in Scottish historiography, see Elizabeth Ewan, 'A Realm of One's Own? The Place of Medieval and Early Modern Women in Scottish History', in *Gendering Scottish History: An International Approach*, ed. Terry Brotherstone, Deborah Simonton and Oonagh Walsh (Glasgow, 1999), pp. 19–36.

[11] T. M. Cooper, 'The Numbers and the Distribution of the Population of Medieval Scotland', *Scottish Historical Review* 26 (1947), pp. 2–9. For the fourteenth century, Cooper suggests a distribution of the population thus: Glasgow 107,000; St Andrews 88,000; Aberdeen 35,000; Dunkeld 34,000; Dunblane 20,000; Argyll 18,000; Moray 18,000; Whithorn 11,000; Brechin 10,000; Ross 5,000; Caithness 4,000; outlying areas 50,000 – giving a total of 400,000, which correlates as one-fifth of the English population of the time, and seems confirmed by a comparison of Scottish ecclesiastical revenues to those of England, four-fifths greater.

[12] This is also a conclusion that Jane Cartwright comes to as a likely explanation for the similar absence of evidence for female anchoritism in Wales during the same period. Jane Cartwright, *Feminine Sanctity and Spirituality in Medieval Wales* (Cardiff, 2008), pp. 207–8.

[13] Many of the hermits of Scotland maintained lighthouses or provided aid to mariners in trouble. Walter Bower recounts the story of the hermit who dwelt on the island of Inchcolm and tended the shrine of St Colm there, and who helped Alexander I in 1123 when the king's ship was stormbound on the island for

able (and recorded) only when combined with a contribution to the small community's welfare would seem to confirm the possibility that anchoritism, a form of the eremitical life which dispensed with this service, would be unsustainable in a community which needed almost every able-bodied adult.

Scottish eremitism

Further to this practical consideration is the cultural face of Scotland, which knew the hermit well, but the anchorite less so. The trend towards eremitism in the Celtic church has been well examined, but it is worth bearing in mind that the Celtic eremitical life did not usually involve enclosure.[14] However, the sixth-century rule attributed to Columba, which would have been known throughout the *Céli Dé* (culdee) communities of western Scotland, has a focus on solitude, which is worth mentioning.[15] Among the measures advised by the rule is that the solitary should 'Be alone in a separate place near a chief city, if thy conscience is not prepared to be in common with the crowd', and to 'Let a fast place, with one door, enclose thee'. The hermit is allowed a servant, and should converse with religious-minded men on holy days. Foreshadowing the later *Ancrene Wisse*, the hermit is counselled against chattering, being told:

three days, for which see Walter Bower, *Scotichronicon*, ed. Donald E. R. Watt (Aberdeen, 1987–91), vol. 3, V.37, pp. 2–23. In 1427 a hermit acted as lighthouse-keeper at the chapel at Seacliff in East Lothian and is recorded in this year as petitioning the Curia for his independence from the abbey of Holyrood: see *Calendar of Scottish Supplications to Rome*, ed. Annie I. Dunlop (Edinburgh, 1956), vol. 2, p. 172. In the sixteenth century, the hermit of the Isle of May combined his eremitical life with duties as the king's gamekeeper: see McRoberts, 'Hermits', pp. 206–7, for the historical inferences which can be drawn from this. There are also place names suggestive of similar hermits at Holyman Head in Lossiemouth, along the Forth and at Cannesbay parish in Caithness. (A cursory search of the RCAHMS *Canmore* database of archaeological sites, monuments, buildings and maritime sites in Scotland reveals how many places in Scotland are connected with a hermit or holy man.)

[14] For an introduction to Celtic Christianity, see Brendan Lehane, *Early Celtic Christianity* (London, 1968); for Scotland more specifically, W. F. Skene's magisterial *Celtic Scotland* (Edinburgh, 1876–80), although deeply contentious, remains authoritative in its handling of sources; see also W. Douglas Simpson, *Saint Ninian and the Origins of the Christian Church in Scotland* (Edinburgh, 1940) for an introduction to Celtic Christianity in Scotland, as well as Alfred P. Smyth, *Warlords and Holy Men: Scotland 80–1000* (London, 1984); see Dauvit Broun and Thomas Owen Clancy (eds), *Spes Scotorum: Hope of Scots* (Edinburgh, 1999) on the Columban contribution, and Clancy's essay, 'Iona, Scotland, and the *Céli Dé*', in *Scotland in Dark Age Britain*, ed. Barbara E. Crawford, (Aberdeen, 1996), pp. 111–30.

[15] The term culdee (an Anglicization of *Céli Dé*, or friend of God) is not without its problems, but here is used loosely to refer to those religious communities which existed in Ireland and Scotland from the eighth century until the twelfth-century reforms of St Margaret and her sons, when they were gradually absorbed into regular monastic communities of the new, European orders, and which were characterized by a return to the sternness of the sixth century. Much of the extant documentary evidence for the culdees can be found in A. W. Haddan and W. Stubbs, *Councils and Ecclesiastical Documents Relating to Great Britain and Ireland* (Oxford, 1873), vol. 2, part 1, pp. 224–8, and pp. 278–85. A range of definitions and attitudes towards this group can be found in: Skene, *Celtic Scotland*, particularly vol. 2; William Beveridge, *Makers of the Scottish Church* (Edinburgh, 1908); William Reeves, *The Culdees of the British Islands* (Dublin, 1864). A thumbnail sketch of the culdee reforms in Ireland can be found in Peter O'Dwyer, 'Celtic Monks and the Culdee Reform', in *An Introduction to Celtic Christianity*, ed. James P. Mackey (Edinburgh, 1989), pp. 140–69. MacRoberts ('Hermits', p. 200) rightly points out that the *Annals of Ulster* 'carefully distinguishes the *disertach* or hermit, Mac Gilladuff, from the *célidé*, as well as from the brethren of the *muinntir*'.

a person too who would talk with thee in idle words, or of the world; or who mur-
murs at what he cannot remedy or prevent, but who would distress thee more
should he be a tattler between friends and foes, thou shalt not admit him to thee,
but at once give him thy benediction should he deserve it.[16]

It is difficult to determine whether the rule envisions a hermit or an anchorite – the
presence of a servant would suggest the latter – but it is by no means solely reflective of Celtic eremitism throughout Scotland. Although St Cuthbert spent time as
a hermit on Lindisfarne, he travelled widely throughout the north;[17] St Serf,
although spending long periods in solitude on the tiny islands of Loch Leven,
nonetheless travelled to Dysart;[18] St Molaise lived in solitude on Holy Island;[19] St
Baldred on the Bass Rock;[20] St Gerardin, after whom Holyman Head in
Lossiemouth is named, was probably a hermit rather than an anchorite;[21] St
Kentigerna, the recluse of the island of Inchcailleach on Loch Lomond, was
enclosed only by the water which separated her from Balmaha on the shores of the
loch.[22] The distinction between the hermit and the anchorite in the early Celtic
church (and indeed later) may have collapsed due to the extreme isolation of the
locations; with few urban centres and no parish churches, as they came to be

---

[16] Haddan and Stubbs, *Councils and Ecclesiastical Documents*, vol. 2, part 1, pp. 119–21 (p.119).

[17] The life of St Cuthbert, a member of the foundation at Melrose from 651AD, can be found in Bede's
Ecclesiastical History of the English People, although an earlier hagiography (MS Corpus Christi
College, Cambridge 183) by a monk of Lindisfarne provides information, and MS University College,
Oxford 165 was the first fully illustrated Life of a saint to be produced in England. See also Thomas
Arnold (ed.), *Symeon of Durham Opera* (London, 1882–5); Reginald of Durham, *Libellus de admiran-
dis beati cuthberti virtuti* (London, 1835); Alexander P. Forbes, *Kalendars of the Scottish Saints*
(Edinburgh, 1872), pp. 317–19; Bertram Colgrave (ed. and trans.), *Two Lives of St. Cuthbert: a Life by
an Anonymous Monk of Lindisfarne and Bede's Prose Life* (Cambridge, 1985); Alan Thacker,
'Lindisfarne and the Origins of the Cult of St Cuthbert', in *St Cuthbert, his Cult and his Community to
AD 1200*, ed. Gerald Bonner, David Rollason and Claire Stancliffe (Woodbridge, 1989), pp. 103–22.

[18] St Serf (*c*.500–53) is generally connected to the Ochil hills in Clackmannanshire: see Forbes,
Kalendars, pp. 445–7; *Butler's Lives of the Saints*, revised by H. Thurston and D. Attwater (New York,
1953–54), vol. 3, p. 5; Edwin Sprott Towill, *The Saints of Scotland* (Edinburgh, 1978), pp. 227–9; Simon
Taylor, 'Seventh-century Iona Abbots in Scottish Places', in *Spes Scotorum*, ed. Broun and Clancy, p. 66,
which situates Serf's floruit in the late seventh century. The RCAHMS *Canmore* database lists a number
of sites in Perth and Kinross which are connected to the island retreat on Loch Leven.

[19] Molaise is also known as Laserian (d. 639), an early Irish monk and, possibly, bishop: see Forbes,
Kalendars, pp. 407–9, and Daphne P. Mould, *The Irish Saints* (Dublin, 1964), pp. 203–4. The RCAHMS
Canmore database also lists a chapel on Arran thought to have been connected to the saint, along with
the cave on nearby Holy Island.

[20] For Baldred (fl. 756), see Forbes, *Kalendars*, pp. 273–4, and *Butler's Lives of the Saints*, vol. 1, p. 502.

[21] Also known as Gervadius. The Life of Gerardin has the saint meeting English soldiers sent by King
Athelstan in 934 AD, which is surely difficult to believe, since he is normally located near Elgin, where
his cave is mentioned in Elgin charters; see Forbes, *Kalendars*, pp. 354–5; and Herbert B. Mackintosh,
Elgin: Past and Present (Elgin, 1914), pp. 268–9.

[22] Kentigerna (d. 733) is listed in the Aberdeen Breviary as being of Irish royal blood. Her father was
Cellach, prince of Leinster, and her marriage to a neighbouring prince produced Fillan. Upon being wid-
owed, she settled in the island church of Inch Cailleach (island of the old (or cowled) woman). The
RCAHMS lists 'Gille Chaointeart' as the site of an old chapel dedicated to St Kentigerna on the south
side of Loch Duich, in the Highlands, and St Comgan's church in Knoydart is traditionally connected to
Comgan, the brother of Kentigerna: Forbes, *Kalendars*, p. 373; *Butler's Lives of the Saints*, vol. 1, p. 20.

known after the reforms of Margaret and her sons, there were simply no locations similar to those of the English urban anchorites of later centuries.

Certainly, place names in Scotland suggest an attachment to the idea of solitude and a connection to the early Christian Desert Fathers – Dysart in Fife is evidence of the derivation of the Gaelic *diseart* from Latin *desertum*, and the chapel of St Anthony on Arthur's Seat is usually connected to the presence of an (unknown) hermit. Several Celtic hermits and their hermitages reappear in the later Middle Ages with a revived cult or simply a new hermit taking their place in the same location. As Michael Lynch points out:

> Ninian, Columba, Adomnan ... and Kentigern, probably the four best-known early Scottish saints, all became subjects of a cult within a few decades of their deaths, but they were all also later recast, both in the twelfth or thirteenth centuries and again in the fifteenth, as born-again saints to fit new fashions of hagiography or the demands of contemporary ecclesiastical politics.[23]

As interest in the Celtic hermits waxed and waned, so too did the presence of hermitages in their old locations, named after the previous occupants and often maintaining shrines to their legend. The revival of the cult of asceticism in the eighth-century Irish church was also felt in western Scotland; over the next 200 years communities of culdees were established in major royal and religious centres such as Kilrimont (St Andrews) and Dunkeld. It is important to remember, however, that the *Céli Dé* were themselves divided by practice into the *disertach* or hermit and *muinntir* or communities of brethren.[24] These 'comrades of God' filled the gap in Scotland which existed after the expulsion of the Iona monks by Nechtan in 717 and the failure of the Roman monks of Northumbria to evangelize in the north.[25] Despite the gradual shift away from indigenous saints towards those recognized by Rome during the reign of Kenneth MacAlpin (d. 858), both traditions maintained an eremitical aspect, and the presence of hermitages continued throughout the gradual 'romanization' of the Scottish church. Dunkeld and St Andrews, the two religious centres of the kingdom under Kenneth and his successors, were dedicated to different traditions of saints, and maintained a harmony

[23] Michael Lynch, 'Religious Life in Medieval Scotland', in *A History of Religion in Britain: Practice and Belief from Pre-Roman Times to the Present*, ed. Sheridan Gilley and W. J. Sheils (Oxford, 1994), pp. 99–124 (p. 100). Recent critical studies of Scottish saints include: John MacQueen, 'Myths and Legends of Lowland Scottish Saints', *Scottish Studies* 24 (1980), pp. 1–21; Alan Macquarrie, *The Saints of Scotland: Essays in Scottish Church History AD 450–1093* (Edinburgh, 1997), particularly chapter 3 on St Ninian (pp. 50–73), and chapter 6 on St Serf (pp. 145–59); and Macquarrie's essay 'Lives of Scottish Saints in the Aberdeen Breviary: Some Problems of Sources for Strathclyde Saints', *Records of the Scottish Church History Society* 26 (1996), pp. 31–54.

[24] Although Irish, this terminology was presumably applicable to the west of Scotland as well. See Alan O. Anderson, *Early Sources of Scottish History: A.D. 500 to 1286* (London, 1922), vol. 2, p. 253.

[25] On the kingship of the eighth-century Pict Nechtan mac Der-Ilei, who expelled the Ionian monks in 717 after being convinced about the rectitude of the Roman dating of Easter by Ceolfrid, abbot of Wearmouth and Jarrow, see Thomas O. Clancy, 'Philosopher-King: Nechtan mac Der-Ilei', *Scottish Historical Review* 83 (2004), pp. 125–49; Alex Woolf, 'AU 729.2 and the Last Years of Nechtan mac Der-Ilei', *Scottish Historical Review* 85 (2005), pp. 131–4.

which Michael Lynch has called 'a distinctively Scottish solution to a Scottish problem'.[26] The very nature of ninth- and tenth-century kingship was composite; so was its church – and so was its eremitism.

The reforms of Margaret, the second wife of Malcolm Canmore, and her sons gradually brought the eremitical practices of the culdees to a close by integrating many of their communities with monastic orders introduced from the south.[27] Margaret maintained a great respect towards these indigenous hermits, and Turgot, her confessor and biographer, tells us that around the year 1100:

> Very many men, shut up in cells apart, in various places in the districts of the Scots, were living in the flesh but not according to the flesh, for they led the life of angels upon earth. The queen endeavoured to venerate and love Christ in them and to visit them very often with her presence and conversation and to commend herself to their prayers. And when she could not persuade them to agree to accept from her anything, she humbly begged them to deign to enjoin upon her some act of charity or mercy. And without delay, she fulfilled devoutly whatever was their will, either in delivering the poor from penury or in relieving the afflicted of the miseries by which they were distressed.[28]

Margaret herself apparently engaged in brief periods of contemplative life in a cave in Dunfermline, now popularly known as 'Margaret's Cave'. Turgot does not mention this periodic withdrawal, and although it is possible, it is perhaps better to understand the anecdote as history's desire to accrue a contemplative aspect to Margaret. Such 'part-time contemplatives' are common in Scottish history, and include Cuthbert, Serf, Ninian, Nechtan and William abbot of Holyrood – the 'failed' hermit of Inchkeith in 1227.[29]

The integration of the culdee communities with the orders brought from

---

[26] Lynch, 'Religious Life', p. 103.

[27] For the attitudes of St Margaret (1045–93) to the culdees and her reforms to the Scottish church, see Alan Wilson, *St Margaret, Queen of Scotland* (Edinburgh, 1993), especially pp. 70–80, and Haddan and Stubbs, *Councils and Ecclesiastical Documents*, vol. 2, part 1, p. 159. See also Geoffrey W. S. Barrow, 'From Queen Margaret to David I: Benedictines and Tironensians', *Innes Review* 11 (1960), pp. 22–38. Although Margaret brought a community of Benedictine monks to Dunfermline in 1070, R. Andrew McDonald argues that it was the twelfth century which saw the Continental religious orders established under the patronage of the royal family, as, for example, with the Augustinian canons at Scone (c.1120), and the great Cistercian foundation at Melrose in c.1136. ('Foundation and Patronage of Nunneries', p. 4). As for the experience of women, McDonald argues that 'although there is some evidence for communities of religious women in the early middle ages, it is doubtful whether any continued into the twelfth century'. Around 1136 David I founded a nunnery at Berwick on Tweed, and later in the twelfth century other members of the royal family founded nunneries at Manuel (Malcolm IV, 1153–65) and Haddington (Ada, Countess of Northumberland). For these, see Easson, 'Nunneries', p. 22; Janet E. Burton, *Monastic and Religious Orders in Britain 1000–1300* (Cambridge, 1994), p. 95; see also Richard Oram's biography, *David I: The King who made Scotland* (Stroud, 2004), particularly chapter 3, 'The Saintly King', pp. 145–65.

[28] From Turgot's 'Life of Queen Margaret', in Anderson, *Early Sources*, vol. 2, pp. 76–7.

[29] On Ninian, whose cave by the shore of Whithorn in Galloway, see Forbes, *Kalendars*, pp. 421–4; see also W. M. Metcalfe, *The Legends of SS Ninian and Machor, from an Unique MS in the Scottish Dialect of the Fourteenth Century* (Paisley, 1904). For Abbot William, see Bower, *Scotichronicon*, vol. 5, IX, p. 141.

England by Margaret seems to have been effected without incident; many of the known communities of brethren simply became integrated with the Augustinian canons, an order with a sympathetic attitude to their eremitical existence. Those who did not join the new communities of canons were usually awarded a life-rent, but were excluded from voting for the new bishop, and by the fourteenth century had become absorbed by the canons. David I granted the island on Loch Leven to the canons in 1150 on condition that a foundation was to be built there, with the provision of expelling those culdees who refused to become regular canons.[30] Many Augustinian canonries maintained some form of hermitage within their walls – the hermit on Inchcolm island who saved Alexander I from the waters of the Forth occasioned the foundation of the Augustinian monastery there, according to its abbot, Walter Bower:

> About the year 1123 the monastery of St Columba on the island of Inchcolm near Edinburgh was founded in a way that was as remarkable as it was miraculous. For when the most noble and most Christian lord king Alexander the first of this name was making the crossing at Queensferry in pursuit of some business of the kingdom, a violent storm suddenly arose as wind blew from the south-west, and compelled the ship with its crew scarcely clinging to life to put in at the island of Inchcolm, where a certain island hermit lived at that time. He was dedicated to the service of St Columba, and earnestly devoted himself to it at a certain little chapel on the island, content with a meagre diet consisting of the milk of one cow, shells and little fish that he gathered from the sea. The king with his very large number of fellow soldiers gratefully lived on this food of his for three days on end under compulsion from the wind. But on the previous day when he was giving up hope of surviving, as he was being buffeted by the very great danger of the sea and the madness of the storm, he made a vow to the saint that if he brought him safely to the island along with his men, he would leave on the island such a memorial to his glory as would serve for asylum and solace to sailors and victims of shipwreck. This is how it came about that he founded a monastery of canons in the same place...[31]

We will never know how the hermit felt about having his solitude disrupted by the building of a new monastic foundation on his small island, but the canonry maintained the hermitage, which can still be seen with a late medieval roof, a little behind the chapel.[32] It is not surprising that the indigenous eremitical heritage was

---

[30] Haddan and Stubbs, *Councils and Ecclesiastical Documents*, vol. 2, part 1, pp. 227–8. On the spread of the Augustinian canons in Britain, see Burton, *Monastic and Religious Orders*, pp. 43–56, and on David I's foundation of the canonry at Loch Leven, p. 54.

[31] Bower, *Scotichronicon*, vol. 3, V.37, p. 111.

[32] An archaeological view of the hermitage of Inchcolm is that it 'must have been the subject of much rebuilding. In its present form the stone vault can hardly be earlier in date than the later middle ages, whilst the internally lintelled doorway looks even more recent. This door may have been rebuilt after the Reformation in 1560, when the cell was used for burial purposes'. However, the building, positioned a little behind the nave of the mid twelfth-century church nonetheless gives an accurate impression of the conditions of these early hermitages and their relations with the canonries into which many were absorbed. See Richard Fawcett, David McRoberts and Fiona Stewart, *Inchcolm Abbey and Island* (Kircaldy, 1998), pp. 4–6.

absorbed into the canons, for no order was closer to the royal house between 1200 and 1450, and it is to this connection with regal power that we owe the few remaining references to twelfth-century hermits in Scotland.

Certainly, there were solitaries who lived without apparent membership of an order – such was 'John the hermit' who, around 1180, received the island on Loch Lunnin and a half carucate of land in Duldavach from William the Lion; Gillecmichel, whose land was donated to the abbey of Coupar Angus only upon his death; and Gyllecrist Gartanach, hermit of Ruthven, whose croft was exempted from a donation made to the bishop of Moray by Alexander II in 1236[33] – but many hermits (or hermitages) seemed to be absorbed into the new Augustinian canonries. Gilbert, Earl of Strathearn, in founding the Augustinian house at Inachaffray in Perth around 1200, provided that Mael-Isu, 'presbyter and hermit', would administer the new foundation and that those who were associated with him would be instructed in the service of God according to the Rule of St Augustine.[34] Similarly, the island of Inchmahome on the Lake of Mentieth may well have harboured a hermit before becoming an Augustinian priory in 1238 – but this is supposition, as nothing remains of a hermitage.[35]

These are the recorded hermits of the mid-twelfth and early thirteenth centuries, often connected to religious foundations and receiving patronage from the crown or wealthy lay patrons. Yet it is worth examining the reasons why there appears to be so little of the 'parish anchorite', those lay enclosed women and men who were not connected to a religious house and who were, physically and in historical record, contextualized within a local parish.

Clergy and the local parish

Many of the hermits or anchorites described so far owe their historical record to their parallel roles as ordained priests or members of a recognized order, often even living within that order's walls. It is perhaps unsurprising that these solitaries should have been recorded, since they existed at the heart of the medieval record-making machine. The lay anchorite, living outside the walls of a monastic foundation in the local parish, was in a precarious position, both in terms of being recorded and of finding a sympathetic milieu in which to pursue his or her vocation. The idea of the parish developed only gradually in Scotland, and Ian Cowan has argued that 'it may be doubted whether many truly urban parishes existed in medieval Scotland … [T]he origins of the urban parish must be sought not in the town, but rather in the countryside surrounding it, in which parishes recognizably

---

[33] These references may all be found in McRoberts' essay and are drawn from the *Registrum episcopatus Moraviensis* (Edinburgh, 1837), p. 4; *Miscellany of the Spalding Club* (Edinburgh, 1841–52), vol. 2, p. 307; and *Registrum episcopatus Moraviensis*, p. 32, respectively.

[34] William A. Lindsay, John Dowden and J. Maitland Thomson (eds.), *Charters, Bulls and Other Documents Relating to the Abbey of Inchaffray* (Edinburgh, 1908), pp. 6–8; Cowan and Easson, *Medieval Religious Houses*, p. 48.

[35] I am grateful for the engineering expertise of Mr Peter Brooker, who surveyed Inchmahome and Inch Talla with me.

antedate the appearance of towns.'[36] In the first half of the twelfth century the term is used imprecisely, and seems to denote areas of jurisdiction enjoyed by a mother church. Diversities disappeared over some 200 years, and the term assumed the current connotation of an area within the jurisdiction of a baptismal church; by the thirteenth century the terms *parochia* and *parochia ecclesia* had become common-place.[37] However, the system was never static; Ian Cowan has shown how the parish of Wiston, for example, had three chapels – Roberton, Symington and Crawford-John – all of which attained parochial status in the thirteenth century. Yet only Crawford-John freed itself from the control of Kelso, to become a fully independent parish in lay patronage.[38] Bishops also maintained chapels on their episcopal lands, endowing them with their own curates, and lay landowners followed the pattern, creating what became known as proprietary churches. Control of parochial status could be maintained, preventing chapels from becoming parish churches by forbidding Easter mass from being said anywhere but in the parish church. There was also the complex pull upon the parish – or rather, upon its *teinds* [tithes] – from lay patronage on one hand and the great monastic and episcopal foundations on the other. By 1300 more than sixty per cent of parish kirks had had their *teinds* appropriated, in whole or in part, to another ecclesiastical foundation – usually the great religious houses or cathedral chapters which needed vast revenues to finance ambitious building programs. This figure would rise to eighty-five per cent by the sixteenth century.[39] The pattern in the urban parish is thus one of no small instability: the 'parish' could have been a wide rural area with very little urban development, where the solitary may be better described as a hermit, living in rural isolation and farming a small tract rather than being enclosed in a parish church with the local population to provide physical sustenance; the revenues of parish churches were an irresistible temptation for cash-strapped foundations, and the honour of providing the incumbent was vied over by bishop and local laird. Under such unstable conditions, the prospect of enclosure in a parish church or urban chapel may have been impossible, unattractive, or unlikely to last long.

If the local parish was in a financially precarious situation, so too were its clergy. Instead of beneficed parish priests, many parishes were beginning to be served by poorly paid, overworked vicars. Michael Lynch has shown that the falling value of the Scots pound, the pressures of intermittent warfare, the slump in trade after the optimism of the 1370s, and the new costs of papal provision to benefices, meant that local clergy were desperately poorly paid, which ultimately led to a slump in vocations:[40]

> There was a drastic loss of the clergy in minor orders, linked to their failing income, in the fifteenth and early sixteenth centuries. Responsibility for this rests

---

[36] Cowan, *Medieval Church in Scotland*, p. 30.

[37] Ibid., pp. 1–2.

[38] Ibid., p. 9.

[39] Lynch, 'Religious Life', p. 109.

[40] Ibid., p. 112.

primarily with a hierarchy which failed to divert enough resources into the ordinary parish system, but it also belongs to the lay patrons who employed chaplains on minimum wages in collegiate churches, hospitals or other lay foundations. The laity expected more to be done for the salvation of their souls, but were unwilling or unable to pay as much for it as before.[41]

With a much smaller population than England, Scotland's loss of clergy must have been instantly noticeable to ordinary parishioners and those who needed intensive spiritual direction, such as anchorites. With an overworked and perhaps disinterested clergy, the provision for spiritual counsel to enclosed men and women would have been limited.

Patronage

The instability of the parish system and the impoverishment of the clergy provide two cogent reasons for a smaller number of anchorites, but it is also useful to look at the provision of patronage and the survival of records to understand why, if such enclosed souls existed, the record of their existence has survived so poorly. A substantial part of the answer may lie in the puzzle of the patronage of anchorites, which was as varied in Scotland as in England, and tied anchorites to monastic foundations, the houses of the nobility, wealthy townsmen and the crown. As Hughes-Edwards has also pointed out, Rotha Mary Clay tabulates some 300 solitaries and their patrons in a useful appendix, which shows that the majority of patrons for English hermits and anchorites were abbeys or other churches, followed by private lay patrons, then the crown, which patronized the smallest number of solitaries. It is difficult to determine whether these proportions are reflected in Scotland, but the presence of the crown, the laity and monastic foundations is representative of the patronage of Scottish anchorites, and of the problems inherent in their historical record. Those patronized by the laity may have combined their vocation with other roles, such as the hermit who advised Black Agnes, the Countess of Dunbar, in the early fourteenth century.[42] The position of the hermit as counsellor is well known, and Mgr McRoberts shows how:

> When the *Scotichronicon* describes how St Catherine of Alexandria went with her mother to consult a holy hermit on the outskirts of Alexandria about her prospective marriage and how she remained 'ad fenestram cum heremita secum diutius disputans' – talking at the hermitage window where the recluse dispensed counsel, it does not give us an authentic picture of what happened in Alexandria in the days of St Catherine but rather what was familiar to Scotsmen one thousand years later.[43]

The relationship of Margaret Countess of Ross and John 'presbiter ac heremita' is recorded by a cross-shaft from Eilean Mor, Kilmory, Knapdale, Argyll, which

[41] Ibid., p. 111.
[42] E. B. Rankin, *Saint Mary's, Whitekirk* (Edinburgh, 1914), p. 5.
[43] McRoberts, 'Hermits', p. 203.

may have been erected to form a sea-mark to guide boats navigating around the island.[44] There may also have been a hermit at the chapel of St Fillan near the castle of Doune in Menteith, as reference is made as late as 1665 to a 'Hermetis-Croft' and there is a small chapel within the castle itself known as 'St Fillan's within the Castle'. Such solitaries, attached to great houses and perhaps acting as counsel to their wealthy patrons, may have been recorded in payrolls as a counsellor rather than hermit, and bequests of land to them are now virtually invisible due to the loss of so many medieval Scottish wills. Similarly, because of their record in bequests, we may hear more about a hermitage than an individual hermit, for many chapels were 'inherited' by further generations and new incumbents.[45] The presence of recluses on lay land is often a matter of local legend, with little truth behind it; such is the case of 'Ossian's Cave' in Atholl lands, some half-hour's walk from the monastery of Dunkeld. The cave which exists there has no medieval record, nor is there an eremitical connection to Oisín or the poet McPherson, and it may be representative of an eighteenth-century desire to see a hermit on Atholl lands rather than any medieval individual.

The patronage of recluses by monastic foundations could be a mixed blessing. Although we owe to a monastery the details of such few solitaries as we know, their presence in the recluse's life was not always beneficial. The appropriations of parish *teinds* by monastic foundations was indicative of a rapaciousness which would stretch even to a poor hermit. The life-rent from the hermit of Ruthven's croft was explicitly exempted from a donation made to the bishop of Moray by the king, and the hermitage of Gillecmichel was only to go to Coupar Angus abbey after the recluse's death. In 1427 John Vussdale, 'layman, poor hermit', whose hermitage fell under the abbey of Holyrood, petitioned the Curia to rule that he 'who is lame and infirm, desires to live a hermit's life in the hermitage and chapel, pouring out prayers to the Most High and exercising the foresaid office for his lifetime', be 'not removed, deprived or molested by the abbot and convent of the said monastery or any other person, removing any occupier'.[46] The abbot of Holyrood also had charge of the hermitage at St Leonard's hospital in the neighbourhood of the abbey, to which he annexed the chapel in 1493.[47] As part of larger monastic institutions, one would expect records of dependent recluses to be more numerous than they are. Yet McRoberts suggests a cogent explanation for this:

> At least in some cases, where the hermit was a priest, the custom may have been
> in Scotland to describe such an individual as a chaplain and his hermitage as a
> chaplainry ... The Aberdeen town records are reasonably complete and there is no
> mention in them of any hermit in the vicinity of the burgh, but we do find evidence

---

[44] Ibid., p. 204.

[45] See also McRoberts' reference to the hermitage of Kilgerre, which was bestowed by James II upon John Smith in 1445 after Hugh Cuminche, the hermit, resigned it into the king's hands. McRoberts, 'Hermits', p. 205.

[46] *Calendar of Scottish Supplications to Rome*, vol. 2, p. 172.

[47] McRoberts, 'Hermits', p. 206.

of chaplains in that neighbourhood engaged on work which, in other lands, would have been in the hands of a hermit ... This suggestion would also explain why, in the lists of different categories of ecclesiastical property, taken over from the medieval church in 1560, hermitages are never mentioned. It is unlikely that hermitages had completely disappeared from Scotland by that year and the explanation may be that hermitages dependent on monasteries are simply included in monastic property and other hermitages are included under 'chaplainries'.[48]

McRoberts makes an excellent point about the difficulties of terminology, but the issue of monastic appropriation of the hermitage or its historical record extends beyond mere terminology; John Vussdale's fear of being 'removed, deprived, or molested', and the abbot of Holyrood's 'annexation' of the St Leonard hermitage to his abbey's hospital indicate the record-maker's general lack of interest in the individuals who inhabited these dwellings, which were perhaps regarded as no more than assets of the great monastic foundations. Further, if the recluses were already in holy orders, they may be absorbed within the records of their order or congregation, since they probably cost little more to run than an ordinary choir-monk.

This pragmatism, consistent with a small population which valued every able-bodied adult, is reflected in the third of the three patronage-groups, the crown. From the reign of Malcolm and Margaret (d. 1093) the Scottish crown had proven itself generous to recluses of all persuasions, and as late as 1526, James V is recorded as giving forty shillings to the hermit Jacob Stobo.[49] Yet such solitaries often only appear in crown records when they combined their vocation with more earthly pursuits, such as the hermit of the Isle of May, who was James IV's gamekeeper. The Isle of May had been a site for recluses since the seventh century, when the death of St Ethernan made it a pilgrimage site. St Adrian of May, the next known incumbent of Ethernan's hermitage, was killed by Norse raiders in 875, and the shrine to the martyrs made it a popular pilgrimage destination. It eventually became a chapel where nine priests were maintained to pray for the kings of Scotland.[50] Shortly before Flodden, the hermit of the Isle of May appears in the Treasurer's Accounts when James IV made several visits to the island to visit the shrine and to shoot seabirds. The hermit apparently brought 'ane selch' [a seal] to the king as well as visiting Edinburgh to present him with 'cwnyngis' [coneys], and he accompanied the boats carrying various local lairds and canons of Pittenweem with the king's boat around the island to 'shut at fowlis with the culueryn' [shoot birds with the canon].[51] What is interesting is not so much the hermit's ability with seafowl as his dual role; he is only recorded inasmuch as he exercises a useful function, and is paid commensurately with his earthly, rather than spiritual, pursuits. Clearly important to the king, the man is nevertheless

[48] Ibid., p. 216.
[49] *Accounts of the Lord High Treasurer of Scotland*, ed. Thomas Dickinson and J. B. Paul (Edinburgh, 1877), vol. 5, p. 306.
[50] On this foundation, see Cowan and Easson, *Medieval Religious Houses*, pp. 53–4.
[51] *Accounts of the Lord High Treasurer*, vol. 4, p. 130.

never named nor has anything of his life recorded, and we have the sense that it is the office, not the office-holder, which is important to the patrons of Scottish recluses. The same pragmatism which would eventually pour scorn on the hermitage of Loretto in Musselburgh, Scotland's last medieval venture of this kind (as documented below), is visible in the method of recording the presence of recluses by their patrons: the laity record them only when they are in the role of counsellors; the monastic foundations only when there is a dispute about the possession of the hermitage; the crown only when the hermit performs another function. Although I have shown that, with Scotland's small population and unstable parish system, the numbers of anchorites might be expected to be fewer than in England, nonetheless the brutal pragmatism of the record-keeping further obscures those anchorites who did exist in medieval Scotland.

The later Middle Ages

By the beginning of the fifteenth century there existed a tension between a spirit of personal piety which accounted for the new feasts of the Crown of Thorns, the Five Wounds, the Compassion of the Virgin, and the new devotion to the Rosary and the Passion, and a pragmatism which caused a negative, or at least suspicious, attitude to new eremitical foundations.[52] The lack of money or the vagaries of interest in the eremitical life can be seen by the failure of Sir John Crawford's scheme for the Borough Muir hermitage in Edinburgh from 1512 to 1517. Despite the fact that the town council, in gratitude for Crawford's endeavour, gave extra land to add to the three-and-a-half acres he had leased from it to build the hermitage, Crawford annulled his foundation of St John the Baptist only four years later and endowed the new foundation of the Dominican Sisters instead.[53] Crawford's instructions for the hermit who would inhabit his foundation were specific:

> Moreover it is appointed and I ordain that a man of advanced age, of good life and sound constitution, shall always live at the said church and shall always wear a white gown, having on his breast the picture of the head of St John the Baptist and he shall be called his hermit and be bound to continual residence and to say daily and devoutly the following prayers for his founder and the souls aforesaid: that is to say, in the morning before the ninth hour, the psalter of the Blessed Virgin Mary, and in the time of masses, fifteen paternosters, as many Ave Marias and one Credo before the Image of the Crucifix.[54]

---

[52] For further reading on the new expressions of personal piety, see Alasdair A. MacDonald, H. N. B. Ridderbos and R. M. Schlusemann, *The Broken Body: Passion Devotion in Late Medieval Culture* (Groeningen, 1998); and Fitch, 'Power through Purity', pp. 16–28.

[53] The women of this foundation have left behind several literary remains, including a manuscript containing gospels for reading in chapter, and a short customary, written for the Sciennes convent in the early sixteenth century, was produced by the Abbotsford Club as *Liber Conventus S. Katherine Senensis prope Edinburgum* (Edinburgh, 1841). Also extant is a *Psalterium Daviticum*, printed in Lyons in 1552, which belonged to Sr Marion Crawford of the Sciennes convent.

[54] *Book of the Old Edinburgh Club* (Edinburgh, 1925), vol. 10, pp. 100–1.

Crawford's removal of his patronage from the foundation – and its apparent demise in favour of the Dominican Sisters – is characteristic of the gradual failure of interest in the eremitical life in central and lowland Scotland during the sixteenth century. It was, however, to have one final boom in the form of the Loretto shrine, the popularity of which, together with the dubious conduct of its hermit, arguably sounded the death-knell for Scottish lay eremitism.

The hermitage of Loretto was created by Thomas Douchtie, hermit of the Order of St Paul the First Hermit of Mount Sinai, who had apparently enjoyed a military career in the Holy Land.[55] It was part of the European enthusiasm for the *santa casa* of Loreto which developed as a result of Julius II's bull of 1507 approving the Italian shrine.[56] In 1534 James V confirmed a gift of the piece of ground from the bailies and burgesses of Musselburgh to Douchtie, who set about building a Loretto chapel around an image of Our Lady which he had brought with him. Despite Douchtie's involvement in the assault and stabbing of a chaplain, the chapel received official approval when James V, foiled in his first attempt to sail to France to marry Marie de Guise, made a pilgrimage to the Loretto shrine. Letters of Protection written shortly afterwards show that the chapel employed some seven chaplains, which implies a great surge of popularity in a very brief period.[57] The popularity of the Loretto chapel coincided with, and no doubt spurred on local manifestations of, growing anti-clericalism and Lutheranism in Scotland.[58] Douchtie was personally involved in the anti-Franciscan propaganda of the time, and 'Ane Epistle direct fra the Holye Armite of Allarit to his Bretheren the Gray Freires' by Alexander, Earl of Glencairn, was included in Knox's *History of the Reformation in Scotland*.[59] Sir David Lindsay, in his 'Dialog betuix Experience and ane Courtear', describes the 'claggit taill of the Armeit' who presides over a place of feigned piety and much fornication.[60] Charges of bogus miracles abounded, and although accusations of fornication and fraud are commonplace in medieval and Reformation descriptions of pilgrimage sites, the Loretto hermitage seems to have suffered heavily from them. Thomas Douchtie disappears, perhaps killed in the battle of Pinkie, fought nearby in 1547, or absent on another pilgrimage to the Holy Lands. By the time that Douchtie vanishes from history, however, the popularity of the Loretto hermitage is waning, and its reputation fodder for the

---

[55] McRoberts, 'Hermits', pp. 209–12 provides a cogent analysis of the downfall of Douchtie and the fall into disrepute of the Loretto shrine. Information about the Loretto hermitage in Musselburgh can be found in *The new statistical account of Scotland by the ministers of the respective parishes under the superintendence of a committee of the society for the benefit of the sons and daughters of the clergy* (Edinburgh, 1845), vol. 1, pp. 270–4; *Fasti Ecclesiae Scoticanae: The Succession of Ministers in the Church of Scotland from the Reformation*, ed. Hew Scott et al. (Edinburgh, 1915–61), vol. 8, pp.75–6.

[56] See Christine Shaw, *Julius II: The Warrior Pope* (Oxford, 1993), pp. 203–4.

[57] *Registrum secreti sigilii regum Scotorum*, ed. M. Livingstone et al. (Edinburgh, 1908), vol. 2, p. 2175.

[58] For more on this, see Alec Ryrie, *The Origins of the Scottish Reformation* (Manchester, 2006), p. 20.

[59] The poem can be found, without Knox's contextualizing vitriol, in *Early Popular Poetry of Scotland and the Northern Border*, ed. David Laing (London, 1895), vol. 1, pp. 175–8.

[60] *Ane Dialog betuix Experience and Ane Courteour (The Monarche)*, in *The Works of Sir David Lindsay of the Mount*, ed. Douglas Hamer (Edinburgh, 1931), vol. 1, pp. 197–386, lines 2661–708, and vol. 3, pp. 347–50, for notes on this.

growing surge of Reformation anti-popery. In 1569 the town council of Musselburgh used the stones from the property to repair the Tollbooth.

With the failure of the Loretto hermitage, Scottish eremitism seems to pass, surviving only in place names such as Ankerlaw, Ankerville, Croftangry, Angreflat and Croftingay.[61] It is easy to see how the Loretto phenomenon could provoke a wane in the public view of eremitism, but Ian Cowan's observation that 'monasticism was certainly out of favour' is perhaps a little premature.[62] Michael Lynch's claim that 'the single *corpus christianum*, which comprised the whole community of the burgh, remained, but each of the new components of urban society was given its own niche'[63] seems more judicious, especially in light of the fact that the only named Scottish anchorite, Helena Grant, was enclosed in Edinburgh as late as 1516. Despite the opportunity for expressions of personal piety in the new popularity of the Rosary, anchoritism was clearly still practised. That Helena's enclosure is mentioned in the *Diurnal of Occurents* suggests a number of things: that anchoritism was (still) practised in Scotland in the sixteenth century; that it provided enough of a public spectacle to be written up in the *Diurnal*; and that no apparent ructions followed this enclosure, since it would be reasonable for unrest to be noted as well. Other than the fact of Helena's enclosure, and its record in history, we know nothing about Scotland's only named anchorite, and her background, life and vocation will pose a tantalizing puzzle to those interested in the phenomenon of anchoritism in the north of Britain.

Conclusion

Evidence for Scottish medieval hermits is, if not flourishing, at least sufficient to establish their existence. For anchorites, on the other hand, it is virtually non-existent. Bequests of land to hermits show that they farmed and lived lives outside their hermitages – and so cannot be termed anchorites *per se*. The difference between the hermit and the anchorite in rural Scotland may have been redundant, since isolation would have effectively enclosed both. Indeed, the possession of sufficient land from which to survive could perhaps account for more recluses than normal, since they would not necessarily have to show financial independence for the remainder of their lives if they could farm. And yet the records do not reflect these possibilities. Medieval Scotland represents an apparent paucity of recluses as well as of information about them. I have attempted to show why this is so, by suggesting that the socio-economic form of medieval Scotland could not sustain many recluses: a small population required the efforts of all able-bodied adults to sustain itself, and the instability of the urban parish system made anchoritism, as it was practised in England, often unfeasible. Cultural considera-

---

[61] McRoberts' essay offers several pages of these names, many more now lost even since the 1960s ('Hermits', pp. 214–16). I have searched for several of these properties and have found that, for example, Croftangry survives in Alloa, along with Croftingay in the Lennox, and Angreflat in Roxburgh.

[62] Cowan, *Medieval Church in Scotland*, p. 173.

[63] Lynch, 'Religious Life', p. 120.

tions also suggest that anchoritism, although known to the Celtic church of early Scotland and respected by its reformer, Margaret, gradually became absorbed by the Augustinian canons brought from mother houses in England. As well as this, there are cogent reasons why structures of patronage may have hampered accurate records of recluses: lay and royal patrons recorded payment for services other than prayer, and monastic patrons absorbed the hermit within records of the general community, treating his hermitage as an asset, not a point of cultural or spiritual interest. Finally, the growing tension between Scotland's anti-clericalism and new methods of pietistic expression rendered the anchorhold obsolete. Helena Grant remains a tantalizing figure, but will, because of cultural circumstances in her own time and the condition of records left to ours, probably be forever obscure. The problem of Scottish anchorites faces the scholar in the same way that the hermitage on the Brigs of Fidra, connected to the nunnery at North Berwick, faces the traveller.[64] Unable to reach the island across the wilds of the Forth, we can only look into the mist and wonder.

---

[64] John Dickson, *Emeralds Chased in Gold; or, the Islands of the Forth, their story* (Edinburgh, 1899), pp. 304–6.

9 Anchorites and medieval Wales

Liz Herbert McAvoy

That there was an anchoritic tradition in the region known as Cymru to many of its current inhabitants, and Wales to the rest of the non Welsh-speaking world, is beyond doubt; and that it was overwhelmingly male seems also to have been the case in the face of little or no extant evidence to suggest otherwise.[1] There are more than sufficient material and textual traces to corroborate the popularity of the solitary religious life for men, although, as is the case in both Ireland and Scotland, the type of detailed records we find within the English tradition are sadly missing. This present essay, therefore, is an attempt to open the debate on the Welsh anchoritic experience, outlining some of the most useful sources and pointing the way forward for more concerted and detailed study which may lead to discoveries so far unenvisaged.

Reclusion and early Celtic Christianity in Wales

Without doubt, the lack of source material on a par with that of England and elsewhere comes as a direct result of the histories of English colonization and conquest which besieged Ireland, Scotland and Wales during the later period, resulting in protracted socio-religious upheavals and regroupings throughout much of the Middle Ages. But, as is frequently the case in such turbulent circumstances, memories are passed down through the generations via oral tradition: hagiographies, folklore, popular practices, myth and legend, prayers, place names etc. As such, they become embedded within a culture and that culture's 'collective psyche' and practices, what Pierre Bourdieu would term the *habitus*, taking on a life which, even if disappeared from view, nevertheless refuses to be eradicated completely.[2]

This aspect of collective memory is something also acknowledged by Oliver Davies in his book on Celtic Christianity which focuses specifically on Wales.[3]

---

[1] This is something which has recently been addressed in part by Jane Cartwright in her magisterial book on female spirituality in Wales, *Feminine Sanctity and Sprituality in Medieval Wales* (Cardiff, 2008). I shall return to the issue of female anchoritism in Wales towards the end of this essay.

[2] On the theories of Pierre Bourdieu, see my Introduction, p. 4.

[3] Oliver Davies, *Celtic Christianity in Early Medieval Wales* (Cardiff, 1996). See also Brendan Lehane, *Early Celtic Christianity* (London, 1994).

From the outset, Davies takes pains to contextualize the romantic appeal that the notion of a golden-age 'Celtic Church' still holds for a twenty-first-century audience, which often likes to re-imagine it as some kind of unified body standing in opposition to an apparently hegemonic Roman Church. For Davies, this is typical of the type of exploitation which the so-called 'Celtic world' has been subject to since the eighteenth century and, as he emphasizes most categorically, 'such an entity is fiction'.[4] Nevertheless, during the Middle Ages, the 'Celtic language cultures' did display some commonalities within their religious sensibilities, reinforced either by their geographical proximities or their shared experiences of colonization and occupation. As was the case in Ireland, Christianity arrived early in Wales, monasticism being already well established by the early sixth century.[5] Its practices, however, did not develop along the same lines as those of the Roman religion and, as a quasi-institutional expression of the religious life, it encompassed both the ordained and non-ordained, the secular and the monastic.[6] As such, it differed radically from the type of monasticism which had spread throughout the rest of Europe; indeed, within Welsh monastic life celibacy was a notable exception, rather than the norm as it was elsewhere,[7] and the Rule of Saint Benedict, so influential within the history of European monasticism, as we have seen, only began to exert influence in Wales after the Norman Conquest.[8] This inherent difference, with a built-in acceptance of sexuality at its core, was something, however, which resulted in a deep suspicion of and anxiety about the Welsh people among English commentators, who frequently considered them ontologically incontinent and somewhat depraved. Without the firm base of a recognizably Roman monasticism to underpin it, Welsh society could only ever be considered marginal and uncivilized. In the *Gesta Stephani* of the chronicler, John of Salisbury (*c.*1120–80), for example, the writer locates Wales as an alien and desolate land 'immediately bordering on England [in which] men of an animal type [*hominum nutrix bestialium*] live'. Moreover, these bestial peoples are 'by nature volatile ... and change their abodes frequently'.[9] It was just this sort of instability and godlessness which, for John of Salisbury and others like him, rendered the Welsh people so resistant to the 'civilizing' forces of the Norman English which alone could offer them a chance of reaching their full humanity.

Yet, it was just such socio-religious differences, both perceived and real, which not only distinguished Wales from its near neighbour but which would allow it the type of romanticized resonances in ensuing centuries to which I have alluded above. As Davies asserts in the context of the imposition of a new religion upon a pre-existing culture: 'the implantation of a world religion will take on specific

---

[4] Davies, *Celtic Christianity*, p. 1.

[5] Wendy Davies, *Wales in the Early Middle Ages* (Leicester, 1982), p. 148.

[6] Davies, *Celtic Christianity*, p. 9.

[7] Ibid., p. 10. On the meaning of monastic terminology in Wales during the period, see Huw Pryce, 'Pastoral Care in Early Medieval Wales', in *Pastoral Care before the Parish*, ed. J. Blair and R. Sharpe (Leicester, 1992), pp. 41–62.

[8] Davies, *Celtic Christianity*, p. 10.

[9] John of Salisbury, *Gesta Stephani, Regis Anglorum et Ducis Normannorum*, ed. Andrea Duchesne (London, 1846), p. 9. My translation.

local colour due to the continuing influence of primal elements'.[10] The specific local colour of Welsh monasticism, therefore, was very much shaped by the culture and practices which it met on its arrival in medieval Wales. Based upon the old social grouping of the *clas*, monastic groups were initially family- or clan-based and there was virtually no diocesan or parochial structure before the twelfth century, as there was in England, for example. This *clas*-based structure thereafter developed in several directions:[11] it formed itself into major monastic centres with disciplined regimes, such as those of Llanbadarn Fawr and Llantwit Major; less rigorous communities also sprang up which were both ascetical in their outlook and undertook hard manual labour as their practice; finally, for those who deemed neither of these models sufficient, it took the form of withdrawal into isolation, with individuals or small groups occupying the many caves and islands dotted around the Welsh coastal areas.[12] In this way, eremitism was clearly fundamental to the type of Celtic spirituality being examined here and, although detailed information about its adherents is yet to be forthcoming, sufficient textual and archaeological traces remain to suggest that the solitary religious life provided an alternative vocation – perhaps even a career path – which was intensely more taxing and disciplined than life within a more conventional Welsh monastic setting. Moreover, it was a way of life which, for some writing in the wake of John of Salisbury, came to characterize Welsh religiosity; for others, it would be appropriated as a nationalistic discourse in the wars and skirmishes which were part of Wales' relationship with England as its neighbour and colonizer in the later Middle Ages.

Narratives of Welsh eremitism

Some of the most high-profile and influential of contemporary accounts of Welsh recluses come from the pen of Giraldus Cambrensis [Gerald of Wales], writing during the twelfth century. In his *Itinerarium Kambriae* [*Journey Through Wales*], an account of his journey through Wales with Archbishop Baldwin on a mission to attract soldiers for the Crusades, Gerald, who was of mixed Welsh and Anglo-Norman parentage, articulates the difficulties of occupying a grey-zone of multiple identities within a time of great conflict.[13] Caught in the space between pro- and anti-Welsh sentiment, Gerald's *Itinerarium* recounts the

[10] Davies, *Celtic Christianity*, p. 2.
[11] On the *Clas* structure see, for example, Glanmor Williams, *The Welsh Church from Conquest to Reformation* (Cardiff, 1962), pp. 17–18.
[12] On this see Davies, *Celtic Christianity*, pp. 10–11.
[13] Giraldus Cambrensis, 'Itinerarium Kambriae', in *Opera*, Rolls ser. 21, ed. J. S. Brewer (London, 1861), vol. 6, Liber II, cap. ix, pp. 1–227. The modern English translation, from which I will be quoting here and elsewhere, is taken from Gerald of Wales, *The Journey through Wales* and *The Description of Wales*, trans. and intro. Lewis Thorpe (London, 1978). For a useful full-length study of Gerald of Wales see Robert Bartlett, *Gerald of Wales* (Oxford, 1982). Gerald's maternal grandfather had been a leader in the early attempts to conquer Wales and, in keeping with the militaristic strategy of subduing through marriage, had subsequently married Nest, the Princess of Deheubarth. Thus, Gerald, as their son, spanned the plastic space between the English and the Welsh, was caught between both and belonged fully to neither, as his writing fully attests.

author's kaleidoscopic travels through this 'degraded land', proving to be a highly popular text which extended to a third edition in 1214.[14] Rather than realistic account of a linear peregrination, however, the text – to quote the words of Jeffrey Jerome Cohen – 'tends to progress via associative logic, wandering the byways of a fertile mind rather than offering a pilgrimage to some secure destination'.[15] Thus, in Gerald's text, individual episodes tend to spark off memories of earlier encounters or written accounts, and also produce a range of hearsay representations replete with multivalent images which are, in every sense, associative. This is particularly true of Gerald's use of the anchorite, who forms a central part of the pro-Welsh 'associative logic' employed by him in this text. Indeed, in his *Description of Wales*, written soon after the *Itinerarium*, Gerald leaves the reader in no doubt as to the superior power and influence of the Welsh recluse:

> Nowhere can you see hermits and anchorites more abstinent and more spiritually committed than in Wales. The Welsh go to extremes in all matters [...] A happy and prosperous race indeed, a people blessed and blessed again, if only they had good prelates and pastors, and one single prince and he a just one![16]

For Gerald, the Welsh religious recluse clearly embodies the best that the Christian religion has to offer in terms of the potential for harmony and religious unity – and his agenda is also clearly a politicized one. This is further corroborated when, drawing on Bede, he recounts the famous meeting of Saint Augustine with seven Welsh bishops whom Augustine was supposed to have summoned from Wales to meet him on what is now the border between Gloucestershire and Monmouthshire.[17] Displaying what Gerald identifies as 'typical Roman arrogance',[18] Augustine manages to insult all seven Welsh bishops by omitting to stand up to greet them upon their arrival. At this point, the insulted bishops turn on their heels and make a dignified retreat to Wales 'with the utmost contempt'.[19] It is here that we learn that on their way to the synod the Welsh bishops had chosen to visit for his advice a 'saintly anchorite of their own nation', obviously a recluse of longstanding whose wisdom was widely renowned.[20] What his advice was we are not told, but as a result 'on their way home they announced to everyone they met that they would never acknowledge Augustine as their Archbishop'.[21] Thus, for Gerald, the independence of Celtic Christianity was built upon a sanctity which was underpinned by the solitary life and on several occa-

---

[14] Jeffrey Jerome Cohen, *Hybridity, Identity and Monstrosity in Medieval Britain: On Difficult Middles* (New York, 2006), p. 96. Bartlett points out the extensive number of extant manuscripts and editions, suggesting widespread readership and popularity of this text in the high Middle Ages: see *Gerald of Wales*, p. 179.

[15] Cohen, *Hybridity*, p. 96.

[16] Gerald of Wales, *Description of Wales*, p. 254.

[17] This is an event first recorded by the Venerable Bede in his *Historia Ecclesiastica*, for which see Venerabilis Bedae, *Historia Ecclesiastica Gentis Anglorum*, ed. Joseph Stevenson (London 1838), § 91, pp. 99–100.

[18] Gerald of Wales, *Journey through Wales*, Book II, ch. 1, p. 164.

[19] Ibid., p. 164.

[20] Gerald suggests that the bishops drew upon the anchorite's 'long experience': ibid., p. 164.

[21] Ibid., p. 164.

sions during his *Itinerarium* he draws upon eremitic founding narratives to prove his point. Llanthony Abbey, on the border between present-day Monmouthshire and Herefordshire, with which Gerald appears to have had close affinities, is described by him as 'originally founded by two hermits, in honour of the eremitical way of life, in solitude and far removed from the bustle of everyday existence and built on the bank of the Honddu'.[22]

Perhaps the most interesting (and amusing) of Gerald's anchorites, however, is one whom he names as Wechelen. Unlike some of the religious and saintly hermits whom he mentions elsewhere (Illtud and Caradog, for example),[23] Wechelen was both a layman and, so Gerald claims, illiterate. Wechelen, like so many laymen and women of the period, had undertaken a lengthy pilgrimage to Jerusalem, the experience of which brought about a desire to embrace a life of holy reclusion. He was duly enclosed at Llowes in Powys upon his return, evidently in a cell abutting the local church, since Gerald tells us that he could understand very little of the liturgy because of his ignorance of Latin.[24] After a miraculous vision in which he saw a loaf of bread on his altar [*super altare meum panem iacere*][25] which, in priestly fashion, he himself took, blessed and ate, he was granted knowledge of the Latin language by God and was thus able to fully understand what was being read at vespers in the adjoining church. By the following day, not only was Wechelen able to translate the gospel from Latin into his native Welsh but also to expound upon it in Latin to a priest who came to him outside his anchorhold window. What is particularly amusing about this incident as recounted by Gerald (and most likely demonstrates a form of suppressed intellectual snobbery which the layman-anchorite may have incited amongst the local 'intelligentsia' such as Gerald) is that Gerald first attempts to capture Wechelen's rustic, vernacular, idiomatic speech in writing ('Och, och ...'), and then has his anchorite use a type of 'cod' Latin which fails to conjugate its verbs, relying instead on the infinitive in each case. Indeed, Wechelen is the first to admit to Gerald his lack of fluency: 'et Dominus meus, qui dedit mihi Latinum linguam, non dedit eam mihi per grammaticam aut per casus' [and my God , who gave to me the Latin language, did not give it to me by means of grammar or cases].[26] Humorous though Gerald's recounting of this tale is, nevertheless it also demonstrates clearly a muted respect for the dignity of the layman-turned-anchorite and the ability of God to distribute his grace in a most egalitarian way.

[22] Ibid., Book I, ch. 3, p. 97. See also ibid., n. 102. On the late medieval history of Llanthony Abbey, see George Roberts, 'Some Account of Llanthony Priory, Monmouthshire', *Archaeologia Cambrensis* 3 (1846), pp. 201–45; and E. W. Lovegrove, 'Llanthony Priory', *Archaeologia Cambrensis* 97 (1938), pp. 213–29. Tradition would have it that one of these hermit founders was none other than the powerful Marcher lord William de Lacy, who, influenced by the Celtic spirituality with which the place was imbued, decided to abandon the military life and live a life of reclusion in the same location as Saint David himself was reputed to have done.

[23] On Wechelen and other Welsh recluses se F. G. Cowley, *The Monastic Order in South Wales 1066–1349* (Cardiff, 1977), pp. 51–2.

[24] For the Latin version of this episode, see Giraldus Cambrensis, *Opera*, vol. 1, pp. 89–92. The editor also offers a partial translation of this episode in his Preface, p. liv and p. lv. Rotha Mary Clay also includes an account of this episode in her *Hermits and Anchorites of England* (London, 1914), pp. 169–70.

[25] Giraldus, *Opera*, vol. 1, p. 91.

[26] Ibid., p. 91. My translation.

Later, however, this anchorite will be compromised by Satan masquerading as a nun [*mulier* [...] *sub specie monialis*] who would incite the warmongering English to attack and kill more than three thousand Welshmen in battle, supposedly on the advice of Wechelen.[27] This, of course, points towards an underlying suspicion of the female religious in Wales as outlined below in the context of Welsh medieval poetry dedicated to nuns.

Elsewhere, Gerald makes use of the figure of the literate anchorite in a similarly political – and self-interested – way. He tells of how an esteemed anchorite [*inclusus*] of Newgale in Pembrokeshire summoned him to his anchorhold by letter. Speaking to Gerald via the anchorhold window [*per fenestrum suum*], the anchorite proceeds to alert him to the various temporal punishments which he foresees will be meted out shortly to various canons of St David's cathedral (who are both his enemies and Gerald's).[28] Nor is this the only Welsh anchorite with prescient abilities focused on by Gerald at this point. He recounts the visionary predictions of another anchorite [*vir bonus anachorita*], this time from Locheis.[29] This anchorite has received a vision of Gerald in the form of an inert body lying in a dark prison, obviously pointing towards the type of institutional attempts to silence Gerald about which he complains on many other occasions in his writing. Upon the behest of this anchorite, however, Gerald is restored to life and released from the prison, to everybody's great joy.[30] It is not difficult here to see writ large the political purpose to which Gerald likes to put the anchorite in his writing, as we saw in the example from his *Itinerarium* cited above. As the most sacred of religious personages, Gerald's anchorites not only display a sanctity which outstrips all those corrupt (and, by implication, anti-Gerald!) ecclesiastics whose aim is to keep him from the highest office – that is the St David's episcopacy – but he also has them ventriloquize, in the form of a vision, the supposed word of God, which, of course, also falls in Gerald's favour.

The recluse and male hagiography

On other occasions, Gerald draws upon Welsh hagiographic narrative, or else folkloric tales concerning saintly Welsh predecessors, to underpin the superiority of Celtic religiosity: Saint Illtud (d. 540), mentioned above, for example, was said to have lived as a hermit at Oystermouth on the Gower peninsula, moving later to Llanhamlach.[31] Elsewhere, Gerald recounts the life of Saint Caradog, who lived a

---

[27] Ibid., pp. 91–2. Such ambivalent attitudes to the figure of the nun are also characteristic of Welsh writing, particularly Welsh poetry, for which see Cartwright, *Feminine Sanctity*, pp. 176–94. See also Helen Fulton, 'Medieval Welsh Poems to Nuns', *Cambridge Medieval Celtic Studies* 21 (1999), pp. 87–112.

[28] Gerald, *Opera*, vol. 1, pp. 178–80 (p. 170).

[29] Ibid., p. 175.

[30] Ibid., p. 175.

[31] Gerald, *Journey through Wales*, Book I, ch. 2, p. 88. Illtud, originally from Brittany, was also a soldier-saint who took up a military life instead of the clerical one for which he was destined. See Elissa R. Henken, *Traditions of the Welsh Saints* (Cambridge, 1987), p. 108. See also G. H. Doble, *Lives of the Welsh Saints*, ed. D. Simon Evans (Cardiff 1971); for Illtud, see pp. 88–145. For the Latin *vita* of Illtud see *Vita Sancti Iltuti*, BL MS Cotton Vespasian S.xiv [BHL 4268], edited in *VSBG*, pp. 194–233.

Anchorites and medieval Wales   201

life of reclusion at St Ismaels in Rhos and then retired to a hermitage on the island
of Burry Holms at the northern tip of the Gower peninsula.[32] There, Caradog was
supposed to have restored the dilapidated oratory of Saint Cenydd, a saint
(focused on below) who had also supposedly withdrawn to the island as a hermit
in the ninth century; Caradog also constructed himself a hut on the island in order
to live the life of religious reclusion there. He was renowned for the miracles he
performed both during his life and after death, as well has for having founded the
nearby priory of Llangennith, to which Burry Holms evidently belonged.[33]
Interestingly, a series of archaeological excavations undertaken between 1965 and
1969 by the archaeologist Douglas Hague on behalf of the Royal Commission on
the Ancient and Historical Monuments of Wales, uncovered on the island not only
a high medieval Romanesque church and burial ground, but also traces of an earlier wooden oratory beneath the church's foundations.[34] Indeed, Hague's conclusions were that this was most likely the remains of the oratory of Saint Cenydd
which Caradog was said to have so lovingly restored. Nearby, the remains of a
wooden hut were also uncovered, the construction of which, for Hague, left much
to be desired: he added playfully in his 'Provisional Account of the Excavations
1965–9' that it was likely built 'by a decayed hermit whose only previous structural experience had been "sticking a row of beans"'.[35] Whoever this 'decayed
hermit' may have been, whether Caradog or somebody else (although the dating of
the hut to the last quarter of the eleventh century certainly fits the time of Caradog's
withdrawal to Burry Holms), neither he nor Cenydd was the first occupant of the
island: beneath the early wooden oratory was an even earlier medieval grave site
which had been disturbed upon the oratory's construction. The occupants, both
men and women, young and old, were most likely the very first Christian occupants of the island, predating even the saintly Cenydd.[36]

Gerald claims in his *Epistola ad capitulum Herefordense de libris a se scriptis*
to have written a *Life of Saint Caradog* and was also responsible for the promot-
ing of Saint Caradog for canonization to Pope Innocent III in 1200;[37] and in most
of Gerald's accounts of anchorites or hermits, an acerbic political agenda is never
far from the surface, as I have suggested. This was something that was echoed in

---

[32] This is confirmed by the twelfth-century *Llyfr Llandaf [Book of Llandaff]*, a register of the cathedral
church of Llandaff. This has been edited by J. Rhys and J. G. Evans (Oxford, 1893). See also J. R. Davies,
The Book of Llandaf and the Norman Church in Wales (Woodbridge, 2003); and Wendy Davies, *The
Llandaff Charters* (Aberystwyth, 1980).

[33] Gerald, *Journey through Wales*, Book I, ch. 11, p. 144. The history of Llangennith priory is recounted
by Latimer Davies in his study of west Gower, *Pennard and West Gower* (Carmarthen, 1928), pp. 21–8.

[34] Very few of the findings from these extensive excavations were ever published. Detailed records, however, are stored (but as yet uncatalogued) in the Royal Commission on the Ancient and Historical
Monuments of Wales archives in Aberystwyth. I am grateful to the archivists there for making this material available to me at short notice.

[35] Hague, 'Provisional Account of the Excavations 1965–9', 1.iv.76. Working on the island at night on a
typewriter in his tent, Hague kept detailed and comprehensive records of the excavations' progress. Those
consulted here are identified by title and date of composition.

[36] Hague, 'Notes on the Burry Holms Excavation, Site D', 18.v.78.

[37] See Gerald, *Journey through Wales*, Book 1, ch. 11, p. 144, n. 228. Gerald's overtures to the pope were
ultimately unsuccessful, thwarted, so Gerald considered, by those clergymen who were antipathetic
towards him.

the contemporaneous enthusiasm for reconfigured Welsh hagiographic narratives which attempt to revive the 'golden age' or 'first wave' of Celtic Christianity embraced during the sixth to ninth centuries in the so-called 'Age of Saints'. According to Ian Bradley, this period was 'a time of missionary zeal, spiritual energy and simple faith in exceptional measures',[38] in which the troubled history of Wales between the twelfth and fifteenth centuries sought refuge. This 'Celtic revival', was, as Bradley also points out, closely associated with the 'new order' of the Norman invasion which brought with it an affection for the old whilst at the same time attempting to effect the new.[39]

As we have seen elsewhere in this volume, the monastic reform movement instigated on the Continent also brought with it a rekindled enthusiasm for the eremitic life, something which in Wales produced a flurry of written saints' Lives in a move towards canonization, no doubt to strengthen the religious foundations of Welsh spirituality at a time when it was most under threat. These Lives included those of male ascetics, monks, hermits and anchorites dating from as far back as the fifth century, and many of them were used as dedications for the new, stone-built parish churches which began to populate the Welsh landscape from the twelfth century onwards under Anglo-Norman influence.[40] Moreover, as both Henken and Bradley have noted, these Lives shared in common a range of national-istic and/or tribal purposes: generically they bore more resemblance to ancient and secular folkloric tales of conception- and birth-miracles, secular conflict and death, suggesting they arose in response to the era of English colonization and, finally, conquest.[41] Indeed, an example of just such a politically motivated revival can be seen in the *Life of Cadog*, which was reworked, developed and embellished by St Caradog himself and circulated in the mid-twelfth century.[42] According to Caradog, Cadog, whose birth and exceptional childhood piety had been accompa-nied by all kinds of marvels, attracted many disciples, eventually founding a monastery on a plot of land known as *Erw Wen* [White Acre]. Nevertheless, desir-ing to intensify his spiritual life, he habitually withdrew into reclusion during the period of Lent on one or other of the islands in the inhospitable Bristol Channel. On another occasion, he is documented as pinpointing the remoteness of the Neath valley as a suitable location for installing 'his clergy' as recluses. Cadog is also cited as the one responsible for converting Saint Illtud from a life as a soldier to one as a dedicated ascetic-recluse. The politico-religious agenda here is, of course, clear. As an English national identity, politics and religious hegemony threatened to encroach upon a region with its own ways of doing things, a revival of the old order and its reinvention as the new could be used to create a distinct sense of

---

[38] Ian Bradley, *Celtic Christianity: Making Myths and Chasing Dreams* (Edinburgh, 1999), p. 1.
[39] Ibid., p. 40.
[40] Ibid., p. 45.
[41] Henken, *Traditions*, p. 2; Bradley, *Celtic Christianity*, p. 45.
[42] The manuscript source of Cadog's *vita*, BL MS Cotton Vespasian A.xix, is an amalgamation of earli-er versions of the text, Cadog's revisions and additions, and further scribal amendment, for which see Henken, *Traditions*, p. 24. See also *VSBG*, pp. 24–141. On further traditions surrounding Cadog, see Henken, *Traditions*, pp. 89–98.

identity within a land which was, to all intents and purposes, increasingly fractured and fragmented.

Until this time, evidence for early Welsh saints' cults suggests that they were mainly local in nature, based on family ties and kinship bonds. This is certainly true of the sixth-century monastic recluse Saint Cenydd (variously written Kennyd, Kenyd or Kenneth) whose popularity on the Gower peninsula is reflected both in place names and church and chapel dedications and who, according to one local historian, therefore left 'an indelible mark on the Gower'.[43] Saint Cenydd's life was recorded in the Middle Ages by John Capgrave from a variety of Welsh sources in his *Nova Legenda Angliae*.[44] In this account, Cenydd was the son of an incestuous relationship between his father, a Breton king, and his sister. Born whilst his parents were visiting Loughor, on the edge of the Gower peninsula, Cenydd had a deformed leg which resulted from his ill-fated conception. Because of this, his father cast him out to sea from the Loughor estuary from where he was washed up onto the rocky crag of Worm's Head on the western tip of Gower at Rhossili. According to legend, he was sustained by the gulls who nested there and by visiting angels who brought him up within the Christian faith. Later, he would be cured of his infirmity by Saint David and go on to found the important priory of Llangennith near Rhossili, mentioned above. At some stage in his life, as we have seen, he retired to the hermitage on the nearby island of Burry Holms.[45] Indeed, scrutiny of the Close Rolls point towards hermitic activity on the island until the fifteenth century when Philip Lichepoll, William Bernard and Thomas Norys are recorded at separate times as living as recluses there,[46] thus drawing to a close an illustrious history of religious reclusion on that small and rocky island.

The influence of the Célí Dé

The eremitic foundation of Burry Holms has also attracted the attention of Oliver Davies whose examination of the *Llyfr Du Caerfyrddin* [*Black Book of Carmarthen*], thought to be the earliest extant manuscript written entirely in Welsh, has identified the poems contained within it as possibly influenced by the Irish *Célí Dé* (culdee) movement (which is focused on briefly by McHugh in the essay which precedes this one).[47] As Oliver Davies notes, this movement was an

---

[43] Latimer Davies, *Pennard and West Gower*, p. 24. The life of Saint Cenydd is retold by Clay in *Hermits and Anchorites*, pp. 8–10. Although Clay claims the Welsh material is beyond the scope of her survey, nevertheless she recounts several instances of Welsh hermits, including Cenydd (Kenyth).

[44] John Capgrave, *Nova Legenda Angliae*, ed. Karl Horstmann (Oxford, 1901), vol. II, pp. 105–7.

[45] *The Life of Saint Cadog* also tells of his retreat to the 'deserted church of St Kined' in the early twelfth century.

[46] See, for example, CPR 22 Richard II, 15 July 1398, p. 382; CPR 7 Henry IV, 27 November 1429, p. 523; CPR 20 Henry VI, 20 November 1441, p. 52. By 1446, Thomas Norys is evidently dead and his 'chapel of Holmes *alias* the hermitage of Holmes' has been granted to a Thomas Car, chaplain: ibid., 24 Henry VI, 16 February 1446, p. 403.

[47] See McHugh's essay, p. 181, n. 15 above.

important influence within Irish spirituality in the mid-eighth century[48] and, in particular, it was associated with eremitism and an ascetic life of prayer and penance. It supposedly produced early Irish religious lyrics which figured prominently in anthologies akin to the *Llyfr Du*.[49] We know that the movement spread to the west of Scotland from Ireland, but Gerald of Wales tells us that it was also to be found in North Wales, in particular Ynys Enlli [Bardsey Island]: 'Beyond Lleyn there is a small island occupied by some extremely devout monks, called the Coelibes or Colidei [...] The bodies of a vast number of holy men are buried there.'[50] For Davies, the poems of this early anthology, perhaps produced by the Cistercians at Hendy-gwyn or the Augustinians at Carmarthen,[51] were very likely inspired by this movement and he rightly points out that the English literary tradition has nothing like the monastic praise-poems contained within the *Llyfr Du*.[52] As Ó Clabaigh points out in his essay on Ireland, however, this perspective on the *Céli Dé* movement has recently been subject to some dispute;[53] moreover, the movement, such as it was in Wales, was associated with areas of North Wales whilst the *Llyfr Du* is undoubtedly of southern provenance, something which Davies is himself quick to acknowledge.[54] Nevertheless, Davies is not the first to associate the activities on the island with a community of the *Céli Dé* type: Hague, in his unpublished papers, was also keen to trace the connections between the Celtic spirituality of the first Christian inhabitants of this island and those of their Irish cousins, particularly the connections between early Gaelic religious verse and that found within the early Welsh tradition, as anthologized within the *Llyfr Du*. This type of Irish connection is one which was also raised by Latimer Davies in his *Pennard and West Gower*, where he points out the many strong Irish influences felt in Gower place names in particular.[55] Indeed, Nora Chadwick goes even further, asserting: 'From linguistic and literary evidence ... it would seem that the peoples of western and southern Wales and south-eastern Ireland shared a common culture in the pre-Norman period.'[56] Close connection between Welsh and Irish pre-Norman traditions is also reflected in the type of saints' Lives referred to above where there is much toing and froing between the two countries and frequent mention is made of important Irish figures. Cadog, for example, is said to

---

[48] Davies, *Celtic Christianity*, p. 46.

[49] Ibid., p. 46.

[50] Gerald of Wales, *Journey through Wales*, Book II, ch. 6, p. 183–4; cited in Davies, *Celtic Christianity*, p. 46.

[51] Ibid., p. 28.

[52] Ibid., p. 46.

[53] See pp. 155–6, above.

[54] The *Llyfr Du Caerfyrddin* has been digitized and can be accessed with full details on the National Library of Wales website at http://www.llgc.org.uk/index.php?id=blackbookofcarmarthen. Last accessed 22 March 2009.

[55] Davies, *Celtic Christianity*, p. 47; Davies, *Pennard and West Gower*, p. 22.

[56] Nora Chadwick, 'Intellectual Life in West Wales in the Last Days of the Celtic Church', in *Studies in the Early British Church*, ed. N. K. Chadwick, K. Hughes, C. Brooke and K. Jackson (Cambridge, 1958), pp. 121–82 (p. 123). See also *Ireland and Wales in the Middle Ages*, ed. Karen Jankulak, Thomas O'Loughlin and Jonathan Wooding (Dublin, 2003).

have sailed to Ireland to seek out the most learned teachers in the land in order to enhance his own spiritual education. Similarly, many of the Welsh saints appeared within Irish martyrologies,[57] suggesting a tradition of early communication and spiritual cross-pollination which had solitary asceticism at its core.

The anchorite of Llanddewi Brefi

In spite of the overwhelming predominance of ascetic monasticism and hermiticism, whether communal or otherwise, in medieval Wales, there are also traces to be found of a specifically anchoritic way of life (as we saw in the writings of Gerald). In this context, probably the most renowned of these is the literary anchorite of Llanddewi Brefi who is best known for his rewriting in Welsh of the *Life of Saint David*, originally compiled in Latin by a monk named Rhigyfarch and dated to around 1095. Rhigyfarch had been part of the esteemed community of Llanbadarn Fawr which had produced a slow procession of scholars whose contribution added much to the culture and learning of both pre-Norman and Norman Wales.[58] Rhigyfarch's *Life* is highly polished and sophisticated and, of course, would have provided eminently suitable reading-matter for an enclosed religious. It may well be significant that both this anchorite and Gerald's Wechelen were involved in translating original Latin material into the Welsh language. Indeed, during the excavation on Burry Holms outlined above, Hague's team uncovered a small cell attached to the twelfth-century living quarters of the community which appeared to have been used as some kind of individual scriptorium.[59] An added attraction of this life for the anchorite of Llanddewi Brefi would have been the fact that one of Saint David's most renowned miracles took place when convening a summit of bishops at Llanddewi Brefi: initially unable to make himself seen or heard, David reputedly caused a large mound of earth to be raised up, upon which he was able to stand to address the crowd – a mound which still forms part of the landscape of the village to this day.

The *Book of the Anchorite of Llanddewi Brefi*, as its compiler helpfully informs his readers, was completed *Anno domini MCCC. Quadragesi Sexto* [in the year of our Lord 1346],[60] and comprises a compilation of devotional texts, most of which

---

[57] This is pointed out by Davies, *Celtic Christianity*, p. 48.

[58] Ibid., p. 20.

[59] Hague, 'Provisional Account of the Excavations 1965–9', 18.i.70, p. 3.

[60] Parts of this manuscript (Oxford, Jesus College MS 2 [119]) have been edited by J. Morris-Jones as *The Life of Saint David and other Tracts* (Oxford, 1912), which is based on the more complete edition of the manuscript produced by himself and John Rhŷs, *The Elucidarium and other Tracts in Welsh from Llyvyr Agkyr Llandewivrevi A.D. 1346* (Oxford, 1894). For purposes of this essay, I will be referring to the latter (here at p. 2). In addition, there is a translation of the text by A. Wade Evans, *Life of Saint David – Rhigyfarch* (London, 1923). Besides the introductions provided by Morris-Jones to each of these editions, very few other commentators have written on the manuscript: see, however, Thomas Jones, 'The Book of the Anchorite of Llanddewi Brefi', *Cardigan Antiquarian Society Transactions* XII (1937), pp. 63–82; and I. Ll. Foster, 'The Book of the Anchorite', *Proceedings of the British Academy* 36 (1950), pp. 197–226. On the dated colophon of *Llyfr yr Ancr* [*Book of the Anchorite*], see Daniel Huws, *Medieval Welsh Manuscripts* (Cardiff, 2000), p. 14. I am grateful to Helen Fulton for alerting me to these two latter works.

were extant in earlier versions.[61] He also informs us that his patron was one Gruffydd ap Llewelyn ap Phylip ap Trahayarn of Cantref Mawr, who seems to have been a friend of the anchorite as well as his patron; but the anchorite himself, in keeping with his profession, opts for anonymity. As if to justify this desire to remain nameless, the anchorite begins his compilation with an almost verbatim extract from the prologue to *Hystoria Lucidar* (or *Elucidarium*):

> This book is called *Elucidarium*, that is, a book that gives light; for in it light is thrown upon various dark subjects. I have not, however, revealed my own name lest these deeds should suffer through jealousy.[62]

The original author of this text was Honorius Augustodunensis, who is thought to have been an anchorite near the Irish monastic foundation at Ratisbon in the early twelfth century. For both men, it would seem that anonymity was crucial, not only to the ethos of relinquishment which was central to the anchoritic life but also because the privileged position of the anchorite within the community could, it would seem, incite envy at the life and achievements which such reclusion entailed. We also see quite clearly reflected in this passage the Bachelardian notion of the cultural meanings attached to the candle burning in the window of the solitary's cell which I quoted in my introduction to this volume. The light and the learning, the architecture and the *modus vivendi* it facilitates, all conflate to present an image of the anchorhold as a liminal and especially sacred space in which its anonymous inhabitant may 'be written in Heaven and [...] his name be not erased from the Book of Life'.[63]

The type of anchoritism embraced by the Llanddewi Brefi recluse appears on the surface to be much more in keeping with the type of anchoritism common throughout Europe in the later Middle Ages, as documented by the other contributors to this volume. The Welsh predilection for peregrination and periodic withdrawal into solitude seems in this case to have ceded to a more static form of the reclusive life, although the two saint's Lives included within the *Book* – those of Saint David and Saint Beuno – would suggest that it was never far away from its origins; indeed these Lives, among others, were read as part of the divine service in Welsh churches, and the collegiate church at Llanddewi Brefi to which this particular anchorite was most probably attached would have been no exception. It is likely, then, that the production of this book in 1346 was part of the religio-political attempt to recapture an essentialized Celtic Christianity, as discussed above in the context of revived interest in the Lives of early Celtic saints.

This church had been founded in 1287 by Thomas Bek, the new bishop of the diocese of St David's. Bek had earlier claimed independence from Canterbury, a

---

[61] Jones, 'The Book', p. 63. The scribe of this particular manuscript was also responsible for other manuscripts including some secular ones. For Daniel Huws it 'represents a contemporary anthology of religious texts from the same milieu as the White Book' – that is to say, it was commissioned by families belonging to the gentry: Huws, *Medieval Welsh Manuscripts*, p. 246. Again, I am grateful to Helen Fulton for pointing this out to me.

[62] *Elucidarium and other Tracts*, p. 2 (quoted and translated by Jones, 'The Book', p. 67).

[63] Ibid., p. 67.

move which had resulted in threats of excommunication from Archbishop
Peckham, in the light of which Bek submitted and was forced to make efforts to
eradicate all traces of the early Celtic Church from current Welsh ecclesiastical
practices.[64] According to Osborne Jones in his account of this process: 'It was the
last shackle which the Latin Church placed upon the Welsh clergy in their successful attempt to dominate the old Celtic Church.'[65] But what had disturbed Bek most
on his arrival at Llanddewi Brefi during the visitation process were the remains of
one of the so-called 'ancient societies' which were in fact part of the Welsh
monastic *clas*-system alluded to at the start of this essay. These *claswyr* were evidently still part of the religious landscape of Wales up until the Edwardian
Conquest and beyond, and Bek's activities at Llanddewi Brefi constituted a concerted attempt to bring the community firmly under the rule of Rome.[66] The
presence of a still 'pro-Celtic' anchorite (specifically named as such in the *Book*
as *agkyr*) at the church just over sixty years later, who is busily translating
important Latin texts into the Welsh language, may well point towards a continued resistance to Romanization as part of a rumbling 'underground' opposition
which would later materialize physically in the context of the rebellion of Owain
Glyndŵr at the start of the fifteenth century. [67]

The likelihood of this being the case can be discerned from the choice of material which the anchorite of Llanddewi Brefi used to compile his *Book*. As Thomas
Jones points out, the manuscript's contents constitute 'a fairly representative
selection of Mediaeval Welsh prose theological tracts', mainly translated from
Latin originals.[68] Absent are extracts from the *Vitae patrum* which we would normally expect to find in similar compilations emanating from elsewhere in Europe.
Instead, two of the most popular of Welsh saints' Lives are chosen for loose translation and inclusion, as detailed above. These Lives, in keeping with much of Welsh
hagiographic narrative, are as much idealizations of a mythical and romanticized
'golden age' as they are 'accurate' accounts of sacred activities. This is further
reinforced by what is, on the surface, a strangely disparate text which the anchorite
also chooses to include: a translated extract from a text entitled *Hystoria Gwlat*

---

[64] In this following section, I am dependent upon the article on Thomas Bek by R. Osborne Jones, 'Coleg
Bek at Llanddewibrefi', *Cardigan Antiquarian Society Transactions* XII (1937), pp. 59–62.

[65] Ibid., p. 59.

[66] Ibid., p. 61.

[67] On the struggles of the Welsh for independence in the Middle Ages see, for example, R. R. Davies,
Conquest, Coexistemce and Change: Wales 1063–1415 (Oxford, 1987), repr. as *The Age of Conquest*
(Oxford, 1991); and *The Revolt of Owain Glyn Dŵr* (Oxford, 1995).

[68] Jones, 'The Book', p. 68. Besides the lives of Saint David and Saint Beuno mentioned above, the manuscript also contains texts taking the form of a dialogue between master and pupil; several apocalyptic
texts; a range of scriptural extracts, sometimes with accompanying commentary; a range of theological
tracts, including a version of the creed of Saint Athanasius (*Credo Seint Athanasius*). Most are translations from the Latin. Whilst Jones laments the lack of information on the translators into Welsh of these
texts, he fails to consider that, in some cases, it may well have been the Llanddewi Brefi anchorite himself. He does, however, acknowledge the debt owed to the translator(s) for their providing the medieval
Welsh lexis with a useful philosopho-theological vocabulary which was not previously available to writers in the medium of Welsh. Ibid., p. 69.

Ieuan Vendigeit or *The History of the Land of Prester John*.[69] This is based on a popular story that took hold in Europe at some stage during the eleventh century regarding a priestly Christian king who reputedly ruled over vast swathes of land in the East. The tales connected with this ruler were highly exoticized and this Welsh extract, translated from the Latin original, is part of a letter, dated 1165, which was supposed to have been written by Prester John himself to Emperor Emmanuel at Constantinople (and thus masquerades as a first-person narrative) – versions of which also appear in most of the other European vernaculars.[70] Prester John was a figure who represented the entrenched position and rectitude of Roman Christianity in the face of the ubiquitous Muslim faith which surrounded his Christian enclave. As such, this can be read as a text which enforces the Roman Church in particular. Interestingly, however, within this anthology this potential enforcement is considerably destabilized by the fact that the majority of the extract in question deals with the enchanted and exotic realm of Prester John himself, rather than the religious ideological work which the text was evidently devised to undertake in its original conception. For example, it concerns itself primarily with phenomena such as a magical and exotic underground river [*ymae auon ydan ydayar*][71] which flows into a waterless sea, and a remarkable fountain [*ffynnyawn arde(r)chawc*][72] which bestows a perpetual youthful energy upon anybody who drinks from it. Moreover, in this marvellous domain, nobody was capable of telling a lie [*nydyweit neb gelwyd yn y plith ni*] but, if a lie were to be uttered, the perpetrator would be considered dead to the world [*dyn marw*].[73] It does not take a long engagement with this text, therefore, to see its correlations with the type of 'otherworldly' tales which have long been part of the Celtic folkloric traditions, and which re-emerge in collections such as the *Llyfr Coch Hergest* [*Red Book of Hergest*] and the *Mabinogion*, for example.[74] The other-world of Prester John is not so far removed from these mythical Celtic pasts, which were to become increasingly important in the years between the excesses of Edward I's conquest and the Welsh rebellion led by Owain Glyndŵr in the fifteenth century. As Ian Bradley points out, part of the purpose of the Welsh rebellion against Henry IV was to free the Welsh church once again from the jurisdiction of Canterbury and restore leadership to the archbishop of St David's.[75] It is hardly surprising then that Owain Glyndŵr himself was deeply responsive to the prophecies of Saint David regarding the eventual routing of the English. Indeed, as Glanmor Williams has also posited regarding the anchorite of

---

[69] *Elucidarium and other Tracts*, pp. 164–71.

[70] Jones, 'The Book', p. 79.

[71] *Elucidarium and other Tracts*, p. 167.

[72] Ibid., p. 166–70.

[73] Ibid., p. 169.

[74] The title *Mabinogion* refers to a group of texts found in two of the most important of Welsh manuscripts, the *Llyfr Coch Hergest* [*Red Book of Hergest*] and the *Llyfr Gwyn Rhydderch* [*White Book of Rhydderch*]. Each of the stories contained within them relates in some way to what is referred to as 'The Matter of Britain' – that is the body of folkloric and pseudo-historical lore which originated within the British Celtic communities.

[75] Bradley, *Celtic Christianity*, p. 81.

Llanddewi Brefi's *Life of Saint David*: '[It] may be best understood as being as much a part of a patriotic protest against the rapidly-growing exploitation of the Welsh Church by the English state in the fourteenth century as Rhigyfarch's Latin text was against the Norman incursions in the eleventh century.'[76] Anonymous and locked away he might have been, but the anchorite within the tiny Welsh community of Llanddewi Brefi was to have a marked influence upon British politics at least until the fifteenth century, and his work would be adopted as part of the statement of hostility against the English. As we have seen, society's use of the anchorite was not necessarily always a benign one.

A female anchoritic tradition?

But what were the circumstances in Wales as far as female solitaries were concerned? It is true to say that we do not know. If the evidence for a more traditional form of male anchoritism is almost entirely missing outside of Gerald of Wales' writing and the often anonymous hagiographies, the same can be said for women too, but more so. To date, virtually nothing has surfaced to suggest there even having been a tradition of female solitary enclosure in Wales – and it certainly does not seem to have been an aspect of Celtic Christianity as practised in the region. Indeed, as Jane Cartwright has demonstrated quite clearly in her important recent study on female religiosity in medieval Wales, the provision for women religious in Wales throughout the Middle Ages was very scant, to say the least.[77] During the later period, there were only ever three religious houses for women, as opposed to 150 in medieval England, sixty-four in Ireland and fifteen in Scotland, a lack of provision which Cartwright rightly deems 'astonishing'.[78] Moreover, these nunneries themselves were equally sparsely populated: in or around the year 1377 there were four nuns and an abbess at Llanllugan (Powys), sixteen nuns at Llanllŷr (Dyfed) and, possibly, up to thirteen at Usk (Gwent).[79] As Cartwright points out, this stands in stark contrast to Eileen Power's assessment of there having been up to 2,000 nuns in English nunneries at the time of the Dissolution,[80] suggesting either that Welsh women did not find religious enclosure an attractive option, or that it simply was not a way of life made available to the vast majority of them.

Of those few who were enclosed in the post-Conquest period we know little: whether they were educated and in what capacity; whether they were literate in Latin or literate in any sense; whether they were noblewomen or otherwise. The only location where the medieval Welsh nun *does* make an appearance is in contemporary poetry, in particular the medium of the *cywydd*,[81] and, as Helen Fulton

---

[76] Glanmor Williams, cited in Bradley, *Celtic Christianity*, p. 81.

[77] Cartwright's survey covers the period 600–1550, for which see Jane Cartwright, *Feminine Sanctity*, op. cit.

[78] The Welsh nunneries were at Llanllŷr, Llanllugan and Usk. Ibid., pp. 177–8.

[79] Ibid., pp. 181–2.

[80] Eileen Power, *Medieval English Nunneries 1275–1535* (Cambridge, 1922), p. 326, as cited in Cartwright, *Feminine Sanctity*, p. 182.

[81] The *cywydd* is a short poem or ode written in rhyming couplets and employing a rich and complex system of alliteration and internal rhyme called *cynghannedd*.

has demonstrated, those secular poets who produced this corpus appear to have failed entirely to take seriously the lives of the nuns about whom they wrote, preferring to make them the objects of, at best, romantic love, at worst, unbridled lust.[82] This stands in distinct contrast to those similar *cywyddau* which were directed at married women, for example, who were often praised highly for their virtues of chastity and piety. It would seem that in the Wales of the Middle Ages, married womanhood was held in much greater esteem than the life of an enclosed nun, something about which Cartwright concludes:

> Women may have been too important within the social, political and economic concerns and interests of the secular community to have been actively encouraged to retreat to more isolated and rarefied religious environments.[83]

In her study, Cartwright also demonstrates comprehensively the widespread devotion to female saints which existed in Wales, particularly amongst women. Very often, this devotion took the form of fully fledged cult status with both local saints and the more universal ones taking centre stage: Saints Non and Gwenfrewy were venerated alongside Saints Mary (Mair) and Katherine (Katrin), for example, and in many cases the cults attached to each suggested an inherent preferment of married life and motherhood to that of the cloister or anchorhold.[84] This again raises important questions about the apparent absence of female anchoritism in Wales: since female devotion to a wide range of female saints was evidently widespread and fundamental to the socio-religious milieu in which these women were operating, one could surely expect quite reasonably the type of identification with and desire to emulate such saintly role-models as was prevalent amongst lay women in England and on the Continent. So, was it simply a case that women were programmed to fulfil other functions within Welsh society, leaving the religious life traditionally to the men? Or, if we search more closely, can we find traces of female solitary enclosure written between the lines of those texts and records available to us, traces which may suggest some kind of precedent for female solitary enclosure?

Saints Melangell, Eluned and Dwynwen

These three native saints are given high priority in Cartwright's study of female sanctity in Wales. In the case of Saint Melangell, the evidence suggests that her Life had long been circulated orally before being written down at some stage during the fifteenth century, and there is similar evidence of a shrine in her name, possibly devised originally to contain her relics, at the church with which

---

[82] Helen Fulton, 'Medieval Welsh Poems to Nuns', *Cambridge Medieval Celtic Studies* 21 (1991), pp. 87–112 (pp. 107–8).

[83] Cartwright, *Feminine Sanctity*, p. 177.

[84] Cartwright draws this conclusion regarding the popularity of the *Buched Seint y Katrin* [*Life of Saint Katherine*] in ibid., p. 175.

she is associated at Pennant Melangell.[85] Like so many of her male counterparts, she is said to have come to Wales from Ireland, in her case to flee an unwanted marriage. Having arrived in the isolated hamlet of Pennant, according to her *vita* as recorded in the *Historiae divae Monacellae*, she withdrew into a life of solitary contemplation *in huius deserto* [in this desert][86] for fifteen years, during which time she failed ever to set eyes on any man. One day when Melangell happened upon a young nobleman hunting a hare, he was so struck by her pious sanctity that he gave her enough land upon which to found a place of sanctuary [*sanctuariam et asylum*], something which allowed her to live the solitary life [*vitam solitariam*] in that 'deserted' location for a further thirty-seven years.[87] Melangell's reclusory was also to be a place of peace, offering safe haven to any fugitives seeking sanctuary – and as her *vita* tells us of the numerous 'virgins' who were attracted to the area because of her, we can presume that Melangell and her location offered an alternative life of piety to those young women who sought her out for *asylum, refugium et tutela* [asylum, refuge and guardianship]. Whilst the events that ensue – involving attempts at the violation of Melangell and her virgin followers, and retribution for the perpetrators – are formulaic and, no doubt, apocryphal, nevertheless, there are clearly anchoritic elements to Melangell's life and precedents are set within it for female religious solitude. In many ways, too, aspects of her *vita* echo those of the English anchorite Christina of Markyate who was equally compelled to flee enforced marriage and take refuge in an anchoritic setting, where she lived for periods of her life before finally entering a nunnery founded for her at Markyate.[88]

Saints Eluned and Dwynwen were two of the legendary daughters of the great leader Brychan Brycheiniog, whom Gerald of Wales claims had twenty-four daughters in all.[89] This family formed one of the most important of ancient lineages within the Matter of Britain which is, of course, what drew the attention of Gerald of Wales. Gerald picks out Eluned for special attention in his *Itinerarium*,[90] although he asserts that all twenty-four sisters were devoted to God. He recounts how Eluned, having rejected a suitor in an isolated location on the mountainside outside Brecon, 'married instead the King Eternal, thus triumphing in an ecstasy of self-denial' [*felici martyrio triumphavit*].[91] We cannot help being struck here by

---

[85] The story of Melangell and its variants (along with details of the extant manuscripts) can be found in Henken, *Traditions*, pp. 217–20. The text has been edited by Huw Pryce in 'A New Edition of the *Historia divae Monacellae*', *Montgomeryshire Collections* 82 (1994), pp. 23–40, which is the edition I have used for my ensuing discussion. For Cartwright's discussion of this saint, see her *Feminine Sanctity*, pp. 76–8. Unlike Cartwright, who considers that Melangell's *vita* configures her as a nun (p. 77), my own reading of the Latin text is that Melangell is depicted in decidedly anchoritic terms.

[86] *Historia divae Monacellae*, p. 38.

[87] Ibid., p. 38.

[88] For an account of Christina's life, see *The Life of Christina of Markyate: A Twelfth-Century Recluse*, ed. and trans. C. H. Talbot (Oxford, 1987).

[89] Gerald of Wales, *Journey through Wales*, Book I, ch. 2, pp. 91–2. As Cartwright points out, Brychan's offspring differ in number from manuscript to manuscript: *Feminine Sanctity*, p. 70.

[90] Gerald of Wales, *Journey through Wales*, Book I, ch. 2, p. 92.

[91] Ibid, p. 92; *Opera*, vol. 6, p. 32.

the combination of the isolated location and Eluned's marriage with Christ. Nor is it possible to ignore the anchoritic connotations attached to the ecstasy which she experiences through self-deprivation and devotion to her heavenly spouse. Moreover, according to Gerald, later devotions to the saint are concentrated on activities and ritual within the graveyard attached to the church of St Eluned, rather than within the church itself, all suggestive of a sacralized location which is exterior to the already sacred space of the church interior (as well as the surfacing of much earlier pagan practices, of course). Could it be that Eluned's place of occupation was also in the graveyard of the church at Brecon?

Eluned as a saint has dropped from public view in contemporary Wales, although the same cannot be said for her sister, Saint Dwynwen, who is celebrated annually on 25 January as the Welsh patron saint of lovers.[92] Unlike her sister, however, or, indeed, Melangell, Dwynwen's religious vocation was spurred on by abandonment by her earthly lover, Maelon Dafodrill, who objected to her retention of chastity until the time when they would be married. Upon being granted three wishes from God, Dwynwen chose to release her lover from his punishment (God had transformed his body into ice), to be able to hear in perpetuity the anguished prayers of abandoned lovers in order to intercede for them, but for herself to be impervious to the feeling of earthly love ever afterwards.[93] She was also granted by God permission to withdraw into a life of solitary contemplation on the island of Llanddwyn off the coast of Anglesey in North Wales.[94] Saint Dwynwen, therefore, is an example of a fifth-century female recluse, one of whose roles was undoubtedly to act as advisor to the lay community and to prognosticate the future in secular matters (primarily problems of love). In this sense, her skills certainly equate to those of the visionary anchorites recorded by Gerald as discussed above, albeit within the social rather than the political arena.[95] If, as seems to have been the case, marriage, childbearing, dynastic continuity and personal devotional practices were of primary importance amongst Welsh women throughout the period in question, then Dwynwen's role as a solitary religious woman offering advice on those matters which most concerned them can be interpreted through

---

[92] For an account of Dwynwen's life, see Cartwright, *Feminine Sanctity*, pp. 88–91. See also Henken, *Traditions*, pp. 227–32.

[93] According to the findings of Henken, Dwynwen was associated with love divination both in North and South Wales, suggesting that 'this aspect of the saint did belong to her originally', for which see Henken, *Traditions*, p. 231.

[94] In fact, today Llanddwyn Island is attached to the mainland by a narrow causeway which is only under water during particularly high tides.

[95] Indeed, Gerald includes his visionary anchorites within a much longer list of visionary religious figures, amongst whom emerges a woman named Ewedas whom he identifies as 'mulier religiosa et monialis omnium opinione sanctissima' [a religious woman and nun, considered by everybody to be most holy]. This woman lived in St David's, so he tells us (although there was no nunnery in the vicinity, as we have seen). Again, she is party to visions of Gerald which bear political import: in this case, she sees him first of all lying spread out across her altar and then across the entire land. True to form, Gerald interprets this vision as evidence of his greatness and popularity. See *Opera*, vol. 1, p. 157. Gerald's use of the word *religiosa* in this context would point towards her being some kind of semireligious or non-regulated holy woman, possibly an anchorite, and has a bearing upon my discussion of the Merionethshire *religiosa* below.

the framework of the female anchorite as proffered by the other contributors to this volume. There is no doubt that for generation after generation (indeed, well into living memory)[96] Dwynwen offered the type of services to the community, albeit in a more secular sense, which we have long come to associate with the female anchorite.

Recorded female anchorites

Writing his history of the Gower peninsular in 1928, Latimer Davies notes the many caves with hermitic associations which pepper the limestone cliffs of the region.[97] Indeed, as we have seen, many of these caves and rocky outcrops form powerful motifs in the lives of the Welsh saints and a good number of their present-day names, along with a range of archaeological findings uncovered during excavations, would appear to corroborate this type of usage during the Middle Ages.[98] One particular cave is of special interest to Davies in his account: that known as 'Minchin Hole' not far from Pennard Castle on the Gower peninsula. As Davies rightly points out, the likely origin of the name 'Minchin' is the Anglo-Saxon *mynecen* which is a term used for a religious woman or, in Davies' words, a 'nun living under vows, an anchorite cell'.[99] Whilst it is highly unlikely that a conventionally professed nun would have occupied such an inaccessible and inhospitable location, nor could this be deemed 'an anchorite cell' in the traditional understanding of the term, it is not beyond the bounds of possibility that it was used as a place of temporary religious retreat for a particularly pious woman, or women of the type we see in the saints' Lives alluded to above. Davies' argument, however, rests upon his claim that 'Mynchin Hele' is listed amongst the possessions of the nunnery of Minchin Buckland in Somerset, suggesting to him that this Gower cave or its environs could have constituted a place of retreat for individual or small groups of female recluses from this nunnery, if only on a temporary basis.[100] The nuns of Minchin Buckland had been granted their nunnery in or just after 1199, before which, as Sisters of the Order of St John, they had been scattered around England. Minchin Buckland was therefore the only priory of the Sisters of the Order of St John in England and was later to adopt the rule of the Augustinian Canonesses for its daily life.[101] The knights of St John were a considerable presence on the Gower during this period, having been handed swathes

---

[96] An aspect of Henken's methodology in her study of the hagiographic traditions of Wales was to collect stories still circulating orally in the relevant communities. On Dwynwen, see, for example, *Traditions*, pp. 229–10.

[97] Davies, *Pennard and West Gower*, op. cit.

[98] Many of these finds are now on display in Swansea museum.

[99] Davies, *Pennard and West Gower*, p. 30. For a definition of this word see *mynecenu* in *An Anglo-Saxon Dictionary*, ed. Joseph Bosworth and T. Worthcote Toller (Oxford, 1848).

[100] Ibid., p. 30. Whilst this provides an interesting – and potentially important – link, Davies is sketchy about his sources, frequently omitting to cite them at all.

[101] *VCH* 2, pp. 148–50. Available online as 'Houses of Knights Hospitallers: the Preceptory of Minchin Buckland', *A History of the County of Somerset*, vol. 2 (1911), pp. 148–50, at http://www.british-history.ac.uk/report.aspx?compid=40938. Last accessed 24 March 2009.

of land and properties in return for the protection they offered to English landowners in the face of repeated – and frequently devastating – incursions by the Welsh
from the north, so it is not beyond the bounds of possibility that there were some
tenuous connections between the two; indeed, at one time, the Hospitallers had
property in almost every Gower parish and many of the lands accrued to them had
been associated with early churches and hermitages.[102] For Davies, therefore, it
would be unsurprising if the women of this same order had associations with the
Gower and had in their possession the site of an ancient hermitage in the cave at
Pennard. Davies' case, however seductive it may be, nevertheless falls down at the
first hurdle: his argument is self-evidently based on a misunderstanding – or care-
less misreading – of the phrase *Thele in comitatu Devonie* [Thele in the county of
Devon] which appears in the list of the possessions of the nunnery of Minchin
Buckland to which he alludes.[103] The word *Thele* actually refers to the manor of
'The Hele', also known as Templand or Templeton in Devon, which had been gifted to the nunnery along with other estates by Loretta, Countess of Leicester, on 16
July 1227.[104] This was the same Loretta who, as a widow, had withdrawn into an
anchorhold at Hackington in Kent in 1219 following the death of her husband in
1204. She lived as an influential anchorite for more than forty-five years,[105] and it
was from there that she obviously administered this charter.[106] It well may be that
the plight of the nuns of Minchin Buckland spoke cogently to Loretta, who was one
of the most high-profile, politically and socially influential of female anchorites of
England during the entire Middle Ages, but it is very unlikely that the nuns themselves had any significant connections with the hermitic cave near Davies's Pennard.

There is, however, a single tantalizing reference to a likely female recluse in
the records, this time associated with Merionethshire in North Wales, a reference
which comes about as a result of what Huw Pryce refers to as 'state power [which
became] more visible ... in parchment rather than stone'.[107] Here Pryce alludes to
the bureaucratization introduced by Edward I in order to maximize the profits
accruing from his recently acquired Welsh lands, a type of record-keeping which

---

[102] Davies, *Pennard and West Gower*, p. 42.

[103] The possessions held by the nunnery on the eve of the Reformation are listed in *Knights Hospitallers in England* ed. L. B. Larking and J. M. Kemble (Camden Society, 1857), here at p. 20.

[104] CCh.R, 1226–57, II Henry III, 16 July 1227, p. 52. Loretta's charter appears here in full and is also reproduced in F. W. Weaver's introduction to the published abbey cartulary, *A Cartulary of Buckland Priory in the County of Somerset: A History of the County of Somerset* (Somerset, 1909), p. xxxi. See also 'Houses of Knights Hospitallers: The Preceptory of Minchin Buckland', *A History of the County of Somerset*, vol. 2 (1911), pp. 148–50, at http://www.british-history.ac.uk/report.aspx?compid=40938. Last accessed: 25 March 2009. Clearly, in spite of her anchoritic enclosure, Loretta was still using her title of Countess of Leicester and the charter still bears her seal [*sigilli mei*].

[105] Loretta is highly visible in the records throughout the forty-six or more years of her anchoritic enclosure, even as an old woman of eighty. For further information on Loretta and the sources in which she appears, see Ann K. Warren, *Anchorites and their Patrons in Medieval England* (Berkeley, 1985), pp. 166–7.

[106] Coincidentally, she was also the Loretta de Braose whose father, William, held large areas of Gower, including Pennard, during the thirteenth century, having been granted custody of the region in 1203 by King John. His family were to retain that lordship for over a century, for which see Davies, *Pennard and West Gower*, p. 14. Davies, however, was clearly unaware of this connection.

[107] Huw Pryce, 'Medieval Experiences: Wales 1000–1415', in *The People of Wales*, ed. Gareth Elwyn Jones and Dai Smith (Llandyssul, 1999), p. 27.

was new to the region. For Pryce, one positive result of this was that 'more Welsh people become visible to the historian than ever before'.[108]

One such person emerging from the list of tax-payers in what is now the county of Merioneth, as recorded in 1292–3,[109] is a woman named Gwladus, a resident of the tiny village of Llanfrothen, which records suggest may have housed up to 400 inhabitants during the period.[110] In this list, Gwladus appears alongside a further 2,600 tax-payers, most of whom are also named. What is remarkable about this entry, however, is not the fact that Gwladus's personal property is valued at 20s. (although that is interesting enough), or that she owed 16d. in tax; it is that the record categorizes Gwaldus as *religiosa*, which Pryce takes to mean 'a woman who had taken vows of religion, perhaps an anchoress'.[111] We know, of course, that Merioneth did not house a nunnery during this period, so Gwladus's status as *religiosa* would point towards anchoritism as her likely profession, or else that she enjoyed some kind of semireligious or vowess status. The church of St Brothen, which still stands in the village, dates from this same period and is the only church in Wales with this dedication to what is now an obscure early Christian saint.[112] It may have been that this was the place of residence of Gwladus and that, as we have seen in the case of Loretta, Countess of Leicester, it was possible for a female anchorite to exercise considerable influence and to retain both money and possessions for her own disposal after entering the anchorhold. That Gwaldus's profession was considered both relevant and important by the compiler of the tax-subsidy record in which she appears is confirmed by the fact that amongst all the women listed by name, only she and one other woman, who is described as *crythores*, are referred to by vocation. *Crythores* refers to a musician – a *crwth* player – suggesting the high status that the player of this traditional Celtic instrument continued to occupy, even after the Norman invasion and the Edwardian Conquest.[113] Indeed, as Pryce points out, whereas well over half the women listed in this tax-subsidy register would have been householders in their own right (the other half being named alongside their husbands), there are doubtless countless other women who failed to make it into the register at all, not owning any property or else married to men who did not.[114] Gwaldus, therefore, and the female *crwth* player, enter the annals of history as two exceptional women, but women about whose actual status within their respective societies we can only continue to surmise.

---

[108] Ibid., p. 27.

[109] This list of tax-payers has been studied at length by Keith Williams-Jones in *The Merioneth Lay Subsidy Roll 1292–3* (Cardiff, 1976). Pryce's discussion relies in part upon this earlier analysis, although his own text is devoid of footnotes.

[110] Pryce, 'Medieval Experiences', p. 33.

[111] Ibid., p. 27. Interestingly, Gerald of Wales includes a visionary *mulier religiosa* amongst those anchorites whom he documents as acting in support of his claims. See pp. 198–2000, above.

[112] Saint Brothen reputedly had a brother called Gwynnin, also a saint, with a church named after him in Llangwynnin: *The Book of the Saints* (Whitefish, 2003; first published 1921), p. 52.

[113] A *crwth* is a traditional Welsh stringed instrument, somewhat resembling a lyre and attested from very early times.

[114] Pryce, 'Medieval Experiences', p. 28.

Conclusion

Evidence for historically accurate accounts of recluses in Wales is sparse and generally unreliable. Very few written accounts remain with which to document the existence or activities of religious solitaries and those that do are coloured by folklore, myth and traditional hagiographic tropology. Moreover, because of the chequered history of colonization to which the country (in Helen Fulton's words, 'a country which is not a nation')[115] was subjected, records were either not kept, or else were not preserved. In addition, the structure within which the Church and the monasteries operated throughout the period was radically different from the rest of Europe: in particular, the clergy continued to marry well into the later period and bishops and abbots tended therefore to hand down these positions of power to their sons.[116] The monastic set-up was originally also family- or clan-based, suggesting that within religious life more widely, the ordinary lay-woman would have had a more inclusive role than her counterpart in the rest of Europe, where she was frequently the source of considerable male ecclesiastical anxiety and antipathy within a culture which insisted on clerical and monastic celibacy. In this way, whilst women were evidently crucial to the social and dynastic economies in Wales, perhaps, too, the ordinary woman was a deeply integral support to the religious scaffold of Celtic Christianity, operating in the way she has always done, that is to say in the background as far as the *historical* eye is concerned. It may also be that the particularly rugged and inhospitable geography of Wales contributed to the lack of an anchoritic community: if the actual terrain inhabited – marginal and liminal to the rest of Europe – resembles, in a literal sense, the wildernesses of anchoritic discourse (Pennant Melangell was, we must remember, described as *desertus*), then each day can be lived out according to the precepts of the Desert Fathers and Mothers, whilst tending to the physical and immediate concerns of family, community and church. This, above all, may be why, in the words of Cartwright, 'private devotion rather than claustration was the mode of religious expression generally preferred for Welsh women',[117] and why anchoritism, such as it was in Wales, appears to have remained primarily male and institutional. Until future research uncovers evidence which suggests otherwise, we must consider it unlikely that the extraordinary tide of female anchoritism that swept through Europe at an unprecedented rate during the later Middle Ages made any significant impact upon a country whose peoples and lands lay at the edge of the known world, their faces already turned towards infinity.

[115] Helen Fulton, 'Writing Nation and Globalisation in the Medieval World', Inaugural Lecture, Swansea University, 6 October 2008. I am grateful to Professor Fulton for giving me access to the full text of this unpublished lecture.

[116] Wendy Davies, *Wales in the Early Middle Ages*, p. 149 and pp. 156–7.

[117] Cartwright, *Feminine Sanctity*, p. 194.

Index